ZEV'S LOS ANGELES

A Political Memoir

From Boyle Heights
to the Halls of Power

To Nadine + Steve —
with gratitude for decades
of friendship. Thanks for
your service to our community.

[signature]

21 September 2023

ZEV'S LOS ANGELES

A Political Memoir

From Boyle Heights
to the Halls of Power

Zev Yaroslavsky

with Josh Getlin

BOSTON
2023

Library of Congress Cataloging-in-Publication Data

Names: Yaroslavsky, Zev, 1948- author. | Getlin, Josh, author.
Title: Zev's Los Angeles: from Boyle Heights to the halls of power, a political memoir / Zev Yaroslavsky with Josh Getlin.
Other titles: From Boyle Heights to the halls of power, a political memoir
Description: Boston: Cherry Orchard Books, 2023. | Includes index.
Identifiers: LCCN 2023001395 (print) | LCCN 2023001396 (ebook) | ISBN 9798887191669 (hardback) | ISBN 9798887191676 (paperback) | ISBN 9798887191683 (adobe pdf) | ISBN 9798887191690 (epub)
Subjects: LCSH: Yaroslavsky, Zev, 1948- | Jewish politicians--California--Biography. | politicians--California--Biography. | Political activists--California--Biography. | Los Angeles (Calif.)--Biography.
Classification: LCC F869.L853 Y27 2023 (print) | LCC F869.L853 (ebook) | DDC 979.4/94--dc23/eng/20230207
LC record available at https://lccn.loc.gov/2023001395
LC ebook record available at https://lccn.loc.gov/2023001396

ISBN 9798887191669 (hardback)
ISBN 9798887191676 (paperback)
ISBN 9798887191683 (adobe pdf)
ISBN 9798887191690 (epub)

Book design by PHi Business Solutions
Cover design by Ivan Grave. On the cover: photograph by Al Seib/Los Angeles Times/via Getty Images

Published by Cherry Orchard Books, an imprint of Academic Studies Press
1577 Beacon Street
Brookline, MA 02446, USA

press@academicstudiespress.com
www.academicstudiespress.com

Contents

Barbara Edelston Yaroslavsky (1947–2018) –
The love of my life.

"I Will Love You Forever, if You Let Me": A Dedication to Barbara Edelston Yaroslavsky (1947–2018)

As I was finishing my daily jog at 9:27 on the morning of December 26, 2018, my mobile phone rang. It was a nurse calling from the California Rehabilitation Institute, telling me that they were sending my wife and love of my life, Barbara, back to Cedars-Sinai Hospital after a fainting spell during a physical therapy session. His tone was more matter of fact than urgent. He suggested that I might want to make my way to the hospital's emergency room, where the ambulance was headed.

Six weeks earlier, a mosquito bit Barbara in our home and infected her with West Nile Virus. She had spent thirty-eight days at Cedars, seventeen of them in the Intensive Care Unit, and it was touch and go for much of that time. But then she began to show signs of miraculous improvement. She was beating back the virus with her characteristic courage and resilience. On December 21, my birthday, the doctors believed she was ready to go to an inpatient rehab center in Century City.

Uncharacteristically, I threw caution to the wind, believing that Barbara had turned the corner. I allowed myself to envision her back at home, the champion multi-tasker, attending to her public service responsibilities, community work, politics, and family—especially to our new eight-week-old grandson, Joshua, whom she adored. My daughter, Mina, my son, David, and my brother-in-law, John Edelston, were also elated. On the morning I received the call, Mina and her husband, Dan, were already setting up a room at our home where Barbara could continue her recovery once she was discharged from rehab. I ran home and told them what had happened. We called David, too and told him to meet us at the hospital.

As we drove the two miles to the hospital, I received another call—this time from the emergency room nurse—asking, "Are you on your way?" I told her that we were two minutes away and inquired about Barbara's condition.

She put her hand over the phone and mumbled something unintelligible to someone nearby. "The doctors would prefer to discuss it with you when you get here," she finally responded. That was not a good sign. As we sprinted to the E.R., memories of my life with Barbara raced through my mind—the home we had established, the birth of our kids, trips we had taken, happy and sad life events we had shared. Barbara and I had been together for fifty-one wonderful, eventful, and remarkable years. I had a sinking feeling that this could be the end of all that.

I met Barbara on a Sunday morning in May 1967, when I was an eighteen-year-old gofer at the Los Angeles Hebrew High School, which met at the University of Judaism on Sunset Boulevard, and Barbara was the university's Sunday morning switchboard operator. What attracted me to her that day was her drop-dead beauty, her bright blue eyes, her infectious smile, and her generous and gregarious personality. All those qualities were instantly apparent to me as we chatted across the counter—she the Lily Tomlin-like operator, and me the disheveled, longhaired mischief-maker. I summoned the courage to ask her out on a date, and she said, "Yes." I never dated another person after that.

I didn't trust enough to enter a long-term relationship with anyone back then. My mother had died of cancer when I was ten years old, and I couldn't bear to have my heart broken again. Barbara sensed my insecurity in the first months of our relationship and confronted it head on. "I will love you forever, if you let me," she wrote to me in a letter that summer. It was a profound promise, and she kept it until the end.

Barbara had an unmatched circle of friends—both in quantity and in the depth of the relationships. I often wondered where she got the bandwidth to bring increasing numbers of people into her orbit. CNN's Larry King once interviewed Robert Strauss, the former US Ambassador to the Soviet Union and prominent Washington influencer, and asked him to describe himself. Strauss responded, "More people know the Pope than know Bob Strauss, but Bob Strauss knows more people than the Pope does." He could have been describing Barbara.

Although I was well known in Los Angeles, Barbara knew more people than I did. She knew whom to call for anything. If you needed an autopsy expedited, she made a call to the coroner. If you needed money for a worthy cause, she would connect you to someone who could help. If your child was single, and you wanted to set them up with someone, Barbara was at your beck and call. As a political spouse, she was the best, my greatest asset and partner. She knew everything about everyone and had uncanny instincts about anyone she met.

But Barbara was much more than that. She didn't just tag along for this journey. She helped blaze its trails from the very beginning. We were a team—a whole that was bigger than the sum of its parts. She also became a forceful public servant in her own right. She served for thirteen years on the California Medical Board, and three of them as its Chair, the first non-physician to do so. Barbara also served on and chaired multiple state, local, community and non-profit boards. She was one amazing woman.

When my kids and I arrived at the emergency room, the doctor came out and told us that nurses at the rehab institute lost Barbara's pulse after she collapsed. They administered CPR, but every time they got a faint pulse, she was unable to sustain it on her own. Multiple efforts to revive her at Cedars failed as well, and in a moment I'll never forget, he said, "We've done everything we can. There's nothing more we can do." Moments later, Barbara was gone.

It never occurred to me that I would survive her. Barbara's mother lived to be ninety-four and her grandmother to 104, although most members of *my* family didn't make it past the age of seventy. Now my actuarial assumptions, and my life, were upside down. Barbara had been by my side every day of my adult life. She raised Mina and David, taught me to celebrate my birthday every day, showed me the difference between formal, business, and cocktail attire, provided a sounding board for my ideas and op-ed articles, and explained me to legions of folks who couldn't figure me out. Above all, she loved me for who I was. And I loved her.

Four days later, over 1,100 of her closest friends filled Temple Israel of Hollywood to honor Barbara's memory and celebrate her life. Mina began her eulogy with a declaration that described her perfectly: "My mother's life was one big mitzvah" (Hebrew for a good or praiseworthy deed). David choked up when he said, "Her love surrounded us like a wish in a well." Father Greg Boyle, a Jesuit priest and good friend wrote, "She was the very shape of God's heart." Those three phrases grace her gravestone. I was the luckiest man on the face of the earth when Barbara agreed to marry me. We could never have imagined the remarkable life that we would make together.

Although this book is about my life and times, none of it would have been possible without Barbara. She was integral to every moment, every aspect of my personal and professional life. Her legacy is enshrined in the more than five decades of public and community service that she performed with grace, generosity, and love. Most importantly, however, Barbara and her soul live on in Mina, David, Sadie, Miriam, Gabriel, Joshua, and Yael, who was born twenty months after she died and who bears her Hebrew name and her big blue eyes. For these reasons and more, this book is dedicated to Barbara.

Introduction

———

Ever since it opened, my family and I have enjoyed memorable nights at the Walt Disney Concert Hall. Designed by internationally renowned architect Frank Gehry, it opened in 2003 and instantly became the crown jewel of downtown Los Angeles. People come from all over the world to savor performances by great classical musicians. But the tone in the hall was decidedly different on a mild November evening in 2014. That night, more than 1,000 guests came to celebrate with me as I retired after four decades of public service to the City and County of Los Angeles. Business, political, cultural and community leaders, as well as colleagues, staff, friends and family mingled in the glittering concert hall—an institution which had transformed the cultural life of the city, yet didn't exist when my career began.

The contrast between Los Angeles then and now was striking, and as the evening went on I couldn't help but reflect on the changes in my own life that brought me to this moment: More than sixty years before, I was a toddler growing up in Boyle Heights on the east side of the Los Angeles River. As a teenager living in the Fairfax neighborhood, I became a social activist fighting for civil liberties, battling to free three million Jews from Soviet oppression, and marching against the war in Vietnam. By 1975 I was walking precincts on the city's Westside, heading to an upset victory in the race for a vacant City Council seat. Two decades later I was elected to the county Board of Supervisors, where I served for another twenty years. It had been quite a ride.

I was a blur of emotions as I stood on the Disney Hall stage that night, humbled by this improbable journey. The child of Jewish immigrants from Ukraine, I grew up in an exceedingly modest household where books were our most prized possessions. My parents lived from paycheck to paycheck, and we rented a small apartment in a duplex in Boyle Heights, a community of immigrants in East Los Angeles, at 724 N. Breed St., where my sister and I shared a small bedroom. Although you could see the lights of the civic center from our home, they might as well have been a million miles away. What were the odds, I thought, that a kid like me could end up helping to govern the largest county in America and its second largest city?

Just as important, who could have imagined how dramatically Los Angeles would grow and change in the same period? Although traffic was as bad as ever that night at Disney Hall, the city was in the throes of a transit revolution, with new subways and light rail networks crisscrossing the region. The county, which nearly went bankrupt twenty years earlier, was in its best fiscal condition in nearly four decades. Although the physical city had long been a punch line for jokes about urban sprawl, it had become one of the world's great urban centers—even as our neighborhoods, beaches, and mountains enjoyed strong protections that would preserve them for generations to come. During these eventful years, Los Angeles had become one of the world's premier cultural centers. All of this and more would have been unthinkable decades earlier, and I was lucky and proud to have been a part of it.

Of course, it wasn't all good news. Los Angeles' homeless population had exploded, and Skid Row was a national embarrassment. Income inequality was preventing vast numbers of people from enjoying the fruits of our economy, threatening our social cohesion. Racial tensions still flared across the region, and the troubled county jail was riddled with corruption and sickening abuse. The streets were patrolled by a police force that, after decades of racial turmoil, was still struggling to transform itself into one that valued constitutional policing and respected the people it served, regardless of the color of one's skin. Immigration, which helped build Southern California, was now a flashpoint for economic tensions and increasingly contentious debate. There was still work to do, but I took pride that I had been in the thick of battles on the most compelling challenges facing our region.

I was all about results and wanted to get things done. And I was determined to learn how to make local government work. To be sure, I made my share of mistakes along the way, and I learned from them. But as we celebrated that night at Disney Hall, I could look back on a career in which I tried to make a difference in the County, the city, and in people's lives.

That's the story I'll be telling in this book. But it's not just an account of my personal journey, or the growth of Los Angeles. The message I hope to convey is that local government is more important today than ever and that we *can* make it work. The stories I'm telling aren't just vivid historical moments. Each one offers lessons about how to use power, how to make government listen to the people it serves, and how to bring about change—all without sacrificing one's values or integrity.

I am named for my paternal grandfather, Volko (wolf in Russian), and my name, "Zev," means wolf in Hebrew. As a public servant, however, I was never a loner. From the beginning I had one foot planted inside the halls of government—pushing the system to change and bend to my agenda—and the other on the outside, challenging the powers that be when they moved too slowly. For me, that's not a contradiction. Being consistent for its own sake was never my objective. I resisted attempts to pigeon-hole me on an ideological spectrum and took comfort in French mathematician Blaise Pascal's observation: "We do not display greatness by going to one extreme, but in touching both at once and occupying all the space in between."

I'm a progressive who believes in paying his bills, so I joined forces with conservative and liberal colleagues to prevent a county bankruptcy. I fought hard for the rights and dignity of working people, but never hesitated to differ with public employee unions when I thought their demands overreached. I partnered with powerful business and real estate interests when we shared common goals, fought them vigorously when I thought they were wrong, and went over their heads, directly to the people, when they gave me no other choice. I was one of the few straight politicians who took up the cause of gay and lesbian rights in the 1970s, an issue that was uncharted territory and perceived to be fraught with political risk for most elected officials. It didn't matter. Then as now, I was determined to be a champion for those who most needed one. I was fortunate to be in public office, and felt obligated to take risks and get things done on behalf of the people who put their confidence in me—big things and little things.

I can be restless, driven, and intense. But also soft-hearted, empathetic, and self-deprecating when you get to know me. Although I've always taken my work seriously, I have never taken myself too seriously. The first time my photo ever appeared in the pages of the *Los Angeles Times*, I was an overweight, long-haired kid who had just been arrested leading a demonstration to save Soviet Jews. Today, my once-unkempt hair is grayer and professionally cut. Material possessions have never meant much to me. I live in the same, modest home in the city's Beverly-Fairfax neighborhood that Barbara and I bought back in 1976. We raised two exceptional children, Mina and David, who are now making their own marks on society, and who have given us five beautiful grandchildren.

During these years, an arc stretching from the 1950s to the present, Los Angeles has been transformed from a sprawling and parochial city into a diverse, international metropolis. The sky's the limit in a region where constant, inevitable change is part of our DNA. And my journey is living proof of this.

Elected office wasn't even remotely on my radar screen as a young boy. But there were some signs that foreshadowed my life to come, like volunteering to be the first in Miss Russell's fourth-grade class at Melrose Avenue School to recite the Gettysburg Address from memory; and later sneaking into the backstage of the Fairfax Theater to hear Eleanor Roosevelt speak on behalf of John F. Kennedy's presidential campaign in the fall of 1960. One of my earliest thrills came after her speech, when she walked over to shake my hand as she headed for the stage door exit. Weeks later, I convinced my father to take me to the Shrine

Auditorium to see JFK at a campaign rally. I nearly poked the future president's eye out with my makeshift "Kennedy for President" sign.

And then there was the day, February 23, 1964, a short three months after President Kennedy's assassination, when I rode my beat-up, barely functional bike with a coaster brake from our Beverly-Fairfax neighborhood to Los Angeles International Airport to see President Lyndon Johnson. I heard that he would be boarding Air Force One after a meeting with the president of Mexico, and decided instantly that I would make the twenty-two-mile roundtrip to be there. This was a foolhardy and dangerous trek for a fourteen-year-old kid to make. Oblivious to the risks, I pedaled from my home to the West Imperial terminal on the south side of LAX. Cars were screaming by me on La Cienega Boulevard—a veritable freeway—at fifty-five miles per hour.

I finally reached the tarmac where the presidential aircraft stood gleaming. A crowd had gathered but I elbowed my way to the front, where Johnson was shaking hands with hundreds of well-wishers. I watched him work the line and could barely believe that he was inching toward me. Then the President of the United States briefly grabbed my fingers and shook them. Mission accomplished! On my ride home, however, anxiety set in. It was now dark; the weather had turned chilly and speeding motorists could barely see me. Yet I was less worried about my safety than I was about telling my father what I had done. To my great relief, my New Deal Democrat dad was more thrilled than appalled when I walked in the door.

Although these early experiences may have provided clues of what was to come, I would have been unconvinced at the time. After all, I was an LA kid who passionately loved the Dodgers and not so secretly coveted Vin Scully's job as the team's radio voice. By the time I was in high school, however, I became obsessed with issues consuming the nation and the world, like civil rights and the Vietnam War. I was anxious to get into the mix because I grew up in a home that lived and breathed social activism. I learned how to fight for what I believed, in part because of my parents, Minna and David Yaroslavsky. They were humble but proud teachers, union activists, staunch Labor Zionists, and lifelong Democrats. At the dinner table and by the lives they led, they tutored my sister and me about right and wrong—about social and economic justice, and about our moral responsibility to make the world a better place.

I never shied away from taking on the status quo, because voters didn't elect me to just mind the store or keep the lid on. They wanted me to move heaven and earth to turn ideas into results. But to me, that was not an obstacle. Barbara understood this clearly when she hung a sign in our kitchen: "A pessimist has no motor; an optimist has no brakes."

Although my door was always open to everyone, my main responsibility was to speak for those who didn't have an army of lobbyists, lawyers, and consultants to represent them. *I* was their advocate, because that's exactly what they elected me to be and what they were paying me to do. As Harry Truman once said, "There are 14 or 15 million Americans who have the resources to have representatives in Washington to protect their interests…The interests of the great mass of the other people—the 150 or 160 million—is the responsibility of the President of the United States."

Unfortunately, we live in an age when millions are skeptical about government, and it's hard to blame them. The once solid foundations of our democratic institutions have come under attack as never before, and support for them is at an all-time low. It's easy to be cynical, but I've lived my entire life convinced that holding public office is one of the most important callings in a democracy—a singular opportunity to improve the lives of those we are elected to represent.

I was born and raised in Los Angeles, and it's tempting to say that my adult life was largely shaped here as a young boy during the '50s and '60s. But if we are all part of a chain linked to past generations, my odyssey actually began long ago, before the turn of the last century in what is now Belarus. My grandfather, Shimon Soloveichik, was a pioneering Hebrew scholar, an avid Labor Zionist, an inventor, and a Renaissance man. Even though he died eight years before I was born, he set an example of morality and integrity that influences me every day. He fought hard to build a new nation for his people, and courageously began a new life in America. He believed in a cause greater than himself, and blazed a trail for his descendants, including me.

That's where my story begins.

CHAPTER 1

Roots of a Legacy:
Shimon Soloveichik

On a warm August morning in 2004, under a deep blue sky with billowing clouds, I walked down the gravel road of a quiet hamlet in western Belarus. It was an isolated dot on the map surrounded by wheat fields, woods, and lakes. Along the way I passed the town's green, white, and brown wooden bungalows, which had no plumbing or hot water, no bathrooms, and few telephones. Halfway between Vilnius and Minsk, the place looked much as it probably had a century or more before—and I was excited beyond words. In my fifty-sixth summer I was searching for the world of an ancestor who had inspired me ever since I was a small boy. I had finally reached Kopach, the birthplace of my maternal grandfather, Shimon Soloveichik.

My parents had raised me and my sister on stories about Soloveichik. He had been an extraordinarily accomplished man with a keen scientific mind, and an outspoken activist who was dedicated to the future of the Jewish people. When I'm asked to name an individual I would most like to have met, his name is at the top of my list. Since I could not meet him, I was determined to do the next best thing by traveling to his birthplace and walking in his footsteps.

Students of modern Jewish history will recognize the Soloveichik name, which includes several revered rabbis. Telling an Orthodox Jewish congregation that you're a Soloveichik is like telling a Boston audience that you're a Kennedy. It was a source of immense pride to be in this family line.

Down by the River

I knew that Shimon Soloveichik was born in 1873 in Kopach. But Kopach was a hard place to find. It didn't appear on any of my maps of the Soviet Union. Whenever I asked my father where exactly it was, he'd simply tell me,

"It's somewhere in the Pale of Settlement," which was one of the only regions of Czarist Russia where Jews had been permitted to live. At one point the Pale encompassed 472,000 square miles of the Russian empire, so looking for Kopach was like trying to find the proverbial needle in a haystack. Ultimately, however, serendipity struck. One of my constituents told me that his son was a cartographer at Stanford University, and he could locate old towns that had long since vanished. I asked if he might help me find Kopach, and three weeks later I received two beautiful, full color maps in the mail pinpointing it in western Belarus, just east of the Lithuanian border.

A place that I could only imagine was now real. My interest in Kopach grew when I asked a friend who was traveling to Belarus to see if he would visit the village and let me know what he found. He reported back with wonderful news. "It's a small little community," he said. "It's fascinating, and you've got to go there." To me, this was like an archeologist telling the world that, yes, the biblical town of Jericho exists and there *is* a remnant of a wall that came tumbling down.

The trip to my grandfather's birthplace was an adventure. I flew to Vilnius, the capital of Lithuania, and headed toward Minsk, the capital of Belarus. What should have been a two-hour drive in my rental car became a maddening half-day trip, including a four-hour confrontation with Belarussian customs officials at the border. The next day, interpreter in tow, I began my search for Kopach. Long after my grandfather died, my parents published a tribute book that chronicled his life in detail. One contributor remembered that Shimon, as a young boy, used to play near his father's mill "down by the river." When I arrived, I began looking for a river with a nearby flour mill. But I was quickly disappointed. There was nothing even remotely like that in sight. Then I spied two elderly women sitting on a bench in front of a small bungalow, with one of them eyeing me suspiciously. I had a videocam and a still camera dangling from my neck, and I probably looked like a foreign agent. Sensing that direct communication might be the best icebreaker, I went to speak with them. Luckily, I speak enough Russian to carry a simple conversation. I introduced myself to the frowning *babushka* and first told her that my grandfather had been born in the village. "I've come back to see where my ancestors came from," I said. Her demeanor changed instantly. She smiled and said that I was fortunate to be able to travel so far. "I can't even remember the last time I traveled to the next town, seven kilometers up the road," she told me.

I asked if there had ever been a flour mill in the village and she said yes, but it was destroyed before the war. However, she added, the foundation was still there. Pointing in its direction, she said, "go take a look—it's down by the river." As I made my way down the road, I saw the old concrete foundation for what must have been my great grandfather's flour mill. Eureka! And then, unforgettably, I saw a young boy kicking a can down the road, as if he were playing soccer with himself. That could have been my grandfather 125 years earlier, I thought. And it could have been me, too, if he hadn't had the courage to uproot his family and begin a new life in America.

Shimon was a larger-than-life figure in my childhood, but I knew little about my paternal grandparents. What I do know is that my grandfather, Volko "Zev" Judah Yaroslavsky, and my grandmother, Miriam "Mindl" Buchbinder, lived in the Ukrainian city of Belaya Tserkov, about fifty miles southwest of Kyiv. Volko was a learned man and a devout Jew who owned a goods store in town. Mindl was a descendant of the great eighteenth-century Hassidic Rabbi Levi Yitzchak of Berdichev, a popular and beloved figure in Jewish history.

When my father immigrated to America in 1921, his plan was to bring his parents and sisters here. But by then the doors to Ellis Island were shut tight for Eastern European immigrants, and the nascent Soviet Union clamped down on emigration as well. My father remained in sporadic contact with his parents until World War II broke out. When the Germans invaded the Soviet Union in June 1941, Volko and his family headed east toward Central Asia on an open-air train, one step ahead of the Nazi armies. Their train was repeatedly strafed by the Luftwaffe, and my father's family would periodically take shelter underneath. They ended up in northeastern Siberia, where both my grandparents died during the war. For a young man who loved history and family, I was sorry to know so little about my father's parents—and was determined to discover as much as possible about Shimon Soloveichik.

The Gold Standard of Yeshivas

On previous trips to the former Soviet Union, I had visited the birthplaces of my mother and father. On this day, however, I found the starting point not only of Soloveichik's journey, but in a real sense of my own. He was a bright boy, and when he turned ten years old his parents sent him to study at a boarding school seven kilometers away. At thirteen, his bar mitzvah year, teachers recommended that he be sent to study at the Volozhin Yeshiva, a legendary place of Jewish learning. Young men studied the Torah and other holy books there, leading to a rabbinical or educational career. This was a perfect fit for a precocious boy like Shimon, but there was a catch: the yeshiva only accepted students at the age of fifteen.

Undaunted, his parents traveled to Volozhin and introduced their son to the head Rabbi. At first, he refused to even see the boy. But the family convinced the rabbi to evaluate him, and see his intelligence for himself. Shimon was quickly admitted to the yeshiva. "And so, a new stage began in Shimon's life," my mother wrote, in the anthology of essays dedicated to him. "Here, for the first time, he was quickly lit with the Zionist flame, which eventually became an all-consuming fire to which he was devoted until his dying day."

Just as important, Shimon learned the basics of physics and mathematics, and the fascinating laws of the natural world, all of which would be part of his intellectual passion for the rest of his life. He was full of energy and driven by a restless curiosity. After only six months at the school a Rabbi wrote to his father: "Had he the same amount of patience as the level of his intelligence, your Shimon would be a genius."

In the late 1890s, Shimon moved to Minsk where he began studying Jewish law and developed broader, more ecumenical social views. "He was influenced by the enlightenment and his religious beliefs began to erode," my mother wrote. "He began to dream of a completely different kind of future. He had a great thirst for understanding the secrets of nature and began to study Russian because he saw it as his gate to the world."

Shimon also began to invent things, if only on paper. Before he knew that such a device existed, he came up with the idea for a bicycle. When a local nobleman showed him a pair of binoculars, Shimon quickly grasped why one side made things appear closer and the other made them appear farther away. He conceived an idea for a helicopter, one of his proudest conceptions, unaware of Leonard da Vinci's design for a similar concept centuries before. When he first saw an airplane years later, Shimon comforted himself with the realization that *his* kind of airplane had still not been invented—one that could vertically take off and land from the same spot.

"We Will Till the Hills with Our Fingernails until the Forest Will Grow"

As Shimon grew to adulthood, the world of European Jewry was in turmoil. The mid to late nineteenth-century was a time of war and bitter ideological conflict over people's rights to determine their destinies in their own homeland. The Zionist movement, founded by Theodore Herzl, sprang from the desire to reconstitute the Jewish state in Palestine. It was time to realize the centuries-old aspiration of "Next Year in Jerusalem," and the appeal was easy to understand. Jews were dispersed from their homeland and had lived in the diaspora for 2,000 years. They lost any sense of security in many of the lands on which they landed. These concerns were especially acute in Russia, where more than three million of them routinely faced economic discrimination, pogroms, and often the threat of Siberian exile.

Zionism offered a brighter future, but it was not universally popular. Some Jews felt it was a pipedream bordering on insanity—a politically naïve, nation-building gambit that would jeopardize the little stability they had. There were also bitter divisions among Zionists themselves. Shimon embraced Labor Zionism and its socialist principles of economic and political equality. This would be the foundation of the Jewish state a half century later. He was an early leader of the Labor Zionist Party, and he imbued his students with the three tools it would take to realize that goal of statehood—a progressive Zionist ideology, fluency in the Hebrew language, and the ability to dream big dreams.

Shimon spoke fluent Russian, which allowed him to participate in the larger society around him, and he was a leader of the generation that transformed the Hebrew language from one of scripture into a modern, conversational, and literary language. By the time he entered his thirties, Shimon was teaching Hebrew at a *cheder* (a Jewish elementary school) in northern Ukraine. There, he met Avraham Gordon, the owner of a successful print shop. Soloveichik gave private Hebrew lessons to Gordon's three daughters, and he became enamored with one of them, Leah, who was seventeen years younger than him. She was intelligent and attractive, and the two fell in love. They were married after a brief courtship and my mother, Minna, their only child, was born in 1909.

As the years passed, Shimon's intellectual commitment to building a Jewish homeland became a fierce political crusade. He lectured widely on the subject, happy to debate skeptics in public forums. "When detractors of the Zionist idea once came to him and commented that Eretz Yisrael (the Land of Israel) was a desert, that her mountains were barren, he became agitated and shouted: 'We will till the hills with our fingernails until the forests will grow,'" my mother wrote.

In 1905 Shimon attended the Zionist Congress in Basle, Switzerland as a labor delegate. At these historic gatherings, which he also attended in 1907, 1909, and 1911, participants debated everything from whether Hebrew should be the only language of a new Jewish state, to what the best strategy was for building a new homeland. In 1911 Shimon sent his young daughter a poignant postcard from the Congress. It read, in part: "I send you greetings from the Zionist Congress in Basle, and I bless you in the hope that you will grow to see Jerusalem rebuilt." My mother cherished that message and lived to see her father's wishes come true. He never got to the Promised Land, but as he wrote to his daughter from Basle, he was embarking on the greatest work of his life.

Preparing His Students for Modern Times

In 1910, the city of Poltava in Central Ukraine offered my grandfather the chance to open his own school. Poltava was a bustling center of artistic energy, and a hotbed of Labor Zionist organizing. Between 1910 and 1923 Shimon launched and operated his life's project—a Zionist school that, in addition to a traditional Jewish curriculum, taught secular subjects such as mathematics, science and history. And he did it *in Hebrew*, a language that for nearly two millennia was exclusively one of scripture. His students remembered him as an engaging, quick-witted mentor, someone who periodically challenged them with questions about the natural world. He was like Bill Nye the Science Guy. As an activist educator, he was determined to bring his students into the modern era.

He was a handsome man with dark, wavy hair, and a thick mustache, an imposing figure who made sure that politics played a role in his classroom. In years to come, students took his lessons to heart and moved to Palestine. As his reputation grew, Soloveichik's household became a welcoming spot, a Grand Central Station for Zionist leaders, students, and everyday people who came to meet him.

As the First World War dragged into 1917, Russia was rocked by revolution. The tumultuous upheavals in St. Petersburg and Moscow fueled a growing belief that profound change—for Jews, for the nation—was at hand. "I can still see the scene before me when (my father) stood on a chair before all the pupils and took down the photograph of Czar Nikolai II," my mother recalled. "With an almost religious fervor he spoke of the future of the Zionist movement in Russia, of a mass aliya (immigration to Israel) of pioneers which would transform the entire structure of the Jewish people. He spoke of the sacred role which we, the Jewish youth, all had. Everyone felt at that moment that Jewish rebirth was our responsibility."

This exhilaration, however, was short lived. The new Communist regime outlawed the Zionist movement, closed Hebrew schools, and throttled the dream of national rebirth for millions of Russian Jews. Shimon's school in Poltava was shut down. It was clear that the new order would not include respect for Jewish education, culture, and identity. Those who didn't conform to the Bolshevik world view paid the price. Like many Zionists, Shimon was arrested in periodic crackdowns, and his deportation to Siberia seemed imminent. Indeed, between 1918 and 1920 thousands of Jews were murdered, beaten or had their properties confiscated in Poltava and throughout Ukraine. What was the family to do?

The answer came from New Jersey, where Shimon's older brother, Yehuda, had immigrated years before. In 1923 he sent Shimon an affidavit for immigration, a letter of sponsorship, to move to the United States. Millions of immigrants saw the US as a bright promise, the "Goldene Medinah," or golden nation, in Yiddish. But moving would not be easy. My grandfather was reluctant to leave behind family, friends, and pupils with whom he was so deeply connected. He didn't want to abandon the world he knew. Most concerning, he would be postponing his greatest dream—to move to the "Land of Israel" and help build a Jewish state.

Shimon was torn, but events forced his hand. The United States Congress was months away from slapping new controls on immigration. They were determined to choke off the stream of arrivals from Russia and Eastern Europe that had been flowing into Ellis Island since the late nineteenth century. After a stressful overland trip, including a train wreck, and a difficult ocean passage from Riga, Latvia, Shimon, Leah, and thirteen-year-old Minna arrived in New York City on October 1, 1923.

Dr. Zhivago on the Hudson

Like millions of other immigrants to the United States, the Soloveichiks grappled with the challenges of building a new life in a strange land. To call them courageous is an understatement. I've often wondered if I would have had the strength and determination to uproot myself and my family under similar circumstances. My grandfather settled into a tenement on the Lower East Side of New York City, where he confronted an additional, deeply personal trauma that made his life far more difficult.

When the family decided to move to the United States, an irreconcilable issue arose between Shimon and Leah. The age difference that separated them on their wedding day was now a chasm. Leah had begun a serious relationship with Mendel, a younger man in Poltava—a relationship that Shimon was aware of—and she was not willing to abandon him, even if it meant staying behind. Ultimately, my grandparents agreed that Leah would accompany Shimon and Minna to New York and help them get settled, but she would return to the USSR a year later to be with the man she loved.

Leah was good to her word and went back to Poltava in November 1924. She and Mendel moved to Leningrad, where they lived out the rest of their lives. They survived the Nazis' brutal, 900-day siege of the USSR's second largest city, a well-documented living hell. More than 632,000 people died—one-third of the city's population—mostly due to starvation. Soldiers and medical workers were given preference for food and other provisions, while others stayed alive, in part by cannibalizing the dead. Leah was a nurse, which is probably why she and Mendel did not perish. She never discussed the war years with members of our family, so all we know of her life in this period is drawn from the testimonies of other Leningrad survivors.

As my father recounted, Shimon had mixed emotions about his new life in America. He was overwhelmed by the freedom of thought and expression, and the kindness of people in America, compared to Russia. But he was also heartbroken, left alone to raise a teenage daughter in a new country without the woman he loved. "I shudder when I think of the terrible distance separating me from all those I love," he wrote to a friend back in the USSR "Everything is strange to me, strange and foreign. Only now do I grasp what has happened to me. Only now do I grasp the terrible choice I have made. Believe me, there are moments when I cannot bear the stifling loneliness."

Nevertheless, he put his talents to use. He taught in several New York yeshivas where he developed a reputation as an excellent pedagogue. Educating young boys in New York City, however, was more challenging than in the old country. "Here the youth…are wild ruffians," he wrote to a friend in Russia. "The question of discipline is most difficult and crucial. When you see a job notice, it will always be written in this manner: 'A teacher wanted who knows how to maintain discipline with the children of America.'" Shimon complained that the boys only seemed to care about "this game called baseball." He wrote that he was beset by "noise and uproar in the halls. The ruffians climb the stairs. And the way they walk! Each one does not walk in his own path but rather in the path of his friend. And they push each other. Shouting. Pushing. I wait for them in the classroom. And suddenly the group explodes in a huge commotion…their mouths don't rest for one minute. And I, the poor one standing before them, helpless…I have to teach Torah to these masses whose language I do not know."

The closest Shimon ever got to the "Land of Israel" was when he vicariously experienced it through my mother. Minna made her first trip there in 1931 at the age of twenty-two. She wrote letters to her father describing the beauty of the land, the magic of finally being in the Jewish homeland, and the people she met. Shimon was filled with pride and savored every word. "The day your letter arrives is a celebration for me," he wrote to her. "I do not read your letters but swallow them whole. Not only do I understand them, but I feel them. I breathe your air and live your life."

To the end of his days, Shimon was a conflicted man. His zeal for teaching and learning never waned, and his commitment to Labor Zionism was as intense as ever. He traveled up and down the east coast and through the Midwest, proselytizing the Zionist ideal and teaching Jewish studies. At the same time, the devastation he felt over Leah's abandonment never left him. I've always thought about this saga as Dr. Zhivago on the Hudson, a Jewish replaying of the classic novel by Boris Pasternak. Only this time the characters were real. When Shimon suffered a heart attack in 1936, his doctor forbade him to work. It was the final blow, as he could no longer practice the calling that had sustained him and his identity since his days in the Pale of Settlement.

As his health deteriorated, my grandfather may have been acutely aware that he was nearing the end. But he could still manage a smile for the world. I learned this through a miraculous discovery I made in my sister's home—her bomb shelter, to be precise—twenty-five years ago during a visit to her home in Israel. There was a box of dusty, 8 mm movie reels, and one bore my father's unmistakable handwriting, reading "Papa 1937." I transferred the old and fragile film to videotape, and when I popped the cassette into my VCR, I was stunned by the last few frames. They showed a crowded Manhattan street scene, with my mother and grandfather walking arm in arm toward the camera. At the very last second Shimon looked directly into the camera and flashed a smile with a twinkle in his eye. That smile, to me, trumped all the unhappiness in his life. Eight decades later, it still touches a deep chord in me.

The same year this film was shot, my grandfather moved with Minna and her husband, David Yaroslavsky, to Los Angeles. They hoped the warmer air and more relaxed pace of Southern California would improve his health. But it was not to be. "His years in Los Angeles could have been years of peace and contentment had it not been for his illness," my mother wrote. "Slowly the joy in his face faded along with his warm and caressing laughter." Shimon Soloveichik died on June 18, 1940, at the age of sixty-seven.

"Did Your Mother Ever Forgive Me?"

Like Shimon, my mother never got over the dissolution of her family. Zina Zisman Levy, a childhood friend from Poltava, recalled wrenchingly sad moments with Minna soon after her arrival in New York City. The two would sit on the steps of the apartment building their families shared, with Minna weeping, pouring her heart out about the pain her mother's actions had caused her.

Minna was by nature a generous, forgiving person, and if Leah had turned her back on the family, she would not do the same. There's no doubt, however, that she felt her mother's behavior had crossed a line. When World War II ended, she sent Leah a letter with a self-addressed return envelope inside, hoping she would receive it. She did, and sporadic communication resumed between mother and daughter. Still, Minna made sure Leah understood her feelings. She mailed two care packages of clothing to Leningrad, and in an enclosed note wrote that she had sent one package to Leah "because you're my mother," and a second package to Mendel "because he survived the war."

As for Leah's feelings, we got a glimpse in 1960 when Shimona visited the Soviet Union. She made plans to meet our grandmother in Leningrad. The morning after she arrived, there was a knock at her hotel room door, and Leah was standing there—a slight woman with light hair, all dressed in black, Shimona recalled. Leah used a cane and had obvious pain walking. For the first few seconds she stood silently in the doorway. Shimona finally moved toward her and gave her grandmother a hug. "I'm a warm person and my parents told me that Leah was a distant person," she recalled. "I don't want to say she was cold, but she was not immediately emotional."

Soon, however, the two warmed up to each other. There was no end to questions about Shimon, Minna, and the family. Leah invited her granddaughter back to her apartment and Shimona remembers that "she wanted to be good to me. She was cooking me food, saying 'eat this.' She wanted to be grandmotherly to me. That day and for several days afterwards, we sat and talked. It would be more correct to say I sat, and grandmother talked. She talked of her life in Poltava." During these visits, Shimona said, "she was deeply sorry that she could not share her life with our mother. Only once did she address the issue that tore our family apart. Looking squarely at me, she asked: 'Did your mother ever forgive me?'"

Shimona thought about how to answer and finally said, "She never spoke of it." She didn't want to add to her misery. She wrote to Leah in the years that followed, and reminded her that she had a family in California—a son-in-law, a granddaughter, a young grandson, Zev, whom she hadn't met. But the chasm was too wide. Leah died four years later. Any private thoughts, any secrets she had, were buried with her.

"A Father's Soul Lives in His Child"

Shimon's spirit lives on in the example he set as a father, teacher, and dreamer. He has always been an inspiration to me. He was a member of one of Judaism's greatest generations, and I am blessed and proud to be his descendant. The things he fought for—the values that drove him—have shaped my life. I can only imagine how elated he would have been to witness the birth of the State of Israel. He once wrote exactly how he hoped that would happen: "We taught the world many things," Soloveichik wrote of the Jewish people. "Let us teach it one more thing. Let us see something that history has not seen the likes of—to build a homeland through peace and justice, without bloodshed, just by toil and culture."

Years after he died, I inherited his 220-year-old High Holiday prayer book that had been in our family for generations. It's an oversized, rectangular volume. The pages are well-used and aged on the edges; the cover is deep brown, almost black. When I take it out every year for Rosh Hashanah and Yom Kippur, I look at the pages, pock-marked with candle wax that dripped on the book before electricity came to Eastern Europe. Shimon Soloveichik could have never dreamed that the book would be in use decades later. That inheritance, like Soloveichik himself, is a bridge between our ancestors, myself, my children, and grandchildren. "Each generation inherits and bequeaths," my grandfather once wrote. "A father's soul lives in his child." And, I would add, in his grandchildren as well. The boy who played down by the river in Kopach embarked on a life-changing journey that would light the way for me years later.

CHAPTER 2

My Parents: Minna and David

The moment was so perfect, it could have been scripted. Except it wasn't. In 1989, as I began walking precincts in the San Fernando Valley to introduce myself to voters in a newly drawn City Council district, a *Los Angeles Times* reporter accompanied me. He wanted to see firsthand how residents reacted to their new councilmember. My campaign for re-election was just beginning, and I was happy to oblige him. Notebook in hand, he followed me onto a residential street in Van Nuys and watched as I knocked on the first door. A pleasant, middle-aged woman answered.

"I'm Zev Yaroslavsky, your new councilman," I said. "I just wanted to introduce myself to you." She reacted with astonishment, saying, "Oh my, I knew your mother! She was my Hebrew teacher years ago at LA City College. One of the kindest, most generous people I've ever known. I'm happy to meet you."

I chatted with my new constituent for a few minutes, always interested in hearing about my mother. Then I thanked the woman, handed her my literature, asked for her vote and for permission to put a "Vote for Zev" sign on her lawn. We began moving on to the next house, but first I wanted to assure the reporter that this was not a set-up. "That precinct and that house were randomly selected," I told him. The larger truth, however, is that it was common throughout my career for perfect strangers to tell me how my mother and father had impacted their lives.

"They Hit Him on His Neck and Killed Him"

Both of my parents fled persecution and uncertain futures in post-revolutionary Russia, but the similarities end there. Although my mother's family secured safe passage with a sponsoring family in the United States, my father's experience was far riskier. David Yaroslavsky grew up in the small Ukrainian city of Belaya Tserkov, about fifty miles southwest of Kyiv. Like Minna Soloveichik, he was raised in a Labor Zionist household. His reason for leaving the "old country" was easy for me to understand, thanks to a constituent of mine from Pacific Palisades. Years ago, she told me that her father came from the same city as my dad. She thought I would be interested in his first-person account of a trip he took back to Belaya Tserkov in 1920—an effort to locate his parents and bring them to America.

It was an eye-opening story. Her father encountered a lawless, violent city plagued by desperate poverty, starvation, virulent antisemitism, and execution-style murders. It was a place where hope was virtually non-existent. He witnessed the cold-blooded killing of an old man, who protested when two soldiers stole a fish from his pushcart in the market. They laughed at his complaints, then beat him to death. "They hit him on his neck and killed him," the visitor wrote. "It's a scene I'll never forget. All I've seen here is people starving." He also learned that soldiers were grabbing girls and sending them into the barracks, to wash the floors and clothes for them. He said soldiers routinely pointed guns at him and shook him down for money, even for the shoes on his feet.

It was a nightmare my father knew well. He grew up with a constant fear of pogroms and remembered hiding with family members in a basement cellar to escape the carnage. The atrocities continued in the immediate aftermath of the 1917 Bolshevik revolution, when Russia was plunged into a bloody civil war. Tsarist sympathizers, bolstered by troops and economic aid from western nations, including the United States, launched a major counterinsurgency and tried to topple the new regime. Russian cities and villages in the Pale of Settlement were engulfed by violence, and bands of soldiers—many of them with ambiguous loyalties—roamed the streets at will. The unrest continued for years, and any hope that Russian Jews would enjoy a better and safer life after the revolution quickly disappeared.

At nineteen, my father left his hometown and joined up with a group of forty others seeking passage to America. They included the grandparents and future mother of Elizabeth Holtzman, who went on to become a member of the United States Congress and served on the Judiciary Committee that recommended the impeachment of President Richard M. Nixon in 1974. Her family's ragtag group made its way to Romania, a place where you could buy travel documents on the illegal market and change your identity, with no questions asked. The group spent about eight months waiting for all the documents they needed before finally arriving in the United States.

Years later, however, no matter how hard I looked, I couldn't find any record of my father's arrival at Ellis Island in 1921. So, I called Liz and asked if she could help me through this predicament. She researched and solved the mystery: "Your dad didn't come in under his family name," she told me. "He came in under my grandparents' name." I looked under the new name and, bingo, there he was. The manifest said that my father was sixteen years old and had blonde hair. I knew I had the right guy (there weren't many Jews with blond hair coming from Eastern Europe). But I also knew that he was nineteen when he got to New York. I suspect that my dad knew that his odds of getting out of Ukraine and into the United States were far better if he came in as a minor, and as a member of Holtzman's family. The subterfuge worked. By 1923 both he and my mother were settled in a new land, with new lives, in New York City.

Builders and Dreamers

Back then, education began early in Labor Zionist households. Minna and David had been members of the movement's Scout groups that sprang up in Russia and other European countries. These organizations introduced children to Zionist values and prepared them for an eventual move to Palestine, to help rebuild the Jewish state. My parents held fast to that dream when they arrived in America. Both graduated from the Herzliya Hebrew Teachers College in New York City and joined the left leaning Hashomer Hatzair youth movement.

David was a chapter leader, and he met Minna at a group gathering. "They became a couple," my sister, Shimona, recalled. "They were sort of going out together…It was like they were in a clan, part of a group." Amid growing tensions in the organization, the young couple joined with others to launch a new Zionist initiative, known as Habonim.

Although it was aligned ideologically with Labor Zionist leaders in Palestine, Habonim also pursued a uniquely American focus on social justice. By the time my parents got married in 1933, they were prominent leaders of the new group. Hebrew would be the dominant language in the movement's schools, and Minna was given a key role in defining and implementing the group's educational agenda.

On May 12, 1935, American Habonim marked its birth with a New York City ceremony saluting its first one hundred members. My mother was the emcee, and my father traveled to the event from a New Jersey farm, where he was helping to prepare Habonim members for agricultural life in Palestine. The new organization published a mission statement:

We are Jews, the sons and daughters of an ancient people that never grows old. However, we are now living in an age when the very existence of the Jews is being threatened. Hitler—Poland—fascist marches even in liberal London!

We are Jews, active Jews, intelligent Jews. We strive to cement friendly relations with other nations, with our American neighbors here, our Arab neighbors in Palestine. We strive to 'know ourselves' so that we may better understand others, they, us. We are Americans. We are Habonim—the builders.

Goldie Meyerson Works Down the Hall

My parents were quite a team, in life and work. In fact, they were often referred to in the collective—"Minna and David." My mother remained devoted to her father, and she cared for him in his declining years. David also adored Shimon, spending countless hours with him. The three lived together in the city, and their daily lives were deeply intertwined.

Years ago, I discovered a remarkable black-and-white photograph of my mother from 1936, standing next to David Ben Gurion, who would later become Israel's first Prime Minister, on a Manhattan street. He frequently visited New York City in those years to raise money and political support for the campaign to create an independent Jewish state. On one of his visits, Minna served as his secretary and body person.

Habonim rented space in the same Lower Manhattan building as the national headquarters for the Labor Zionist Party, and my parents became familiar with VIPs who came and went. One of them was a young Goldie Meyerson, who worked as Labor Party representative in New York. She would later be known as Golda Meir, Prime Minister of Israel. Her office was down the hall from my parents during that period.

Minna and David brought different skills to the table. My father had strong executive abilities and was an obsessive organizer. He was the more introspective of the two, with a temper that flared from time to time. My mother was a generous and outgoing person. Though she often stood on principle, she had a talent for bringing people together. My parents were gratified by their lives in America, but never doubted that they would one day settle permanently in Israel.

That decision was complicated, however, because my grandfather had developed arteriosclerosis and respiratory problems and seemed frailer with each passing day. His doctor recommended a change of scenery, far from the pollution and frenetic pace of New York City. He suggested a place with clean, dry air—and Los Angeles fit the bill. Labor Zionist leaders on the west coast let the couple know they'd be welcome if they chose to relocate and offered to help them find work. At the same time, growing fears of war in Europe and uncertainties in the Middle East made a move to Palestine difficult, if not impossible. Although my parents' plans had been deferred, their Zionist dreams remained strong.

A Little Bit of Palestine in Los Angeles

When Shimon and Minna Soloveichik, and David Yaroslavsky, set foot on American soil in the early 1920s, Jewish immigrants from Russia and Eastern Europe were flooding into the United States in record numbers. More than two million had arrived since 1880, settling mainly in east coast and Midwestern cities.

In the ensuing years, waves of Jews within the United States began moving west across the continent, especially to California. In 1937, my family arrived in Los Angeles. Boyle Heights, the East Los Angeles community that welcomed them, was a polyglot of immigrants; among them, tens of thousands of Jews. These new arrivals were beginning life all over again. If New York City was teeming with established Jewish institutions, the City of Angels was a place where people were building them from the ground up.

Boyle Heights soon became the nation's largest Jewish community west of Chicago. It was a place where one could buy challah bread and rugelach more easily than tacos and burritos, according to Los Angeles journalist Gustavo Arellano. The neighborhood had long been a port of entry for new arrivals, a home to working-class residents and progressive political groups, and the influx of new Jewish residents deepened that tradition.

At one point, Jews comprised nearly 40 percent of the community's population. Amid the worsening international climate, the community and religious leaders helped organize a 1935 mass meeting at the Philharmonic Auditorium at Fifth Street and Olive in downtown, to protest the treatment of Jews in Nazi Germany. Jewish organizations built synagogues, opened schools and ran community centers. Neighborhood branches of powerful labor unions opened on Brooklyn Avenue, the area's main thoroughfare, now known as Cesar Chavez Boulevard. Business was booming at the original Canter's Deli. Kosher butcher shops, bakeries, and small groceries dotted the neighborhood. Yiddish was the primary language for many residents, as more than 2,000 Jewish families a month moved to Los Angeles by 1946. By the end of the decade nearly 300,000 Jews called the city home—no longer just in Boyle Heights but branching out to West Adams, South Los Angeles, the Fairfax neighborhood and eventually the San Fernando Valley.

My parents and grandfather moved into a small apartment on Soto Street in Boyle Heights, and they took their place in the community. The national Labor Zionist organization had sponsored a Hebrew school in nearby City Terrace, a small unincorporated community in the hills above East Los Angeles. My mother, with her passion for education, became a teacher at the school, known as the Folk Shule. The building included two classrooms and a small auditorium, and the structure at 4018 City Terrace Drive still stands today, as the Plaza Community Center. My father soon joined Minna on the faculty, as did Miriam Getzler, a close friend who had traveled to Palestine in 1931 with Minna and David. Within months, my parents took over the leadership of the school and quickly expanded its mission.

The school became a gathering place for community and political groups. There were rallies for the sale of United States Bonds to support the war effort; protests and demonstrations against the Ku Klux Klan, and a community drive to store and protect the belongings of Japanese-American citizens, who had been uprooted from their Los Angeles homes during World War II by our government and transported to remote detention camps. The first local chapter of the B'nai Brith was organized in the school building, along with two branches of the American Jewish Congress. It was a busy place.

The community was overjoyed on November 29, 1947, when the United Nations approved the partition plan establishing a Jewish and Palestinian homeland in Palestine. On the day of the vote, Shimona recalled, "my mother gave me a whole bunch of little blue and white ribbons, and we attached them to a pin. We gave them to anyone who walked into the school." David and Minna viewed the Folk Shule as a powerful community force in building support for the Jewish state. According to my sister, the school "was like a little bit of Palestine in Los Angeles.

Planting the Seeds of Habonim

My parents were determined to teach and pass on a value system based on the Jewish concept of "Tikkun Olam," which in Hebrew means repairing the world. Helping to build a Jewish homeland was paramount, but David and Minna were realists, too. They knew that the school experience had to connect with most students who would remain in Southern California. Both my sister and I attended the Folk Shule in our early years, and Habonim became part of our daily lives as we grew older. We learned that life was not just about grades and textbooks. It was also about social justice, workers' rights, civil and human rights. We were taught that people should be valued for their intrinsic worth, not for the size of their bank accounts, or their religious, racial, national or ethnic origins. Whether it was in Israel or Los Angeles, the same values had to apply. Our teachers and counselors led by example and encouraged us to have the courage of our convictions, to live the life we believed in.

Habonim ran summer camps throughout the country. One was Camp Kvutzvah in Green Valley—nestled in a canyon in the northern outskirts of Los Angeles County just north of what is now the city of Santa Clarita. My father was the camp's business manager during the mid-1950s. Even though I was too young to be a camper, I spent wonderful summers there with my parents. At first glance Kvutzvah looked like most summer camps, with swimming, sports, hiking, and scouting. But it was modeled on an Israeli kibbutz—or collective farm—and the goal was to give campers a taste of what life in such a world was like.

Everyone was treated equally. If I came to camp with a box of bubble gum, I'd have to throw it into the community pot, to be redistributed equitably to all campers. They were divided into age groups, and held robust discussions with counselors about Zionism, social justice, philosophy, leadership, and the difference between right and wrong. These values helped frame a world view that would guide me for the rest of my life.

J.J. Goldberg, the former Editor-at-Large of *The Forward* newspaper and my cabin-mate in a Habonim leadership training camp during the summer of 1966, has pointed out that graduates of Habonim went on to become leaders in North America and Israel—in politics and the rabbinate, in communal work, education, and labor. He said Habonim, for all practical purposes, was an officers' training academy for young activist Jews in the latter half of the twentieth century. Amen!

A Call to Action

Mark Twain once wrote, "Don't let your schooling interfere with your education." I got my schooling in the classroom and in camp discussions, but I got my education at home. As a young child in the 1950s, I was schooled at our dinner table. My parents didn't teach me and my sister what to think or what to do. But they insisted that we commit our lives to something greater than ourselves. If we had strong beliefs and dreams, it was up to us to turn them into reality. Social justice wasn't a checklist of causes. It was an urgent call to action.

Shimona and I were raised to make a difference, and we had sterling examples at home. My father helped organize the Los Angeles Hebrew Teachers Union, fighting for fair wages and benefits for teachers in the Jewish educational system. My mother helped organize anti-fascist marches and pro-Israel demonstrations. She opened students' eyes to injustice, at home and abroad. My parents still planned to move to Israel, and in 1954 my mother took a six-month sabbatical trip there, with my sister and me.

I was only five years old, and I hated the place. To begin with, Israeli milk was not homogenized, so the cream rose to the top, causing me to gag every time I took a sip. Strike one! The hamburgers were not finely ground like they were back in Los Angeles, making them tough to swallow. Strike two! Finally, eggplant was ubiquitous in Israel, and it made me nauseous. Strike three and Israel, you're out! (To this day I refuse to touch eggplant.)

My mother, however, knew that a six-month trip to Israel would be a formative experience, even at my early age, and I do have profound memories of the trip. I was fascinated that there was a place where *everyone* spoke Hebrew, not just those of us who learned to speak it at home in Los Angeles, as Shimona and I did. Hanukah was not a holiday celebrated by a handful of people in our living rooms, but by the whole country in the public square. Most important, I felt like I belonged. In time, the memory of the milk and burgers faded (not the eggplant), and the feeling that I had been in the homeland of the Jewish people was palpable.

When we arrived back in America, shortly after my sixth birthday, major changes awaited us. Thousands of Jewish families, lured by housing opportunities, had begun moving from Boyle Heights to the western part of Los Angeles and the San Fernando Valley. The communal infrastructure that had sustained the Jewish population in our neighborhood began to disintegrate. Synagogues, Jewish bakeries, kosher butchers, and Jewish schools were disappearing one by one. What was once a diverse community of Mexicans, Japanese, Jews, and Russians was now predominantly Mexican.

My parents held on, refusing to move as long as the Folk Shule's doors remained open. But by the end of the 1956 school year Minna and David couldn't fill one classroom for the next year, and they were forced to shutter the school. We left Boyle Heights and moved into a new home at 710 North Martel Ave., at the corner of Melrose Avenue in the Fairfax neighborhood.

At first we were exuberant, because we owned our own home, with a lovely back yard and garden. I loved baseball. Gilmore Field, the home of the minor league Hollywood Stars, was walking distance from our new house. Kids got in free on Saturdays, and I took full advantage. When the Dodgers came to town, I followed them religiously. I badgered my dad to take me to the 1959 All-Star Baseball Game at the Coliseum. It's a moment seared in my memory. I spent the afternoon transfixed by Ted Williams, Stan Musial, and Mickey Mantle. My father sat quietly next to me in the center field stands, reading four Yiddish newspapers he had brought with him to while away the hours.

At that point in my life, my ambition was to succeed Vin Scully as the Dodgers' broadcaster. This was more than fantasy. I used to pretend I was Scully. I would sit in front of our television set with my father's tape recorder and broadcast my play-by-play of games onto old magnetic tapes, a few of which I still have.

One day, when the St. Louis Cardinals were in town to play the Dodgers, I called the Statler Hotel where the visitors were staying and asked to speak to Stan Musial. The operator asked no questions and connected me to the room of one of the greatest men to ever play the game. I was surprised when he picked up the phone. Straining to make my pre-pubescent voice sound as deep as possible, I identified myself as Bob Price, host of the Bob Price radio sports show. "I just want to do a short interview with you about the Cardinals," I said.

I asked him to talk about the team's hitting, and he answered as if I was a real sportscaster. "Well, we've got some great hitters—Ken Boyer and Curt Flood come to mind," he said. "How about your pitching?" I followed up. "Oh, we've got a great young right hander by the name of Bob Gibson," he obliged. And so, it went. "Thank you, Stan Musial, for being with us on the Bob Price Sports Show," I concluded. "You're welcome, *son*," he answered. He wasn't fooled for a second, but no matter. It was great practice in case the Dodger broadcast job suddenly opened up. But it's a good thing I didn't wait around for Scully. He retired more than five decades later.

I'm sure I wasn't the first kid who had the audacity to call Musial's hotel room, and I certainly wouldn't be the last. But he made time for this eleven-year-old, who just wanted to talk baseball with a future Hall of Famer. Decades later, thanks to a mutual friend, a package arrived from St. Louis and was sitting by my front door. Inside was an official major league baseball that was inscribed: "To Zev. A great fan. Stan Musial." He was a real mensch.

I liked hanging out with friends, but my mother had laid down a strict rule in our home: First you work, then you play. Although my father spent as much time with us as he could, Minna was the CEO of our household. And she never missed a beat in raising Shimona and me. She took us to doctor's appointments and held us accountable for our schoolwork. Every Saturday morning, my mother would sit me and Shimona down, separately, and go over a chapter of the Torah. We were not a religious family, but we were traditional. Our parents believed that it was important to read the bible for its historical significance and for the important moral issues it raised. Take the story of Cain and Abel. At one of our weekly study sessions, when I was seven years old, my mother asked: What does it mean to kill your brother, and then lie about it? What would have been the right thing to do, the ethical thing to do?

January 17, 1959

I was a happy kid, but the joy of our new surroundings was short lived. My mother was not well, and doctors discovered that she had developed breast cancer. It was not clear how far it had spread, but the prognosis was not good. At the age of seven, my father did not convey the seriousness of the situation to me.

Minna didn't slow down, despite her debilitating illness. By then she had been teaching Hebrew at Los Angeles City College for nearly ten years. She worked day and night, reading term papers, grading exams, and helping students who fell behind. Our home remained a busy place that welcomed friends, family, and community activists like my mother's childhood home in Poltava decades before.

It was inconceivable to me that something might be seriously wrong with my mother. Shimona, eight years older, understood the gravity of her illness. But even she insisted that our mother would overcome this challenge. The doctors said she needed to live five years without a recurrence of the cancer to be out of danger, and we were confident she would. They held out the possibility that further treatment or another operation would bring her back to health, and we believed them.

By January 1959, my mother's condition deteriorated. She had to be propped up in her bed to keep working. It was deeply upsetting to me to watch her struggle. It was also miraculous to watch her engage in incredible acts of human kindness. One example came to me in the mail years later, from a friend of my parents whose wife had died in mid-December 1958. My mother had sent him a handwritten note of condolence on December 24, and he thought I'd like to have it. The fact that she could write such words while dealing with her own pain and mortality was astonishing:

When I heard of your tragedy, I wanted to wait until the seven days had passed so that I could open my letter with 'shalom.' Then I myself became ill and I couldn't sit down to write until today. What can I say? We knew that Mrs. Sheraga was ill and even very ill—but did not imagine the depth to which her human condition had reached…What can we say to you? How will we comfort you? We hope you will find solace in your work for Zion and Jerusalem.

The irony is that this was precisely how I felt, watching my mother fighting for her life. On January 16, 1959, doctors said my mother's last, best hope was an operation that she might not survive. We visited her at Kaiser Hospital in Hollywood that day, but I wasn't allowed to go to her room because of my age. So, my mother went out on her room's seventh-floor balcony and waved to me as I stood on Sunset Blvd. waving back. The next thing I remember is waking up suddenly at 4 a.m. the next day to see my mother's childhood friend, Zina Levy, washing dishes in our kitchen. She had comforted Minna years before when my mother was devastated by *her* mother's abandonment. Now, Zina had flown to Los Angeles to say goodbye.

As the sun rose, my dad took me into his bedroom. He had been crying and said simply, in Hebrew: "*Ima Enena.*" Mother is no more. Years later, I learned that my father had kept our mother's deteriorating condition from my sister and me. He shielded us from the dreadful inevitability of her passing until the very end. Minna Yaroslavsky was forty-nine years old when she died.

When you're ten years old it's hard to process such a life-changing event. My mother was the rock of my life. She was everything. And now she was gone. As the hours passed, I felt the need to be alone. In a household filled with grief and the flurry of preparations for a funeral, no one noticed when I slipped quietly out the door. I began walking down Melrose Avenue early on Saturday morning with a basketball under my arm, heading for the Fairfax High School gymnasium, 10 blocks away. Once inside I began shooting hoops over and over, trying to make sense of an unfathomable truth. I felt truly alone.

Who Was That Woman?

To those who knew Minna, the huge crowds that turned out for my mother's memorial service at Temple Beth Am on La Cienega Blvd. would not have been a surprise. She influenced so many people, and over 700 of them showed up to pay their respects. My sister remembers pedestrians passing by, asking in wonder, "Who was this person who drew such a crowd?" For me, the answer has come from those who still take me aside decades later, remembering my mother's spirit, integrity, and kindness. She had all of that, and more. But I couldn't put any of this into words on that raw January day.

Minna Yaroslavsky died too soon, and she left behind a shattered family. I've carried her loss for a lifetime and wish she could have been in my life longer. But I'm also profoundly aware of the values she imbued in me—a legacy I carry to this day.

CHAPTER 3

The Sandman Awakens

—————

As 1959 dawned I began the painful process of learning to live without my mother. There was a gaping hole in my life, and as a boy I would only slowly begin to realize how much I had lost. The woman who had shaped me, upon whom I relied on more than anyone, was suddenly gone. And then I had to contend with another loss.

Within a year, in 1960, my sister kept a promise she had made to my parents. She made "aliya"—permanently immigrating to Israel, where she lives today. My father, still grieving over Minna's death, tried to convince her to delay that decision. She could do this later, he pleaded. But Shimona was determined to move. After all, this is precisely what my parents raised her to do. Even though my sister was older than me, we were close. We shared great times and heartbreaking sorrow. We had shared a bedroom in our Boyle Heights apartment and now she was moving 10,000 miles away.

That left me and my father. He became my mentor, my supervisor and sole parent. He was the one who would now hold me accountable for school, homework, grades, chores, and extracurricular activities. He did his best in his new role, but it wasn't easy. Although we talked a lot, he couldn't replace my mother. We had radically different schedules. He taught at the Los Angeles Hebrew High School, and his workday typically began at 4 p.m. By the time I got home from school he had already left for work, and most days he wouldn't return until 10:00 p.m. By then I was usually asleep. We were like ships passing in the night, and long before I knew what the term meant I became a latch-key kid. I had to prepare my own dinners, do my own homework, and tackle my household responsibilities largely without parental supervision. It was now up to me to make decisions that most kids my age would not make until years later. With apologies to Tennessee Williams, I learned to rely on the kindness of family members, friends, teachers, and neighbors, and on my own wits.

To be sure, I had chores to keep me busy. I took out the trash cans, which gave me my first encounter with local politics. For decades, Los Angeles had allowed homeowners to burn garbage in backyard incinerators. In a landscape that already had a natural propensity for air pollution (Indigenous populations of the Los Angeles basin called it the "Valley of the Smoke"), the blackened air pouring out of hundreds of thousands of backyard smokestacks severely aggravated the region's air quality. Choking smog was pervasive from the San Fernando Valley to San Pedro, and there were days when my friends and I were prohibited from playing in the school yard. It was my job every week to clean out the ashes from the bottom of our incinerator, put them in the "ash can," and haul it to the curb for pickup. When the practice was finally banned in 1957, my workweek was cut, but my allowance wasn't. What a great system! My thrill turned to elation four years later, when newly elected Los Angeles Mayor Sam Yorty fulfilled his campaign promise to end the practice of separating trash into two or three separate receptacles. Once again, my workload was reduced, and once again there was no reduction in income. Like any constituent, I was thankful for small favors.

I was also gratified that my father and I were together on Friday nights, the beginning of the Sabbath, and on weekends. We went on vacations and spent time with family friends. Three months short of my eleventh birthday, I entered the city's Hebrew High School, which I attended twice a week after my regular school day was over and on Sunday mornings. I experienced the privilege, and the burden, of having my own father as a teacher. I loved him and I cared deeply about him. Aside from DNA we had one other thing in common: We had both lost Minna Yaroslavsky, and we would both spend a lifetime grappling with that tragedy.

Someone to Watch over Me

Shortly after taking my seat on the Los Angeles County Board of Supervisors in 1994, I got a call from a constituent, Molly Ann Rubin. She wanted to meet with me to discuss a grant proposal for the Hollywood Canteen, an agency that served wayward teens. As it turned out, Mrs. Rubin had been my sixth-grade teacher at Melrose Avenue School, and when we met she startled me by saying, "I remember when your mother died." She explained that it caused great concern to the staff at the school. Ms. Groves, the principal, called all the teachers and staff together and said, "We must embrace Zev. Keep an eye on him because he has suffered a great personal trauma." Molly added poignantly, "I doubt you were aware that the entire staff of the school had you on their radar screen." I didn't know it, and I was moved to tears to learn four decades later that they were watching over me.

I made a lot of friends in the years that followed, including kids in school and kids from Habonim. One particular friend, Harry, was the only boy my age on our block. He and I played almost every day; baseball in our front yards, with the Lionel trains in his garage, and just about everything else. He also had cerebral palsy. The first day I met him I couldn't help but notice his disability, but before long I ignored it entirely. He was an all-star in my book.

Many years later President Jimmy Carter would launch an economic stimulus package, the linchpin of which was the Public Works Employment Act (PWEA). Any city that had a "shovel ready" project would be eligible for millions of dollars in federal largesse. At the time, the one thing Los Angeles had ready to go were thousands of curb cuts. These are ramps that make it possible for people with physical disabilities to safely move from a sidewalk to the street at intersections throughout the city, without having to step off a curb. Mayor Tom Bradley led the effort to secure the funding and I aggressively supported his efforts, even as many of my constituents scoffed at what they considered a waste of taxpayer funds. Easy for them to say. Thanks to my boyhood friendship with Harry, I knew what a difference these curb cuts could make to people experiencing disabilities. I was determined to get them built. To this day, whenever I see the ramps, I think of him.

Keeping out of Mischief

Although I got myself into my share of mischief as a youngster, it's a miracle that I didn't get involved in more serious trouble. I was lucky that my plate was full when I entered Bancroft Junior High School in 1961. Once again, friends came to the rescue. Yoni Shultz and his brother Norm also lived on Martel a few blocks away. They were two of my best friends. Yoni played a strange instrument in the school orchestra—the oboe—and I watched enviously as he performed on opening night in a school production of George and Ira Gershwin's "Girl Crazy." I wanted to be in show business, too.

So, I made a beeline for the beginning woodwind class. The teacher, Robert Williams, asked what I was doing there, and I told him that I wanted to play in the orchestra. "OK, we need an oboe player," he said. He told me to grab one from the shelf, go into the cubicle, and teach myself to play a C major scale. When I thought I was ready, I could join the rest of the class. A day later, I was ready. The oboe makes a beautiful sound when played well, but a beginner makes it sound more like a duck in heat. Nevertheless, I passed the test and played for three years in the school orchestra. Classical music had always been a staple in our household, but playing in the orchestra gave me a deeper appreciation and understanding of the genre. It would play a pivotal role later in my public service career.

Around the same time, I was also beginning to develop a political conscious-ness. I was determined to accept President John F. Kennedy's challenge to take a fifty-mile hike, for example, until my father explained I'd have to walk from our Fairfax neighborhood to San Clemente in Orange County to complete the journey. I also won my first political contest during this period for the post of Boys League Vice-President. I began my campaign speech to the student body by saying, "I have a friend here who'd like to speak on my behalf." Turning my back briefly, I spun around wearing a JFK mask, and in a thick Bostonian accent told nearly 1,000 students that they should vote for Zev "because he has great vigah." This brought the house down. I also suggested they "vote for the candi-date with the shortest first name and the longest last name." This would not be the last time I would exploit my three-letter given name.

Like so many others, I followed the perilous course of the 1962 Cuban Missile crisis. It's hard to imagine now the psychological impact those thirteen days had on me and my generation. I was thirteen years old, and the threat of nuclear war was palpable. "Duck and cover" drills were de rigueur for school age kids, as if our 1960s-issue school desks would protect us against a ballistic missile attack. Fallout shelters were for sale all over, and I thought having one under our backyard would make a great club house. But my father would have none of it. As the crisis built, so did my anxiety level. I sensed that the stakes couldn't be higher. Only later did we all realize how close we came to being incinerated.

The following year, during the summer of 1963, my father took me on an eight-week trip to Israel to visit my sister and her husband, David Kushner. Being together with my dad and Shimona for the first time in two years was special. We rented an apartment in Jerusalem for two months, but also traveled throughout the country. My dad even took me to the Prime Minister's office, where one of his old Labor Zionist friends was a senior advisor. I was offered the opportunity to sit behind Prime Minister Levi Eshkol's desk, but I declined. Presumptuous, I thought to myself. One day we drove to Eilat at the southern tip of Israel. Our driver and tour guide was Yitzchak Ulitzky, my mother's child-hood classmate in Poltava. In the desolate Negev desert, a rock struck the oil pan under Ulitzky's 1954 Plymouth station wagon. Oil began to stream onto the road, and the nearest service station was dozens of miles away. What to do? Ulitzky stopped the car, took out a handkerchief from his pocket, and stuffed it into the hole in the oil pan to stop the leaking. And off we went. This was Israel, after all, where necessity was the mother of invention. We got to the next gas station without further incident.

As it happened, the World Zionist Youth Congress was meeting in Jerusalem that summer, and I attended the opening reception hosted by the President of Israel. When I made my way through the receiving line to shake hands with President Zalman Shazar, I introduced myself in Hebrew: "I'm Zev Yaroslavsky from Los Angeles." The President's eyes lit up: "Are you Minna's son?" I said I was. My parents had known Shazar since they met in New York in the 1930s, when he was an emissary for the Labor Zionist movement. Shazar insisted that I have my father contact his office the next morning, so our family could come to the presidential residence for afternoon tea.

My father, sister, and brother-in-law were invited along with me, and they were all extremely excited. As for me, I was 10,000 miles away from home, missing Sandy Koufax's greatest season to date. I still had issues with Israeli cuisine, and apparently I could do nothing but complain to anyone who would listen. Before we left to meet the President, my father and sister took me aside and admonished me: "We are going to meet the President of Israel in his official residence. Please don't embarrass the family. Whatever you do, keep your complaints to yourself." My response was, "I'll think about it." When the President greeted us in his reception room, he looked me in the eye and asked: "So how are you enjoying Israel?" I paused as my family members held their collective breath. "It's OK," I responded. This was my first brush with international diplomacy, and my family was relieved.

November 22, 1963

I was moved by President Kennedy's mystique from the moment he declared his candidacy, and I followed everything he did. We had seen him up close when my dad took me to a 1960 campaign rally at the Shrine Auditorium, and our family displayed a JFK bumper sticker on our Plymouth Valiant. I watched every press conference he held and followed his policy initiatives. I related to his youth, vision, and modern ideas, and thought he could do no wrong.

President Kennedy challenged the nation to embrace civil rights, and laid down a marker to send astronauts to the moon, and more. Then, on November 22, 1963, a hall monitor came into my third-period Spanish class and handed a note to our teacher, Ruth Land. She was standing right in front of me as she read it to herself, and then she blanched. I had no clue what was up, and she seamlessly continued with the lesson. At approximately 11:20 a.m., when the class was about to end,

Principal Paul Schwartz came on the public address system and announced that President Kennedy had been shot and killed in Dallas, Texas.

My heart sank. Ms. Land broke down, and I slowly connected the dots. The note she got minutes before had simply said that the president had been shot. She learned of the President's death at the same time as the rest of us. I was stunned. In the days that followed, I was obsessed with the non-stop television coverage of the tragedy. I can remember every moment of that long November weekend: the cortege carrying Kennedy's casket to the Capitol, John Jr.'s salute to his father coffin, the procession to St. Matthew's, and the motorcade to Arlington National Cemetery. I can still see Jack Ruby pointing his gun at Lee Harvey Oswald as though it was yesterday. I wondered how they let someone with a gun get that close to the assassin.

A sudden, unexpected death, whether it's a parent or a president, can turn one's life upside down in a millisecond. I felt for the President's two children, because I knew what it was like to lose a parent and wondered how they would cope. On that dark weekend, however, we couldn't begin to know what the assassination portended for the nation as a whole, in what turned out to be a tumultuous and tragic decade.

"Pick It up, Yaro, You Can Do It"

I entered Fairfax High School in February 1964, and I look back on my high school years with gratitude, nostalgia, and a bit of cynicism. Our school featured a lineup of academic go-getters, talented thespians, some decent athletes (but mostly not), and some of the greatest teachers any high school student could want. Most of us did not fully appreciate the comfortable middle-class bubble in which we were living, isolated from many of the city's social problems. Our school's pompous, overbearing alma mater, "Hail to Thee, Lord Fairfax," was an anachronism in the maelstrom of the 1960s. Still, I couldn't have asked for a better high school education. I became a math and science major because that's what many Fairfax students did in those days. Although I earned decent grades, I wasn't headed for Cal Tech.

If you can still remember the names of teachers who made a difference in your life by the time you're on Medicare, you're lucky. I have my share. George Schoenman, my tenth-grade English instructor, taught me how to write a composition. He showed me how to coherently organize my thoughts and persuasively present ideas. To this day, when I write an op-ed column or a speech, I outline it exactly the way Schoenman taught me. He also taught how to look critically at advertising. "Winston Tastes Good like a Cigarette Should," Schoenman would say, quoting the slogan of one of America's top-selling cigarettes. "What the hell does that mean? How *should* a cigarette taste?" It sounds good, he would explain, but it means absolutely nothing. Besides, a cigarette doesn't taste good. This taught me not to accept at face value what people in authority say—whether they were hucksters selling a product, or government leaders selling disastrous policies. This was a profound lesson, with the war in Vietnam revving up and domestic turbulence sweeping the nation.

Marty Biegel, a colorful and outspoken government teacher, encouraged us to debate political issues in class. We had the freedom to dispute his views, but God help us if we couldn't intelligently defend our own. Our class met in the choir room and students were seated on risers as Biegel paced back and forth like a coach on the sidelines, randomly calling on students to discuss that day's current events. I loved Biegel's class because it was so relevant to the things that really interested me. I got to talk about politics, policy, presidents, and governors—whatever was on the front page of the morning newspaper. We were judged by the degree and cogency of our participation, not by our points of view. He counseled us to be prepared and to bring our best to class every day. Years later, when I was well advanced in my public service career, I learned that Biegel took pride in telling people that "Zev was one of my boys." As I told him before he died, I was proud to be one of his boys.

Biegel's gifts, however, went beyond the classroom. At the time, Fairfax High School's population was largely white and mostly Jewish. All of that changed four years after I graduated. District boundary lines were redrawn, and Fairfax became a more racially diverse school. The pace of change was accelerated by the destructive 1971 Sylmar earthquake, which forced the temporary closure of nearby Los Angeles High School. Overnight, half of its largely Black student body began sharing space at Fairfax High School for half-day sessions. Some parents didn't embrace these changes, but Biegel saw enormous opportunity.

He counseled the Fairfax community to seize the moment and set an example for interracial harmony that would resonate with the rest of the city. Looking back, students and their parents credit him with building bridges at a time when white families were threatening to leave the public school system entirely. Los Angeles was caught up in a bitter legal battle over school integration, a fight that would drag on for twenty-five years. Yet Fairfax High School safely navigated these uncharted waters, in part because of Marty's firm hand and reassuring optimism. There was also a collateral benefit to these changes: Biegel became coach of the school's varsity basketball team, and his dramatically improved squads began to win conference championships. The school's now well-established tradition of basketball dominance began with Marty.

When I entered Fairfax, I joined the cross-country and track teams. Our coach, Dean Balzarette, was more interested in my ability to run a two-mile race than in my academic pursuits. A wiry, compact man who had been a star quarter-miler at USC, he became the coach of the Fairfax cross-country and track teams in 1965. His athletes either loved him or hated him. There was no middle ground. I fell into the first category, but earning Balzarette's respect was no easy task. He demanded a special kind of excellence, invoking the wisdom of John Wooden, UCLA's legendary basketball coach: Living up to your full potential, measuring yourself against your abilities instead of others', is the most important goal of all.

Balzarette was a strict disciplinarian who imposed a rigorous workout schedule. He put us through punishing sprints and long runs, and even though I wasn't one of the top runners on the team he treated me like I was. When I improved my performance, he complimented me like I had just helped the team win a championship. When I didn't, he let me know it. He demanded that I train as hard as I intended to run on race day. As a result, Balzarette made me the best runner I could be. During my last year at Fairfax I ran my fastest ever two-mile race, in a track meet against Hamilton High—eleven minutes and fifty-nine seconds. Remarkably, the first half of that race represented my fastest one-mile time ever, 5:59, and I never got close to that time again. I had set two goals for myself in my three-year competitive running career—to improve my racing time each week, and to earn an athletic letter. More than any other teacher, Balzarette taught me that success isn't handed to you; it's earned through preparation and effort. Years later, as I walked door to door soliciting votes in my first election, I could hear Balzarette's voice: "Pick it up, Yaro. You can do it."

Balzarette offered one more teachable moment in the fall of 1966. After our final league meet, our cross-country team was waiting for a bus to take us back to Fairfax from Pierce College in Woodland Hills, a suburban community in the far west San Fernando Valley. Republican Ronald Reagan was running an aggressive campaign for Governor against the incumbent, Democrat Pat Brown. So, what's a group of Fairfax students to do while waiting for a bus? Talk politics, of course. "Anybody who votes for Reagan has to have his head examined," I said confidently to my teammates. Suddenly I heard Balzarette's booming voice behind me: "Yaro, watch out who you're talking about." He wasn't pleased, and my face turned as red as my crimson running shorts.

This was the first time I had knowingly come face to face with someone who thought Republicans should be spoken of respectfully. In our Beverly-Fairfax neighborhood, Franklin D. Roosevelt was like a god. Actually, God was like a Roosevelt. The late president's son, Jimmy, was our congressman, and Fairfax residents still had vivid memories of the depression and the New Deal.

My exchange at the bus stop showed me that not everyone loved Franklin and Eleanor, or Pat Brown, or even JFK, for that matter. There was a whole other world beyond Fairfax High School. It was a lesson learned! I made it a point to never again assume anything about anyone's politics.

Living in a Cocoon

Beyond the partisan divide, it was dawning on me that the comfortable world in which I lived was part of a racially segregated city. By design, Los Angeles had rigidly separated its white population from communities of color. This was the result of more than a half century of discriminatory lending policies, racial covenants, and plain unvarnished racism. When thousands of Black people and Latinos migrated to Los Angeles during and after World War II, these inequalities became more pronounced.

In fairness, high school students like me might be forgiven for not thinking beyond their neighborhood or their school. I could live my entire life in Los Angeles without encountering people who didn't look like me. Yet there was no mistaking the fury that exploded in the 1965 uprising in Watts, a predominately Black community in South Los Angeles, about a dozen miles from my home. It was driven by Black community anger over police abuses and economic inequalities. Still, for all the violent pictures filling our TV screens during that awful August, I'm sure that I and most of the kids at Fairfax thought of the uprising in Watts as an event far away, in a part of the city they never visited.

My sense of isolation, however, began crumbling in 1964. While the presidential election between Lyndon Johnson and Barry Goldwater dominated the nation's attention, there was a growing furor in California over Proposition 14 on the state ballot. It was sponsored by the California Real Estate Association and aimed to repeal the Rumford Fair Housing Act, which banned racial discrimination in the sale or rental of housing. This battle galvanized California liberal voters in a fight against racial bias. I went to a massive Hollywood Bowl rally to protest the initiative, put a "No on 14" bumper sticker on my dad's car (with his permission) and volunteered in the "No" headquarters. The top leadership of the Democratic Party campaigned furiously against the measure, but we were trounced on Election Day, losing by 2.3 million votes—more than a two-to-one margin. The campaign against the Fair Housing law had won support from nearly 68 percent of Los Angeles County voters, which meant that a healthy percentage of county Democrats also voted to repeal the law.

It was the most powerful manifestation of racism I had witnessed to that point in my life. Until a 1953 Supreme Court ruling ended the practice, many homes across the city were governed by covenants limiting sales and rentals to whites only. Throughout the county, neighborhoods like Bel Air, Hancock Park, Los Feliz, and Toluca Lake were off limits to Black people, Mexicans, Asians, and Jews. Indeed, Los Angeles was a city of ethnic and racial enclaves, with Jews largely on the Westside and in the San Fernando Valley, Latinos on the Eastside, and Black residents in South Los Angeles.

Racial covenants had a very human face. In 1950, when future Los Angeles Mayor Tom Bradley was starting a family and rising through the ranks in the Los Angeles Police Department, he wanted to buy a home in the Crenshaw District's Leimert Park neighborhood. But the only way he, a Black man, could purchase the house was through the aid of a white intermediary, who fronted for him. Years after restrictive racial covenants were outlawed, their legacy was kept alive through an informal covenant among property owners and real estate agents who simply wouldn't sell or rent to non-whites. In the late 1950s and early 1960s, even high-profile Black players on the Los Angeles Dodgers faced obstacles when they tried to buy homes in "white only" neighborhoods.

After Proposition 14 passed in 1964, there was no sense that these restrictions would be ending anytime soon—certainly not with the conservative political wave that was sweeping California at the time. A sign of the time was Ronald Reagan's 1964 assertion that "if an individual wants to discriminate against Negroes or others in selling or renting his house, he has the right to do so."

The Proposition 14 battle took place in the same year that the 1964 Civil Rights Act was signed into law, and one year before President Lyndon B. Johnson launched his Great Society programs. California had taken a giant step backward, while the nation was moving forward with an ambitious social experiment. Even though the United States Supreme Court eventually overturned Proposition 14 on constitutional grounds, the scars were long lasting. Meanwhile, anxiety grew over America's escalating war in Southeast Asia. There was ferment everywhere. People could still tune it out, especially high school students, and many did. But I took a different path.

The Sandman Awakens

Although I had a diverse group of friends in high school, I was closest to the kids I met in Habonim. Some attended Fairfax High with me, but most hailed from throughout Southern California. I spent virtually every weekend with them in movement activities, or going to movies and ball games. As we grew older, we began to take the lessons of the movement more seriously. You had to be a participant in life, not an observer; an activist, not a bystander. So, I was thrilled when I got an invitation to attend Habonim's national leadership training camp in the summer of 1966 in Hunter, New York. There would be 60 or so of us, brought together from across the country, and I assumed the experience would underscore things I already knew. I couldn't have been more wrong.

When I left Los Angeles that summer, it was the first trip I had ever taken by myself. I first went to Washington, DC to take in the sights. I spent a few days as a guest in the home of J.J. Goldberg, who was also headed to Hunter that summer. He would later become an important author, journalist, and close friend. From there I boarded a bus to New York City, where I stayed several nights with Zina Levy, my mother's childhood friend, and her husband, Arthur. Then it was off to the camp, nestled in the Catskill Mountains.

All the campers were extraordinary in their own way, which initially intimidated me. Our cabin had a stellar cast of characters: Goldberg was an articulate intellectual who could speak eloquently on most any issue. David Twersky, a flaming red head, was an anti-war zealot. He started a campaign to protest the raising of the American flag every morning. Yehuda Rubin was an avowed radical. He would eventually move to Israel and become a West Bank settler.

Day and night, we engaged in debates over American politics, Israel, the Vietnam War and LBJ. Believe it or not, I was a little shy back then. During nightly debates in the cabin I'd argue my positions in low-key monotones, in marked contrast to the fiery arguments made by my East-coast cabinmates. They were fast-talkers and knew more about verbal sparring than I did. My pals soon nicknamed me "Sandman," because when I spoke, I tended to put them to sleep. Although we were the most controversial boys' cabin, I was one of the token moderates. At this point in my life, I didn't fully grasp what Martin Luther King, Jr. called "the fierce urgency of now." Over the course of the summer, my sense of purpose markedly intensified.

Indeed, my experiences at "Machaneh Bonim" (Hebrew for Camp of the Builders) sharpened my instincts to challenge authority, to ask questions of people in power. The kid who rode a bicycle across town two years earlier to shake LBJ's hand was now ready to campaign fiercely against him and a war that was tearing our nation apart. Most important, I decided I was going to fight for human rights behind the Iron Curtain and advance the cause of the young State of Israel. The world looked quite different by the time I got back to Los Angeles. Put simply, I was transformed.

Last Lap at Fairfax High

I began my final semester at Fairfax in the fall of 1966, restless and anxious to move on, but still facing twenty more weeks of academic rigor. I also had one more cross-country season to pursue an athletic letter. By the end of January, I expected that I would march across the stage, pick up my diploma, and head off to college. But then, there was a bump in the road.

During this period of my life I did wicked impersonations of show business personalities, politicians, and especially my teachers. At Fairfax it was traditional for the graduating class to be entertained by a handful of their classmates in a talent show. For the senior breakfast, as it was called, our class had a deep bench of talented actors, singers, and musicians who were asked to perform. Then there was me. I was asked to do an impersonation of our legendary chemistry teacher, Mr. Sawyer, an older chap who hailed from the Northeast. He spoke with a thick, Ichabod Crane-like New England accent and had several well-worn idiosyncrasies. In all humility, my Sawyer impersonation that morning was spot on. It was such a hit that our principal, Jim Tunney, who was also a National Football League referee, came up to me afterwards, put his arm around me and said, "Zev, you did a wonderful job this morning." I was on cloud nine.

I also did a mean impersonation of our Analytical Geometry teacher, Leonard Taafe, and he knew it. Due to a space between his two front upper teeth, he had a unique speaking trait. Every time he pronounced a word with an "s," it came out like a whistle. One day in class, he intentionally positioned himself right next to my desk and made what he called an important announcement: "Classsss, next Monday we are going to have a sssssurpise quiz, and the subject will be conccccccentric ccccircles." It was all I could do to control myself. Then he added, "sssso classsss, thisssss weekend I want you to sssssstudy ccccircles, ccccircles and more ccccircles." At that point I lost it. I burst out laughing so hard, that I literally fell out of my chair onto the classroom floor. The last thing I remember was Taafe, staring down at me. Not surprisingly, he gave me a "U," an unsatisfactory, in cooperation and behavior on my report card.

I also got a "U" from my social studies teacher, but this one was decidedly undeserved. Mark Lit was an ardent defender of the Johnson administration's Southeast Asia policy. I decided to stand up to him and challenge his position. For doing so, and defending my beliefs, I got a second "U" on my final report card.

This posed a problem, because if a graduating senior received two "Us," he or she could be barred from participating in the graduation ceremony with the rest of the class. After twelve years in the Los Angeles public school system,

I was about to be prevented from walking across the stage to get my diploma. Jim Tunney summoned me to his office to advise me of the school's policy. Then, to my surprise, he asked what I thought he should do. I told him it didn't matter to me whether I graduated on stage or not. I'd get my diploma either way. However, it would deeply hurt my father, who had experienced enough pain in the preceding eight years. My graduation would give him a strong dose of happiness, which he deserved.

As for the two "Us," I told Tunney that I strongly objected to the one I received for differing with Mr. Lit on the Vietnam war. It flew in the face of everything I had been taught at Fairfax. Although I was not contesting the "U" I received for impersonating Taafe, I told Tunney that "I don't know why I should be punished so severely. In fact, sir, when I impersonated Mr. Sawyer at the senior breakfast, you took the time to come over and congratulate me." The office fell silent for a moment. Then Tunney turned to me and said, "So I did, so I did."

That's how my high school career ended—walking across the stage and accepting my diploma from Jim Tunney. As an NFL referee he had never reversed a call, so I was relieved he reconsidered his original decision in my case. It turned out to be a wonderful week. I graduated with my class, and also got my long-coveted athletic letter for cross-country running. For all the pomp and circumstance, leaving high school was somewhat anti-climactic for me. I had already experienced more defining transitions in my life, and graduation couldn't begin to compare. I was sorry to part with my classmates, some of whom would not live through the next chapter in their lives, and many of whom I would never run into again. I would miss my great teachers and the whole high school experience. But it was time to move on. I was now headed to UCLA, where a whole new world awaited me. I was ready to embrace it.

CHAPTER 4

Coming of Age

———

When I arrived at UCLA in the spring of 1967, it was as if a black-and-white movie suddenly changed to technicolor. I was in a state of wonder. Although the sprawling Westwood campus had opened decades earlier, it was a shiny new landscape to me—an academic Shangri-La. Right away, I was swept up in an upbeat, contagious energy. The university was packed with people and ideas from all over the world, and I wanted to soak it all up. I met new friends and remained close with old ones from high school and Habonim. Over the next four years we'd see our lives—and the world around us—change dramatically.

My biggest initial challenge was figuring out which courses to take. All the other questions that make first-year students nervous, like what I was going to do with the rest of my life, remained unanswered and understandably so. How many people can tell you at the age of 18 what their future path will be? But one thing remained absolutely clear: I had a strong belief in the importance of social activism and a responsibility to make a difference in the world. That inner drive would continue to shape me in the years ahead. However much I might change on the surface, my core values would never change.

On a personal level, I was now a bit more removed from the emotional shock of my mother's death. Although I was feeling more secure and confident, my father and I still had to watch every penny. I continued to live at home and drove a 1954 Mercury convertible, carpooling to school every day with friends. College life seemed to fit me like a glove.

The Math Just Didn't Add Up

I entered UCLA as a Math major, largely because science and math were my focus at Fairfax High. It seemed like the logical thing to do, but my future as a mathematician didn't last long. All of the Fairfax brainiacs envisioned themselves going into engineering or the sciences. Some aspired to launch a career in the space program. Although I was fairly good at math and science, it wasn't my passion like it was for some of my classmates. I couldn't see myself spending the rest of my life solving equations or developing formulas, not when there was a world out there to save. I decided to merge my math background with a subject that I could apply to social policy, so I became an Economics major.

I shifted academic gears, again, when I took an elective class in the history of Southeast Asia with Professor Damodar Sar Desai. This turned out to be a transformative decision. The Vietnam war was dominating the headlines, and I thought I would benefit from knowing something about the region's modern history. So you can imagine my surprise on the first day of class when Sar Desai announced: "This is History 156A, the History of Southeast Asia from pre-historic times to the tenth century."

It was not exactly what I had in mind, but I couldn't disrespect the professor by walking out at the outset of class. So, I stuck it out for an hour, and I'm glad I did. Sar Desai brought ancient history to life, as though I was watching a travelogue in real time. I had never experienced such a vivid, interesting, and dynamic history instructor before, and I decided to stick with the class. The rest, you'll pardon the expression, is history. I took every other class that Sar Desai offered, and it became clear to me that I was in love with the discipline. I became a double major in Economics and History. My interests soon gravitated to British Empire History under the tutelage of one of that subject's great scholars, John S. Galbraith (not the economist). He would become my advisor through the rest of my college years and a personal mentor as well.

I stayed connected with Professor Sar Desai until he died a few years ago. At one point, as he recovered from stomach surgery, he sent me a signed copy of a book he had written about the history of India. I sent him an email thanking him and recounting the story of the day I stepped by accident into his class. He responded with an email of his own: "That story made me laugh so hard, I thought I was going to bust my stitches."

Enter Barbara Edelston

In May of 1967, I was working at the Los Angeles Hebrew High School from which I had graduated three years earlier. They paid me to be an errand boy on Sunday mornings, relaying messages to teachers and ensuring students didn't make mischief the way I used to. One day, I noticed an attractive woman working the switchboard in the lobby. I had known her casually through Labor Zionist youth circles, but we never really had a serious conversation. On the spur of the moment, I asked if she would go out with me the following Saturday night to a new comedy club that had just opened on the Sunset Strip. She agreed, and that was my first date with Barbara Edelston, the only woman I'd ever date from then on. We went to see "The Committee," an improvisational comedy group that included two of her high school classmates—Richard Dreyfuss and Albert Brooks. Most importantly, we began a relationship that changed and later anchored my life for more than fifty years.

Barbara was beautiful, gregarious, and whip smart. She was a member of Hashomer Hatzair, the more leftist branch of the Labor Zionist movement that my parents broke away from in the 1930s, and we'd joke in later years that we were an inter-faith couple. We started dating exclusively and did virtually every-thing together. I just loved her genuine affection for people, her warm personal-ity, and the way she made every person in her life feel important. This is who she was. She had a keen radar for phoniness in people, which she could sense immediately. Over the years, she helped shape the person I ultimately became.

Barbara had lost her father at a relatively early age, so she was raised by her mother. Over the years I grew to appreciate Ruth Edelston, but we didn't hit it off at first. Actually, that's an understatement. I made every effort to steer clear of her, because she was deeply suspicious of my intentions. It didn't help that my car broke down constantly and made a lot of noise. I also had longish hair and didn't exactly dress like a preppy. What's a mother not to like? Barbara and I had to find ways to meet surreptitiously, which made for a unique courtship. I couldn't just knock on the front door of her huge house in Beverly Hills and expect to be admitted.

I frequently wanted to stop by and visit Barbara, late in the evening, on my drive home from UCLA. The challenge was how to get into the house without Ruth knowing. I came up with a plan: I'd accelerate my car about a block away from her house, then cut the engine and lights and coast quietly into her drive-way. Barbara would then meet me at the side door. Occasionally, however, the Beverly Hills police took notice of my jalopy and long hair. They wanted to know what I was doing in the neighborhood. I explained the situation, and they even-tually aided and abetted my scheme.

All the while political turbulence was growing in America and abroad, and I followed those events closely. I hosted and produced a public service program that was broadcast on FM radio, sponsored by the Jewish Youth Council of Greater Los Angeles. In 1967, I interviewed Yael Dayan, daughter of Israeli Army general, Moshe Dayan, who was passing through Los Angeles on her way home from a visit to Vietnam. She gave me a blunt assessment of the war: America couldn't win without winning the hearts and minds of the Vietnamese people.

"And you're losing them," she added. It was a prophetic appraisal. She delivered another assessment, however, that turned out to be way off the mark. Dayan said confidently that there was no likelihood of war between Israel and her neighbors at that time because neither side wanted it.

Six Days in June

By the spring of 1967, most of us felt that Israel's very existence was hanging by a thread. President Gamal Abdel Nasser of Egypt had moved his armies into the Sinai Peninsula, and ordered a blockade of the Straits of Tiran, cutting off the vital shipping corridor to Israel's southern port of Eilat. Nasser had been threatening to wipe out Israel for years, and he now appeared ready to make good on that promise, with the help of Syria and ultimately Jordan.

At that time, you wouldn't have given Israel good odds for surviving a multilateral attack from its three strongest neighbors. The expectation was that such a conflict, if it occurred, would at best be brutal and ugly. Tensions were at an all-time high for one month, and a major conflagration seemed inevitable. There have been hundreds of books and thousands of articles written about this period, offering myriad analyses and conspiracy theories, and I don't intend to revisit the history of the Six-Day War here. What matters is what I knew and how I felt in real time. The Israeli military was massively outnumbered, and Nasser's provocative moves posed an existential threat to the nineteen-year-old Jewish state. Israelis were warned to prepare for the worst, and they were instructed to dig mass graves just in case.

War broke out on June 5, and the experience impacted me in a very personal way. Two decades after the Holocaust, I couldn't imagine a world without Israel. I had already visited there twice. I had friends and relatives there whose lives hung in the balance. Some of my Habonim buddies had immigrated to Israel, and some were serving in its army. The country to which I had grown emotionally attached was now in the cross hairs.

Getting news out of the Middle East in the first hours of the war was difficult. When it's daylight in Israel, it's the middle of the night in Beverly-Fairfax. That's when the bulk of the military action was reported. So, when the war started, I left my radio on next to my bed all night, every night, so that I would get the news as soon as it was broadcast. I never broke that habit. To this day, I continue to leave news radio on next to my bed at night.

At first the Arab nations were reporting great victories. In fact, Israelis immediately gained the upper hand after a preemptive attack, and I was relieved.

The war underscored how important Israel was in my life. In the Soviet Union, however, three million Jews only got the news as reported by Radios Cairo, Damascus, and Moscow. The only reports they heard during the first days were that Arab armies were overrunning the Israelis. They believed that the Jewish state, a nation that had given them a semblance of psychological security, was in shambles. When the truth finally reached them, they swelled with pride, feeling more emboldened in a hostile land.

More than any single event in my lifetime, those six days in June awakened Jewish self-confidence and pride around the world. Throughout, there were daily debates and arguments over the conflict on the UCLA campus at Meyerhof Park, the school's free speech zone. We had pro-Arab students, including visiting students from Arab countries at UCLA, and the back and forth got heated. I was taking to political activism like a duck to water.

Century City—The Beat Goes On

Back home, another war came to dominate my life as well. On June 23, 1967, as my first quarter at UCLA came to an end, a coalition of 80 anti-war groups organized a huge protest march in Century City. President Johnson was the headliner at a Democratic Party fundraiser at the Century Plaza Hotel, and I went there to join the protest. We heard rousing speeches by Dr. Benjamin Spock, Muhammed Ali, and others, but the march quickly turned into a police riot. I was in the back of the crowd and didn't witness the violence, but there was no question that something had gone terribly wrong at the front of the march. It became an explosive national story.

As Johnson arrived at the hotel, more than 15,000 peaceful, largely middle-class demonstrators were marching up Avenue of the Stars, where they planned to file past the hotel in protest and then disperse. Whatever speech LBJ made that night was lost to history, because riot police began moving on the crowd, swinging batons in an effort to break up the march. A handful of protestors at the front sat down on the pavement, refusing to move. Los Angeles Police Chief Tom Reddin ordered his officers to shut down the march, as he peered down on the scene from a high-rise command post inside the Century Plaza. The air was suddenly filled with the sickening sounds of clubs smashing into bodies. I could hear the screams of protesters trying to get away from the advancing police phalanx. Chaos was all around us. As darkness fell, the crowd was trapped and unable to move.

When the confrontation de-escalated, I went home infuriated by the LAPD's unnecessary and excessive use of force. But Century City was more than a case of police misconduct on a massive scale. By 1967, the Vietnam War had become the dominant issue in America, with thousands of soldiers coming home in body bags, victims of a bloody conflict that made no military, diplomatic or ethical sense. The mayhem in front of the hotel that night was yet another harbinger of the political storm that would sweep the nation. I joined with millions of other Americans in believing that the Democratic Party, and the nation, needed to find an alternative to LBJ.

Taking Care of Business

As the summer began, however, I had to find a way to support myself financially and help pay for my education. Family members came to the rescue. Sidney Solow was as close a relative as our family had in Los Angeles. His father, Yehuda, was my grandfather Soloveichik's brother. He had shortened his name to "Solow" when he landed at Ellis Island. Sid and my parents remained close to one another after they arrived in America in the early 1920s. To me, Sid was like a second father. One of the greatest honors you can give someone in the Jewish tradition is to ask him to hold an infant boy during the circumcision ritual. He was one of two people to whom Barbara and I gave that honor when our son, David, was born.

Sid Solow was president of Consolidated Film Industries (CFI) in Hollywood, a film developing laboratory second in size only to Technicolor. He was a legend in the film industry and won several Academy Awards for technical achievement. Although I wasn't going into the film business, CFI hired me for a summer job that paid $100 per week, enough to cover my tuition and books for an entire academic year.

Aside from the income I earned, I'm grateful to Sid for exposing me to the real world of factory work. My job was a clock-punching one. CFI developed films for the top TV shows in Hollywood, and my assignment was to pick up empty film cans that had been inked with the name of a show—say, "Mission Impossible"—then clean the cans with acetone and bring them back to the beginning of the assembly line, where they'd be filled with another film print. That's what I did all day, every day. I was always looking at my watch. How long was it until my lunch break? How long until quitting time? The workday seemed like an eternity, and the experience gave me an appreciation for people who worked these jobs. It also showed me the importance of labor unions. I joined one of them—IATSE, the International Alliance of Theatrical Stage Employees—to work at CFI, a union shop.

Actually, CFI was not all monotony. One day Sid called me into his office and introduced me to Quincy Jones. He asked if I could give Quincy a ride back to 20th Century Fox film studios where he was working on a film. Although I wish I could remember what we talked about, I do recall how that genius, who profoundly impacted America's cultural landscape, took an interest in who I was and what I planned to do with my life.

Annus Horribilis

By my sophomore year at UCLA (1968), the simmering political protests of the summer had reached a national boiling point. America and the world were plagued by one traumatic event after another, month after month, in a steady parade of urban uprisings, campus shutdowns, electoral clashes, assassinations, military invasions, and political revolutions. It felt like the world was coming apart at the seams.

The domestic disorder was in large part rooted in America's involvement in Vietnam, as well as what LBJ called "the crippling legacy of racism" in cities across the country. As for Vietnam, the question I kept asking was, "why were we there?" The reasons for that growing involvement, which began with small teams of military advisors and soon morphed into full-scale war, would have been hard for even the most erudite observers to explain at the time. The true facts—that LBJ and his administration knew the war was unwinnable but kept fighting to save face—would only come to light years later.

The lack of purpose and transparency was fully revealed in January 1968, when the Tet Offensive, mounted by North Vietnamese and Viet Cong forces, destroyed the Johnson administration's narrative that America was turning the tide and winning the war. In coordinated, surprise attacks, they launched crippling assaults on urban centers and overran key military targets through-out South Vietnam. At one point, they briefly seized control of part of the US Embassy in Saigon. The debacle prompted Walter Cronkite, who at the time was the nation's most trusted television journalist, to air a scathing critique of the war, leading President Johnson to conclude that "if I've lost Cronkite, I've lost Middle America." Indeed, our government's credibility had fallen to an all-time low, a credibility gap that hasn't really been closed since.

During that same month, US Senator Eugene McCarthy (D-Minn.) addressed a packed house of 12,000 students at UCLA's Pauley Pavilion. The crowd cheered his insurgent campaign to unseat Lyndon Johnson as the Democratic Party's nominee. I was part of that audience, and desperate for an alternative to LBJ. McCarthy had me at "hello." He was the only game in town, and I readily volunteered for his campaign. The improbable crusade caught fire on March 12, when McCarthy garnered an impressive 42.3 percent of the vote against Johnson in the New Hampshire primary. It was an astonishing upset, even though the president had won more votes. What once seemed like a fantasy—nominating an anti-war Democrat and ending the war—now looked like a genuine possibility. I was exhilarated at the prospect that a grassroots presidential campaign could lead to the end of the Southeast Asian bloodbath once and for all.

But the month was still young. Four days later, Sen. Robert F. Kennedy entered the race for the presidency. On March 16, the same day he announced his candidacy, US ground troops in Vietnam assaulted the village of My Lai, slaughtering more than 500 Vietnamese civilians. The month's climatic political moment came on the 31st, when Johnson, facing grim political realities, announced that he would not seek re-election. I was sitting in our living room watching his speech, and as he spoke the fateful words—"I shall not seek and will not accept the nomination of my party for another term as your president"—I erupted in cheers, much to my father's chagrin (he was a Johnson supporter). It now seemed that the anti-war movement would prevail in the presidential election. But then, four days later, Martin Luther King, Jr., was shot to death as he stood on a balcony at the Lorraine Motel in Memphis. The murder of the leader of the American civil rights movement was a body blow to the nation, especially to Black Americans. I learned of the assassination as I was walking across the UCLA campus that afternoon. King was a beacon of hope to those who believed in racial justice. That included me, and as we experienced the second assassination in less than five years, I asked, "What the hell is going on?" The tragedy triggered civil unrest across the country, leading to forty-six deaths and hundreds of injuries.

The drumbeat continued in June, when California voters cast ballots in the bitter Democratic presidential primary fight between Kennedy and McCarthy. Although I admired Bobby Kennedy and would have eagerly supported him had he entered the race earlier, I remained loyal to McCarthy. I walked precincts for him in Westchester, a quiet community in southwest Los Angeles which is home to LAX. In those days, it had an even distribution of Democrat and Republican households. Once again, I was reminded that each community in Los Angeles was distinct. You could walk for blocks in my Fairfax neighborhood and never see a Republican voter. In Westchester, many of my fellow Angelenos didn't care a whit for liberal politics, nor were they interested in the nasty Democratic primary clash. They were going to happily vote Republican.

On election night, June 4, 1968, Robert F. Kennedy was shot after proclaiming victory before his supporters at the Ambassador Hotel in Los Angeles. Barbara and I were just leaving McCarthy headquarters at the Beverly Hilton Hotel when we turned on the car radio and heard the news. I was devastated. Enough was enough, I thought to myself. What is happening to our country? The next day I joined with hundreds of others in a vigil outside Good Samaritan Hospital where Bobby lay unconscious. We were hoping against hope that he would somehow survive, but that was not to be. He died early the next morning, June 6, twenty-six hours after being shot. His death appeared to signal an end to the hopes and dreams—not to mention the primary votes—of millions who believed they would propel an anti-war candidate to victory. McCarthy quickly faded into the background. Vice President Hubert Humphrey, LBJ's protégé who had not entered a single primary, went on to win the nomination at the Democratic National Convention in Chicago later that summer.

I watched on television as Chicago police began violently dispersing anti-war demonstrators at the Democratic convention. The bloodbath repulsed millions who watched it on live TV, and Mayor Richard Daley made history of a sort when he defended the attacks by his police department on unarmed protestors, saying: "The policeman isn't there to create disorder. The policeman is there to preserve disorder." A week later, Tommie Smith and John Carlos, US athletes who won medals in the 200-meter dash, made headlines around the world when they raised their fists in the Black power salute during the playing of the Star-Spangled Banner at the Mexico City Olympics. It was a sobering reminder that Vietnam wasn't our only national grievance. The War on Poverty had failed to lift the hopes of America's most vulnerable and marginalized citizens.

As I watched the tumult of 1968 unfold, it was clear that the United States was not alone. Uprisings and conflict swept the globe. In May, the "Bloody Monday" riot by Parisian students and a massive general strike ignited revolts across France. Sympathy strikes erupted in one city after another until French President Charles de Gaulle suppressed them with thousands of military troops. The drama continued on August 20, when the Soviet Union invaded Czechoslovakia with more than 200,000 Warsaw Pact troops and 5,000 tanks. It put a brutal end to the "Prague Spring" and President Alexander Dubcek's hope that his nation might become more democratic and eventually free itself from Soviet domination. In October, police and soldiers killed more than 300 students at a political protest in Mexico City. Ten days later that city hosted the opening of the Summer Olympics, which thirty-two African nations boycotted because of South Africa's participation in the games.

Nixon won the Republican nomination in Miami that summer, promising to crack down on dissent and honor the nation's conservative "Silent Majority." On November 5, he was narrowly elected president. His victory was a slap in the face for those of us who worked so hard to end the war. Although I was too young to vote in 1968, I initially told myself that, if I could, I wouldn't vote for Humphrey because of his pro-war stance. But I changed my mind about two weeks before the election, coming to the conclusion that as deficient as Humphrey was, the stakes were too high to elect Nixon. So, I would have grudgingly, but affirmatively, voted for Humphrey. I've always wondered whether he would have beaten Nixon if eighteen-year-olds had the right to vote in 1968. To this day, I'm not sure.

Millions of people were dispirited the day after the election. I remember Nixon holding a press conference and joking "I know how it feels to lose a close one and how it feels to win a close one. Winning is better." Some thought it was a funny line, but I didn't see the humor in it. When I looked back at the carnage of 1968—the lives lost, the leaders killed, the hopes destroyed—Nixon's trivial crack was like an exclamation point on a disastrous year. As the clock struck midnight on New Year's Eve, I literally heaved a sigh of relief, grateful that the horrors of 1968 were now in the rear-view mirror. But the damage had been done. The country was bitterly divided and shaken to its core.

The Good Earth

For all the despair, there was one bright moment at year's end. In late December, the Apollo 8 astronauts were the first to orbit the moon, and they beamed pictures of its ghostly, pock-marked surface back to earth. I was watching the event on television at home, utterly transfixed by the images of the earth rising above the moon's horizon, a blue and white "marble bowling ball" that Joni Mitchell and others would later describe. I was greatly moved when Astronaut Frank Borman read from the opening lines of the Book of Genesis as Apollo circled the moon. They were the same words that my mother had me read aloud at our kitchen table nine years earlier:

> And God said, 'let the waters under the heaven be gathered together unto one place, and let the dry land appear: and it was so. And God called the dry land Earth; and the gathering together of the waters he called the Seas: and God saw that it was

good'…And now from the crew of Apollo 8, we close with good night, good luck, and Merry Christmas—and God bless all of you, all of you on the good Earth.

It was a reminder of how precious and fragile the earth is, and I felt a rare glimmer of hope in a world gone berserk. But there was no sugar-coating what America had just been through. Queen Elizabeth may have popularized the phrase "Annus Horribilis" in 1992, when she fretted about Royal Family travails, but 1968 truly deserved the title. Millions of people were confused and disheartened, wondering what to do next. For many the answer was to tune out reality, forget about politics, and drop out. But I was the son of two parents who didn't raise me to watch life from the sidelines, or shy away from confrontation. I had been taught to act, and as the New Year began I was more determined than ever to do just that.

CHAPTER 5

The Walls Have Ears

If an aspiring activist was looking for ways to change the world in the late 1960s, there was no shortage of opportunities. The Vietnam War continued to rage, the civil rights movement was still traumatized by Dr. King's assassination, and the War on Poverty was imperiled by a new, conservative Republican administration in the White House. It seemed that all a person had to do was pick a cause and get to work. The question was not whether to act but which path to take, and quite often the answers were found in our personal histories. As Shakespeare wrote, "What's past is prologue."

For me, a clue lay in my Bar Mitzvah seven years earlier. On the surface, it was a warm and joyous affair. My sister flew in from Israel and I was surrounded by family and friends. The speech I gave saluted my mother and grandfather, and their lifelong work as educators and pioneering Labor Zionists. I spoke of the times in which we were living: "There is no difference in the attitude you should have toward someone just because his opinions are different than yours, just because he worships differently than you do—or just because his skin is a different color than yours," I said. "God created all men equal, and it is the responsibility of men to keep it that way."

And then there was a surprise telegram. It came from my father's two sisters in Kharkiv, Ukraine (then in the Soviet Union). It simply read: "Congratulations on your birthday." This sounded strange to me. I was celebrating my *Bar Mitzvah*, not just my birthday. In Jewish tradition it's a holy rite of passage, an ascension to adulthood. Every other greeting I received said, "Mazel Tov on your *Bar Mitzvah*," or "We wish we could be with you on your *Bar Mitzvah* day." So, I asked my dad, "What's with 'happy birthday?'"

He explained that his sisters lived perilous lives as Jews in the Soviet Union. Since 1917 the government had shut down all but fifty-five synagogues in a nation of 3 ½ million Jews. (There were at least that many synagogues in West Los Angeles, where I lived.) My father said Jews in the Soviet Union were prevented from speaking, teaching, reading, or writing Hebrew. They even took risks celebrating the Sabbath. Mail was routinely screened and often went undelivered. On top of it all, they were not allowed to emigrate to more hospitable nations, and they faced horrific consequences if they tried. At bottom, they were persecuted for being born Jewish.

My father told me that if my aunts had used the words "bar mitzvah" in their congratulatory wire, they would have risked arrest. So, "happy birthday" would have to suffice. I took careful note of this reality. In a world where people were fighting for their rights and basic freedoms, Jews living in the Soviet Union, *my people*, were experiencing a cultural and religious genocide.

I kept thinking that we in the free world weren't doing enough to protect our fellow Jews. This gnawed at me. Had we not learned *any* lessons from the world's silence during the Holocaust twenty-five years earlier? Soviet Jewry needed champions, and I was determined to be one of them.

Persecution and Terror

In 1966, Elie Wiesel, Nobel Laureate and conscience of the Holocaust, published *The Jews of Silence*, an eye-opening book telling of his visit to the Soviet Union. He described his rendezvous with hundreds of Jews who recalled in humiliating detail the discrimination they experienced. The Jews of Silence to whom he referred were actually Jews in the West who remained silent while their brethren suffered behind the Iron Curtain.

Buoyed by Israel's victory in the Six-Day War, small numbers of courageous pacesetters—roughly several thousand Soviet Jews—began to seek visas to immigrate to Israel, their ancestral homeland. Officially, Jews had the "right" to leave as long they received invitations from a close relative in Israel. Yet this was an illusion, because the Soviets had no interest in honoring these requests. In any event, Moscow had severed diplomatic relations with Israel at the onset of the 1967 war, so processing the invitations was difficult, if not impossible. Moreover, Soviet antisemitism was a way of life, exacerbated by official anti-Israel policies amplified in the Soviet media and press. Applying for an exit visa was extremely risky and would usually result in the loss of one's job or apartment. It could also result in arrest, internal exile, or years in the Siberian gulag. Either way, there was a heavy price to be paid.

"The Walls Have Ears"

I made my first trip to the Soviet Union with my dad in September 1968. This visit profoundly changed my life. Moscow was gray and drab, and people didn't smile much. The food was of substandard quality. Few people had telephones, and many didn't have bathrooms in their residences. Apartments were small and cramped, and some didn't even have hot and cold running water. On the brighter side, if you could call it that, Russian black bread was the best I'd ever had, and I largely lived on it during my stay.

I was eager to meet my aunts and cousins for the first time. They lived in Kharkiv, Ukraine's second largest city. When I arrived at the Moscow airport, I quickly picked my Aunt Rosa out of the crowd. Her facial features were the spitting image of my father's. She had traveled 500 miles to meet me, and we instantly hit it off. Rosa was kind and welcoming, and for the first few days she was my tour guide. We went to the Kremlin, Gorky Park and even the Bolshoi Ballet. My aunt was the quintessential "Yiddishe Mama," a classic Jewish mother. I had taken one year of Russian at UCLA in my first year and was able to carry on a conversation with her and others.

On this trip I asked questions about Jewish life in the Soviet Union. When my aunt and I got to the middle of Red Square, I couldn't wait to ask her what it was like for Jews there, and had she experienced antisemitism, herself? When I finally did, my aunt looked nervous, put her fingers to her lips and said, "Ssshhh…the walls have ears." What walls, I wondered? The nearest wall was 100 yards away, or more. She let me know that Red Square wasn't the place to talk about such things. In fact, there was no safe place to talk. In the USSR, you never knew who was listening. People believed that the regime's surveillance was ubiquitous. This sense was all that really mattered. Fear and paranoia were the grist for tyranny in a dictatorship.

After a few days, my Aunt Rosa and I traveled to Kharkiv to join my father and my Aunt Nyura. On Friday night, Rosa prepared a sumptuous Sabbath dinner that had to have blown through much of her monthly income. The whole family was there, except for Rosa's husband, my Uncle Miron. I asked where he was, and Rosa told me he was at a meeting and would be joining us soon. Nothing more was said. Later, on a streetcar back to our hotel, my dad explained that Miron was attending a secret Sabbath service with other Jews in a private apartment. Kharkiv, with a Jewish population approaching 100,000, did not have a single synagogue. When my uncle toasted all of us at dinner later that night, he *whispered*, "L'Chaim," because he was afraid that the KGB might be listening.

I brought a Magic Slate with me on my early trips to the Soviet Union. This was a cellophane covered board on which one could write a message and then make the text disappear by lifting the cellophane. That's how we communicated when discussing sensitive subjects that we didn't want the authorities to hear.

By now, I had seen all I needed to see. Although the walls in Red Square might have ears, I wasn't going to be silenced. I had ears, too, plus eyes, feet, and one big mouth. I promised myself that when I got home, I was going to take on the cause of Soviet Jews. This was not a mainstream issue for my generation, but I would leave popular issues to others. I had found a cause that needed a champion.

"What You're Doing Is Counter-Productive"

During the 1960s thousands of activists across the United States adopted Martin Luther King, Jr.'s strategic approach to social change. He believed in using civil disobedience to focus attention on the moral issues of the day. By organizing peaceful protests and sit-ins to educate the public, he would build a constituency for civil and voting rights legislation. When I returned from the Soviet Union, I decided to apply some of those tactics to a movement demanding human rights for Soviet Jews. It didn't take long for me to identify my first target.

For a number of years, American and Soviet teams held highly competitive track and field meets, alternating every other year in their respective countries. The Los Angeles Memorial Coliseum was set to host the next competition in July 1969. When the Soviets came to town, they were housed in the University of Southern California (USC) dormitories, walking distance from the Coliseum. I put out the word asking students to join me in "welcoming" our guests to the City of Angels with picket signs and chants of "Let My People Go." We had no organization and no experience in this sort of thing. I was making it up as I went along.

We alerted the media to our protest, and I immediately heard from a representative of the Jewish Federation of Greater Los Angeles, the umbrella organization of the city's organized Jewish community. He was not pleased with our plans and urged me to cancel the protest. "What you're doing is counter-productive," he said, because the Soviet government would retaliate against its Jews if we proceeded. At first, I was speechless. Then I got angry. "That's absurd," I told him. "Nobody's going to prison because a twenty-year-old sophomore at UCLA pickets the Soviet track team."

We went ahead with our plans. Dozens of protesters and a large contingent of local media showed up. It was the first time anyone in Los Angeles had picketed a Soviet delegation on behalf of its persecuted Jews, and we made quite a splash. That first demonstration led to others. My goal was to ensure that, from here on out, no Soviet delegation could come to Los Angeles without being confronted on the issue of Soviet antisemitism. I soon formed a group called "California

Students for Soviet Jews," and we built a coalition with like-minded students on other California college campuses. I began writing op-eds in the UCLA Daily Bruin and other publications under the pseudonym Yehuda Ben Russi (Hebrew for Judah, Son of a Russian), because I planned to return to the Soviet Union in the fall and I didn't want to jeopardize my ability to get a visa. This time I wasn't going on a family visit. Whether it was due to my pen name or not, the Soviets let me in.

The Leningrad Synagogue Riot

By the fall of 1969, student activism on behalf of Soviet Jews was growing from coast to coast. I traveled to the Soviet Union with two other college students from New York. We met with "refuseniks," Jews who had unsuccessfully applied to leave the Soviet Union, and we expressed our solidarity. I brought a suitcase full of books with me, including Leon Uris's "Exodus" translated into Russian, beginning Hebrew books, Russian-Hebrew dictionaries and other texts that would be of interest to Jews seeking to immigrate to Israel. We also collected the names and addresses of emerging leaders in the nascent emigration movement.

I arrived in September at the onset of the Jewish High Holy Days, with visits planned to Moscow, Riga (capital of Latvia), and Leningrad. On my first night in Moscow, I attended Yom Kippur services at the Choral Synagogue, which was a stone's throw from KGB headquarters. Ushers escorted me to a partitioned VIP box for foreigners in the front of the sanctuary. I sat there with half a dozen other foreigners, while hundreds of parishioners spoke to me only with their longing eyes. It was eerie and emotionally draining. When the service was over, I left the synagogue to find thousands of young Jews gathered outside. Such assemblies were among the few permitted ways they had of declaring their Jewish identity and meeting foreign visitors. I stayed and talked with them until late into the night.

Next we traveled to Riga, where I went to the city's synagogue to visit with congregants. Afterward, a group of young Jews took me to a nightclub. A band was playing mostly Russian folk music, but they spontaneously broke into "Hava Nagila" as a welcome to their Jewish-American guests. As it turned out, several of the musicians were also Jewish. It was a politically daring thing for them to do. Once again, we took down names and contact information for Jews hoping to emigrate.

The most dramatic moment of the trip came at the end. I visited the Leningrad synagogue for the celebration of Simchat Torah, a holiday marking the conclusion of the yearly cycle of Torah readings. It was a traditionally joyous occasion, a night when thousands of young Jews would gather outside the synagogue under the careful watch of the local police. They mingled with each other and sought out foreigners like me as they danced and sang. It was also an opportunity for them to find like-minded Jews with whom they could establish ongoing—sometimes romantic—relationships.

On the night I arrived, however, police suddenly charged into the crowd to break up the gathering. They began beating the participants, arresting a few and shoving the rest out of the area. Some were injured and bloodied. The swinging of clubs instantly brought back memories of the Century City demonstration against the Vietnam War.

On my way home, I spent a night in Helsinki, Finland, where I made phone calls to the United States to alert the Jewish press about the Leningrad event. When the JTA (Jewish Telegraphic Agency) published a story, the news was out. As I headed home across the Atlantic, the world was learning about the Leningrad Synagogue riots.

Back in Los Angeles, I participated in a solidarity rally for Soviet Jews and marched with then-Councilman Tom Bradley. I gave a speech recounting my trip, underscoring the point that the Soviet Union was not a safe place for Jews. The media covered my remarks, and I was soon in demand as a speaker at synagogues and college campuses throughout California and across the country. I did not know it at the time, but my life as a public figure had begun.

Weeks later, I gave an eyewitness account of my trip to the Jewish Federation's Commission on Soviet Jewry. I had seen hundreds of young Russian Jews sticking their necks out, demanding the right to go to Israel. If *they* could take enormous risks, I said, the least we could do here in America was to be their voice, their comrades in arms. I called for an active response that was worthy of their courage. The commission's answer was disturbingly bureaucratic. They ruminated about what kind of articles to write, where to send letters, and when their next meeting would take place. They seemed out of touch with the urgency of the moment.

Their attitude underscored a great divide emerging in the Jewish community. Many establishment organizations went out of their way to avoid conflict and confrontation. But my generation believed the stakes were too high to sit idly by. The Jews I met in the USSR demanded that we take bolder action. They implored us not to remain silent as our parents' generation largely did during World War II. As author, Yossi Klein Halevy said: "The Soviet Jewry movement gave us the chance to retroactively fight the Holocaust."

Although some leaders at the Jewish Federation shared my impatience, the people who ran the organization stifled a more activist approach. I walked out of the meeting disappointed and angry. We were fiddling while Rome burned, I thought to myself. Afterward, as I stood outside the Federation headquarters, a middle-aged man who had been in the meeting walked up to me. "I was impressed by what you had to say," he said. "I feel the same way, and we should get together and talk."

His name was Si Frumkin.

The Sha-Shtil Syndrome

For the next forty years, Si's life and mine were totally intertwined. Apart from Barbara and my family, no one influenced me as profoundly. He had survived the Holocaust, the Kovno ghetto in Lithuania, and the Dachau concentration camp. His father and other family members perished at the hands of the Nazis. If one believes there is a reason for everything, then Si survived for a reason. He was a voice of conscience who insisted that Jews must never again be threatened without a fight.

When I first met him, he was living a perfectly normal, comfortable, upper-middle class life. Si owned a wholesale drapery fabric company in downtown Los Angeles and lived in a home with a pool in the suburban hills of Studio City. He had it made. However, Wiesel's "Jews of Silence" galvanized him as it did me. And like me, Si was inspired by the actions of Soviet Jews who risked everything for the right to live in a society where they were free to be who they were.

This was the backdrop as the two of us met for the first time. We decided we had to do something, *anything* to kick-start a social action movement. He formed his own organization, the Southern California Council for Soviet Jews and gave me crucial advice about launching my own. "Get a letterhead," he said, giving me a crash course in public relations and grassroots organizing. Without a home base or a fixed address, California Students for Soviet Jews would never be taken seriously. I watched as Si put his own organization on the map. He mocked up a letterhead with his own business address, got a local print shop to run off hundreds of copies, and created a distinctive logo showing a Star of David with a chain and padlock around it. Just like that, he was in business.

But I was just a college kid. Who would let me use their address? The obvious place was UCLA Hillel, the main Jewish student organization on campus. I asked Rabbi Richard Levy, its newly appointed director, for permission. He told me that he wanted to think about it, and I knew exactly why. The organized Jewish community was a major funder of Hillel, and they would not look kindly on him if he endorsed my efforts. It might even cost him his job. Yet it took him less than twenty-four hours to agree. He gave me a pigeonhole where our mail could be delivered, and he let us use the organization's telephones. It was an act of personal courage. Levy's view was that if an activist Jewish college student is not welcome at the Jewish students' umbrella organization, what's the point of having such an organization? Suddenly, I had a logo, an address, a phone number, and stationery. All of this may seem like a minor skirmish half a century later, but Levy's integrity inspires me to this day.

As 1970 commenced, I had a fledgling organization to run, a key ally in Levy and a mentor in Frumkin. Si didn't suffer fools, coining a phrase that came to describe those who shunned activism: the "Sha Shtil Syndrome." Translated from Yiddish it means, "Be Quiet and Be Still." An old Jewish joke illustrated the meaning: Two Jews are up against a wall during the Holocaust, waiting to be executed by a Nazi firing squad. The first one begins cursing the killers, when the other interrupts him. "Sha! You're going to get us in trouble."

Nothing was more abhorrent to Si than free people sitting on their hands while others suffered, and his passion was contagious. As time went on, we ignited that urgency in each other and in an army of committed activists. Working as a team, we helped put the Soviet Jewry issue on the map in Los Angeles, joining with other like-minded activists across the nation.

"And Don't Forget to Bring a Candle"

Frumkin, a left-of-center liberal in those days, was willing to create alliances with conservatives if it advanced our cause. That is exactly what happened when we turned George Putnam, one of Los Angeles' most politically conservative TV news anchors, into a staunch ally. Most people would never have expected to see George Putnam interview me, a longhaired kid who opposed the Vietnam War. But Si made it happen.

Soon after my return from Leningrad, he told me that I should appear on Putnam's KTLA broadcast to tell my story. He explained that Putnam would *love* to hear a young anti-war activist blasting the Soviet Union for its persecution of Jews. It would be a win-win for both of us. With me standing by, Si cold-called Putnam on the phone and told him what I had witnessed in Leningrad. "You should interview this kid on your show," he told Putnam. Then he handed me the phone, and the newscaster questioned me about my recent trip. Putnam asked if I could make it to the studio that evening for an on-air segment. After a brief pause to supposedly glance at a calendar, I said, "OK, tonight sounds great."

This was the beginning of a long and improbable relationship. In the coming years, I appeared on his show dozens of times.

On the night of that first broadcast in October 1969, Putnam asked Si and me to join him for dinner at Nickodell, a venerable Hollywood restaurant on Melrose Avenue next to Paramount Studios. He proposed that we hold a huge candlelight rally on Hannukah in downtown Los Angeles, demanding justice for Soviet Jews. In his deep, booming voice, Putnam was convinced that thousands of people would attend the event, which would be scheduled after sunset. "What a sight it will be! We'll call it the 'Candlelight Walk for Soviet Jews,'" he said. I told him that we were still a fledgling group, and it would be difficult to attract so many people. "Leave that to me," Putnam said confidently. He promised to promote the event on his nightly newscast.

Putnam was good to his word. The plan was to march down the City Hall Mall on the first night of Hanukah, from the Department of Water and Power building on Hope Street to the Spring Street steps of City Hall. His nightly advocacy of the march—capped by his trademark phrase, "And don't forget to bring a candle"—worked its magic. Si and I arrived at 5:00 p.m., an hour before the scheduled start of the march, and we were stunned to see hundreds of people already gathered and holding candles. Ultimately more than 5,000 Angelenos arrived, despite a cold and windy night. The optics were powerful. We had stressed the non-partisan character of the event and persuaded Mayor Sam Yorty and his bitter rival, Councilman Tom Bradley, to co-anchor the march. Folk singer and actor Theodore Bikel was the emcee. Si and I spoke to the large crowd, and we drew heavy media coverage for the cause. The next year we held the march again, and we doubled its size to 10,000. Steve Allen was the emcee, and an even larger contingent of political figures and celebrities joined us.

When I look back at this period, I realize how naïve we were to think we could make a difference, and wildly idealistic to think we might free our brothers and sisters from the USSR. But our initial results spoke for themselves. With a little help from George Putnam, a college student and a small businessman put the Soviet Jewry issue on the local map for good.

My frustration with the Jewish establishment grew between 1969 and 1972. Among the activist groups around the country, six of them—in Cleveland, San Francisco, Miami, Washington, and the two in Los Angeles—joined to form a national organization under the leadership of Dr. Lou Rosenblum, a NASA scientist in Cleveland and one of my early mentors. We called it the Union of Councils for Soviet Jews (UCSJ). The national Jewish establishment went nuts. They could not handle the thought of an independent national organization "competing" with them, an odd notion inasmuch as we were all presumably on the same side. Using every tool at their disposal, they tried to nip our effort in the bud.

At one point, the Federation hired me on a part-time basis to staff their Soviet Jewry effort. It was a short-lived relationship that was *not* a match made in heaven. They clearly hoped to co-opt me, while I hoped to leverage their resources to ratchet up the community's efforts. We were like oil and water. When word got out that the California Students for Soviet Jews, my organization, was going to be one of the founding members of the UCSJ, Federation officials bluntly told me that I would be fired. I didn't back down and was terminated after 90 days on the job. Frankly, I was relieved, but my closest allies were livid. Rosenblum wrote a blistering letter to the Federation, excoriating their heavy-handedness. What was behind the establishment's opposition was that we made their bureaucrats look bad to their lay leaders. If a group of unpaid activists could raise the profile of this issue as we had, why was the Jewish community paying comfortable salaries to fulltime executives? In the ensuing years, the UCSJ grew exponentially, with members in Moscow and Israel. It became an important force in the Soviet Jewry cause here and abroad.

David Drabkin, You're on the Air

By the early 1970s our Soviet Jewry media campaign was shifting into high gear. Putnam, now firmly in our corner, persuaded conservative radio talk show host, Ray Briem, to help us spread the word. I became a regular on his all-night KABC radio show, frequently spending all five hours with him, from midnight to 5:00 a.m. I remember asking him halfway through one of those programs, "Who the hell is listening to us at 3:00 a.m.?" Briem explained, "You may not be aware of this, Zev, but there are one million people in Southern California who work the graveyard shift at various jobs, and they like companionship. They are listening to us." He was right. I was amazed at the number of people who told me that they heard me on one of those all-nighters.

One evening I suggested to Briem that we directly call David Drabkin, an English-speaking activist in Moscow, and put him on the air. It was rare for a refusenik to have a working telephone, and I had his number. It could be a dramatic broadcast. Briem loved the idea, and I arranged the call. For nearly twenty drama-filled minutes, Drabkin talked on live radio to an American audience. In chilling terms, he described the anxious, unsettled life of a Jew in the USSR. He told us he lost his job when he applied for permission to emigrate to Israel and that he faced other reprisals as well. The interview became a national news story, and calls to other Soviet Jews soon became a staple on Ray Briem's show. This brought expanded attention to our cause.

We got comparable results when Si conceived the idea of sending Jewish New Year cards to refuseniks. Some said this would jeopardize their security, but we didn't buy it. We launched a national campaign at Si's kitchen table that sent tens of thousands of New Year's cards to refuseniks from Moscow to Baku. A sizable portion of the cards got through to them, and they learned that they were not alone. We also created "Prisoner of Conscience Medallions" calling attention to imprisoned refuseniks. Sales took off like wildfire. This increased the visibility of the issue, and helped fund our organization for years.

Sometimes we took on issues beyond Soviet Jewry, like our 1973 boycott of Standard Oil. The California based corporation had sent a letter to shareholders, calling for a more "evenhanded" US policy in the Middle East. The conglomerate was attempting to weaponize its shareholders against the young State of Israel, and the organized Jewish community was slow to react. Not us. We called on Angelenos to boycott Standard gas stations, urging them to cut their credit cards in half and mail them to us. We, in turn, would burn them in a very public bonfire in front of the company's downtown offices. We received nearly 5,000 destroyed credit cards in the mail. A *Los Angeles Times* survey showed that business at Southern California Standard stations had plunged by as much as 60 percent at some stations. After a multi-week boycott, Standard Oil backed down, sending a second letter to its shareholders apologizing for the original message.

The Great Toilet Plunger Caper

On occasion, our campaigns had mischievous overtones. We were always on the lookout for new ways to spread the word, and a golden opportunity arose on December 17, 1973. Learning that a Soviet freighter, the Pskov, had docked in Southern California, we launched a plan to "welcome" it to Los Angeles. Three of us would rent a small dingy at Ports of Call in San Pedro and make a two-hour voyage to Long Beach Harbor, where the Soviet ship was docked. When we reached the Pskov, I would spray paint "Let Jews Go" on its hull. We'd take a photograph of my penmanship and deliver it to the *Los Angeles Times*, where it would hopefully run in the next day's newspaper.

We were all set to go when Si—invoking the laws of physics—asked how we expected to stabilize our dingy in the harbor's churning wake. "Take two toilet plungers with you," he said. "When you get to the ship, two of you should attach the plungers while the third sprays the slogan on the ship." It worked. I painted the message on the ship's massive hull, we snapped the picture and got it to the newspaper. The next day our protest was splashed on the front page of the Metro Section, and the caption described our caper as a "naval assault" carried out by "raiders in motorboats." It was also picked up by wire services and published around the world. The principal benefit, of course, was that word of these protests would quickly reach Soviet authorities, and inevitably reach the refuseniks, boosting their morale.

Our plans weren't always as successful. On one occasion we bought tickets to the performance of a Soviet Balalaika orchestra at the Shrine Auditorium. The plan was to unfurl three large banners reading "Let My People Go" from the first row of the balcony during intermission. "Somehow" the Los Angeles Police Department had advance knowledge of what we planned to do, and after we displayed our banners we were quickly arrested for "disturbing the peace" and hustled out of the auditorium. A photo of me being led out of the Shrine in hand cuffs appeared in the next day's *Los Angeles Times*. Although we hoped to air the Soviet Jewry cause in a court of law, we never had a chance to present our case. The judge dismissed it, finding there was no evidence of a disturbance of the peace.

In the aftermath, I received thoughtful feedback from my UCLA academic advisor, Professor Galbraith. He called me into his office after the Times photo appeared, and gently asked when my academic pursuits were going to command as much of my attention as my extracurricular activities. He had a point. By then I was in my first year of a doctoral program in British Empire History, and I couldn't see myself spending the rest of my life sitting in libraries researching Colonial Office minutes. I gathered up my courage and told Professor Galbraith that my plan was to get a master's degree at the end of the academic year and leave the program. Breaking this news to him was one of the hardest things I ever had to do, but he was supportive. "I understand," he said. "Good luck and stay in touch." It was the right decision for me and for the UCLA History Department.

By the time I left UCLA in June 1972, my activism had begun attracting attention in political circles. I was hired to be the California Jewish Community coordinator for George McGovern's 1972 presidential bid. During that campaign, I helped draft remarks for McGovern when he came to town on the night of the terrorist massacre of eleven Israeli athletes at the Munich Olympics. I also advanced my first political event, when Vice Presidential candidate Sargent Shriver visited the Jewish Home for the Aging in Boyle Heights. I wrote political mail, drafted newspaper advertisements, and made speeches on behalf of the Democratic Party ticket throughout Southern California. Although the Nixon campaign made a concerted effort to peel off Jewish votes for the Republican ticket, we held our own in California and across the nation. After the election, Si asked me to take over the job of running the Southern California Council for Soviet Jews, and I accepted.

The Jackson-Vanik Amendment

Although the Soviet Jewry campaign was gaining traction across the country, we wanted to raise the stakes. Many of us began demanding that the United States use its economic clout to pressure the Soviets on the emigration question. The issue heated up in 1972 when the USSR imposed a crippling tax on Jews leaving for Israel, charging $100,000 per person if they had received a college education in the Soviet Union. The "exit tax" as it came to be known sparked international outrage and galvanized us in Los Angeles. We asked local Congressman Tom Rees (my Congressman) to introduce legislation that linked US economic credits to a Soviet promise to let Jews emigrate freely. The bill went nowhere, but it presaged the historic Jackson-Vanik legislation. That measure linked the Soviet Union's bid for Most Favored Nation (MFN) status to free emigration for tens of thousands of Jews annually. MFN would have granted the USSR the most favorable trade terms and the lowering of tariffs and other barriers from the United States. Although the executive branch traditionally negotiates such agreements, they require congressional approval.

The amendment to the MFN bill by Sen. Henry Jackson of Washington and Congressman Charles Vanik of Ohio was a bold initiative. Prospects for its approval were slim, however, because Nixon and powerful business interests were pushing hard for the deal, and the amendment could tube it. Meanwhile, some Jewish community leaders were torn. They were reluctant to alienate President Nixon, because the Nixon administration made it clear they would not look favorably on the Jewish community's support of this legislative effort. They argued that the legislation was a threat to detente, warning that the Jews would be blamed if the push for better US-Soviet relations went up in smoke. Other leaders stood shoulder to shoulder with Jackson and Vanik. They considered this amendment to be the most important human rights legislation in generations, arguing it would be an historic mistake not to support the efforts of these two legislators. Indeed, Jackson reportedly cajoled Jewish leaders to hop on board, arguing that if he, a Lutheran senator from Washington, could fight for Soviet Jews, the Jewish community could do no less.

MFN was an economic boon to the Soviet Union as well as to some of Nixon's biggest donors, including the Pepsi Cola Company, which was in line to get a monopoly on cola sales in the USSR. It made no sense to us that Nixon or the Soviets would walk away from such a lucrative trade agreement over the fate of a few hundred thousand Soviet Jews.

Our coalition, the Union of Councils for Soviet Jews, enthusiastically endorsed Jackson-Vanik from the beginning. There would be no repeat of World War II inaction on our watch; we would use every bit of leverage at our disposal. Eventually, most established Jewish communal organizations came around to support the legislation. Fighting for the amendment became my principal focus between 1972 and the end of 1974. I savored the high-level legislative strategizing as we built a national coalition to support Jackson-Vanik, and I was fascinated by the legislative process in Washington, DC, the biggest stage of them all. In short, I caught the political bug.

Moscow and Leningrad: 1974

To help pass the Jackson-Vanik amendment, we wanted to document the strong, unconditional support of the Soviet Union's refusenik community. This would send a clear, unambiguous message to US lawmakers that those who had the most at stake strongly backed the legislation. In the spring of 1974, while America was consumed with Watergate, I joined with Frumkin, Rosenblum, and Bob Wolf, who headed our Florida organization, for a one-week trip to the Soviet Union. Our goal was to meet with prominent Jewish activists there and to document their support for the bill.

This trip proved to be exhilarating. But it was also risky, because we were no longer anonymous to the Soviet government. They knew exactly who we were, they had heard our speeches, they followed our social action exploits, and they could track our movements. We weren't fooling anybody by arriving on Soviet soil under the cover of an American Express tour from New York.

To succeed we'd have to play a cat and mouse game with Soviet authorities. We knew they would methodically search our luggage upon our arrival and departure. We were carrying suitcases full of books and other materials, and took our chances that they wouldn't be found. I brought a 16-mm motion picture camera and multiple rolls of film with me, courtesy of my cousin Sid Solow. We also brought audio tape and recording devices, something that was particularly frowned upon by the Soviet authorities.

Our group left Los Angeles with high hopes, but disaster struck before we ever got to Moscow. Although our bags had been checked through to the Soviet Union, we missed our connecting flight from London to Moscow because of a travel agent's clerical error, delaying our arrival until the next day. It meant the Soviets would have access to our luggage for a full twenty-four hours while we were stuck in London. Our "contraband" would be evidence enough that we were not innocent tourists. When we got to Moscow, however, we were relieved to find that our luggage was undisturbed—at least to the best of our knowledge.

We immediately plunged into meetings with leading refuseniks. Operating on two hours of sleep each night, we were determined to make every minute count. The main gathering, held at the apartment of refusenik leader Alexander "Sasha" Luntz, was a veritable summit of the movement's leadership, including Anatoly Sharansky, Victor Polsky, Alexander Lerner, Ida Nudel, and Vladimir Slepak. They were accomplished people—engineers, scientists, and academics—who had sacrificed their careers for the dream of repatriation to Israel.

I brought my motion picture camera with me to the meeting. Polsky, who was under surveillance for teaching Hebrew, took me to the balcony and pointed out a KGB car outside staking out Luntz's apartment. I took out my camera and filmed the agents for posterity. He then told me that he was going to leave the apartment and board a bus. "Watch what happens when I get on the bus to go home," he said. "A KGB car will immediately follow the bus." His prediction was spot on, and I filmed it in living color, too. On the balcony of Luntz' apartment, we recorded one refusenik leader after another imploring Congress to pass the Jackson-Vanik Amendment.

We held similar meetings in Leningrad. The most poignant gathering took place in the apartment of Valery and Galina Panov, two internationally acclaimed dancers with the Kirov Ballet. When the Panovs sought permission to emigrate a couple of years earlier, the government didn't simply deny their request. It set out to destroy their careers, firing them from the Kirov. They instantly became an international *cause celebre*. Determined to stay in shape, all they could do was practice in their one-room apartment using a homemade exercise bar. It was painful to watch because great ballet dancers are like great athletes. They only have a limited number of years to perform at an elite level. Watching Valery and Galina doing their exercises was like watching two brilliant careers dying before our eyes. I captured it all with my camera.

By the end of our trip we had thirty minutes of film—six rolls—and the challenge was to get them out of the country safely. I couldn't take the film, because my bags would certainly be searched. Luckily, I befriended a married couple from Cleveland, who were part of our American Express tour. They knew what we were up to and agreed to smuggle the film out in their carry-on luggage. I handed the six rolls to the husband in the men's room of the Leningrad airport, and we arranged to reclaim the precious cargo once we were back in the US.

Meanwhile, as a decoy, I placed six rolls of exposed film in my suitcase. As we expected, Si and I were searched thoroughly as we checked in. We were taken into a side room and interrogated. We feigned indignation when the Soviets confiscated the decoy film. Then we boarded our plane for the long flight home.

The film would tell an explosive story, just not as quickly as we had hoped. I gave the footage to CBS News back in New York, which they developed and were prepared to use. But not immediately. Three months later, when the Panovs were freed, our film of them in their Leningrad apartment was finally broadcast on the CBS Evening News with Walter Cronkite. However, the rest of my handiwork sat unseen in my closet for more than thirty years. Then, out of the blue, I was contacted by Laura Bialis, a young and gifted filmmaker. She was working on a documentary about the Soviet Jewry struggle and asked to interview me. When we met, I offered her the use of my film. That visual record of our 1974 visit was incorporated into her award-winning 2007 movie, "Refusenik," chronicling the movement's story.

Victory in Washington

The Jackson-Vanik amendment was finally approved by Congress and signed by President Gerald Ford at the end of 1974. But, surprisingly, a debate over whether it ultimately helped or hurt our cause continues in academic circles to this day. I have no doubt that it was successful. Within three years 35,000–50,000 Jews emigrated annually from the Soviet Union, and practically all remaining restrictions were lifted when the Berlin wall fell fifteen years later.

In coming years, Jewish emigres would thank me for my work on their behalf, but I thanked *them* for awakening a keener sense of purpose in me and my generation. They taught us what courage and sacrifice was all about while we were living relatively carefree lives in the West. Senator Henry Jackson became one of my greatest political heroes. Lou Rosenblum was a strategic leader of our national organization, and he remained a revered friend until his death in 2019. And, of course, my life would have taken a completely different trajectory had it not been for Si Frumkin. He remained as close a friend as I had until he died in 2009.

The Soviet Jewry movement was a transformative period in my life, and while I was only a soldier in an international army of human rights activists, I consider it one of my most significant undertakings. When the Soviet Union collapsed and the gates to free emigration flung open, one of our colleagues, Michael Sherbourne of London, spoke for all of us when he said "I just couldn't believe it. I never thought I would live long enough to see this." Amen!

Now Is the Time

As the Soviet Jewry battle was playing out, there were also momentous developments in my personal life. Barbara and I got married in 1971, after a four-year
courtship. From the day we started dating, it was love at first sight. We started
talking about getting married that first year, and we agreed that's where we were
headed. But there was never that moment when I got on my knee and proposed
to her with a ring in hand. Frankly, I couldn't afford a ring yet. But this was our
destination, and we knew it.

When I look back at our relationship, I am struck by the parallels with my
father and mother's relationship. We were two independent people who learned
to survive and thrive on our own. But when we met, the whole became much
larger than the sum of its parts. Our lives were so intertwined that it would have
been impossible for us to disengage if we had wanted to. And that relationship
only strengthened in the decades that followed.

In February 1970, Barbara and I announced our engagement, and we had a
party for our family and friends at the Budapest Restaurant on Fairfax Ave. I
recently found an undeveloped roll of film which turned out to be from that
party. Barbara looked absolutely radiant. We set August 22 of the following year
as our wedding day to accommodate my father, my sister, and her family.

Rabbi Richard Levy of UCLA Hillel was one of two rabbis who officiated at
the ceremony. Si Frumkin celebrated like we were his own family, and George
Putnam attended, creating quite a stir when he took his seat in the synagogue
sanctuary. Our families and friends came to celebrate with us, too. Barbara was
absolutely beautiful in her wedding dress, which she had knitted herself over
several months. I was happy thinking of our future together, and gratified that
my father and sister could be a part of our joy. At the same time, I was sad that my
mother didn't live to see that day. She would have loved Barbara.

My father, who had realized his lifelong dream of moving to Israel a year
before, made a huge concession to Barbara by agreeing to wear a tuxedo for the
first time in his life. David Yaroslavsky was a working man, a union founder, and
a socialist Zionist. To him, the tuxedo was a distasteful bourgeois symbol. But he
wouldn't disappoint Barbara, whom he adored. Truthfully, he looked downright
smashing in formal attire.

After the wedding, we got in our car and headed to the Beverly Hilton Hotel
for our first night as a married couple. About an hour after we checked in, there
was a knock on the door. The hotel had decided that was the most propitious
time to send us a wedding gift—a bottle of champagne. Timing is everything!
Halfway through our honeymoon, while Barbara and I were driving from Lake

Tahoe to Yosemite, I suggested that we go back to Los Angeles. "Who knows when we'll see my father again?" I said. I knew we could always go to Yosemite. I wanted to hang out with my dad until he returned to Israel. Barbara enthusiastically agreed. When we arrived back home, he was thrilled.

Despite the physical distance between us, my father and I had grown closer since he had moved to Israel. We communicated mostly by mail, since telephone calls were prohibitively expensive. It had been easier for my father to put thoughts down on paper than discuss them face to face. It was easier for me, too. The last week before he returned to Israel was an opportunity to spend quality time together.

On May 16, 1973, a Wednesday, I was driving home after teaching a Confirmation class at Long Beach Temple Beth Shalom. As was my custom, I stopped to play a few hands of poker at the Normandie Club, a card parlor in Gardena, south of downtown Los Angeles. (Poker was a passion of mine during those years, and helped supplement my income.) I would usually play until I netted $25, enough to cover my expenses for a week. Then, just before leaving, I'd call Barbara to let her know I was on my way home. On this night, however, the line was continuously busy. This was highly unusual, and I started getting a sinking feeling that something was wrong. When I got home, Barbara was waiting at the window of our upstairs apartment on Vista Street. As soon as she saw me, she began shaking her head. "Shimona just called from Israel," she said. "Your father died a couple of hours ago."

I immediately called my sister. She told me that our dad had suffered an apparent heart attack, and he probably died before he hit the floor. It was a wrenching shock. The grief I felt fourteen years earlier over the loss of my mother came rushing back like a tsunami. My dad was seventy years old, and he seemed to be in good health. He never had a sick day since his bout with typhoid as a teenager in Ukraine. Just like that, I had no mother *and* no father. My sister and I were now the last living survivors of the Yaroslavsky family.

I have often been asked if I have any regrets in life, and I do. I regret that neither my mother nor my father lived long enough to see how I turned out. In truth, in mid-1973 I didn't know what was in store for me either. With only half-hearted enthusiasm, I was set to begin an MBA program at UCLA's Graduate School of Management. Then the city's political landscape shifted, and my life's plans suddenly changed.

In 1974, Los Angeles City Councilman Ed Edelman, who represented the Beverly-Fairfax district where we lived, won a seat on the County Board of Supervisors. This created a vacancy on the City Council that would be filled in a special election the following year. Friends, colleagues, and people I had worked with in the McGovern campaign began to ask if I might consider running for the seat. I was surprised and flattered, but it was definitely a longshot. Moreover, I never had a burning desire to run for local office, but I had to admit that I wasn't repelled by the idea either.

I was growing politically active in my neighborhood, even though my policy interests clearly lay in the federal sphere. I had lived in the Fairfax area since 1956, and I could see that senior citizens were increasingly burdened by rising rents. I had ideas about how to improve parks and transportation. Fairfax was still a center of Los Angeles' Jewish community, something that I felt was worth preserving. Maybe I could make a difference, I thought, warming up to the idea.

Before I could throw my hat in the ring, however, I had to cross a few "t's" and dot a few "i's." I wasn't going to make such a move without Barbara's enthusiastic support. When we discussed this prospective detour in our lives, she was 100 percent on board. We didn't have kids yet, and we had enough savings and income to sustain us for the duration of a campaign. "Now is the time. You should do it," Barbara said. I took a leave of absence from the Council for Soviet Jews at the end of 1974, continued teaching, and deferred my admission to the UCLA business school, to which I had been admitted.

There was one final question. Although I had never shied away when advocating for a cause, I was deeply uncomfortable about promoting myself. But that's exactly what a candidate must do. A campaign is a job interview. If I wanted the job badly enough I'd have to let voters examine my ideas and character up close. There was no getting around this. When I added it all up, I was all in. It was now or never. With no more roadblocks in the way, Barbara and I took a deep breath and began to prepare for my first campaign.

CHAPTER 6

"Why Zev?"

On a mild December day in 1974, I launched my campaign for the Los Angeles City Council in front of Canter's Delicatessen—one of the most iconic delis in the heart of the city's Jewish community. It was a contest that would ultimately shake up the Los Angeles political establishment, but you wouldn't have known it at the time. The press conference on Fairfax Avenue received little coverage, and I wasn't flanked by prominent members of the community or elected officials. Even Barbara couldn't attend because she was working at UCLA that Monday morning. People passing by may have wondered what was going on, if they paid any attention at all. It was me against the world that day, a theme that would intensify in the coming months.

Speaking without a podium (we couldn't afford one), I touted my independence and pledged that I would run a clean, grassroots campaign. "I'm unbought and unbossed," I said, hoping the message would resonate. Richard Nixon had resigned the presidency in disgrace four months earlier, and the voters in the city's fifth council district, not to mention the rest of the nation, were clearly disgusted with politics as usual. They were weary of establishment hacks and skeptical about campaign contributions from special interests. They were fed up with political machines picking their representatives, and they hungered for transparency in government. There were myriad issues facing the district, and voters wanted a champion.

From the start, the powers that be either ignored or dismissed me and my candidacy. The field included two formidable candidates—former 5th district Councilwoman Roz Wyman, and Fran Savitch, Mayor Tom Bradley's Administrative Coordinator. Understandably, Roz and Fran got all the early media attention. In a rundown of the candidates who entered the race, the *Los Angeles Times* barely acknowledged me or my community credentials. Who was this guy Yaroslavsky, insiders asked, and how in the world did he expect to win?

For all the talk about political reform, money still talked in most elections, and few expected me to be competitive in that department. They were right.

Although it was tempting for me to call this a David versus Goliath contest, it would have more accurately been called David versus Goliaths: Me, a longhaired kid two-and-one-half years out of college, up against the amassed power and influence of the press, the money of the business community, and the power of the city's political establishment.

The lone bright spot seemed to be that I was running in one of the city's most progressive districts, where voters were historically inclined to take a chance on underdogs. The best examples were Roz Wyman's 1953 election at twenty-two years of age, the youngest person ever to win a council seat, followed by Ed Edelman's insurgent victory over her twelve years later, when he campaigned against City Hall.

The 5th, in West Los Angeles, included some of the most affluent neighborhoods in the city, including Bel-Air, as well as a high percentage of renters and seniors, some of whom lived close to the poverty line. It had the city's highest percentage of Jewish voters. The district was generally bounded by Highland Ave. on the east, the San Diego Freeway on the west, Venice Blvd. on the south and Mulholland Drive on the north.

It's hard to imagine today, but there was a time when there were no Jewish elected officials representing this section of Los Angeles. That began changing after World War II when Jews migrated from Boyle Heights and South Los Angeles to the Westside. By January 1975, thirty years after these postwar demographic changes began sweeping through West Los Angeles, nearly 50 percent of those likely to vote in the April primary for the 5th district seat were Jewish, according to Fran Savitch's own pre-election survey.

I thought I had a chance, given the electoral map, but it was a long shot. Winning would take a lot of effort and more than a little bit of luck. Although I had little or no money, and no formal campaign headquarters, I was thankfully not alone. Peter de Krassel, a politically active attorney who was one of the first to urge me to run, introduced me to Jack McGrath—a real estate broker, former assembly candidate and off-and-on political consultant. He agreed to join my campaign as a strategic advisor. In the beginning, however, he wasn't prepared to leave his day job for my quixotic quest, and who could blame him? So, he introduced me to Wayne Avrashow, a young, twenty-three-year-old Cal State Northridge student, and he soon became my day-to-day campaign manager. Wayne was an emerging political junkie who was eager to get involved in a political campaign, and he took a leave of absence from college to do so. When he told his father what he had done, he asked who was I running against? When he heard Roz Wyman's name, he told his son that I had no chance.

For most of the first 12 weeks of the campaign, Avrashow ran the operation. He was the first one to arrive at our one-room headquarters in the morning and the last one out late at night. He assumed all the responsibilities that multiple campaign staff would typically manage—including strategizing where I should campaign, preparing me for appearances, scheduling, dealing with the press, coordinating volunteers, organizing our field operation, and drafting our campaign materials, and more. He took to the job like an old pro.

My first order of business was qualifying for the April 1 primary ballot. To do so, I could either pay a substantial fee and collect signatures from 500 registered voters, or avoid the fee by garnering 1,000 qualified signatures. I chose the latter strategy, taking advantage of my grassroots support. As it turned out, I was the first candidate to hand in my signatures—2,000 of them just to be sure—and the first to qualify for the ballot. That should have been a sign that I had something going. I was boosted by an army of volunteer petition circulators from every walk of Barbara's and my life. They hit the streets on my behalf: Soviet Jewry activists, former UCLA classmates, friends, and relatives helping me pass the first test.

This was a prelude to what my campaign would look like. I spent day and night walking door to door, standing in front of supermarkets, hustling for support at bowling alleys and visiting senior citizen centers. During our signature gathering campaign, Barbara was hospitalized for four days with an emergency tonsillectomy. No matter. I spent those evenings near Cedars Sinai Medical Center, positioning myself where large numbers of people passed by, and I gathered signatures. Then I snuck into Barbara's hospital room after hours, giving her a full report on the day's progress. I could sense her frustration at not being able to help in this initial phase. She loved people, and there was no better way to meet them than by approaching them to sign her husband's nominating petition.

The real work began once I qualified for the ballot. Before I took the plunge, McGrath offered me advice which, to be honest, was more like an order: "Get some suits and get some endorsements," he said. I went to Malibu Clothes in Beverly Hills and bought two suits—one pinstripe charcoal and one plain tan—which would become my uniforms for the next five months. These were the first suits I had acquired since my Bar Mitzvah. Up to this point, I had traveled around town in a pair of jeans and a distressed corduroy jacket.

Next, we recruited three community leaders to be my campaign co-chairs, and to give me much-needed credibility in the mainstream political community: Si Frumkin, my comrade in the Soviet Jewry cause; Rabbi Albert Lewis of Temple Isaiah, a Tom Bradley, commissioner, civil rights leader, and pillar of the Westside Jewish community; and Ed Sanders, a former Jewish Federation president and longtime supporter of Mayor Bradley. In time, I would pick up endorsements from KNX, the all-news radio station, the Santa Monica Evening Outlook, and the Los Angeles Police Protective League. In the case of the League, it wasn't their love for me, rather their dislike of Tom Bradley, that "earned" me their support. It wasn't long before they had buyer's remorse over their endorsement. But my strength was not in big name support. It came from hundreds of community folks who signed on to endorse and work for my campaign.

They Talked, I Walked

I knocked on doors day and night like a human machine. It was a non-stop journey that would eventually cover more than 100 miles of city sidewalks. This was nothing remarkable to those who knew me, but as a political neophyte neither my opponents nor the political elite took me seriously. Indeed, the more my opponents ignored me, the more I was able to execute a game plan underneath their radar. They talked, I walked, and that was the key to my success.

McGrath suggested that I devote my mornings to fundraising and spend the rest of the day pounding the pavement. Although I'd had a taste of this as a McCarthy volunteer in 1968 and as a volunteer for Tom Bradley's mayoral campaign in 1973, nothing prepared me for the tough regimen of my own campaign. I walked in neighborhoods of single-family homes and apartment buildings, in areas of great affluence and in apartment complexes with senior citizens on fixed incomes. I shook every hand I could, anticipating the advice of Michael Berman, a Los Angeles political consultant who told me years later that "every hand you shake is a vote you've banked."

When voters opened their door to me, my pitch was straightforward. Handing them my walking brochure I'd say: "Hello, I'm Zev Yaroslavsky, and I'm running for the City Council and would be honored to have your vote." If they declined, I'd move on to the next house. If they signed on, I'd ask if they'd let our campaign put a "Sold on Yaroslavsky" sign on their front lawn. By the end of the race we had a couple of thousand lawn signs throughout the district, and I used to joke that if I lost the election, I could always become a real estate agent. I had more signs on district lawns than Fred Sands, the Westside's most prominent realtor. If a voter wanted to know my position on the issues, I was happy to oblige them. I was committed to reducing crime and improving public transportation, building new parks, and controlling overdevelopment. I was fighting to control rising rents and property taxes. In short, I was the personification of a community-based candidate running against the City Hall machine, and that message seemed to be gaining traction with every passing day.

Wherever I went I handed out my signature blue and white bottle-tops emblazoned with my first name (my last name wouldn't fit). I also handed out emery boards to voters sitting underneath dryers in beauty parlors. When it was too late to knock on doors, I worked the bowling alleys and Westwood movie lines, especially the Fox and Bruin Theaters, two of the few places one could see a first run movie in Southern California. I was soon struck by the fact that I never saw any of my rivals on the hustings. They had ceded the grassroots battlefield to me, and I intended to take full advantage.

I'm not the kind of person who likes to make small talk at cocktail parties. No one would ever confuse me with a touchy-feely guy. But I had no choice. I forced myself to invent a more gregarious personality. I was a man on a mission, and once I broke the ice it was almost as if I was gliding from one encounter to the next like Fred Astaire on the dance floor. I became so comfortable asking strangers for support that during one precinct walk in a driving rainstorm, I actually invited myself into a voter's home so I could watch the last minutes of the UCLA/Kentucky basketball game for the NCAA championship, John Wooden's final game. The voter was happy to oblige, and we hit it off. Once the Bruins had won, I asked my host for his support and if I could put a "Zev" sign on his lawn. And so, it went, every day for five straight months, rain or shine.

As the campaign progressed, I realized that I was meeting the same people again and again—at their doors, in supermarkets, movie lines, bowling alleys, and at candidates' forums. They were unfailingly friendly, but by the time Election Day arrived they were also getting tired of meeting me. "I'm voting for you, I'm voting for you. Don't worry," they'd say.

The Nibblers Group

Even though I became a prolific fundraiser over the years, I always hated asking for money. And raising funds was exponentially more difficult in the beginning, when I was a longshot candidate. Yet, I couldn't fully communicate my message without a modicum of resources—and a modicum is what I amassed. I was helped by a small group of supporters from different walks of professional life. They were river-boat gamblers willing to take a chance on an overweight 26-year-old candidate, a man with two suits to his name who didn't look like a winner under the most optimistic scenario. Some of them had supported my work for Soviet Jews while others simply wanted to shake up City Hall. Years later, many would become extraordinarily successful Los Angeles businessmen. But no thanks to me, as they'd be quick to tell you.

In the beginning, none of them thought they were investing in a future city councilmember. We met every Friday morning at Nibblers, a Wilshire Boulevard coffee shop. And the Nibblers group, as it came to be known, was the nucleus of my modest fundraising effort. When the campaign reached crunch time and we didn't have enough money to pay for our mail, we came up with an idea that each member would loan the campaign up to $1,000. If I won, the campaign would pay them back; if not, it wouldn't. We called it a "winner's loan." The group loved the idea, and six of them signed up immediately. My mother-in-law kicked in as well. In all, we raised a respectable $27,000 for the primary, a little over one-third of what Savitch and Wyman had each amassed. This was the bare minimum I needed.

It's Better to Be lucky Than Smart

There was a sign that once hung in the Fairfax High School locker room: "Luck is where preparation meets opportunity." Our campaign had more than its share of luck. When Ed Edelman won his 1974 race to fill a seat on the Los Angeles County Board of Supervisors, the City Council faced a major decision. It could order a special election to replace him in February, in which case the leading vote getter would be the automatic winner, with or without a majority. Or it could consolidate the 5th district election with the city's regularly scheduled election, in which case candidates would run in an April primary. If no one got a majority, the top two vote getters would meet in a May runoff. It may sound like an arcane distinction, but the choice was important and backroom politics played a critical role in the council's eventual decision.

Savitch's own pre-election poll showed Wyman getting 38 percent of the vote, while she and I were tied at 5 percent. In a special election, the former councilmember would be the heavy favorite to snare a plurality and win the contest outright. This did not suit the Bradley-Savitch camp, because they didn't see any way they could beat Wyman in a February winner-take-all election. So, they convinced the City Council to consolidate this election with the Spring city election. This decision was made before I even qualified for the ballot, but it benefited me enormously. It would have been impossible for me to get the most votes in a winner-take-all contest, given my formidable and well-funded opposition. At least now I'd potentially get two bites at the apple—in a primary election and, if I came in second, in the runoff.

The shifting fortunes of the two top candidates played an even bigger role in the race. Wyman was attempting a political comeback. She and her late husband, Eugene, were prominent Democratic Party leaders with a long history in Westside and national politics. She had been instrumental in helping to bring the Dodgers to Los Angeles from Brooklyn and had widespread name recognition. But after twelve years in office, she lost her seat to Edelman in a 1965 landslide.

Savitch, on the other hand, was making her first bid for elected office, and she had major league allies in the Democratic power structure. At the time, Bradley was at the apex of his popularity, two years removed from a smashing win over Sam Yorty in the mayor's race. It was no secret that he wanted to elect a councilmember whose vote he could count on, and Savitch fit the bill. As the race began, the two candidates viewed each other as principal adversaries, likely to battle it out in a runoff election. Wyman largely ran a positive campaign, a prudent strategy given her commanding lead. What she didn't fully anticipate was the brutally negative campaign that Savitch would run against her, mercilessly dredging up all the issues that Edelman used against her a decade earlier. As a result, Wyman's once commanding lead went into free fall, and Savitch's fortunes began to rise. Decades later, I had a chance to look at Savitch's campaign files, now in the California State Archives. Based on internal memos, her campaign didn't consider me a threat. This gave me the chance to make my case to voters with little or no interference.

I continued my marathon trek through the district, knocking on thousands of doors. When people opened their homes to me, I was able to share my ideas with them, just as they shared their aspirations and frustrations with me. This was better than a poll, which I could hardly afford. I was actually engaged in a giant, ongoing focus group that allowed me to have my finger firmly on the pulse of the voters. After months of campaigning, the notion that I might squeeze into the May runoff election began to seem real.

I had some lucky breaks, dodged a few bullets, and met voters wherever I could find them. The headline on my brochure read, "For a Change, We Have a Leader," but the real message was inside. "Why Zev?" Unlike other candidates, it said, "Zev Yaroslavsky is not cast from the old political mold. He is not sponsored by big-name politicians who would expect to control his every move once he is in office. He will not have the big financial interests behind him, nor will he have the lobbyists who want to control City Hall." The brochure listed my allies on the back page—fifty-seven names that wouldn't make a Hollywood gossip column but were well-known to district neighbors and community activists. What might have been liabilities in another race were assets in the post-Watergate environment. Less was more, and I seized the moment.

Every candidate stumbles at some point, and my first blunder came at a candidate's forum sponsored by the homeowners association in the Westwood-Holmby community, one of the Los Angeles' most affluent neighborhoods. Sara Stivelman, the group's general manager asked me to outline my position on density—the term commonly used to describe how much a developer could build on a parcel of land. It was a simple question and a big issue in neighborhoods throughout the westside. However, the last time I had heard the term "density" was in my eleventh-grade high school chemistry class. My heart sank out of sheer embarrassment. I paused for a moment, then humbly asked, "Could you explain exactly what you mean by density?" Without a hint of condescension, she told me what the word meant, and I proceeded to answer. Of course, I was concerned about overdevelopment. I was a UCLA alum and quite familiar with the issues of West Los Angeles development and traffic. Neighborhoods should be consulted before such development is approved, and I was committed to a partnership with the citizens I would represent in helping shape the future of their communities. It could have been a disastrous moment, a not-ready-for primetime embarrassment, but I was able to salvage it. Stivelman came up to me after the forum and complimented me on how I answered that question. "It would have been much worse if you had tried to fake your way through an answer," she said. "The audience appreciated your honesty."

Meanwhile, the daily grind of walking precincts occasionally yielded great surprises. One morning I came to an address on Holt Avenue north of Olympic Boulevard, and the precinct sheet I carried with me showed that seven single women lived at this one address. How odd, I thought to myself. I straightened my tie, brushed my hair, rang the doorbell, and was stunned when a nun opened the door. I hadn't noticed that the property was adjacent to Saint Mary Magdalen Catholic Church. The sister smiled and said, "You look surprised to see me." I was, but quickly added: "My name is Zev, and I'd love to have your vote and the support of the other sisters here as well." She asked me for extra brochures and "Zev for City Council" buttons. "I'll pass them on to the others. I'm sure we'll all vote for you," she said. I walked away not quite believing what had just happened. It was either a message from God, or the campaign equivalent of hitting the jackpot in Vegas, or both. Getting seven votes at one address was a bonanza for any precinct walker.

Wishing You a Happy Easter

Jack McGrath had sharp political instincts, but he also had a reputation for wild, unpredictable ideas. It was said that nine out of ten of his suggestions were crazy, but the tenth would be a stroke of genius. I benefited unexpectedly from one such idea when he suggested we could broaden our base by sending an Easter card to non-Jewish voters throughout the district—upwards of 50,000 of them. The message would hit their mailboxes ten days before the election.

I was understandably skeptical. How could we identify which voters celebrated Easter? His plan was simple enough. We would cull the voter data base for all Jewish surnames using the "Jewish Surname Dictionary," a list pioneered by Michael Berman, the political consultant. We would assume that the remaining names were not Jewish. *They* would be the ones to get the Easter card. In a close race, this kind of outreach could make a difference. Years later, Berman told me how to split hairs when identities were not so clear. If a voter was named Newman he could be a Catholic or a Jew. If his full name was John Francis Newman, Berman explained, one could assume he was Catholic. If it was Isaac Herschel Newman, he was likely Jewish. And so forth.

We sent out 50,000 Easter greeting cards to voters and used our apartment as the return address. This would make the mailing as personal as possible. It was a home run. We got 600 Easter cards back with warm, personal handwritten messages from voters. I was thrilled, because I always believed that anyone who has taken the time to print the name "Yaroslavsky" by hand will never forget the experience. The 600 people who addressed envelopes to Barbara and me probably had our surname in mind when they went to the polls one week later.

Meet My Father, Irving Kaddish

Nobody should ever under-estimate the importance of political volunteers, and one name stands out in my first run for office. Early in the primary an older man named Irving Kaddish walked into the back of Peter de Krassel's law office, which had become our de facto headquarters. Irving said he'd like to help. He was tall, thin, and unshaven and had a lonely air about him. We were grateful for any offer of help and gave him a bunch of brochures to hand out along Fairfax Avenue. He came in every day asking for another batch, and we obliged. Honestly, I was never sure he was handing out our stuff, but we couldn't say no.

Suddenly, people began telling us about their encounters with a man who looked just like Irving in front of Canter's Deli. "I met your father the other day handing out your literature," one voter told me when I knocked on her front door. "He seemed like a really nice guy." You can imagine my surprise. My dad had been dead for two years. "Please vote for my son," Irving would tell voters. "He's a good boy and he'll be a great councilman." At first, I was concerned that

I might be accused of recruiting an impostor to pose as my dad, but I decided to let it go. From what we could tell, Irving needed somewhere to go and something to do. He lived alone in an apartment in the Fairfax area, and working in my campaign was the focal point of his life. To tell him to cease and desist would have broken his heart.

In a political race you're grateful for any volunteer who puts in a couple of hours a week. Irving put in twenty-thirty hours. Soon there were Kaddish sightings throughout the district. He was spotted in front of the kosher butcher shop on Pico and Shenandoah, at the market on La Cienega and 18th St., at Juniors Deli at Westwood and Pico, and at the legendary Pinks hot dog stand at La Brea and Melrose. Kaddish handed out our literature for three solid months. He reached thousands of people—more than anyone else in our campaign except for me. He could easily have been responsible for swinging hundreds of votes my way, which would have made the difference between winning and losing. Sadly, we lost touch with him after the election. He had come in off the street, adopted me as his son, and helped get me elected to the Los Angeles City Council. I've never forgotten him.

Election Night, April 1, 1975

The conventional wisdom on Election Day was that Savitch and Wyman would fight it out for the top two spots, and I'd be the odd one out. But I sensed my campaign was gaining momentum. Everywhere I went people told me they had seen me, read my literature, or used my bottle top. They wished me well and assured me that I had their vote. The media and political pundits may have consigned me to also-ran status, but our ground game kept nailing down votes until the polls closed.

On the night of April 1, we gathered at Si Frumkin's home in Studio City, well outside the boundaries of the 5th district. The first returns were absentee votes cast by mail before Election Day, and they seemed to confirm what everyone else had predicted: I was running a distant fourth behind Savitch, Wyman and Dori Pye, the Westwood Chamber of Commerce leader, and a Republican. But then the Election Day votes began pouring in, and my totals began rising. As the night wore on, it was clear that Savitch would come in first with one-third of the vote, but Wyman and I were in a dog fight for second place.

When McGrath saw this, he told me that there was an excellent chance I would come in second, in which case we needed to be at City Hall where the media was gathered. It was imperative that I seize the moment and frame my general election message for the battle ahead. In those days, there were only a handful of television stations in Los Angeles, and all of them would be covering the results of our race as their lead story on the 10:00 pm or 11:00 pm news broadcasts. I quickly thanked 100 or so supporters and raced down the 101 freeway to the City Council chambers where vote totals were being reported.

I sat down in the front row next to Wyman. Although we had exchanged a few shots in the campaign—I accused her of being a City Hall insider, and she pointed out my lack of government experience—we had never attacked each other personally. As more returns rolled in, I vaulted into second place. When my lead grew to several hundred votes, she leaned over to me and offered her congratulations. I was surprised, since the last batch of votes had not yet been counted. Wyman was a veteran of election nights, however, and she explained that there simply weren't enough uncounted votes to close the gap. I was in the run-off. When the campaign started, I just wanted to make a respectable show-ing. Now, I could hardly believe the primary results.

When the dust settled, Savitch ran first with 33 percent of the vote, I received 19 percent and Wyman 18 percent. The difference between me and Wyman was only 359 votes. As I sat in the council chambers I wondered where those votes had come from. Was it the Easter card mailing or my precinct walking? Was it my adopted father, Irving Kaddish? Or was it because Wyman, confident that she would be in the runoff, held off spending the last $30,000 in her campaign account, instead saving it for the run-off?

As the news spread, the media woke up to the fact that an earthquake had just rocked the fifth council district and the city's political establishment. Reporters who had been distant before were now descending on me for interviews, ask-ing how I had done it and what my message would be. For the first time in this campaign, I actually believed I could win, and I remained true to what I had said from the beginning: I was an independent voice, running against the City Hall establishment and beholden to no one except the voters of the 5th district.

One postscript to the primary election: The Savitch campaign's decision not to opt for a winner-take-all election was a costly strategic mistake. Had they done so, Savitch would have become a Los Angeles City Councilmember with 33 percent of the vote, and who knows what would have become of me? As the saying goes, "Sometimes it's better to be lucky than smart."

The General Election

As we pivoted to the run-off, I kept my foot firmly on the gas pedal. But it was another gas pedal that became the symbol of my campaign. Shortly after the primary, I crashed my beloved 1966 Rambler into an oncoming car not far from home. No one was hurt, but my left fender was grotesquely crushed. I didn't have the time or money to fix my car, so I drove it all over the district for the duration of the campaign. Nothing conveyed my "man of the people" persona like my mangled Rambler. The medium was the message.

Meanwhile, Savitch was flummoxed. Confident that she would be facing Wyman, Savitch planned to present herself as the reformer, a breath of fresh air, and an ally of popular Mayor Tom Bradley. But her game plan fizzled when Wyman failed to make the run-off. Savitch was suddenly transformed into City Hall's candidate, and I was the independent outsider in a district that historically elected such individuals. It was a stunning reversal of fortune for her.

Still, she continued to enjoy the backing of incumbent political figures, organized labor, and the downtown business establishment. She raised more than twice as much money as our campaign, and when the Los Angeles Times endorsed her in the runoff, it didn't even mention my name. Ironically, all that establishment power proved to be her undoing. Every one of her endorsements and every contribution she received was evidence that she was the handpicked choice of political insiders, while I wouldn't owe anything to anyone. I didn't know it at the time, but I was in the driver's seat—even though I couldn't open the hood of my Rambler.

You've Got Mail

After the primary, McGrath quit his day job and signed on to help run the campaign fulltime. He was a brilliant strategist when it counted, and we fought hard to make our case. While the odds were shifting in my favor, we had to launch an aggressive strategy to counter Savitch's financial edge. In those days, before social media, the principal way to communicate with voters was through the United States mail. Fran could afford to send out far more mailers than me, but McGrath conceived an ingenious plan that caught everyone by surprise.

Data from the April 1 primary showed that 33 percent of the district's voters had turned out to vote. It was almost certain that these voters would vote again in the May 27 runoff, but it was unlikely that most of those who sat out the primary would turn out. Given our limited resources, McGrath proposed that we only communicate with those who had voted in April and ignore everyone else. Savitch didn't have to make this kind of decision, because she had enough money to saturate all registered voters with mail. With our strategy, we would mail to the same number of *likely* voters as Savitch, but she would be spending three times more trying to reach a majority of people who weren't likely to vote.

It was a shrewd gamble on our part, and it paid off. Savitch's campaign team didn't realize what we had done. They cried foul, suggesting that we were funding our mail program with a secret slush fund. How else to explain how we matched her volume with only a fraction of her financial resources? Her campaign didn't figure it out until after the election, when we revealed what we had done.

Endorsements can make the difference in a close race, and a crucially important message of support came my way about one month before the general election. Roz Wyman and I had run neck and neck in precincts in the eastern half of the district—from Century City to Beverly-Fairfax. I would beat her by 20 votes in one precinct, and she would beat me by fifteen votes in another. If I could win over her voters, I had a real shot at prevailing on Election Day.

So, shortly after the primary I called Roz and asked if she would consider endorsing me. After thinking it over for a couple of weeks, she agreed to do so. Then she asked me to send a draft message that I would want her to sign. I wrote a hard-hitting letter, and asked Avrashow to take it to her home for her approval. An hour later the phone rang in our headquarters. It was Roz. "Zev, I've read your letter, but I can't sign it," she said. Thinking that the text was too tough, I responded, "Don't worry, we can tone it down." In words that are seared in my memory, Roz responded, "Tone it down? It's not *strong* enough!" I laughed and asked her to draft what she felt comfortable signing, and we'd go with it. Forty-three years later, her letter's potency still resonates:

> Mrs. Savitch's campaign represents everything that is repugnant to me in politics…Watergate could learn from this campaign… In contrast, Zev Yaroslavsky has discussed the issues and run an honest campaign. Zev has spent his entire life in the 5th District, not elsewhere as Mrs. Savitch has.

We sent the letter to precincts where Roz had done well and consolidated our base with hers. In the ensuing years, she and I became good friends and found common ground, especially on the cultural arts and their importance to the region's economic vitality and social fabric.

Wyman, who died in 2022 at the age of ninety-two, is a historic figure in Los Angeles politics. She played a key role in bringing the Dodgers to Los Angeles, and in increasing the region's cultural footprint. She truly helped lay the groundwork for LA's transformation into a world-class city. I am indebted to her, not only for my election, but for what she did to help make Los Angeles what it is today.

All in the Family

Running for office is stressful. I can't imagine what it would have been like to hit the streets every day and make my case without Barbara's love, steady support, and keenly intelligent advice. She was my partner in every sense of the word. My bet is that Barbara was as responsible as I was for the votes I received throughout my political career, and probably more.

In 1975, however, I got additional family help from an unexpected quarter. My mother-in-law, Ruth Edelston, had moved to Santa Cruz, California years before, but she paid close attention to the race. She drew on years of her own political activism to send me a stream of letters packed with support, observations and, needless to say, advice. Her missives were as clear and perceptive as any I received from my campaign team:

> May 4: "Is there any way your opponent's image can be associated with unpopular occurrences as it relates to the mayor without naming him? (It would be counter-productive to pan the mayor anyway)... Even though I am not physically in LA, doing something to help you during these very important days in our lives, I couldn't be more interested, more concerned, or relate more deeply with you. And if you need me to come to LA, call me and I'll come."

> May 6: "Don't be surprised at anything that happens in politics. Don't let an opponent upset or bait you. It is a common tactic to find a short fuse. Do what is necessary for you to be relaxed and confident. A broad smile and a sense of humor helps... Hold back your big salvos until the last days of your campaign."

> May 21: "Read the account in the Tuesday, 5/20 LA Times, of the KTTV program about the race. You scored again. The contrast between yourself and your opponent was on target. Good going."

I must admit, at the time I didn't appreciate her input as much as I should have. After all, it was coming from my mother-in-law. As I've read those letters in the years that have passed, I realize what gems they were.

Throughout the runoff, the Savitch campaign was in a box. They couldn't figure out how to run against someone like me. I had no political track record they could attack. Even my arrest in the 1972 Soviet Jewry demonstration would have helped me if her campaign had raised it. Shortly before the run-off election,

Savitch and I squared off in a debate on KCET, Los Angeles' public television station. One of the first questions came from *Los Angeles Times reporter*, Doug Shuit, who covered our race from the beginning. He pointed out that I had received a campaign contribution from the Personal Freedom Campaign Fund, a first amendment advocacy group that counted the Pussycat Theaters as one of its supporters. Was it appropriate for me to accept campaign contributions from a porn theater? I was prepared for the attack and responded that this political action committee defended *everyone's* rights under the First Amendment. A movie theater had the right to operate without government censorship. This was a matter of settled law. Then I turned the tables on Savitch, whose father was the highly respected Superior Court judge, Alfred Gitelson, a longtime defender of First Amendment freedoms. I told her that I was certain her father would agree with me, as would the *Los Angeles Times*, which also had a vested interest in defending the First Amendment. Checkmate!

Election Night 1975

Dean Balzarette, my high school track coach, used to tell us that, "unless you're nervous before a race, don't bother running. Nervous energy is what gives you the competitive edge you need to win." Well, I was plenty nervous on Election Day. I had a pit in my stomach all day long, and by my coach's metric I was ready for the race. I continued to campaign until the polls closed, hitting the old reliable places where prospective voters were busy working, shopping, or playing shuffleboard at senior citizen centers. I asked for their votes one last time, and the response was encouraging. Our volunteers stood at freeway off ramps leading into the district and at major intersections, displaying "Vote for Zev" signs. Win or lose, I felt good that we had left it all on the playing field. Now, all we could do was wait for the votes to be counted.

My supporters gathered on election night at the Westwood home of Ed Broida, a charter member of the Nibblers Group. When I arrived shortly after 8:30 pm, the first thing I noticed was a battery of television trucks parked outside, setting up to cover our election night party. There were over 100 people already gathered inside, with more were on their way. Tonight, we wouldn't have to rush down to City Hall to meet with the press. The news outlets came to us.

The media sensed the contest was up for grabs, and this time nobody had to ask, "Who the hell is Yaroslavsky?" I was trailing 62 percent to 38 percent when the absentee votes came in. But I announced this was good news, to the surprise of my supporters. My reasoning was simple: In both the primary and the run-off,

Savitch had captured over 60 percent of the absentee votes cast in convalescent homes throughout the district. The owners of those facilities supported her, so her campaign had been able to gain access to their clients and sign them up to vote by absentee ballot. I had no doubt these folks were vulnerable to being influenced or pressured to vote for the candidate who brought them their ballot. Based on the convalescent home votes that were cast in the primary, I calculated that unless Savitch got more than 67 percent of the absentee votes in the runoff, I'd win. I was right. It wasn't long before I took the lead, and the final tally wasn't even close.

I won the election 54.5 percent to 45.5 percent, a victory margin of slightly more than 4,000 votes. The next day, the Santa Monica Evening Outlook, which served the western part of the district, ran a banner headline: "Yaroslavsky Wins." My new life as an elected official was about to begin.

My first emotion was relief. It had been a long, improbable journey. I was a 26-year-old novice, whose political experience was relatively sparse. At the outset, it was a race that I didn't expect to win. I don't think I'd been inside City Hall more than five times in my life—and two of them had come during this campaign. I knew my life was going to change, but I didn't know what was in store, what the life of a councilmember would be like. Just like my campaign, it was going to be a learning experience, this time on steroids. I ran for office to enter public service, and I had just been given that opportunity. As for Barbara, she was the eternal optimist. She never doubted that I would win. For her, this would be a seamless transition. She was a public servant in her own way, and she would embrace this new life. I was as happy for her as I was for myself.

I got a call from Savitch at 9 o'clock the next morning. She sincerely congratulated me, conceding graciously that "you wanted it more than I did." I had always felt she was a reluctant candidate, and her words confirmed that. I was touched by the call. I told her that I looked forward to working together, and that my door would always be open to her. Indeed, our relationship from that day on was friendly and collaborative. Mayor Tom Bradley called to congratulate me minutes later. He was also very gracious, and he asked to meet with me as soon as I was ready. I told him that I looked forward to it.

Later that morning I pulled my battered Rambler into the parking lot of the Los Angeles Press Club on Vermont Avenue, where a mob of reporters asked what I planned to do in office. I told them my mission was the same as it was on the day I declared my candidacy in front of Canter's Deli. I was independent, and I wouldn't be constrained by party labels. I'd represent and focus on the needs of the people who had put me in office. Above all, I'd call them as I saw them. "Don't try and pigeonhole me; I'm not necessarily going to be predictable," I said. Despite our victory, reporters and pundits were still shaking their heads.

As I left the press conference, a Times photographer asked me to pose next to the left fender of my car. That picture ran on the front page the next day and became the enduring image of my improbable campaign. I was an average-looking guy with a jacket slung over his shoulder, standing next to a hopelessly unglamorous vehicle. Governor Jerry Brown, who had put his own stamp on frugality with his battered Blue Plymouth, joked that I had one-upped him. The truth was that we both got extraordinary mileage—and messaging—from our cars.

After the press conference I decided to drop by the Jewish Federation offices across the street from the Press Club. It was a day of victory laps, but I didn't go there to settle scores. The people who greeted me at the door—and gave me hugs of congratulation—took pride in my election. In the years that followed I partnered with the Federation and its social service agencies in serving our mutual constituencies. The hatchet was officially buried.

I received kind notes and phone calls from people who had supported me, as well as those who had not, and there was a blur of press interviews, meetings, and receptions. A congratulatory note that I cherished came from Professor John S. Galbraith, my UCLA doctoral advisor. "The British Empire's loss is Los Angeles' gain," he wrote. "And I hope that the city is in better shape than the empire."

The day after the election, the mayor's office phoned to say that they were sending me a copy of the city budget, along with Bradley's veto message. What happened next was absurd. A shiny Cadillac limousine pulled up in front of my Pico Blvd. headquarters. There, on the plush leather back seat, sat the budget. Like an arriving dignitary! A messenger delivering the document in a Ford compact would have sufficed. Apparently, City Hall didn't get the memo that Angelenos were irate over wasteful spending.

One event, however, had great personal meaning to me. On a June evening in the Fairfax neighborhood, I went to a celebration at the home of Jacob and Miriam Getzler, my parent's closest friends. My parents had known Miriam since their Labor Zionist days in the late 1920s in New York. They had traveled with her to Palestine in 1931. All told, there were three dozen of my parents' closest friends there that evening—people who knew me and my sister since we were born. They spoke of how proud my parents would have been. They had not lived long enough to see this day, and that was a hard pill to swallow. Then, Jacob spoke of how he felt their presence in the room. I did, too. He raised his glass and toasted, "L'Chaim, To Life."

My new job began officially on June 10, when I stood in the City Hall chambers with Barbara at my side and took the oath of office. Mayor Bradley marked the occasion with humor, saying it would be good if I got some extra suits and a haircut. "Zev, you are now part of the establishment," he said with a chuckle. I looked him squarely in the eye as I began my remarks and answered: "I may be part of the establishment, but the establishment is not part of me."

CHAPTER 7

Be Indispensable to Your Constituents

———————

My life was about to change dramatically, and I really had no idea what to expect. But I had a guiding light: I was a student of history and the lessons it offers to understand the world around us. History helps us put events in perspective, and it can provide a moral compass in times of political ferment. A book that profoundly influenced me in later years was Barbara Tuchman's "The March of Folly." With brilliant analysis, she explored leaders' persistent pursuit of policies that were clearly not in their best interests—stretching from the Fall of Troy to America's Vietnam War. It's a lesson we never seem to learn.

Another question debated endlessly by historians seemed equally relevant as I began my new duties: Do individuals drive great moments of change, or do external events generate historic transformations? I knew that idealistic and committed people could change the world, a fact that history has repeatedly confirmed. This was the reason I had run for public office in the first place. At the same time, I knew that political change doesn't happen in a vacuum. Events and social forces shape us profoundly and unexpectedly, sometimes in ways we are slow to understand. Historical context is everything, and it was certainly in play in June 1975.

The Vietnam War had ended, and a disgraced Richard Nixon was living in seclusion in San Clemente. Jimmy Carter, an obscure ex-governor and peanut farmer, was launching a quixotic campaign for the presidency on a pledge that he would never lie to the American people. In Sacramento, newly elected Democratic Governor Jerry Brown was laying out an agenda focused on frugality, environmentalism, and a New Age approach to traditional politics.

For me, however, the biggest changes were taking place in my own backyard. Mayor Tom Bradley, halfway into his first term, was solidifying his grip on City Hall. His victory two years earlier over Sam Yorty had ushered in a dramatic new era of reform and coalition politics in Los Angeles. With support from Black and white liberal voters, many of them Jewish, he amassed a strong and powerful political base linking South and West Los Angeles. Liberal forces had taken control of City Hall, replacing Sam Yorty's conservative regime with a broad-based multiracial coalition. Local government was now open to people who previously had been denied a seat at the table. Although my victory over a Bradley-linked candidate showed the limits of his burgeoning power, the mayor and I would soon become allies on most issues as the new political winds began to blow.

To be sure, there were problems galore. The city was grappling with rising crime, property tax rates, and rents. Neighborhood groups were angrily pushing back against unwanted development and traffic congestion that was eroding their quality of life. Black people, Gays and other marginalized groups were bitterly protesting their treatment by the Los Angeles Police Department, and a long-simmering dispute over busing and school integration was boiling over. I was eager to make a difference in what is now considered the onset of the city's modern political era. But first I had to learn the ropes.

Getting Started

There was a staff to hire. I had to build bridges to fourteen colleagues on the council and begin the transition from insurgent candidate to city councilman. There were big promises to keep, but I would never get anything done without a full understanding of the council's rules and traditions. The very first vote I cast drove this point home. As I settled into my chair in the council's ornate chambers, my colleagues were debating a trivial matter that I and several other members opposed. One colleague called for the "previous question," a strictly procedural motion to close debate. I mistakenly thought the vote was on the item itself, and when the clerk called my name, I proudly (and pointlessly) voted "no." The vote was 14 to 1, and the clerk handed me a printed copy of the roll call sheet memorializing my first vote as a councilmember. I asked myself, "What just happened?" Whatever embarrassment I felt, however, was dissipated when my amused colleagues gave me a copy of "Roberts Rules of Order" that they had all autographed. I wouldn't make the same mistake again.

As my learning curve continued, I got invaluable advice from United States Senator Henry (Scoop) Jackson. I came to know him while working to pass his historic human rights legislation that helped increase the numbers of Soviet Jews given permission to emigrate. He memorably told me: "Zev, surround yourself with staff who are smarter than you are. If you don't, you'll end up doing their job as well as your own, and it will be a colossal waste of your time and resources." I took that to heart and have given the same advice to newly elected officials who sought me out for my "wisdom" ever since.

In addition to appointing Jack McGrath as chief of staff, I hired a formidable team of deputies—some who worked on my campaign, some who were experts in their fields and others who had the capacity to grow and master their jobs. Several of my first staff members remained with me for most of the forty years I served in City and County government, something that few, if any, politicians can say.

I was also the first member of the council to appoint a fulltime press secretary, which proved to be a controversial move. Jackie Brainard was one of the best hires I ever made. She was smart and innovative, and the envy of the other fourteen councilmembers. Contrary to widespread belief, our press strategy was not primarily focused on getting my name in the paper or my mug on television. It was designed to help me inform the public about my proposals and rally them to my side. As best I could, I wanted to control my own messaging and, when possible, build a constituency outside my district for my citywide initiatives. If I was going to take on Police Chief Daryl Gates, or a powerful oil company, I wanted Angelenos to hear directly from me what I was proposing and why. Many of my colleagues were initially resentful of the press coverage that came my way. John Ferraro, who would later become president of the City Council, used to joke: "Don't ever get between Zev and a TV camera. You'll get crushed." Still, if imitation is the sincerest form of flattery, I was soon flattered by my colleagues, many of whom hired their own press deputies. Any councilmember who was serious about governing in the 1970s and beyond would have been crazy not to.

As I was preparing to take my seat on the council, I met with Mayor Bradley and spent time getting to know my colleagues. He was a tall man of few words, an intimidating presence both physically and politically. It was hard to read him. But he was always unfailingly gracious. As for my new colleagues on the council, there were five Republican members and three Democrats who often voted like Republicans. Some were old enough to be my grandparents. John S. Gibson, the council president, was a deeply conservative, elderly man from Kansas with whom I had little in common. I felt the age difference between us acutely, and other colleagues as well. But I knew my vote counted as much as any other member's.

I got another piece of important advice from Councilman Art Snyder, who represented East Los Angeles. He had a checkered reputation when it came to ethics and campaign finance, but his friends and adversaries agreed that he was a smart attorney and shrewd politician. When I asked for his thoughts about life on the council, he said simply: "Be indispensable to your constituents." As I got my sea legs at City Hall, those words were never far from my mind.

Being indispensable meant many things. If you were an elderly social security recipient who missed a check, my office wasn't just going to tell you who to call. We'd make the call for you. If you were a renter who couldn't get a landlord to make a necessary repair, we would get the Building and Safety department to run interference for you. Sometimes we'd even call the landlord. On occasion the issues were grand in scope—like a neighborhood fighting a massive commercial development; a hillside community fearful of catastrophic landslides during winter rainstorms; or residents tortured by the roar of overhead planes. Whatever the problem, we had to make sure that people knew we were their advocate and that we would get results. After walking door to door for five consecutive months, the last thing I wanted to do was lose touch with the voters who put me in office. If I was going to take on big issues, including controversial ones, I first had to make sure that I took care of their needs. As former House Speaker Thomas "Tip" O'Neill famously said, "All politics is local."

The Sabbatical Light

During my campaign, I heard growing concerns about traffic from residents who lived in the Westwood-Holmby Hills area. They wanted four-way stop signs installed at the corner of Warner and Loring Aves. adjacent to Warner Elementary School. They rightly believed that kids walking to and from school were in danger from cars speeding to the nearby UCLA campus. They had failed to get action from City Hall in prior years, so they raised the issue again with their new councilman. I had something to prove to the neighborhood, so I committed to get this done.

I ran into a brick wall, however, when I contacted the city's Traffic Department. Sam Taylor, the agency's legendary general manager, told me the four-way stop couldn't be approved because, as he put it, the request "didn't meet the national warrants." When I asked for a translation, he said there wasn't enough cross-traffic to justify adding the stop signs. I wasn't satisfied, so I contacted George Buchanan, the Assistant City Attorney assigned to give legal advice to the City Council. He told me that I could override the department by having the council pass an ordinance (a law) requiring the city to install the stop signs. I introduced a motion to do just that. When it was clear that I had rounded up enough votes, Taylor conceded the point and told me he would install the signs if I withdrew my proposed ordinance. He didn't want to be forced to install the signs by his bosses, because he would have been embarrassed in his traffic engineering world. "Just don't make a big deal out of it," he said. We came to a mutual under-standing, and I never had another problem with Sam.

The neighbors were thrilled by this achievement, and they threw a thank you party for me at the home of Sidney and Frances Brody, who lived next door to Hugh Hefner's Playboy Mansion in Holmby Hills. The Brodys were major donors to the Los Angeles County Museum of Art, and they had a large personal art collection in their elegant home. After finding myself face to face with a stunning Picasso in the restroom, I went up to our hostess and said, "Mrs. Brody, that's a great looking Picasso in the powder room. Is it an original or a print?" She looked at me with barely concealed disdain and answered, "Young man, *it's an original*." I could only imagine what was hanging in the master bedroom. This was the beginning of the acculturation of Zev Yaroslavsky.

Some constituent stories stand out. In 1975 the city began to install electronic "walk/don't walk" signals on traffic lights throughout Los Angeles. A pedestrian who wanted to cross a street had to push a button to activate the "walk" sign in order to legally cross. This innovation was generally well-received, but not by orthodox Jews. They were not permitted to activate electricity on the Sabbath, so when they wanted to cross a major thoroughfare like La Brea Ave. on their way to synagogue on Friday nights and Saturdays, they only had one option—to cross against a "don't walk" sign, which was a jaywalking violation. Soon, the LAPD began issuing tickets to people simply trying to make their way to religious services. To make matters worse, jaywalking ticket recipients were required to sign the ticket as proof of service, and Orthodox Jews were prohibited from writing on the Sabbath. Soon, congregants were getting *arrested* and taken to the local police station, all because of the new pedestrian signals. It was a heartburn-inducing problem, and I once again sought help from Sam Taylor.

Thankfully, he had just the solution. "Each traffic signal is computerized," he said. "We can program the computer from Friday evenings to Saturday night in these neighborhoods, so that the pedestrian 'walk' sign will activate automatically. Nobody will have to press anything." I loved the idea and asked Sam, a Mormon, to get it done. He appropriately named this technical fix the "Sabbatical Light," and the city eventually installed it in the Fairfax, Pico Robertson, North Hollywood, and other communities with large orthodox Jewish populations.

Then there was the urgent message I received from Mrs. Abe Goldberg. When I called, she told me her husband had just died. In a chipper voice that belied her sudden widowhood, she said, "I'm sure you remember my husband, Abe. He was very active in the community." It didn't ring a bell, but I asked her to remind me. "Oh, you know, they called him the 'Honorary Mayor of Fairfax.'" I had absolutely no clue whom she was talking about. "Well, Abe passed away on Wednesday, and he would have loved for you to speak at his funeral. It's on Sunday at 11:00 a.m. at Mt. Sinai Cemetery." I don't' know what I was thinking, but I agreed to do it.

When I arrived, the chapel was overflowing with mourners. I thought there would be multiple eulogies, but the Rabbi told me I was the *only* speaker. I asked for a few facts about Abe, but he knew nothing about him. "I'm only the chaplain for the day, but I know the family appreciates this," he said. I'll bet they did.

What was I to do? When I got to the pulpit, I said, "We're not here to mourn Abe Goldberg's death, but to celebrate his life." I looked at the hushed crowd and continued: "As many of you may know, Abe was known as the Honorary Mayor of Fairfax. He cared deeply about seniors," I said, riffing for two minutes on senior citizen services. "He cared deeply about affordable senior housing," I added, and I reviewed some of the things we had done in that realm, giving Abe all the credit. And so it went for ten minutes. All the while, many of the more than 200 mourners were overcome with emotion. Mercifully, the service ended.

I had just eulogized someone who was a complete stranger to me, apparently to great effect. As I walked to my car, an old friend who had known the Goldbergs came up and thanked me for my remarks. "We've known the family for twenty-five years and never realized that Abe was so active in the community," he said. I paused and answered: "Well, he was the kind of guy who pretty much kept this stuff to himself." I was beginning to learn what it meant to be indispensable.

Too often it came at moments of profound tragedy. On a warm Sunday evening in 1980, four innocent people were randomly gunned down while taking strolls in the Pico-Robertson community. Two gang members committed the murders, probably as part of an initiation ritual. The killings sent shockwaves throughout the neighborhood. As a councilmember, I came to understand that from time to time I had to be a consoler-in-chief.

In this instance, I strongly believed we needed to restore confidence to this shattered neighborhood. Simply sending thoughts and prayers wouldn't cut it. So, I talked to the police captain for the area and suggested we close down the street where the killings had taken place, set up a few hundred chairs, and invite all of the residents to attend a community meeting with me and LAPD representatives. I thought it would help them psychologically take back their streets. The captain agreed, and the strategy worked. Hundreds of people came out at dusk to be with their neighbors, declaring that they wouldn't surrender to fear. Darkness descended as the meeting ended, and the community had been backed off the edge.

One of the murder victims was a nineteen-year-old French citizen, Jean Louis Vernin, who was fulfilling a dream to visit California. His family couldn't afford to bring his body back to France for a proper burial. Enter serendipity. One of the residents at our community meeting was a French-American who worked as a pilot for Flying Tiger Airlines. Jean-Claude Demirdjian contacted me and offered to return Vernin's body to France, at no charge, on one of the company's planes in a coffin that it would pay for. Demirdjian personally accompanied the young man's body back to his parents in Paris.

When he returned, Demirdjian wrote to tell me that Vernin's grandmother had expressed profound gratitude to the people of Los Angeles. "She remembered the American soldiers from World War II, who were buried in cemeteries all over Normandy, their graves flying French and American flags," he wrote. "She had tears in her eyes, and told me that 'When your American boys died in France, we couldn't afford to send them back in such nice coffins.'" As I read his letter, I was moved to tears, as was my staff. Loving kindness wasn't in Jean-Claude's job description, nor was it in ours. But it was assuredly part of our jobs.

The Slave Auction

I grew up adjacent to West Hollywood, then an unincorporated part of Los Angeles County. From an early age I got to know my gay and lesbian neighbors. We shopped at the same stores and attended the same schools. There were numerous gay bars and bath houses in our neighborhood as well. I met many of them playing softball at Poinsettia or West Hollywood Park, and I vividly remember how talented the female players were. When it came to pitching, hitting, and fielding, they killed it. I knew many of them on a first-name basis, and they were warm and outgoing to me. As a teenager it never occurred to me that they would face attacks on their constitutional liberties just because of their sexual orientation. But the Los Angeles Police Department saw things differently. Uniformed and plain-clothed officers routinely harassed gay men and lesbians on the streets, in bars, movie theaters, and throughout the city. This orchestrated violation of their personal freedoms was common across the country, not just in Los Angeles.

Today, it's hard to remember how harshly the LAPD once treated the LGBTQ community. In 1975, Police Chief Ed Davis was invited to participate in the local Pride parade, an annual celebration of the gay community that drew tens of thousands of people in West Hollywood. Davis rejected the written invitation, saying "I would much rather celebrate 'Gay Conversion Week,' which I will gladly sponsor when the medical practitioners in this country find a way to convert gays to heterosexuals."

On the night of April 10, 1976, more than 100 LAPD officers, including a fleet of police helicopters, descended with overwhelming force on Mark IV, a gay bar on Melrose Avenue, not far from where Barbara and I lived. The club had been hosting a slave auction—a social services fundraiser where consenting gay men "auctioned" themselves off to each other. Police broke up the event and arrested forty people for violating an 1899 California law against slavery, if you can believe it. The crackdown was extensively covered by local media which had been alerted in advance by the LAPD. Members of the gay community and its straight allies, including me, were infuriated.

About a week later, Morris Kight, an elder statesman of the city's LGBTQ community, called for a mock slave auction and community protest to be held at Trouper's Hall on La Brea Avenue in Hollywood. It was billed as a solidarity rally with those who were arrested the previous week, and Barbara and I decided to attend. When we arrived, the hall was jammed, standing room only. Morris privately asked if I wanted to say a few words, but I told him I was just there to lend support and didn't need to speak. I thought that just being there was enough.

When the event began, it looked like every TV camera in town was in the room. Morris began the evening by telling the crowd that there were some "very important guests" present. "I'd like to acknowledge our new councilman, Zev Yaroslavsky, who is standing way in the back of the room," he proudly declared. Every camera in the room pivoted 180 degrees to get a good close-up of us, and we got a rousing ovation. I was proud to be there, realizing how much my presence as an official representative of the city meant to the community that night. Yet I was also embarrassed by my initial reluctance to be called out. If I didn't show up for the gay community, who could they count on in the straight community? They needed allies who were prepared to use their political capital to stand up and speak out, and I needed to be one of those persons.

To criticize the LAPD in the mid-1970s meant taking on Davis, a popular and powerful police chief. The city's seventeen police divisions were not only organized to fight crime throughout the city; they provided the chief with political tentacles into every one of its neighborhoods. If he wanted to pressure a councilmember to toe the line, all Davis had to do was send talking points to his community relations officers, and within forty-eight hours every homeowner group, church, synagogue, Chamber of Commerce, and Rotary Club would get the message. Few councilmembers dared to tangle with him, but I wasn't intimidated. In my view, when the LAPD attacked the civil liberties of gay persons, it attacked the rights of every citizen—gay or straight.

Ironically, Chief Davis's bigoted views about gay people evolved over the years. As a Republican state senator he had a profound change of heart and became an outspoken advocate for gay rights. In fact, he was condemned by one of his Republican colleagues as "the legislature's leading crusader for homosexual rights," after voting for the first California bill banning discrimination against gay persons. Despite our prior clashes, he wound up endorsing my 1989 re-election campaign.

Looking back, Kight taught me a great lesson that night at Trouper's Hall. When civil liberties are on the line, there's no virtue in standing quietly at the back of the room. If you're going to fight for a principle, be up front, stand tall, be seen and be heard. Two years later I was one of the first straight elected officials in Los Angeles to openly oppose Proposition 6, a pernicious state ballot initiative authored by State Senator John Briggs that would have banned the employment of gay teachers in California's public schools. I campaigned against it throughout Southern California.

I was the first straight politician to debate Briggs in a confrontation that took place on Sam Yorty's weekly television talk show. By then, Yorty was a curmudgeon with a dwindling following of elderly conservatives. I'm happy to report that I shredded Briggs. When I pointed out that his measure also called for firing teachers who simply knew gay teachers, even Yorty agreed that the measure went too far. A few weeks later I was again scheduled to debate Briggs on NBC's nationally televised "Tomorrow" show with Tom Snyder, but the Senator was a no-show. I ended up eviscerating one of his surrogates, with eloquent support from Snyder. Thankfully, the Briggs amendment went down to defeat.

I had come a long way from the baseball diamonds of West Hollywood Park, and my alliance with the LGBTQ community became one of my strongest and most heartfelt bonds. Years later I sponsored a city ordinance providing benefits to domestic partners, which at the time was a profound advance for same sex couples. The City Council resoundingly approved it. I authored a similar law when I arrived at the County Board of Supervisors, winning domestic partnership benefits by a 4 to 1 vote. I was pleasantly surprised to even get the vote of conservative Republican Deane Dana.

But my education on this issue was still evolving. Years later, as the debate shifted to same-sex marriage, my daughter, Mina, asked about my views on the issue. I told her that same-sex couples now had domestic partnership rights that bestowed all of the benefits of marriage, so that should settle the issue. But she kept pressing me and finally said: "Dad, if two people love each other and want to get *married*, what difference does it make to you?" It was a pointed question, especially coming from my grown-up daughter, who for years had been able to intelligently challenge my views. It was a moment every parent experiences. She succeeded in changing my thinking.

This was not just an abstract question. When the State Supreme Court upheld the constitutionality of same sex marriage in 2008, June Lagmay, Los Angeles' City Clerk and a former clerk of the Finance Committee which I chaired, asked if I would officiate at her marriage to the woman she had loved for twenty-one years. I was honored and accepted the request. Performing the ceremony was a deeply meaningful moment for me.

Yaroslavsky v. The United States of America

Traffic impacts everyone's life in Los Angeles, whether they make daily commutes on the freeways or visit here briefly. It's part of our culture and identity, and late-night comedians have mined the subject with immense success. Several years ago, Conan O'Brien quipped: "There is a rumor that the San Diego Chargers might move to Los Angeles. The Chargers could be here for the 2016 season, or the 2017 season, depending on traffic." Southern California car congestion is ubiquitous, and commuters have learned to live with it. What they won't tolerate, however, is a foolish, man-made traffic catastrophe, and that's what the infamous Santa Monica Freeway Diamond Lane project proved to be. It remains a textbook case of bureaucratic arrogance run amok, a reminder of the price that government pays when it doesn't listen to the people it serves.

The story began on March 15, 1976, when Caltrans, the state's transportation agency, launched the "Santa Monica Preferential Lane Project." Under the program, the freeway's fast lane between Pacific Coast Highway and downtown Los Angeles would be reserved strictly for buses and vehicles with three or more passengers, between 6:30 a.m. and 9:30 a.m., and 3:00 p.m. and 7 p.m. on weekdays. All other cars would be confined to the freeway's three remaining lanes. Motorists would receive hefty tickets for violating the new policy, which Adriana Gianturco, Governor Brown's Director of Transportation, had promoted to boost ride sharing and reduce congestion on one of the world's most heavily traveled freeways. It marked the first and last time that the state would remove an existing lane from general use in favor of a Diamond Lane, and the results were appalling from the moment the project began.

Drivers were infuriated that their cars were brought to a standstill in the three mixed lanes, while a car in the diamond lane sped by in what seemed to be every fifteen seconds. Widespread protests erupted almost immediately. According to a retrospective report by the US Department of Transportation, the project caused "significant physical and emotional dislocation among freeway drivers, public officials, and other residents of Los Angeles, and generated considerable controversy regarding the reported and actual impacts of the project. The first day of operations was disastrous, featuring bumper-to-bumper traffic, long queues at on-ramps, a malfunctioning ramp meter, many accidents, outraged drivers, poor press notices and derisive news commentary." No government report has ever been more truthful.

As bad as the optics were, the practical impacts were worse. Daily travel times lengthened and what once were routine commutes became marathon ordeals for hundreds of thousands of motorists. Surface street traffic worsened as drivers left the freeway, seeking out less congested neighborhood streets. Although many citizens were angered by the idea of a lane set aside for special vehicles, I wasn't in that camp. I believed then, as I believe now, that carpool lanes could be a constructive tool if state officials *added* a lane and designated it for carpools, instead of removing a lane from general circulation. That's not what Caltrans did, and they set back the concept of carpooling for years as a result. Gianturco had imposed the project with little outreach to local officials and without conducting a required environmental impact analysis. She failed to gauge how the Diamond Lane would affect traffic on the freeway, as well as on adjacent city streets.

The most insulting thing of all, however, was Caltrans' continued insistence that the project was working, even when it was plain for all Southern Californians to see that it wasn't. Commuters painted obscene graffiti on the carpool lanes, while others scattered nails on them. Caltrans maintenance officials feared for their safety, and Gianturco became perhaps the most reviled public administrator in Southern California. The agency's press releases, insisting that the Diamond Lane was a success, reminded essayist Joan Didion of the absurdly dishonest appraisals that the Pentagon made of our progress during the Vietnam War.

However, Paul Conrad, the *Los Angeles Times'* Pulitzer Prize-winning cartoonist, said it best when he launched an attack on the freeway boondoggle. In a parody of the old Burma Shave billboards that dotted America's highways, Conrad lampooned the Diamond Lane by drawing a consecutive, five-sign display that read:

> The Diamond Lane
> Is Working Well
> If You Don't Like It
> Go to Hell
> *Caltrans*

Although scores of elected officials condemned the project, none had been able to end it. When I joined City Attorney Burt Pines at a press conference demanding that Governor Jerry Brown halt the project, Caltrans ignored us. Amid the handwringing, I decided to take action that was controversial but also necessary. I joined with the Pacific Legal Foundation—a conservative legal defense fund with which I had nothing in common—to file a lawsuit against Caltrans. We argued that state officials had failed to produce a legally required Federal Environmental Impact Statement (FEIS), and that an injunction should be issued against the project. Although the foundation provided legal firepower, I gave them the legal standing to proceed in court. I was a commuter who often used the freeway and was adversely impacted by the project, and I testified to that during a court appearance.

A handful of people criticized me for joining with the foundation, given its conservative history, but this was a classic case of politics making strange bedfellows. I couldn't find an environmental attorney who was willing to take on the Brown Administration, so I could either sit on the sidelines and do nothing or join forces with "the enemy." Since my goal was to bring relief to hundreds of thousands of daily commuters, the decision was easy. As George Washington noted in his Farewell Address, there are times when "we may safely trust to temporary alliances for extraordinary emergencies." This was such an emergency.

In August, our case was heard in federal court by US District Judge Matthew Byrne. We won a huge victory when he issued a restraining order halting the project. He agreed with us that the state had failed to comply with the National Environmental Policy Act. The next day local papers led with the story, and you could hear cheers erupting all over the region. One paper called me a "Giant Killer," which wasn't bad for a twenty-seven-year-old who had been on the City Council for barely one year. Jerry Brown had no stomach for a battle that was politically embarrassing to his administration. So the state decided to pull the plug on the failed project and declined to appeal Judge Byrne's decision. The freeway nightmare was finally over.

When reporters asked for my reaction, I said simply that the Diamond Lane lawsuit was a great victory for the people, which it most certainly was. It was also a milestone for me. I had challenged an arrogant, tone-deaf bureaucracy and won. It's rare in public life when an elected official helps to scuttle a debacle, and with a stroke of a judge's pen ends a misery that plagued the daily lives of so many people. This was just such a moment.

Water, Power, and Politics

I was elected to fill out the balance of Ed Edelman's term on the City Council. But a mere two years later, I had to stand for re-election in a regularly scheduled contest. There was little drama this time. I won 91 percent of the vote, earning my first four-year term and piling up strong majorities in neighborhoods that didn't support me the first time around. The political world now realized that I was not some flash-in-the-pan who pulled off a freakish upset. I acquitted myself well in my partial term, and I developed a strong base in my vote-rich district. People who needed my backing were not hesitant to ask for it. During his 1977 re-election campaign, I accompanied Mayor Bradley on a walk down Fairfax Avenue, introducing him to voters and merchants whom I had known since childhood. Two years after I toppled his candidate for City Council, the two of us were allies. It was hard to ignore the irony of that stroll. I was walking him through my base, soliciting votes for him in front of Canter's Deli where I had launched my first campaign. Bradley didn't really need my support. He was re-elected in a landslide.

On July 1, 1977, John Ferraro replaced the aging and increasingly feeble John Gibson as council president by a unanimous vote. The president of the City Council traditionally makes new committee assignments following his election, and Ferraro asked me for my preferences. As a relatively new member I could not realistically hope to unseat more veteran colleagues on their powerful and influential panels. So, I asked to chair the Water and Power Committee, a post that no one on the council coveted. It was hard to blame them. The main thing that committee did was to periodically recommend water and electricity rate increases. Not exactly a politically remunerative job.

Still, I saw this assignment as an opportunity to start a conversation about reforming the Los Angeles Department of Water and Power, the largest publicly owned utility in the United States. This was no easy task. Second to the LAPD, there was no more powerful political force in city government than the DWP. Water and electricity were essential for industry, commerce, and residential living. Any attempt to mess with the built-in advantages that manufacturers and homeowners enjoyed could be politically riskier than taking on Ed Davis.

My task was made easier by a young deputy I hired to help me run the committee. Smart and indefatigable, Alisa Belinkoff had graduated from Brandeis University and the Coro Fellowship program, and earned a master's degree in Public Policy at Occidental College. I had known Alisa and her family since we were both teenagers in the Habonim movement, and our parents had known each other since their early days in Los Angeles.

When my mother died, my father created a scholarship fund in her memory for high school graduates wanting to study in Israel before beginning college. Alisa received one of the first scholarships. Hiring her was a smart move as

I began work on the Water and Power committee. It commenced a nearly four-decade relationship, the last twenty-nine of which she served as my chief of staff.

From the beginning, Alisa showed impeccable integrity and intelligence. She saw the big picture while mastering the intricacies of detailed policy issues. Alisa had her fingerprints on all my policy initiatives, large and small; on every legislative proposal, speech, article, and press statement coming out of our office. She helped me turn promising ideas into reality and toss bad ideas into the circular file. In short, we had a special professional relationship—the kind where you finish each other's sentences and speak the same language. And all the while, she administered a growing office with an increasingly complex agenda. Alisa was there for it all.

The first item on my DWP agenda was to revamp its antiquated electric and water rate structure. The agency charged large water and electricity users less per unit than small ones—your basic volume discount. This was a throwback to the days of abundant energy and water when the city was attempting to attract new businesses and promote more residential development, especially in the San Fernando Valley. It may have been a good pricing strategy from the 1930s to the 1960s, but it made no sense in a period of increasing scarcity. For example, Anheuser-Busch's beer production facility in Van Nuys paid less for a cubic foot of water, and the Playboy Mansion in Holmby Hills paid less for a kilowatt hour of electricity, than Barbara and I paid in our modest Fairfax area home. If the City wanted to encourage water and energy conservation, it made sense to charge large consumers more, not less. Making the rates more equitable and environmentally sensitive was a heavy lift, but we got a good portion of the work done.

Second, I wanted to establish a more open relationship between the city and the Owens Valley. There was historical enmity between the two communities. Los Angeles began diverting vast amounts of water from the eastern Sierra Nevada Mountains watershed just prior to World War I to accommodate the city's explosive growth. Over time, the diversion project caused the saline Owens Lake to go dry, creating a serious air pollution problem when the winds swept menacing saline dust up the valley. Resentment ran deep in Inyo and Mono counties, and I knew we weren't going to change anything overnight. Still, I was young, idealistic, and not constrained by sixty years of DWP orthodoxy.

Beyond wanting to defuse the tension, I love this region of California. The Eastern Sierras are the most beautiful part of the state, along with Highway 1 along California's coast. I spent a lot of time skiing at Mammoth Mountain, and I always enjoyed the drive on US Highway 395. I wonder to this day how much more beautiful the Owens Valley and Mono Basin would be if so much of its water hadn't been diverted to serve the city's growth machine.

When I made diplomatic overtures to officials in these remote counties, they were understandably skeptical of this Los Angeles politician's intentions. Did I *really* want to address the inequities in Los Angeles' water diversion policy? I tried to convince the local officials that this wasn't just talk. It marked the first such outreach by a Los Angeles elected leader to officials in that region, and laid the groundwork for profound reforms that were implemented years later.

To demonstrate my seriousness, I invited Johnny Johnson, the Chair of the Inyo County Board of Supervisors, to testify before my committee on August 16, 1977. We asked him to drive all the way to Los Angeles City Hall to lay out his aspirations and frustrations over DWP's water policies. This was the first time in memory that an Owens Valley official had been invited to testify before a Los Angeles City Council committee. Unfortunately, when Johnson made the four-hour trip from Independence, California, he learned that it was all for naught. There was a good reason. Barbara was pregnant and she began having contractions during the night; by dawn I was driving her to the Tarzana Medical Center. The imminent birth of our first child was the only thing that would cause me to abruptly cancel this meeting. Later that morning I called Johnson to apologize. He told me there was no need to do so. He headed back to the Owens Valley after leaving a beautiful note in my office congratulating us on the birth of our first child. Thankfully, he and I bonded after the scheduling mishap.

When I arrived at the hospital, I was asked to sit in the waiting room until the doctors were ready for me to apply the Lamaze technique that Barbara and I had practiced. As I was waiting, a bulletin flashed across the television screen that Elvis Presley had died. Moments later, I was in the delivery room helping to bring Mina Yaroslavsky into this world. Named after my mother, she was a beautiful baby who was calmly taking in her new surroundings. As we both took our first look at her, Barbara had a radiant smile on her face, and I felt tears of joy streaming down my cheek. To call it a life-changing moment would be the ultimate understatement.

Eventually, my focus returned to water policy. We launched initiatives to reduce the diversion of water from Mono Lake, whose water levels were dropping precipitously, beginning the slow process of restoring this unique environmental resource. We promoted water conservation through a more progressive rate structure, which resulted in a significant drop in the city's per capita water consumption. According to a 2016 report on usage rates in Los Angeles, "the Los Angeles Department of Water and Power (LADWP) has seen the city keep its water demand at about the same level for the last forty-five years, despite population going up by one million people, thanks to conservation measures, incentives and mandates to cut down on [water] use…" In addition, the city implemented a more progressive electrical rate structure and developed sources of clean energy, ultimately reducing the city's carbon footprint.

Many of my colleagues chuckled when I took on this committee post, chalking it up to my lack of experience. But it was a pattern I would repeat throughout my career. I've always looked for opportunities that others passed on, then tried to make the most of them. In this case I took over a moribund committee and became a champion for reform. Indeed, I felt vindicated when a *Los Angeles Times* article said I was now chairing "a key Los Angeles City Council committee." Our efforts made it politically palatable for future city leaders to double down on the initiatives we undertook in the late 1970s. Today, the Los Angeles Department of Water and Power is a far more conservation and environmentally sensitive utility than anyone could have imagined prior to 1977.

"I Think the People Should Vote for It"

One day, during my first City Council campaign, I was walking precincts in the Fairfax neighborhood, and knocked on the door of a home on North Crescent Heights Blvd. A registered Republican homeowner answered the door. His name was Howard Jarvis. It was three years before the passage of Proposition 13, a popular tax-cutting measure that would make him an international celebrity. But I recognized his name. At the time of our encounter on his doorstep he had authored several failed property tax reform measures. But unlike many people, I didn't dismiss him as an irritating gadfly. When I told him I was running for the City Council, he was delighted to have a captive audience.

He spent the next fifteen minutes lecturing me on the inequities of the property tax system. I was impatient and wanted to move on because I didn't think I had a shot at getting his vote. Nonetheless, I listened politely. "I hear you, I understand," I said. Then, much to my surprise, he promised to vote for me, saying I appeared to be a "fine young man." When I asked if he'd put up a lawn sign for me, he quickly agreed. It was a friendly but not particularly memorable encounter. Three years later, it proved to be worth its weight in gold.

By 1978 Los Angeles was caught up in a bitter, protracted legal battle over the desegregation of its public schools. A 1963 lawsuit backed by the American Civil Liberties Union (ACLU) had accused the Los Angeles Unified School District of a deliberate pattern of racial segregation. The evidence spoke for itself: City schools were populated with predominantly white students in the San Fernando Valley and Westside, and mostly Black and Latino students in South and East Los Angeles. In part, this was one of the legacies of discriminatory housing and lending policies that confined persons of color to certain areas of the city. Tensions began to grow on both sides of the racial integration issue after a 1969 ruling by respected Los Angeles Superior Court Judge Alfred Gitelson—Fran Savitch's father—ordering the integration of district schools. But that anger erupted nine years later when Superior Court Judge Paul Egly ordered the busing of students in order to accomplish racial balance throughout the district.

By then, voters had begun to weigh in on the issue. Bobbie Fiedler, the leader of the anti-busing organization, "Bus Stop," was elected a year earlier to the Los Angeles Unified school board. More anti-busing activists were lining up to run for other board seats two years later. Meanwhile, it was clear the school board didn't reflect the district's steadily increasing racial and ethnic diversity. Five of the seven school board members were white, one was Black, and only one was Hispanic. The lack of diversity resulted from board members being elected at large, meaning they didn't run in geographic districts like members of Congress or city councilmembers. Since whites voted in greater numbers and percentages than non-whites, communities of color were underrepresented on the board of education.

The time had come to reform the school district's electoral system. With the teachers' union support, I authored Proposition M to be placed on the November 1978 ballot. Backed by the City Council, it required that school board members be elected in seven geographically distinct districts, each containing about 450,000 residents. It was imperative that Los Angeles' racial and political diversity be represented on the board as it dealt with Egly's mandatory busing decision.

Although Proposition M had considerable political support and the endorsement of the Los Angeles Times, the anti-busing forces vigorously opposed it. We were clearly the underdogs in this fight. We needed a prominent conservative voice who could speak to voters in the suburbs and elsewhere about the need for accountability. It was then that I hit on the idea of asking Howard Jarvis to endorse the measure. Proposition 13 had passed overwhelmingly several months before, and he was riding a wave of unparalleled popularity. It was a long shot, but his endorsement could turn the tide.

So, I called Jarvis at home late on a Monday afternoon and asked if I could meet with him to discuss an important issue. He remembered meeting me during my campaign and invited me to come over. I grabbed my chief deputy, Jack McGrath, and we raced down Beverly Boulevard to the Jarvis home. His wife, Estelle, welcomed us at the door and we found Howard sitting comfortably in the den in his Archie Bunker chair, sipping a Scotch and soda, and watching the Monday night football game between the Chicago Bears and Minnesota

Vikings. After a quick chat I explained Proposition M, asked for his support, and was elated by his answer. "Of course!" he said, signing a typed statement we had prepared a couple of hours earlier, just in case he said "yes."

As we left, I told McGrath to get the statement to City News Service as soon as possible, so they could run it on their overnight wire and disseminate it to their clients in the print and electronic media throughout Southern California. I woke up early the next morning to hear KNX News radio leading with Jarvis's Proposition M endorsement. Later that day, Jarvis held a previously scheduled press conference on an unrelated matter, and we knew he'd be asked about his endorsement. I sent Jack to the Press Club with a tape recorder, just in case he said something we could use in the campaign. Unbeknown to us, Jarvis had previously given a letter to Bobbi Fielder opposing the measure. So, when the question was popped, Howard looked and sounded confused. "Prop M? What's that?" he asked. When a reporter explained it to him, he responded, "Oh, Prop. M! I think the people ought to vote *for* it."

That's all we needed in the way of an endorsement. We turned that sound bite into a radio ad in the waning days of the campaign. A voice boomed, "Howard Jarvis on Proposition M." Then Howard's voice confirmed, "Prop M? I think the people ought to vote for it." Then a voice described the measure and wrapped up by saying, "Vote Yes on M, for *local* control of schools." The ad aired heavily on Los Angeles radio until Election Day. Proposition M passed with 54 percent of the vote, creating a district-elected board structure that remains in place to this day. It marked the first time I undertook a winning campaign for a ballot measure—a strategy I would use again and again in the years to come.

To be sure, Proposition M didn't immediately bring political balance to the school board. In 1979, busing opponents recalled School Board President Howard Miller, a supporter of the Egly busing plan. Roberta Weintraub, a busing opponent, was elected to take his place. The board now had an anti-busing majority, including Bobbi Fiedler and two others. Over time, however, the board began to look like school district voters and its students, a long over-due outcome.

Although it was an imperative that schools be desegregated, I didn't believe that busing kids as much as thirty miles each way to and from school was neces-sarily the answer. Neither did most parents in the school district. (Years later, my children were voluntarily bussed forty-five- and twenty-mile-roundtrip respec-tively, to Monroe and North Hollywood High Schools in the San Fernando Valley.) To my mind, the school board needed to be more responsive to its constituents—parents *and* students—and Proposition M could provide the framework to achieve that goal.

In retrospect, my first years as an elected official were remarkably eventful. I was honing my skills as a politician, taking deep dives into long neglected policy issues, and establishing my credentials as someone willing to challenge powerful political and institutional forces. But as heady as those first years were, the upbeat feeling was short-lived. There was an epic political storm headed California's way, and this time government would pay a far higher price for its failure to listen.

CHAPTER 8

The Taxpayer and Renter Revolt

Over the years, I coined many an axiom. One of my favorites was that when a politician goes to a public meeting and can't find a parking place, it's not going to be a good meeting. That was the case on a November night in 1977, when I arrived at the Cheviot Hills Recreation Center in West Los Angeles to meet with residents who had just received their property tax bills. Warm Santa Ana winds were whipping through the southland, but the temperature was even hotter inside the gymnasium. Although the room had the capacity for 180 people, more than 400 were jammed inside waiting to hear from several elected officials, including me. They were in a foul mood, because their tax bills had exponentially increased over the previous year.

As it turned out, my sister, Shimona, was visiting me from Israel for the first time since my election to the City Council, and I asked her to join me at the meeting so she could see her brother in action. Neither of us was prepared for what transpired. Residents were infuriated, voicing legitimate anger—and fear—that higher taxes would force them out of their homes. They believed local and state government officials had ignored their steadily worsening financial burden, and it was hard to argue with them. I took a pummeling that night, along with other officials in attendance, but it wasn't personal. The people I represented had every right to demand that something be done, and fast.

The 1970s were an economically turbulent decade across the country, and in many ways Los Angeles was ground zero for this upheaval. Inflation hit the nation as the decade began. Prices of goods and services were rising while wages were not keeping pace. Then the national economy slipped into recession, further fueling economic insecurities among consumers. Finally, in the latter part of the decade, hyperinflation and rising interest rates eroded Americans' purchasing power, calling into question many of the economic assumptions they had relied upon since the end of World War II. Economic stability seemed like a faint memory to the average Angeleno when the Consumer Price Index—the average change over time in the price of a basket of groceries—rose to nearly 18 percent in 1979, and interest rates exceeded 20 percent.

To complicate matters, property values that had been relatively stable in the middle of the century dramatically increased during the 1970s. Property taxes, which were tied to a property's assessed value, dramatically rose as well. Homeowners were apoplectic. The increased value of their real estate existed only on paper, much like owning stock that appreciated in value. In the case of stock, you don't owe the IRS a penny until you sell it—and only if you've made a profit. But if you owned a home that appreciated in value, you paid taxes based on the higher value, even if you hadn't yet sold the property and realized a profit.

The *ad valorem* (value-based) property tax became a budgetary opiate for cities, counties, and school districts. They had no incentive to cut tax rates, which would have limited some of the increases. In fact, their elected representatives often argued to burdened homeowners, "Don't blame us; we didn't raise your taxes, the assessor did." All the while, homeowners were grappling with an existential threat to their homeownership, especially those on fixed incomes.

This simple but devastating predicament sparked an explosion of protests, like the one I encountered in Cheviot Hills that night. At the conclusion of the town hall meeting, one elderly widow approached me, and the ensuing conversation has been etched in my memory ever since. She showed me copies of her 1976 and 1977 property tax bills. The '76 bill was for $1,500, an amount she could barely afford, but the '77 bill rose to $7,500, *a five-fold increase.* "I'm going to have to sell my house. I'm going to have to leave the home in which my late husband and I raised our family," she said. "I don't want to leave. Where will I go?" She didn't want to leave her church, her doctors, and her social network. It was a crushing blow. This story was playing out in hundreds of thousands of households across our region.

I had knocked on every door in Cheviot Hills during my 1975 campaign, including a visit to this widow's home. As we spoke, I tried to put myself in her shoes. My initial councilmember's annual salary was $30,000. Based on that income and our savings, Barbara and I were able to buy our modest Fairfax area home in 1976. However, if our property taxes had quintupled in one year, we would have been forced to sell it. We also would have been hard pressed to afford another home anywhere in the fifth council district. And I wasn't even retired on a fixed income.

As we left that difficult homeowners meeting, my sister wondered aloud, "Is this why you walked all those precincts? To deal with these problems?" In truth, that is precisely why I ran. I didn't realize it at first, but I lived for moments like these. For all of democracy's challenges, I passionately believed in the right of our citizens to petition their elected representatives and to redress their grievances. It's what our political system is supposed to be about. The give and take with constituents made me a better representative. I welcomed those town hall meetings, and I never turned an invitation down. I often felt like an evangelical preacher trying to recruit converts, and the fundamental tenet of my "old time religion" was that government could work for them.

In the ensuing years, I convened hundreds of town halls and attended just as many homeowner and tenants' meetings. I held court in supermarket lines, coffee shops, gas stations and even at my front door. I took painful beatings at many of these encounters, some of them lasting for hours. But it was all worth it. Unfiltered access to my constituents gave me a sense of voters' aspirations *and* frustrations. When government ignores citizen anger, the results can be bloody. Unfortunately, that is exactly what happened as 1978 approached.

Howard Jarvis Is Mad as Hell

The smoldering protests over rising property taxes in 1977 erupted into a prairie fire the following year, when 65 percent of California voters approved Proposition 13. Among other things, the sweeping ballot measure authored by Howard Jarvis and Paul Gann capped property taxes at 1 percent of a home's assessed value, slashing property tax revenues in California by an astonishing 57 percent. Going forward, one's property taxes could only rise by a maximum of 2 percent per year, or until the home sold. Then, its value would be reassessed based on the sales price. Future increases would again be capped at 2 percent annually. Moreover, anyone who had purchased a home before the 1978 election, like the Cheviot Hills widow, would have their taxes rolled back to pre-1978 levels. It's no wonder the initiative was successful, winning 67 percent of the vote in the state's largest and hardest hit county—Los Angeles.

There was one more important wrinkle to the measure. It mandated that new or increased state taxes be approved by a two-thirds vote of the legislature, and local tax increases would require voter approval, sometimes by two-thirds, in a given jurisdiction. These were almost insurmountable hurdles.

While property taxes were skyrocketing, voters were infuriated that the State was sitting on a fat budget surplus that totaled $7 billion. Hyperinflation had generated increased income tax revenues, which swelled state government coffers. But the Governor and legislature refused to utilize the surplus to ease the taxpayers' burden, despite repeated pleas from citizens and local governments to do so. It was a fatal error.

Given the lopsided vote, there was no percentage in trying to weaken or nullify the measure, as some elected officials hoped to do in its immediate aftermath. Indeed, Proposition 13 quickly became a political "third rail," something too dangerous to touch. Jarvis and Gann rode a wave of unprecedented public fury that has transformed the politics of the Golden State to this day. The campaign turned Jarvis into a potent political force, and he became an overnight media star. Three months after the election, he told me that when he boarded an airplane, he received standing ovations from the passengers. A tough, belligerent populist who cussed like a sailor, he even landed an iconic cameo role in the hit film "Airplane," and he was featured on the cover of Time Magazine. It all came as a shock, especially to Democratic Party leaders and major media outlets who had strongly opposed the ballot measure and confidently predicted its defeat.

Can the City Pay Its Bills?

Proposition 13 sparked similar insurrections in seventeen other states, with varying results. Some historians have suggested that the firestorm over taxes and government spending fueled a movement to shrink government and set the stage for Ronald Reagan's victorious presidential campaign two years later. But California was the guinea pig.

In the immediate aftermath of Proposition 13, California faced a staggering fiscal crisis. Funding for vitally important services that came from property tax revenues—such as public schools, parks, libraries, and public safety—were in jeopardy. Local elected officials from Eureka to San Diego were in a state of panic, and Los Angeles was no exception. We had to keep our city running without the wave of crippling cutbacks that were predicted during the campaign. Although the city had recently passed its budget for the 1978–79 fiscal year, that blueprint would now have to be revisited. Life on the City Council became a sprint to cut costs and re-invent ways in which Los Angeles could preserve local services, and we were under a daily microscope. The media watched our every move, and taxpayers insisted that we faithfully implement the fiscal reforms they had approved.

State government was feeling the heat as well, and it was fascinating to watch Gov. Jerry Brown turn on a dime after the tax cutting measure passed. Within a matter of hours, he went from being one of its most vocal opponents to its biggest advocate. Smartly, he was determined to make the measure work, realizing the futility of trying to stem a popular tidal wave. Instead, he rode the wave like a champion surfer.

Until 1978, property taxes were the principal source of funding for schools, counties, and cities. After Proposition 13, however, there weren't enough tax revenues to pay for all three. Amid lengthy wrangling in Sacramento, the state took over much of the funding for education, averting a breakdown of the California public school system. This was a seismic change. At the same time, the chastened legislature returned a portion of the $7 billion State surplus to local governments, to help them adjust to the new reality. But it was hardly enough.

Los Angeles and other cities would be forced to cut spending dramatically to balance their budgets. Opponents of Proposition 13 had said that the measure would lead to massive layoffs of police and fire personnel, closing firehouses, and shuttering schools and libraries. Now, no one wanted that to happen. Facing reality, we sought ways to avert such a cataclysmic development.

The council's task was complicated by the fact that public safety unions (police officers and firefighters) were demanding salary raises of as much as 10 percent, even as the City was trying to keep from falling off a financial cliff. Few of us wanted to slash vital services in other departments to pay for a double-digit pay raise to any city employee. The message in the post-Proposition 13 environment could not be clearer: Every department and every service had to bear a share of the financial burden, and that included public safety departments.

The union demands were excessive and ill-timed, but there was an intelligent middle ground between laying off police and giving them the raise they demanded. In concert with other councilmembers, I proposed that we hire civilians to work police desk jobs and free up more officers for patrol duty. At the same time, we would freeze salaries citywide, preserving as much of the workforce as possible. This earned me the wrath of Daryl Gates, the city's newly appointed police chief. He told me to my face that I didn't know what I was doing and publicly called me a "snot-nosed kid." It commenced a relationship between us that, to put it charitably, would not be a bed of roses. Our budget plan prevailed, however, because if we simply gave in to the demands, the money would come out of the hide of other services, like garbage collection, parks, libraries and, ironically, the number of officers patrolling the streets of our city.

Ultimately, the city budget took a painful but survivable hit. As noted in a *Los Angeles Times* analysis of the tax initiative's impact, the city's property tax revenues dropped by $239 million in the first year after the passage of Proposition 13, while the state contributed only $80 million in funds to reduce the deficit. The next year, the bail-out was cut by nearly 40 percent. To soften the fiscal impact, cities opted to impose user fees that were not precluded by Proposition

13. The pubic was now going to be charged for services that were previously underwritten by their taxes. Fees were assessed or increased for garbage collection, building permits, parks, libraries, and more. Hiring freezes as well as cuts to services like tree trimming and street maintenance were also instituted. This was the new normal. Amid the declining State bailout, user fee increases and budget cuts, City Hall managed to function.

On a personal note, Barbara brought our ten-month-old daughter, Mina, to one of the council's marathon budget sessions. I hadn't seen her in days, so I placed her on my lap as we thrashed out the financial details. A *Los Angeles Times* photographer took an iconic picture of the two of us—me poring over a budget document while Mina posed for the camera. The photo was prominently featured in the next day's newspaper, prompting one reader to write me a letter complaining that I shouldn't babysit on the taxpayers' dime. I generally avoided responding to moronic letters, but this person deserved an appropriate response, and he got one from me.

The post-Proposition 13 era marked the beginning of a professional relationship with two of the most stand out public servants with whom I worked on an almost daily basis: Keith Comrie, the city's Chief Administrative Officer, and Ron Deaton, the city's Chief Legislative Analyst. Keith was the top budget and labor negotiator for the city, and he was accountable to both the mayor and the City Council. Ron was the council's top policy advisor on all matters—budgets, water and power, federal and state legislation, and most policy initiatives. He engaged in shuttle diplomacy between councilmembers who sometimes didn't speak to one another.

Both men loved the city and its institutions, and they dedicated their professional careers to them. They were the filter through which we all vetted our crazy ideas in order to get a reality check on their wisdom, and they never failed us. They became indispensable to me as chair of the council's Budget and Finance Committee in my last eleven and a half years at City Hall. Both Keith and Ron died in 2020 as I was working on this book. They had become close personal friends of mine—friendships that lasted until the end. It all started as we were trying to figure out how to extricate ourselves from the Proposition 13 morass.

Remaking the budget was hard, the pressure was intense, and the stakes were high. But we made it work. The experience, you'll excuse the expression, was taxing. It was seared into my psyche for the rest of my career. But there were glaring inequities built into the new law that bedevil California to this day. Longtime homeowners would enjoy a much lower property tax than a neighbor who purchased an identical home next door years or decades later. And thanks to a legal loophole, many new commercial property owners were not taxed based on the purchase price, avoiding a substantially higher tax. This was a benefit not afforded to a new homeowner. Over the years, calls to correct that inequity have proven politically too hot to handle. In November 2020, a State constitutional amendment that would have ended this exemption was narrowly defeated by California voters.

Despite the approval of alternative fees and taxes, local government never fully recouped the financial losses caused by Proposition 13. Adopting budgets became an annual struggle to make ends meet, and vital social, capital, and operational investments were deferred or never made. The consequences fell most heavily on economically and racially marginalized communities, further exacerbating the structural inequities that plague our society.

The Price of Arrogance

I do not believe we would have had a Proposition 13 if the Legislature had not been oblivious to voters' fears and anger. The message sent by voters that year was much the same as in the Diamond Lane fiasco: If you don't listen to the people you serve, they will take matters into their own hands with a vengeance. Back then, the crisis cried out for a complete overhaul of the state and local government tax structure. It remains one of the state's most important pieces of unfinished business.

Years later, I went to see "Seinfeld" star Jason Alexander in a play at the Geffen Playhouse in Westwood. After the show, he was asked if he preferred to perform in live theater or in a television studio in front of a camera. Without hesitation, he said live theater. His answer resonated with me. In the theater, he could see and feel his audience in real time. He could watch how they reacted to his interpretations of dramatic or comedic lines; what made them wince or laugh.

In my case, the "live audiences" were the community meetings where I could see what made my constituents nod in agreement or shake their heads in disgust. That's why, after a hot autumn night in Cheviot Hills, I realized that if the Jarvis measure ever made it onto the ballot, it was destined to pass. Although I opposed Proposition 13, like most local elected officials in urban California, I fully understood the grassroots anger that powered it to victory. It was a veritable tsunami.

Rent Control: The Other Side of the Coin

If Proposition 13 was a victory for homeowners, the City Council's approval of a permanent rent stabilization law four years later was a godsend for renters.

But the story of how we passed rent control could not have been more different. Instead of an overnight change driven by voters, we went through a protracted debate in City Hall before tenants finally got relief from soaring rents. I was in the thick of that struggle, and the high stakes were underscored when I got a breakfast invitation in late September 1977 to discuss rent control with several of the donors whose support had been crucial to my first City Council race.

The late California Assembly Speaker Jesse Unruh famously said of the relationship between politicians and their donors, "If you can't eat their food, drink their booze, take their money...and vote against them, you don't belong in politics." Although I instinctively knew this, that maxim was driven home to me when I arrived for the breakfast meeting at Ollie Hammond's steakhouse on La Cienega Boulevard. I was ushered into a wood-paneled basement hideaway that served as a watering hole for the rich and famous, and after a few pleasantries, my hosts got right to the point.

As apartment house developers and owners, they were disturbed by the growing calls for rent control by tenants across the city. They said these controls would threaten their investments, and they feared that what started in Los Angeles would soon spread like a virus to other California cities. They wanted a firm promise from me that I would oppose rent control and punctuated the demand with a line I rarely heard in the give and take with donors: "We were there for you, and now we need you to be there for us."

I was subjected to a John Wooden-like full court press during the meeting, which lasted a couple of hours before I called an end to it. When one donor finished a pitch, another picked up where the last one left off. They were part of the old Nibblers Group and clearly expected me to meet their demand. But they should have known better. Most of them had taken a chance on me because I was my own man, unattached to the political establishment or to any special interest. What were they thinking? I told them that I understood their concerns. But more than 23,000 voters, many of them renters, elected me and I knew firsthand the financial hardships they faced because of never-ending rent increases. I had knocked on their doors and felt their pain. I was not going to sell them out.

The disbelief and anger in the room was palpable, but my answer was final. It would be an understatement to say that the breakfast meeting ended badly for my donors. The city's battle over rents was slowly turning into a political war, and I would hear their arguments many times in the ensuing years: Imposing rent control would stifle new apartment house construction needed to meet the city's growing housing demand. The city would never recover from such a move, they said, nor would the officials who supported it—like me.

In truth, however, Los Angeles was no stranger to rent controls. The federal government had imposed them during World War II to maintain the affordability of the area's limited stock of affordable housing. Tens of thousands of new tenants were streaming into the region to fill wartime industry jobs, and that new demand threatened to drive rents sky high. The emergency rent control rules affected more than 550,000 units countywide, because preserving the affordability of Los Angeles' housing units was deemed to be in the national interest. Even so, some residents were driven to extremes. "I do not know what we are going to do," said John W. Brooks, a veteran returning to Los Angeles, whose wife was expecting a child. His story was cited by Marques Vestal, now an Assistant Professor of Urban Planning at UCLA, in a 2018 study on the history of rent control in Los Angeles by the UCLA- Luskin Center for History and Policy. "At present I am living with 18 other ex-servicemen in a crowded apartment house," Brooks said. "We have even tried to remodel and fix up a chicken house to make shelter."

The wartime controls ended in 1950, but the issue resurfaced with a bang twenty-eight years later. The same pressures that led to passage of Proposition 13—a dramatic rise in real estate values—were affecting renters, principally in middle class neighborhoods in the Westside and San Fernando Valley. As property values in those communities increased, real estate investors had to pay higher prices for apartment house properties. They, in turn, charged higher rents to service the debt on these new investments and to pay their rising property tax bills. This seemingly never-ending cycle hit senior citizens particularly hard. Tens of thousands were living in apartment buildings, surviving on fixed incomes. The crisis forced many of them from their homes and threatened thousands more.

Grassroots Agitation and Political Response

These pressures eventually jumpstarted a tenant activist movement that staged rent strikes, pressured landlords to repair buildings, and promoted state and local legislation to curb what many of us called "rent gouging." Tenant leaders, however, faced an uphill battle. In 1976, the California legislature defeated a rent control bill and passed another measure disallowing rent control altogether, although Governor Jerry Brown vetoed it. The story was the same in one neighborhood after another: Renters were protesting, property owners refused to relent, and the media filled front pages and TV screens with heartbreaking stories.

Rent control was a potent statewide issue. Tenants comprised 45 percent of California households, and many of them had their rents doubled or more in a single year. But Los Angeles was the epicenter of this inflationary earthquake.

During the summer of 1977, the State Consumer Affairs Department reported receiving 3,000 calls per month about rent issues in its Los Angeles office alone. Mayors' and city councilmembers' phones were ringing off the hook, and their mailboxes were filled with letters from seniors on fixed incomes for whom no relief was in sight.

During the Proposition 13 campaign, Jarvis, who was also the executive director of the Apartment Association of Los Angeles County, sought to reassure renters that property owners who benefited from the new tax-cutting law would pass these savings on to tenants. But his pledge wasn't binding, and most apartment house owners made no such promises. Many who did, reneged once the election was over. Less than a month after Proposition 13 passed, the tenants of one Sherman Oaks building went on strike after receiving rent increases ranging from 20 percent to 29 percent per month, the second round of increases that year. So much for campaign promises.

The Fairfax neighborhood in my district was a focal point for the rent rebellion. I met hundreds of articulate, well-organized tenants at the neighborhood's senior center on Melrose and Hayworth. People were furious over the recurring assaults on their wallets, and the center's auditorium that normally held 250 people was frequently packed with 500 renters demanding action. But the most vulnerable people could not make it to these rallies. They were the infirm, the frail elderly, and they felt powerless. The people I met walking precincts, in their apartments and at community meetings, couldn't afford to hire blue-chip lobbyists and consultants to fight their battles at City Hall. They only had me and other elected officials to represent their interests.

Although I was an outspoken advocate for rent relief, the main credit goes to Councilman Joel Wachs for his leadership on this issue. He took on rent control as one of his core causes. His intellect, political acumen and perseverance made him the leading political force behind what ultimately emerged as the city's landmark Rent Stabilization Ordinance (RSO). Pressure grew for a solution when it became clear that most landlords had no intention of passing on rent savings to tenants. Mayor Bradley, who had not previously spoken out on the matter, finally called for "dramatic action" to halt what he termed "outrageous" rent increases. As a result, the council passed a rollback and moratorium on rents in August 1978. The following year, after a furious battle, the City Council renewed the RSO. It did so each year until it approved a permanent law in April 1982.

This was a difficult battle, however, because councilmembers were bitterly divided. Rent control, at least then, primarily affected Anglo neighborhoods. Two of the city's three Black councilmembers opposed the RSO. Their reasons were understandable. Rents were not skyrocketing in their districts and rent control opponents convinced them that the legislation would stifle apartment development in the communities they represented—neighborhoods that needed new housing the most. Meanwhile, the council's conservative members, including some Democrats, were firmly allied with the apartment house industry. We were divided right down the middle, and if we wanted to get a law passed we were going to have to make uncomfortable compromises.

The law that finally passed allowed Los Angeles rents to rise with the cost of living, but never by more than 7 percent in any one year. However, once the apartment unit was vacated, the landlord could raise the rent to whatever the market would bear. Future rent increases would again be tied to the cost-of-living and capped at the 7 percent maximum, a system known as "vacancy decontrol/re-control." The new law also exempted all apartment buildings built after June 1978, addressing the argument that rent control would discourage new construction. At the time, it seemed like an easy concession to make in order to get a permanent law on the books. Because of this exemption, however, the tens of thousands of new rental units built in Los Angeles over the next four decades were *not* subject to rent control. So, what were once "new" units, are today largely unaffordable to middle- and low-income renters.

Condomania

Some hoped that the city's landlord-tenant battles would die down with passage of the new law. *Au contraire.* They continued to erupt when apartment owners began to convert their units into condominiums, removing thousands of apartments from the rental housing market and evicting their tenants to boot. It was another way to monetize their real estate investments. Condo conversions were largely unregulated by State or City law, and they spread with impunity through my district and adjacent middle-class neighborhoods. Although the law required owners to give existing renters the option of purchasing their units, the practical reality was that most of them, especially seniors, could not afford to do so. Owners were looking to make a quick killing, and neighborhoods in West Los Angeles and the San Fernando Valley that had been rent control battle-grounds now faced a different crisis with the same results. Local newspapers carried at least three or four stories every week about "condomania." In 1977 alone, developers applied for permits to convert some 11,000 units, according to the UCLA- Luskin report.

I had a front row seat to this struggle as chair of the City Council's Planning Committee from 1979 to 1981, and every contested condominium conversion came before us for review. I was appointed to the post by Ferraro after he removed Art Snyder when questions were raised about his ethics. In truth, we had little leverage. The deck was stacked in favor of the owners. If they followed the rules of the California Subdivision Map Act, they could force out tenants in order to make a quick buck. I felt the existential fear that many city residents were experiencing in the face of this deluge. In time, our committee found a way to slow down the conversion train and mitigate its impacts, even if we could not stop it entirely. I authored legislation putting conditions on conversions, allowing them only in planning areas where the rental vacancy rate was greater than 3 percent. In those days this was considered the equilibrium point between a rental housing shortage and a surplus. We also required owners to provide relocation assistance to renters who could not avert displacement.

Still, the conversions continued. They contributed to a higher rent burden and increased poverty in segments of Los Angeles' elderly population. Some of the most vulnerable tenants had to choose between rent and food, between rent and medicine. It was a dreadful predicament that continues to plague Los Angeles to this day.

The city's tenant rights laws were not perfect, but we found a way to keep thousands of renters in their homes. Los Angeles faced a rent crisis not over the supply of rental housing, but over the supply of *affordable* housing, according to a 1981 report by the Rand Corporation. "What Los Angeles has, along with most of the rest of the United States, is a double-digit price inflation that increases the cost of producing housing services, and therefore increases rents," the report said. "Tenants on fixed, low incomes justifiably argue that price inflation is unfair to them."

Indeed, the disparities built into the cost of rental housing in the 1970s and '80s foreshadowed the explosion of homelessness a few decades later, a problem that has now become one of the region's foremost socio-economic challenges. Over time, rents became increasingly unaffordable to the growing number of Angelenos who lived at or below the federal poverty line, and this took a punishing toll on our most vulnerable residents. Many of them were forced into homelessness, and Los Angeles became known as the homeless capital of America. Dating back to the late nineteenth century, Skid Row, a fifty-block area covering 2.7 square miles, just east of downtown, was the epicenter of the city's homelessness crisis. Today, the unhoused and their encampments can be found throughout the Los Angeles region. They are under freeways, in automobiles and public parks, on beaches and boulevard parkways. The homeless crisis is a virtual billboard for government ineffectiveness, and it remains at the top of Los Angeles' "to do" list.

Housing Crises Then and Now

Although the city's Rent Stabilization Ordinance has remained in place, the compromises we made in the early 1980s have become an anachronism in today's world. Under our law, even if the consumer price index (CPI) rises by less than 3 percent, landlords can still raise rents 3 percent. Since the CPI has rarely reached that level in the last decade, landlords have been able to continually raise rents by more than the rate of inflation—and these are increases which many tenants simply cannot afford. To make matters worse, in 1985 the State enacted the Costa-Hawkins law that prevented Los Angeles and other cities from strengthening their rent control ordinances. The cities' hands are tied.

A key reason for this is that the State legislature has always been susceptible to the influence of the real estate and apartment industry lobbies. Many of its members represent suburban or rural communities, where escalating rents do not pose as much of a problem as they do in coastal California, where housing prices are exceedingly high. I continue to believe that, although rent control may not be the best cure to the affordable housing crisis, it is better than simply letting the free market run its course and steamroll vulnerable renters. As history has shown repeatedly, the free market has no conscience.

Today, I don't sense the same level of urgency on the part of lawmakers over rent protections that dominated my years on the City Council. Back then, the notion that we could have ducked our obligation to protect the most vulnerable would have been unthinkable, even to most of my pro-business colleagues. There was a crisis unfolding, and it demanded that we act. Failure to act was not an option. The political landscape has shifted, and cities today are constrained in the ways they can respond to the rent crisis. In the 2020 election, California voters soundly defeated a state ballot measure that would have repealed the Costa-Hawkins law, and would have given cities more authority to stabilize rents.

The Los Angeles housing wars continued without end during my forty years of public service. And they were just as much about integrity and accountability as property tax bills and skyrocketing rents. As I left the contentious meeting with my donors at Ollie Hammond's in 1977, our relationship would never be the same. Rent control and the issue of affordable housing had opened up a deep and irreparable divide between us. Indeed, I hardly had any communication with most of them for the rest of my career. But standing up for what I believed was the right thing to do. It prepared me for future confrontations in the public arena—and in the summer of 1977 they were just beginning.

CHAPTER 9

The Untold Story of the 1984 Olympics

Napoleon famously asked, "What is history, but a fable agreed upon?" And he had a point. Our understanding of the past often reinforces what people have been made to believe, whether it's true or not. The search for historical *truth*, however, is something else entirely. If we want to know what really happened in an earlier era, we've got to keep an open mind, reconsider what we thought we knew and rewrite the story, if necessary. For me, an example is the history of the 1984 summer Olympic Games that were held in Los Angeles.

Most of the books on the 1984 Olympics offer glowing tributes to the event, and deservedly so. The Los Angeles games were only the second to generate a profit; the first were the 1932 Olympics, also held in the city. All other modern Olympics ran in the red, some with crippling deficits. By maximizing revenues and minimizing costs, the 1984 games ended up with an astonishing $235 million surplus.

Yet the story of how all this came to pass is not well known. The financial success of the 1984 Olympics changed, and perhaps saved, the Olympic movement. Still, that narrative glosses over the initial effort by Olympics boosters to crush a November 1978 ballot measure—a proposal I co-authored—that all but prohibited the use of city general funds to finance the Games. Ironically, that measure became Los Angeles' most powerful weapon in staging the most financially successful Olympics ever. Indeed, the overwhelming passage of Proposition N, a city Charter Amendment, protected taxpayers from a boondoggle that could have cost them several hundred million dollars. The victory was one of my most satisfying moments as a public official.

The Olympics That (Almost) Nobody Wanted

For much of the twentieth century, major international cities competed vigorously to host the Olympics. They were traditionally a source of prestige, a chance to showcase themselves to the world. Los Angeles was no different. It had applied unsuccessfully to host each of the Games since 1932. The allure began to fade in 1968, however, when Mexico's military brutally cracked down on students just before the opening ceremonies in Mexico City. Four years later, the Munich games were tragically scarred when pro-Palestinian terrorists kidnapped 11 Israeli athletes in their Olympic village dormitory—an abduction that led to their deaths. In 1976, Montreal got an international black eye when the Olympics it hosted ran up a price tag of $1.5 billion, with a deficit of $500 million that took thirty years to retire.

In each of these cases, the International Olympic Committee (IOC) demanded that the host city contractually guarantee that it would cover the cost of the Games, including any cost overruns, as a condition of getting the bid. In 1978, Lord Killanin of Ireland led the IOC, and he ran it with an iron fist. The financial clause was a non-negotiable part of the standard Olympics contract, as far as the IOC was concerned. But cities that had once competed fiercely for the games were now reticent to assume the risk of hosting the Olympics. By 1977 only two cities, Los Angeles and Teheran, expressed interest in securing the bid for the '84 Games. Iran, convulsed with revolution, was not considered a serious contender. Los Angeles officials, led by Mayor Tom Bradley, saw a golden opportunity to bring the games back to Los Angeles for the first time in fifty-two years. It looked for all the world like a done deal.

But major trouble was brewing in Bradley's own backyard, a fact he was slow to recognize. As his plans took shape, city taxpayers were becoming increasingly angry about runaway property tax bills. The furor which eventually led to Proposition 13 was pervasive, growing more intense with every passing month. In 1977 Bradley commissioned a survey of Los Angeles residents' attitude about hosting the Olympics. The survey, conducted by Mervyn Field, the most respected California pollster of his day, found that more than 70 percent supported bringing the games to Los Angeles, but only 35 percent wanted to do so if city taxpayers had to pay for them.

Shielding taxpayers from cost overruns, however, was a non-starter with the IOC. They expected our city, like others before it, to take total responsibility for financing the Games. Many of us feared that the city couldn't or wouldn't hold the line with the IOC or the international sports federations, which had a habit of demanding excessive gold-plated facilities. So, Bradley and others pledged to run a "Spartan Olympics." He and his team argued that Los Angeles was well-positioned to do so, because the city's many existing sports venues would alleviate the need to build the new facilities that previous Games required. This would be a core part of the Los Angeles bid proposal, and it made sense. But major undertakings like the Olympics had a way of financially spinning out of control. The mayor's word was not enough of a guarantee for me and some of my colleagues. We wanted the taxpayers to be protected by strong, legally enforceable provisions enshrined in the city charter, not by a list of political promises.

For my part, I genuinely wanted Los Angeles to land the Olympics. I had continued to be a passionate fan of track and field, attending every major track competition in the area. I savored the prospect of the world's best athletes competing in my hometown. As I told my colleagues, I was surely the only one of them with a subscription to *"Track and Field News."* But I wouldn't allow the city coffers to become an ATM to pay for the event. I worried that the games could wreck a city's finances.

The Forgotten Man

Bob Ronka is not a name that comes to mind when one thinks about Los Angeles political history. A Harvard-educated attorney, he was elected to represent the First District on the City Council in June 1977. His largely conservative, working-class constituents were nested in Sylmar, Sunland-Tujunga, and Pacoima—all in the northeast San Fernando valley. Bob was a smart and intense man with a compulsive attention to detail. But it would be an understatement to say that some of his colleagues took an instant dislike to him. He was unapologetically ambitious and his frequent press conferences on a flurry of issues did not endear him to other councilmembers. Ronka served only one term on the council before losing a 1981 bid for City Attorney, and he faded from the headlines soon after. For all of that, however, he has been unfairly ignored as one of the most consequential figures in the success of the '84 Olympics. He was the unquestionable City Council leader in the successful effort to protect the city treasury from a fiscal train wreck over the Olympics.

I supported Bob in 1977 when he ran to replace the retiring Louis Nowell, an old-guard, conservative Republican city councilman. Intervening in the political affairs of another council district was a move rarely undertaken by incumbent councilmembers. In this case, however, I saw an opportunity to help elect a young, modern candidate to a body that needed new blood. We found common ground on the Olympics issue shortly after his arrival at City Hall. Frankly, his determination to hold the line on costs far exceeded my own.

Almost immediately, we got caustic criticism from powerbrokers who couldn't believe anyone would put obstacles in the way of LA's Olympic bid. It is not an exaggeration to say that the intensity of their hostility made the two of us feel as if we had been branded as traitors. Even though I had just been elected to my first full term on the council, my push for fiscal controls prompted some to suggest—ridiculously—that I was already eyeing higher office.

I was struck by the notion held by many civic leaders that Los Angeles *needed* to win the 1984 Olympics. They believed it would show the rest of the nation that we were now a sophisticated, international city. Local boosters were embarrassed by the fiction that Los Angeles was a cultural backwater, a suburban wasteland forever playing second fiddle to more established metropolises like New York, Chicago, or even San Francisco. As they saw it, an Olympics bid would be a good place to start changing that image.

I had a radically different view. Born and raised here, I was proud of Los Angeles for what it was—an emerging, vibrant multi-cultural center that was the envy of the world, a place that millions dreamed of visiting and moving to. We had nothing to prove. Although it would be wonderful to host the Olympics, it wasn't worth bankrupting the city because of a civic inferiority complex. I thought too many people had "Olympic fever" for the wrong reasons, and I made these points at the time. Most of us were comfortable in our Los Angeles skin and were not concerned with what the east coast or bay area residents thought of us.

At first, Ronka and I tried to push legislation through the council to protect the city's treasury, but we got nowhere. I could count votes as well as anyone, and we didn't have the support needed for passage. Instead, we decided in late 1977 to threaten to go over the heads of our colleagues by taking the matter directly to the people via the initiative process. The plan was to put a charter amendment on the city ballot that would prohibit the spending of city tax dollars to stage the games.

We began making immediate plans to circulate petitions and place our measure on either the June or November 1978 ballot. Others joined us. In late 1977, a new group, "Concerned Citizens Olympics," was also preparing to support a ballot drive, backed by twenty-three neighborhood and taxpayer organizations. At this point Ronka went to Bradley and City Council President John Ferraro, the council's biggest Olympics booster, telling them that we were willing to deal with them on the language of a charter amendment. Their initial reaction was dismissive. We were told that pushing a ballot measure about the Olympics would mean the end of the LA bid. It "creates a real threat by all means," said Anton Calleia, the mayor's able budget director and deputy mayor on all things Olympics, in a *Washington Post* column by political scientist Joel Kotkin. "We could not in good faith go into Athens [where the IOC was poised to award the games] and put in a bid with a referendum hanging over our heads. We'd be the laughingstock of the world."

As our negotiations continued into 1978, public support for what would become Proposition 13 was building. Anti-tax sentiment in Los Angeles was intense. Whether Bradley liked it or not, Los Angeles voters were in no mood to give local government *carte blanche* to pay for the Olympics. At the same time, it was hard to ignore a 1977 report by the city's Chief Administrative Officer which estimated that Los Angeles could face a deficit of between $200 and $336.5 million if the city bankrolled the games on its own. The writing was on the wall. The IOC was either going to hold Los Angeles taxpayers harmless for the Games' finances, or it would have to find another host.

Welcome Aboard, Tom Bradley

Facing reality, the mayor made some strategic compromises. A City Council ad hoc committee was formed to negotiate the language and content of an Olympics ballot measure. In what was correctly seen as a snub, I was appointed to the panel, but Ronka was not. We agreed on our end not to place a measure on the ballot calling for a simple up or down vote on whether the Olympics should come to Los Angeles. In return, we won tough language barring the city from spending more than $5 million in local tax dollars on the games—a paltry sum, in the big picture—*unless* Los Angeles identified in advance the source of those funds. Just as important, the only tax dollars that could be used to generate revenue for the games had to be Olympics-related levies, such as the city's hotel tax, which was mostly paid by tourists. For the first time, a city had decided in advance to hold the games without financially guaranteeing them. As a practical matter, this meant that the 1984 Olympics would have to be self-sustaining.

The language we negotiated eventually became Proposition N and was placed on the November 1978 ballot by the City Council. Getting final approval, however, was anything but easy. Some councilmembers continued to blast the move as a self-serving end run, and the national media ridiculed our concerns as a distraction from the larger goal of returning Olympic glory to the United States.

Personalities also got in the way. Council President John Ferraro never hid his intense dislike for Ronka, refusing to speak with him, even as crucial elements of the ballot measure were being negotiated. The mere mention of his name seemed to get Ferraro's blood boiling. The chasm between the two men was disturbing, and an incident in the City Hall garage illustrated how wide it was. One morning, Wayne Avrashow, then Ronka's chief of staff, entered the cramped VIP elevator reserved for councilmembers and top staff. As the door began to close, someone blocked it with his hand. It was John Ferraro, who was carrying the morning *Los Angeles Times* in his hand. The paper had run a front-page story chronicling City Controller Ira Reiner's latest attack on the City Council for what he called profligate spending. Face to face with Ferraro, Wayne tried to diffuse the tension. "Reiner is a real prick," he told the Council President. The hulking Ferraro glared down at him and replied, "He's not the *only* prick in the building," a clear reference to Avrashow's boss. Given the total lack of communication between the two councilmembers, it fell upon me to sometimes serve as an intermediary, practicing a Henry Kissinger-like shuttle diplomacy over a period of months.

By late February 1978, the outline of a ballot deal was in place. None of us were under any illusion about the roadblocks that lay ahead because the IOC had never awarded the games with a gun held to its head. Doing so threatened their authority to run the Olympics as they saw fit. But Los Angeles had extraordinary leverage. It was the only bidder.

Who Blinks First?

In May 1978, the IOC held a meeting in Athens, Greece, where it would award the 1984 games. In one sense the outcome was no mystery, because Los Angeles was the last bidder standing. Publicly and behind the scenes, however, the IOC remained fiercely opposed to the idea of a privately financed games that would not be guaranteed by the host city. Lord Killanin continued to insist that Los Angeles abide by the basic terms to which every previous host city had agreed. What bothered him and the IOC most was the precedent that would be set if Los Angeles didn't agree to their demands. Negotiations grew tense, and local politics spilled into the mix. Ronka, who had not been invited to participate in Bradley's presentation in Athens, flew there on his own nickel and tried to attend the meeting. Calleia, the mayor's budget director, blocked him at the door and told him he was not welcome. Ronka demanded to come in. According to press accounts, Calleia threatened to deck him if he stepped foot inside the door. The councilman did not participate in the negotiations but instead held press conferences in Athens and later back in Los Angeles, blasting the IOC and the city's lack of transparency. In a radio interview he called Bradley and Calleia "innocents abroad" who were being "double-crossed by landed gentry and brittle, archaic, arcane aristocrats."

Amid the furor, Bradley held firm. He told Killanin that the city would be more than able to finance the games with private support, adding pointedly that his hands were tied by our impending ballot measure. Voters were overwhelmingly behind him, and he was not about to bargain away their rights in a closed-door meeting. Ironically, the mayor became a leading advocate for a position he once opposed, much like Jerry Brown's post-election conversion after the passage of Proposition 13. As the Athens talks concluded, Los Angeles won provisional approval for its bid. Still, the IOC insisted that negotiations should continue over the specific terms. The matter was far from resolved.

Weeks later, when Los Angeles refused to back down, Killanin dropped a bombshell. Unless the city capitulated, he said, the IOC would withdraw its approval of the bid. Bradley, not missing a beat, sent a letter to the City Council asking it to withdraw the city's bid. In a matter of hours, Killanin blinked. Although the media treated the mayor's comments like the end of the world, it was in fact a head fake, a smart negotiating tactic. Ferraro had been alerted in advance and referred Bradley's request to the City Council's Ad Hoc Committee on the Olympics, which he chaired. Ferraro never scheduled it for a hearing and never seriously considered bringing it to the floor of the City Council for a vote. The mayor played the issue like a Stradivarius, and the IOC finally capitulated. Further negotiations could resolve the deadlock, Killanin said, throwing in the towel.

In June 1978, the mayor and the United States Olympic Committee (USOC) struck a deal that helped turn the tide. Joined by local business leaders, they formed a private, seven-member committee—the Los Angeles Olympics Organizing Committee (LAOOC)—that would take over the responsibilities of negotiating the Los Angeles bid. They agreed from the outset that the committee's main responsibility would be to stage the contests without any financial liability to the city. Meanwhile, USOC, not Los Angeles, would "guarantee" the finances of the games. To the extent that Killanin demanded an insurance policy to make sure that the Olympics would be fully funded, this was it. The deal was a total fiction, however, since USOC didn't have the financial resources to be a credible guarantor. But everyone was able to save face.

With the creation of the LAOOC, Los Angeles and the IOC finally reached an agreement. Killanin signed off on the deal, the council gave its approval and both parties approved the contract at a White House ceremony in October 1978. The following month, city voters approved Proposition N by a whopping 74–26 percent margin.

There remained an inconsistency in the final contract, which I thought posed potential liability to the city. For that reason, seven of us opposed the contract. In truth, however, it turned out to be a non-issue, because neither Bradley, the City Council, nor the LAOOC had an appetite for putting taxpayers at risk. At that point, any city official who went back on the spirit of the deal, or the text of Proposition N, would pay the ultimate political price. Moreover, there were seven of us watching the issue like hawks. Bottom line: The 1984 Olympics would not become a municipal boondoggle.

The Rise of Peter Ueberroth

One of the first orders of business for the LAOOC was appointing a CEO to oversee both the funding and the running of the games. The final choice came down to corporate leader Ed Steidle, CEO of the May Company department stores in Los Angeles, and Peter Ueberroth, an ambitious young entrepreneur who founded and ran one of the nation's largest travel agencies. The committee picked Ueberroth in early 1979, and it proved to be a brilliant choice. He was energetic, smart, and hungry to make his mark. He seemed to be bursting with novel ideas. Ueberroth faced a massive challenge but was totally confident in his abilities. Just the kind of man the task required.

From the minute he took the reins, Ueberroth ran the games like a business. He won a pivotal victory by persuading the IOC to award him the bulk of the proceeds from the sale of the Games' television rights. That alone earned LAOOC a $225 million payday from the ABC television network, an unprecedented amount for an Olympics telecast to that point. It was just the beginning. "Ueberroth succeeded in pioneering a new model of exclusive licensing and sponsorship," according to *Lessons Learned from the 1984 Olympics Games and the Los Angeles Bid for 2024*, a report by the UCLA- Luskin Center for History and Policy, to which I contributed. "Rather than having hundreds of corporations participate as sponsors, he auctioned off exclusive sponsorship rights for each product area and required each sponsor to make a minimum contribution of $4 million and/or in-kind donations to the LAOOC."

It was a game-changer. In short order, Coca-Cola beat out Pepsi for the soft drink sponsorship by paying $12.6 million. Other lucrative sponsorships followed. Ueberroth wasn't sentimental. When the choice for the games' official film sponsor came down to Kodak, an American company that was widely expected to win, and Fuji, a Japanese company, Ueberroth awarded the sponsorship to Fuji because it was the higher bidder. That stunning decision sent a message to other would-be sponsors: There would be no "hometown" favorites.

The sale of television rights, corporate sponsorships, and ticket sales covered most of the Olympics' expenditures. Ueberroth deserves credit for that and for the overall success of the games as well. However, the initial skepticism of city officials, and Proposition N, played a decisive role for this success.

Ueberroth acknowledged this in his memoir, *Made in America: His Own Story*, in which he wrote that the need to save taxpayer dollars drove him to invent an entirely original approach to the Olympics. "Even I was one of the vast majority who voted for Proposition 13 and later against taxpayer money being used to underwrite the Games," he wrote.

Given the passage of Proposition N, he had no choice. If Ueberroth heard complaints about the booming prices of sponsorships, he could tell bidders that there were no deep pockets to bail out the games if they went belly up. If sports officials complained about using existing venues instead of building new ones, he could blame it on city voters who would not bankroll new and expensive capital projects. How could he justify spending lavishly on the games at a time when the city was having trouble paying to put cops on the streets?

This would be the first Olympics run on tough love and common sense. The LAOOC housed athletes in existing dormitories at UCLA, USC, and UC Santa Barbara. Although the Los Angeles Memorial Coliseum, near the city's dense, urban downtown, would be the hub of Olympics activity, many other contests were held at existing facilities throughout the southland. Overall, Ueberroth estimated that the total costs of the games would be $472 million. This was 5 percent of the costs of the Moscow Games and about 30 percent of the Montreal games. As a result, the 1984 Olympics became a hugely profitable, sixteen-day television spectacular that was the envy of cities around the world.

Real History and Lessons to Be Learned

For the 1984 Olympics, taxpayer protections were the product of tough compromises and a contentious legislative process that brought out both the best and the worst in local politics. However, as Los Angeles prepares to host the 2028 games, the Covid pandemic and its impact on the Tokyo Olympics demonstrates the risks that cities take in assuming total financial liability for hosting this event. This time, there is no charter amendment protecting Los Angeles taxpayers. It will be up to city leaders and Olympics organizers to hold the line.

We are often counseled to learn from past mistakes. But sometimes we can learn from past successes. The 1984 Olympics were a success by any metric, and it's an event worth emulating.

There was one more person who contributed mightily to public awareness and understanding of the Olympics bid. *Los Angeles Times* reporter Ken Reich covered the Olympics saga from beginning to end, ultimately writing more than 1,000 articles about the games. A belligerent, curmudgeonly character, Reich was nonetheless a rigorous reporter who held all stakeholders in this saga to a punishing level of accountability. I was pleased when he complimented me in print on my skills as a behind the scenes dealmaker at the conclusion of the '84 games. Truthfully, Reich's skepticism about Olympic boosters and his oversized media influence buttressed our cause.

Tom Bradley was covered with glory on the day the Olympics came to town, and his celebration was well-deserved. Peter Ueberroth won international plaudits for his business acumen and became Time Magazine's "Man of the Year." These accolades were also well-deserved. Yet they were not the only players who could have taken victory laps during the opening ceremonies. One person deserved high praise for his role—Bob Ronka. The newly elected councilman led the effort to ensure that local government held the line on Olympics spending. Yet his name is not mentioned in the LAOOC's official history of the games, Ueberroth's memoir, or Los Angeles Times reporter Ken Reich's history of the games. Not once.

History has been kinder to Proposition N. The "Official Report of the Games of the XXIII Olympiad" conceded that the amendment "was extremely important to the future direction and structure of the Olympic organizational efforts." When the 1984 games generated a huge surplus, $93 million of it helped finance the LA 84 Foundation, which has since invested more than $200 million in grants to more than 1,100 local youth sports organizations.

There was one other unexpected benefit to the 1984 Olympics. Although most Southern California residents were convinced that the sixteen-day extravaganza would be a traffic nightmare, this was a disaster that never happened. People either stayed home or left town because of official warnings. For ticket holders, the LAOOC funded a massive transit program aimed at transporting them to every event without having to use a car. No parking was provided at the Los Angeles venues, so patrons had no choice but to use the highly effective bus and shuttle services they were offered. Traffic was dramatically lighter than anyone expected, with smoothly flowing freeways day and night that seemed like a throwback to an earlier era.

City traffic engineers later estimated that traffic was reduced by 3.5 to 5 percent during the games. It was astonishing that such a relatively small dip in vehicular traffic would be the difference between stop and go traffic and free flow. By all accounts, Angelenos enjoyed their two-week "staycation." More than three decades later, people still ask me, "Why can't we reduce traffic like we did in the 1984 Olympics?" It's a good question.

On a warm July afternoon, Barbara, Mina (then seven years old) and I arrived at the opening ceremonies of the XXIII Olympiad. We were higher than a kite.

The city was ready to host the nations of the world, and I took it all in like a kid in a candy store. I looked forward to the next sixteen days, and the opportunity to see some of the world's greatest athletes compete at the highest levels. It seemed as though Los Angeles had been transformed with pastel-colored banners on many of its power and light poles. The explosion of color and pageantry on the Coliseum's floor had given the old stadium new life.

But of all the thrills of the games, one is etched in my memory. As we were leaving the stadium, one of our athletes was jubilantly running toward his bus. He caught a glimpse of Mina out of the corner of his eye and suddenly stopped. He took off the visor that US team members wore as they first marched into the Coliseum, and he put it on her head. Then he resumed his sprint to the bus—as giddy to have parted with it as Mina was to receive this precious memento. It typified the spirit that would engulf the city for the next two weeks.

But I also commiserated with Barbara about the saga we had been through to get to this day. We had taken on the city's entrenched establishment, and we prevailed. Our efforts paid off. The Olympic movement and its local organizers succeeded, too. Ueberroth had turned Los Angeles into one giant television studio, with a billion people tuned in around the world. The games were the most successful of any to that point.

As the three of us sat in the Coliseum on opening day, surrounded by 90,000 cheering spectators, I couldn't help but remember Winston Churchill's classic observation: "You can always trust American democracy to do the right thing— but only after exhausting all the alternatives."

CHAPTER 10

Taking on the LAPD

___

As a candidate, I was often asked where I stood on a variety of issues. Did I favor or oppose capital punishment? What was my position on gun control? Did I support a woman's right to choose? But the most important question was never asked: over what issue would I be willing to lose my next election? This speaks to a politician's core values, and mine have long been ingrained in my DNA. I would never compromise my views on civil liberties, civil rights, freedom of speech, the right to privacy, protection from government abuse, and the constitutionally enshrined separation of church and state. With due respect to Bruce Springsteen, these were the principles on which I would neither retreat nor surrender.

I was tested on these questions early and often during my first ten years in office, and the battles often involved the Los Angeles Police Department. I had many friends and allies in the LAPD. Some of the smartest, most dedicated public servants I came to know were among its ranks. They taught me a great deal about law enforcement and leadership, and two of them—Deputy Chief Dan Sullivan and Commander Joe Gunn—became close personal friends. At the same time, I clashed with the LAPD over its aggressive and unconstitutional surveillance activities, as well as its chronic use of excessive, sometimes fatal force against people of color. These practices damaged the department's relationship with the communities it served, and over the years cost the city treasury hundreds of millions of dollars to boot.

These abuses were impossible to ignore. But in truth, both had been on my mind long before. I trace my awareness back to the Century City demonstration against LBJ in 1967, to my conversation with my Aunt Rosa in Moscow's Red Square ("the walls have ears"), and to my own experiences as a student and social activist at UCLA. As a result, when I became a councilman and began dealing with citizens who complained about the LAPD, I didn't dismiss them as anti-police gadflies. I took them seriously and vowed to do something about their concerns. Most of my political advisors warned me not to take on the

LAPD. They knew the department, headquartered downtown at Parker Center, had ways of getting back at its critics. They feared I would become one of its targets soon enough, and that my political career could evaporate in a voter backlash. I appreciated their concern, but these were the issues for which I was willing to die on a hill.

I had spent nearly eight years of my life fighting antisemitism in the Soviet Union before I landed in City Hall. Perhaps I had been too young or naïve to believe that a teenager in Los Angeles could challenge a superpower thousands of miles away. But I did. Compared to the USSR and its much-vaunted KGB security network, doing battle with the LAPD was a walk in the park. Besides, I knew my district and its residents, and they knew me. They didn't elect a twenty-six-year-old social activist to play it safe. They *expected* me to speak truth to power and they made it clear that they would have my back. Nevertheless, as I got my sea legs in City Hall, I updated my aunt's mantra to fit my new digs: The walls have ears—and so does Parker Center.

The LAPD's abuses had been festering for decades. Beginning in the 1920s, officers started infiltrating and harassing progressive political groups, labor unions and social justice organizations. Similar units operated in Chicago, New York, and other major cities, but Los Angeles' so-called Red Squad stood out for the intensity of its surveillance of law-abiding citizens. Author Carey McWilliams, writing about this era in Los Angeles, suggested that a prominent civic leader had been hired by business organizations to spy on the activities of liberal and progressive groups, noting that she was on the board of directors of numerous organizations and regularly reported about them to the police. The Red Squad's aggressive tactics sometimes violated the constitution that officers were sworn to uphold. But their tactics were embraced or tacitly accepted by city officials who either supported the LAPD's policies or were too timid to challenge them.

In 1950, toward the end of his administration, Mayor Fletcher Bowron appointed William Parker as the LAPD's new Chief of Police. The good news was that he brought a long-overdue sense of professionalism, discipline, and commitment to root out corruption in the department's ranks. The bad news was that Parker—the product of a strict, conservative upbringing in South Dakota—intensified the LAPD's crusade against liberals and other groups he disliked. Moreover, the new Chief was by any measure a racist who didn't hide his hostility to people of color, especially Black people. Parker maintained the LAPD as a mostly white male organization, offering few jobs and even fewer promotional opportunities to minorities and women. He belittled politicians who didn't toe his line, and few dared get in his way.

The Chief was a master at public relations, developing a close relationship with Jack Webb, an actor/producer who launched the popular "Dragnet" series on television. Each episode told a harrowing and uplifting story about the LAPD arresting "bad guys" and keeping the public safe. Parker's team helped shape each primetime script, enshrining the department's national image as a no-nonsense crime fighting force. He was one of America's most famous law enforcement officials, along with FBI Director J. Edgar Hoover.

Parker also became the most powerful and influential person at City Hall. His relationship with Mayor Sam Yorty was a case in point. During his victorious 1961 mayoral campaign, Yorty sought support from Black voters by criticizing police abuses and vowing to bring the department under control. This message was well received, and Yorty's share of Black voter support was enough to narrowly defeat two-term incumbent Norris Poulson. Parker's response was swift and chilling. Shortly after Yorty's inauguration, Parker is said to have arrived for a meeting in the mayor's office on the third floor of City Hall with a briefcase in hand. The contents of the briefcase remain a mystery, and the one-on-one conversation lasted approximately one hour. After Parker left the meeting, Yorty never uttered another negative word about him or the LAPD. On the contrary, he became one of Parker's staunchest allies.

For all his political savvy, however, the Chief failed to understand the profound demographic, social and cultural changes that were sweeping across the city. Between 1940 and 1970, the number of Black residents in Los Angeles County increased dramatically—from more than 75,000 to over 700,000. The region's Hispanic population also swelled during this period, transforming the demographics of the white city America saw every week on "Dragnet." During the Parker era, Los Angeles' communities of color and white progressives became increasingly outspoken on issues of police brutality, civil rights, and the growing war in Southeast Asia. It was only a matter of time before these tensions would explode in the streets.

The Watts Rebellion

On a hot August night in 1965, the heart of the Black community in South Los Angeles erupted in anger when a white California Highway Patrol officer arrested Marquette Fry, a Black man, for drunk driving in Watts. Family members and neighbors gathered at the scene, tense words were exchanged, police reinforcements were called in and the spark was lit. Angry community members started to set buildings and cars afire. Six days later, thirty-four people were dead, more than 1,000 were injured, 4,000 had been arrested and the community suffered an estimated $40 million in property damage. It was the first major civil uprising in the nation's modern era.

Although the root causes of the Watts uprising lay in the corrosive effects of poverty, housing discrimination, and economic inequality, the unrest was principally sparked by growing friction between police and the community. Parker's racist rhetoric ramped up during the disturbances when he compared Black participants to "monkeys in a zoo." Many observers hoped that the rebellion in Watts would lead to more evenhanded policing, but Yorty and Parker dug in their heels.

After the chief collapsed and died of a heart attack at a testimonial dinner the following year, the LAPD remained as politically powerful as ever. The men who succeeded him largely followed in his footsteps. Ed Davis, who became chief in 1969, was a smart, blunt, tough-talking conservative who once said that airplane hijackers should be publicly tried, convicted, and hanged at airports. He consolidated the department's political power in City Hall and throughout the city.

Indeed, when he was later asked whether he had an interest in running for mayor, he demurred, saying the chief's job was more powerful. The department's intelligence gathering apparatus expanded on his watch, with the LAPD operating a modern version of the Red Squad. I personally experienced this in my college years, sometimes directly and sometimes indirectly.

In 1970, my junior year at UCLA, I took a course from history professor Hayden White, an outspoken opponent of the Vietnam War. Chief Davis had just formed the Public Disorder and Intelligence Division (PDID) and, incredibly, Professor White's History class became one of its targets. The LAPD planted an undercover officer in the classroom, posing as a student. When White discovered the infiltration he confronted the agent, joined by a colleague and several students. The undercover officer panicked and got into his unmarked car adjacent to Haines Hall in the heart of the campus. He gunned the engine and floored the accelerator, hitting History Professor Geoffrey Symcox in the process.

The incident drew national attention, and it infuriated me. Professor White was as much a threat to public order as my grandfather, who had been dead for thirty years. White's civil liberties were violated, as were those of his students and Professor Symcox. There was no reason for an undercover cop to be lurking in a UCLA classroom. My professor sued the city and the LAPD, and he won a resounding victory five years later in the California Supreme Court, which led to a substantial financial settlement with the city. In a splendid irony, I had the privilege of voting for this settlement agreement when I became a new member of the City Council.

More evidence of unlawful police surveillance emerged during the ensuing years. The LAPD had clearly declared war on the city's progressive activists, targeting the women's liberation movement, anti-war protestors, and civil rights organizations. City Hall finally acted in April 1975. With Mayor Tom Bradley's blessing, the Los Angeles Police Commission ordered the destruction of PDID files relating to more than 55,000 people, a move the *Los Angeles Times* reported would purge two million dossiers. It seemed like a bold move, but as I took my seat on the council two months later the controversy was alive and well. The LAPD took the attitude that mayors and councilmembers come and go, but the department lasts forever. Indeed, they'd be around long after we were gone. Its culture was part of its DNA, certainly since William Parker's reign.

"I've Seen Your File"

On March 28, 1978, Daryl Gates became the new permanent LAPD chief, succeeding Davis. He had joined the department in 1949, shortly after I was born, and rose rapidly through the ranks, including a stint as William Parker's adjutant, a coveted department job as the Chief's personal driver and assistant. Gates wrote in his memoir that he learned a lot from his boss about policing, politics, and putting department interests above all else. During his fourteen years at the helm, he helped launch innovative crime-fighting strategies, notably SWAT (the Special Weapons and Tactics unit), which became a national model for dealing with hostage or barricaded suspect situations. But he is best remembered for his arrogant handling of police scandals, including excessive use of force, the unlawful surveillance of private citizens, and his complete failure of leadership during the 1992 Rodney King civil unrest. Although we had one thing in common—we both liked Barbara very much— he and I became bitter adversaries.

Shortly after Gates assumed the LAPD's top job, the ACLU filed a lawsuit over unconstitutional police surveillance. Through discovery motions, the plaintiffs gained access to documents showing the extent and absurdity of the unit's spying efforts. I joined with activists to unveil a list of more than 200 organizations that had been targeted for police surveillance. The list included the ACLU, the National Organization for Women, the First Unitarian Church of Los Angeles, the National Council of Churches, Vietnam Veterans Against the War, the Gay Community Services Center, the East Los Angeles Community Union, the United Farmworkers of California, and the Southern Christian Leadership Conference. There were also prominent clergy and community leaders on the list such as John Mack, head of the Los Angeles office of the National Urban League.

I wasn't shocked to learn that there were two other organizations on the list with which I had a direct involvement: California Students for Soviet Jews, which I founded in 1969, and the Southern California Council for Soviet Jews, for which I worked between 1972 and 1974. And then there were two names on the list that caught my attention: Si Frumkin and Zev Yaroslavsky. All I could think was, "Holy shit!" On one hand, I wore this recognition as a badge of honor, much like the people who found themselves on Nixon's enemies list in the early 1970s. On the other, I immediately understood the implications. When I thought of the citizens whose civil liberties and right to privacy were abridged, not to mention the tax dollars that had been squandered doing so, I was outraged. I was also determined to push for major reforms. Civilian oversight of the LAPD was a fiction, and that had to change. It was imperative that the department be held accountable for these abuses.

I wondered what might be in the file that the department had on me. That my parents were socialists? That I was arrested at the Shrine Auditorium for *not* disturbing the peace in 1972? That I occasionally played poker at the Normandie Club while in college? These weren't just trivial thoughts, because unconstitutional government surveillance poisons the lifeblood of our democracy. It can have a profoundly chilling effect on people's willingness to speak and act freely.

My worries became real when a former PDID officer took me aside during a 1979 police retirement dinner at the Sportsmen's Lodge in Studio City. A lieutenant who had been custodian of the unit's records put his arm on my shoulder and told me that he had seen my file. "You've got nothing to worry about," he said. I didn't need him to tell me that I shouldn't worry. But I was astonished because he had casually confirmed the existence of a file that Gates publicly said *didn't* exist. He explained that it contained information on my participation in political demonstrations and a trip to Pennsylvania to address a civil liberties conference in my City Council capacity—a trip I never made. I felt personally violated. The LAPD had spent tax dollars to monitor my appointment calendar, even as police response times were increasing and the ranks of police officers were shrinking due to budgetary cuts.

The following year, the ACLU unmasked an undercover LAPD officer who had been posing as a civil liberties advocate. Documents revealed his attendance at three meetings of the Coalition Against Police Abuse, where he observed the organization's strategic planning to sue the city and the LAPD. He even participated in stakeholder meetings in *my* office as we drafted a municipal Freedom of Information Ordinance. Clearly, police spying was out of control in the LAPD.

The arrogance of a police department that believed it had the right to infiltrate meetings in a councilman's office might even have made J. Edgar Hoover blush.

Still, Gates showed no intention of backing down. His condescending attitude toward civil libertarians could be summarized as follows: If you're a law-abiding citizen, you have nothing to fear from the LAPD's surveillance. The *LA Times* blasted him, arguing that such reassurances were "wide of the mark." If these allegations were true, they wrote, all citizens who simply exercised their constitutional rights might fear that they would be targets of police spying. Mayor Bradley also weighed in on these disclosures. He denounced the surveillance as "absolutely unacceptable." When I asked Gates for budgetary data showing how much had been spent on surveillance, he said that disclosing such information would put undercover officers at risk. This cat and mouse game got us nowhere.

Endgame for PDID

New revelations in 1983 finally broke the PDID scandal wide open. Evidence surfaced that the surveillance unit had compiled personal dossiers on Bradley and Police Commission President Stephen Reinhardt (a future Ninth Circuit Court of Appeals judge), as well as Police Commissioners Steve Yslas and Reva Tooley. An extensive file was compiled on respected Superior Court Judge Jerry Pacht (whose daughter was a classmate of mine at Fairfax High School), along with information on his liberal political affiliations dating back to 1945. In addition, a detective with the Organized Crime Intelligence Division (OCID) testified that he was ordered to investigate the sexual orientation and extramarital relationships of some top city officials. One prominent police critic's file contained detailed, highly private medical information. And the beat went on.

Los Angeles Times reporter Joel Sappell then dropped the bombshell that a substantial number of PDID files, which the Police Commission ordered destroyed in 1975, had instead been secretly stored in the home garage of PDID Detective Jay Paul. This was a brazen act of defiance. Later that year, two LAPD detectives told Internal Affairs Division investigators that they had been ordered by PDID Captain Robert Loomis to compile a file on me as early as 1980. As Police Commissioner Sam Williams, a former president of the California State Bar, said with wry understatement, the commission's guidelines "have not been followed." Finally, enough was enough. The Police Commission disbanded PDID, replacing it with a new scaled down intelligence unit. The "Anti-Terrorist Division" suggested that there would be a narrower police mission going forward, focusing on bona fide violent threats to public safety.

In the maelstrom of deceit and revelations, I was startled to learn a new detail about my own case. My file indicated that a death threat had been made against me. That might have been the only legitimate use of intelligence resources involving me except for one thing: The LAPD never bothered to tell me about the death threat. Just a bookkeeping error, I'm sure.

There was one last piece of unfinished business. I believed that the city had to enact a law patterned after the federal Freedom of Information Act, which would allow citizens to access files that government agencies compiled on them. This was an effective tool in fighting unconstitutional surveillance. I assumed that if it was good enough for the FBI, it would surely be good enough for the LAPD. I was mistaken. The department reacted to my proposal as though it would open the gates of Los Angeles to every terrorist on the planet.

Assistant Chief Robert Vernon, second in command to Daryl Gates, launched a campaign aimed at killing the proposal, and his fearmongering got some traction on the City Council. The 1984 Olympics were only months away, and Vernon warned that my ordinance would make it far more likely that we would have another Munich atrocity right here in Los Angeles. The council was divided right down the middle, with seven votes in support and seven members opposed. My colleague, Joel Wachs, was the swing vote. He proposed an amendment to the measure that significantly watered it down. The council approved the amendment by a vote of 8 to 7, and then passed the measure as modified. It was a bitter pill to swallow.

The $300 Dollar Blow Job and Heidi Fleiss

One of the tactics that law enforcement officials can use to intimidate critics is to spread scandalously false information about them. Fears that rumors will go viral, whether true or false, can cause politicians and other public figures to stand down. The LAPD and its allies were masters at this, and on at least three occasions they attempted to target me in such a campaign.

In 1992 I got a phone call from a sympathetic deputy chief, asking if I would meet him for breakfast to discuss a sensitive matter. When we met at Nibbler's on Wilshire Boulevard, my old haunt, he told me he had heard that Chief Gates' adjutant, a former officer in OCID, was investigating my alleged weekly visits— every Friday at noon, he said—to a home in West Hollywood, where I paid $300 for a blow job. "I know that's impossible," he said with a straight face. "You're too cheap to pay that much for a blow job." At that instant, I didn't appreciate the humor. Aside from the utter falsehood of the allegation, I couldn't believe that any intelligence officer familiar with the City Council schedule would peddle a story that so transparently lacked credibility. The City Council met three times a week, including Fridays, and our meetings went well into the lunch hour. It would have been easy to determine that no member could have possibly been in City Hall and West Hollywood at the same moment before wasting time purveying this salacious gossip. Then again, that's why "police intelligence" is often considered an oxymoron.

The deputy chief wanted me to know that Gates' office was monitoring the location in question. They hoped to catch me in the act, and I suppose he wanted to warn me off this alleged pattern of behavior just in case it was true. I asked him for the West Hollywood address so I could have someone check to see if there was a van or some other kind of police presence there at noon on Fridays. Alisa Katz, who by this time had been promoted to my Chief of Staff, drove to the site with her camera on a couple of Fridays to conduct her own stakeout. If she saw something suspicious, I asked her to take a photograph so that we would have verification and could launch our own inquiry. She went on several consecutive Fridays and found nothing.

A few years later, on the late afternoon of Monday June 6, 1994, the council met in a closed session to discuss a contentious labor contract negotiation with the Los Angeles Police Protective League, the union that represents LAPD's officers. Their contract had lapsed, and we were far from reaching agreement. I remember the date clearly, because it was the day before my first election to the Board of Supervisors.

We walked out to a gaggle of media and press when our session ended around 5 p.m. They wanted to know if there had been a breakthrough, and a young reporter from KCOP Channel 13, whom I had never seen before, asked her cameraman to start rolling as she thrust a microphone in my face. "What happened in there?" she asked. "Did you reach an agreement?" I told her I couldn't discuss the status of labor negotiations in public. "Well," she continued, "what if I told you that your name is in Heidi Fleiss's black book?" Fleiss was a well-known and well-publicized madame who oversaw a stable of high-priced "ladies of the evening." As the camera rolled, I tried to compose myself. "If I'm in her black book," I shot back, "it's under tree trimming and street maintenance, because I believe she's a constituent."

I could only surmise that this line of questioning was hatched by someone affiliated with the police union, and the reporter was carrying his water. It was designed to frame a story that said, "Yaroslavsky denies he's in Fleiss's black book." When the interview ended, I went into my office and got the Channel 13 news director on the phone, indelicately expressing my outrage.

"I'm up for election in twelve hours," I said. "You can't put that crap on the news tonight. Why didn't she ask me if I was having sex with pigs? I can deny that, too." He apologized for the young reporter's behavior and assured me the interview wouldn't air. It didn't, and I never saw that reporter again.

Three days earlier, the police union's spokesman told the press that "we are going to be soliciting adverse information on city council members." Indeed, there was an unabashed campaign to intimidate elected officials, including Jackie Goldberg, who was the first openly gay or lesbian member of the City Council. When I told her my Fleiss story the next day, she said I wasn't alone. Unmarked cars had been following her to community meetings and to her home at the end of the day in an apparent effort to intimidate her. "Why?" I asked. "Are they trying to prove you're straight?" We both had a good laugh. You can't make these things up.

The final example of a campaign to smear me surfaced during my first year on the Board of Supervisors. My press deputy, Joel Bellman, came into my office to tell me that Heidi Fleiss was going to be a guest on Michael Jackson's KABC morning show, the most popular and respected talk radio program in Los Angeles at the time. The Channel 13 interview story was no secret in my circle of staff and friends, so Joel suggested that he tape the interview in case anything interesting came up. I agreed.

Well, we weren't disappointed. At one point, Jackson asked Fleiss about her relationship with the LAPD. Sometimes it's hostile, and sometimes it's friendly, she said. For example, an OCID officer whom she knew felt comfortable enough to ask her to set me up. Jackson was aghast and responded, "you mean the Supervisor?" She thought I was still a councilman and allowed that she doesn't really follow local politics. Jackson asked her what came of the request. Nothing, she responded, adding that she had never met me. (I can attest to that) These false and pernicious tactics might have intimidated someone else, but in my case they had the wrong guy.

Shootings, Chokeholds, and Excessive Use of Force

On January 3, 1979, two LAPD officers responded to a disturbance call in Watts. Eulia Love, a thirty-nine-year-old Black woman, was arguing with two gas company employees in front of her home over an unpaid bill. She was waving an eleven-inch knife, and when one of the officers knocked it out of her hand with a baton, she picked it up and threw it at the officers. They fired twelve shots from their service revolvers in response, killing her instantly. The fatal shot was fired as Love lay on the ground, according to a Police Commission report.

Chief Gates admitted that "any way you viewed it, it was a bad shooting." Nevertheless, an internal department investigation exonerated the officers, saying they had fired in self-defense. Love's shocking death sparked an angry debate over the LAPD's use of force. A woman lay dead for not paying her gas bill on time, and this didn't sit well with the community.

It was not an isolated incident. LAPD officers had shot 278 people between 1975 and 1978, killing 123 of them. Most were people of color. To reduce the use of guns, the department began relying on a controversial tactic known as the chokehold. Unlike some other big city law enforcement agencies, Los Angeles police were permitted to use the tactic when confronting suspects, even when they didn't pose an existential threat to them. As the use of PCP and crack cocaine dramatically increased during this period, officers encountered a growing number of suspects with drug-enhanced strength who were difficult to control. The LAPD saw the chokehold as the best alternative to the gun.

There were two versions of the chokehold: The "bar arm," where an officer puts his arm around a suspect's throat, cutting off oxygen and the ability to breathe, and the "carotid" where an officer puts his arm around a suspect's carotid arteries, cutting off the flow of blood to the brain and causing him to stop resisting and to pass out. Although both were approved tactics in the LAPD training manual, the "bar arm" was particularly perilous. Either way, the chokehold was responsible for fifteen deaths in Los Angeles from 1975 to 1982, and most of the victims were people of color. As anger grew over the tactic, more than $200 million in claims were filed against the city. A federal judge limited use of the bar arm hold in 1981, but the United States Supreme Court reversed that decision on a 5–4 vote. Nonetheless, the Police Commission then banned the bar arm hold entirely, as Gates conceded that the carotid hold was enough for the LAPD's needs. Police officials clearly hoped this would end the controversy, but events proved otherwise.

When Policy and Politics Intersect

It was clear to me that no civilized society could permit the unchecked use of a tactic that turned officer-citizen encounters into death scenes, especially when there were alternatives. I said as much during council debates, but never dreamed that I would be thrust into a position to actually help end the chokehold. Yet that's exactly where I found myself in the summer of 1981.

On July 1, the City Council elected a new president. A bare majority of the members felt it was time for a generational and ideological change in leadership and moved to topple then-President John Ferraro. The challenge came in the person of Councilwoman Pat Russell, who was on track to be elected. At the last minute, however, Ferraro turned to Councilman Joel Wachs, who had been committed to vote for Russell, and offered to deliver his seven votes to Wachs if he would jump ship and vote for himself. That's exactly what he did. The City Hall world, which had gone to breakfast that day certain that Russell would lead the council, went to lunch with Joel Wachs as its new council president. I felt terrible for Russell, whose family was in the chambers to celebrate what would have been the election of the first woman to lead the council.

Policy and politics are often two sides of the same coin, and this was certainly the case in Los Angeles city government that day. One of the council president's most important powers is appointing the chairs and members of council committees, and that responsibility now fell to Wachs. At the time, he and I were political rivals, both looking to succeed Tom Bradley when the time came. This was not a fanciful idea. Bradley was preparing to run for governor the following year and was heavily favored to win. I fully expected Wachs to banish me to some obscure, powerless panel. Instead, he stunned me and the rest of City Hall by appointing me to chair the Police, Fire and Public Safety Committee. The *Los Angeles Times* noted that an outspoken critic of police policies was now running the committee that monitored them. Wachs told the paper that he thought no one was more qualified than me to take on this job, adding that he made the assignment without regard to politics.

With all due respect to Joel—who would turn out to be more of an ally than a rival once our political careers took different paths—this was pure baloney. He was as smart a member of the council as anyone, and I suspect he knew that my new committee chairmanship would be a minefield for me. It stood to reason that the more I challenged the LAPD, the more I would alienate conservative white voters; the less I challenged Daryl Gates, the more I would anger communities of color. City Hall gnomes couldn't be faulted for concluding that I was being put in a politically no-win position. For his part, Gates couldn't resist a condescending comment, saying: "Zev, who is a very energetic young man, wants to get ahead in this world, and I think he will really take the time to examine the department." On that last count, he was spot on. I told Gates to "be careful what you wish for."

James Mincey

As I assumed my new post, it was impossible to ignore the growing anger in Los Angeles' minority communities over the chokehold. When the sixteenth death occurred, it changed the debate forever. James Mincey was a twenty-year-old teaching assistant in the city's public schools, when he was stopped by police on the evening of March 22, 1982, for speeding and driving with a shattered windshield. Officers issued him a ticket and he drove away. Less than half an hour later, he passed another police officer who also noticed his broken windshield and signaled him to pull over. Mincey refused, leading police on a high-speed chase which ended in front of his mother's Lake View Terrace home. As officers approached him, he resisted and began to fight, warning them that he would "kick your asses" if they tried to put him in handcuffs.

LAPD officers sprayed Mincey with tear gas to no effect, and they finally subdued and handcuffed him as a police helicopter hovered over the scene. At that point one of the officers applied the carotid chokehold for twenty to thirty seconds. Police said Mincey was conscious as they brought him to Pacoima Memorial Hospital, but medical records indicated that he had already lapsed into a medical coma. His mother, who witnessed the violent arrest in front of her home, told police "You killed him" after blood poured out of her son's mouth while its flow was cut off to his brain. He died two weeks later, and the cause of death was ruled blunt-force trauma to the neck.

Community tensions were inflamed when the LAPD blamed Mincey for his own death, especially as more facts became known. First, he was not armed. Second, the police officers chasing him did not consider him a threat. And most important, the evidence showed that he had been killed after he had been put in handcuffs, with no chance to escape.

I had been a strong critic of the chokehold long before Mincey's case, but his death gave my new committee the chance to significantly raise public awareness of this tactic, and to do something about it. We were determined to see if there was a more humane and less risky alternative to its use. Activists across the city were demanding action, so we took our panel on the road to the two communities where tensions were highest: In South Los Angeles, the site of a disproportionate number of chokehold deaths, and the northeast San Fernando Valley—a predominately Latino area which also had an active but diminishing Black population—where James Mincey died. We held hearings before standing room only crowds at the historic Trinity Baptist Church on Jefferson Blvd., and the Calvary Baptist Church in Pacoima. The anger at both hearings was intense. Young Black men testified that they feared for their safety, even for their lives, every time they were pulled over by an LAPD officer. People chanted angrily that Gates should resign, but he countered that the department's new policy of only using the carotid hold would prevent future deaths. No one believed that in the aftermath of Mincey's death. And then Gates granted an interview that, for all practical purposes, ended the discussion.

On May 8, two days after banning the bar arm hold, Gates told the *Los Angeles Times*: "We may be finding that in some Black people when it [the choke hold] is applied, the veins or arteries do not open up as fast they do *in normal people* [emphasis added]." His comments triggered an uproar. Gates may have thought he was simply making a physiological observation, however ill-informed, but he was in way over his head making such judgments. Bluntly, he didn't know what the hell he was talking about. Much of Los Angeles heard the chief calling Black people abnormal, sparking renewed calls for his resignation. Every attempt he made to clarify his comments fell flat.

Our panel demanded that the LAPD completely end the use of the choke-hold, except when a police officer's life was in danger. This was the same standard required of officers for using their gun. The Commission agreed, first imposing a six-month moratorium on the carotid hold, and then extending it permanently. It was a decision that should have been made years earlier. To find an alternative, we didn't have to look further than next door, to the Los Angeles County Sheriff's Department, where a deputy's toolbox did not include the chokehold. To subdue suspects who violently resisted their directives, deputies carried large fishing nets in their patrol cars. When necessary, they tossed the net over an unruly suspect, bringing the resistance to a relatively uneventful end. This approach was far safer for officers as well as suspects.

The chokehold was now history. Gates' reputation in communities of color was in tatters, and the department's clout continued to erode. Looking back on these tragic events, it was clear to me that Mincey's death triggered one of the most significant changes ever implemented by the LAPD at that point in history. Eventually, Mincey's family settled their civil lawsuit with the city for $1.5 million, but no amount of money could ever compensate them for the loss of his life.

In 2017, more than three decades after Mincey's death, I attended a screening of *Let It Fall*, a brilliant documentary by producer-director John Ridley, commemorating the twenty-fifth anniversary of the Rodney King uprisings. Among those in attendance were James Mincey's mother and his son, who was in utero when his dad was killed that night in Lakeview Terrace. I teared up as I looked them both in the eye and explained the historic significance of James' death. We can't bring him back, I told them, but there are people alive today because of what happened to him. "If it's any solace," I said, "you should take comfort in knowing that James' life had a profound impact on this community."

My stint as Chair of the Police Committee ended abruptly in September 1982, one month after our hearing at Trinity Baptist. If Joel Wachs' decision to appoint me fifteen months earlier was intended to put me between the proverbial rock and hard place, it hadn't turned out as planned. Instead of falling into a political trap, our committee showed what could be done when public officials had the guts to stand up and do the right thing. It's called leadership. As Chairman of the police panel, I had earned respect among constituencies that I didn't represent and who hardly knew me. Many observers believed that my efforts as chair of the police committee had enhanced my prospects in the mayor's race that was increasingly likely because conventional wisdom was that Bradley would be elected governor in 1982. If he succeeded, an election to replace him would pit me and Wachs against one another the following spring. As a result, I was banished to a non-descript post in political Siberia—the Personnel Committee.

I understood the political calculations, but in this case expanding my base was not my objective. There were far easier ways to do that than taking on the powerful and still popular LAPD. But as my friend and former Congressman Howard Berman told me early in my career, "Good policy makes for good politics." It was policy, not politics, that motivated me to take on LAPD excesses.

In the midst of these tumultuous times, another life-changing event helped me put things in perspective. On the evening of June 30, 1982, I was preparing to give a speech at the annual fundraiser for Alternative Living for the Aging, an innovative senior housing provider founded by my longtime friend, Janet Witkin. As I was preparing to approach the podium at the Beverly Hilton Hotel, Heidi Evans, my press deputy, came looking for me with an urgent message from Barbara. She wanted me to know that she had gone into labor and was being driven to the hospital to deliver our second child. She would meet me there, the message ended.

I delivered an abbreviated speech, explained to the audience that I had a good reason for cutting out early and rushed to the Tarzana Medical Center where Barbara was already in the delivery room. At approximately 2:30 a.m. our son, David (named for my father), entered this world. It was just as moving an experience as we had nearly five years earlier when Mina was born. When the sun rose, I made my way home to inform Mina that she had a baby brother. She was thrilled and was already making plans for her new role as "big sister." Our family of four was now complete.

As it turned out, Bradley lost his 1982 gubernatorial election to Attorney General George Deukmejian by 1 percent of the vote. He remained mayor, and all of us on the council who hoped to succeed him—including me, Wachs and Ferraro—would not be facing off in a special election. Whatever passed for political normalcy in Los Angeles City Hall was restored, at least temporarily, and on July 1, 1983, the City Council unanimously elected Pat Russell as its president. Better late than never.

Looking back, I have no doubt that our battles with the LAPD made a difference. On the day I arrived at City Hall, it was virtually unheard of for a politician to challenge the department and its leaders—especially those of us who represented white, middle-class constituencies. Now, it was clear that a mayor or a councilmember could hold the LAPD accountable and live to talk about it.

Some observers hoped that tensions over LAPD abuses might finally subside, as controversies over police spying and the choke hold began to die down in the late 1980s. Perhaps a new era was dawning at Parker Center. But that was an illusion. Friction between law enforcement officers and the communities they served continued to grow, and the biggest shock was yet to come. The resulting explosion would shake Los Angeles to its core and fundamentally transform the culture of its embattled police force.

CHAPTER 11

Big Money and the Battle to Preserve Neighborhoods

In the summer of 1986 Barbara and I took our two children on a road trip to the Grand Canyon and the National Parks in Eastern Utah. On a blazingly hot afternoon we pulled into a gas station in Kayenta, Arizona, a barren town on the Navajo-Hopi reservation and the last before descending into Monument Valley. The Wall Street Journal once identified Kayenta as the most remote zip code in the continental United States. As I pumped gas, Barbara went into the convenience store. She loved to collect local newspapers from places we visited, and I'll never forget the look on her face when she brought me a copy of the *Navajo-Hopi Observer*, the reservation's daily publication. A screaming banner across the front page read: "GROWTH CONTROL SOUGHT IN KAYENTA." I took another look at the town—which consisted of the gas station, an urgent care facility, some small adobe houses, and a lot of open space—and shook my head. Kopach, the obscure village where my grandfather was born in Belarus, appeared to have more density than Kayenta.

The story beneath the headline explained that the town's urgent care facility wanted to expand, sparking local controversy. I laughed out loud. How could the modest expansion of a much-needed medical service institution trigger a call for growth control? After all, we were literally in the middle of nowhere. But then I realized that there was a larger truth to this dispute. When it comes to growth and other quality of life issues, *everything* is relative. It all depends on where you live. In West Los Angeles, too much growth might be an invasion of high-rise buildings adjacent to low-rise residences. In South Los Angeles it was the proliferation of liquor stores. In San Pedro it would be the rapid expansion of the harbor or the Wilmington oil refineries. In Boyle Heights it might be the intrusion of freeways that carved up the community. And in Chatsworth it would be threats to historic horse-keeping districts that allowed equestrians to keep horses next to their homes.

To be sure, protesting overdevelopment is not unique to Los Angeles. In New York City, neighborhood residents rose up and helped defeat a 1955 plan by Robert Moses, the state's development czar, to build a four-lane expressway through Washington Square Park. In San Francisco, neighborhood resistance crushed a 1964 freeway project that would have run through Golden Gate Park and the Panhandle. The instinct to preserve one's quality of life, beginning with one's own neighborhood, is universal—and elected officials ignore this at their peril. As I took a final look at Kayenta, the urgent care's expansion didn't seem to pose a major threat. But who was I to judge?

If residents there were exercised about growth, it shouldn't have surprised anyone that Los Angeles—a metropolis with millions of people—was wrestling with similar anxieties on a much grander scale. And my district had become the epicenter for this debate. I often described the 5th district as the donut, with Beverly Hills, a separate city, as the hole. Most of it included real estate that brokers refer to as "Beverly Hills adjacent," meaning that I represented some of the priciest land in the country.

The pressures to develop and densify this part of Los Angeles were constant, because they offered investors the potential for high economic returns. Yet developers never seemed to be satisfied with the size of the projects that zoning ordinances on their property permitted them to build. And residents were never satisfied that zoning was sufficiently restrictive to protect *their* investments. This tension could surface in an issue as minor as a new restaurant's application for a beer and wine license, or in a massive development proposal for hundreds of acres of undeveloped land. Every square mile of my district had its zoning controversies, and they preoccupied my office for nearly two decades.

As I took my seat on the council in 1975, plans were afoot in Los Angeles to replace blocks of mom-and-pop stores or nostalgic amusement parks with major shopping malls. High-rise commercial buildings were sprouting without warning near residential neighborhoods. Communities were inundated with increased traffic congestion and crippling parking shortages, and once-quiet neighborhoods were being transformed into mega centers. It's no wonder I laughed when Barbara showed me that headline in the *Navajo-Hopi Observer*.

The development battles that raged in the 1970s and '80s were legion, but it would be a mistake to think they bubbled up out of nowhere. The friction had its roots in the economic boom that transformed Los Angeles during and immediately after World War II. The city's anachronistic zoning code, dating back to 1946, encouraged rapid and massive growth. Huge commercial buildings, single-family housing subdivisions and apartment complexes were built at a record pace.

Indeed, the post WW II zoning code would have accommodated a population of 10 million people, more than five times what it was on VJ Day. As vacant land started to become scarcer, however, bitter conflicts broke out between developers looking for new opportunities and residents determined to protect their homes. These clashes took center stage, and although I may have fumbled a question about density as a rookie candidate, common sense dictated that I quickly learn the ropes at City Hall. It was a baptism by fire.

Welcome to the Bazaar

Long after World War II ended, Los Angeles mayors and City Councils showed little inclination to plan thoughtfully for the city's future. They preferred to encourage growth without constraints. Elected city officials subscribed to the boom-or-bust approach to real estate, and their campaign coffers swelled with contributions from builders who stood to benefit handsomely from their cooperative attitudes. Those policies came under fire in the early 1970s, however, when the city's Planning Director, Calvin Hamilton, proposed a modern land use plan for what Los Angeles would look like in the future. It came to be known as "Concept Los Angeles" or the "Centers Concept." This visionary blueprint divided the city into thirty-five communities. Hamilton asked stakeholders in each area to create a balanced plan for future high, medium, and low-density growth, both commercial and residential. Citizens eagerly accepted the challenge and spent years drafting these plans. One by one they were approved, taking nearly two decades to complete.

Then a problem emerged. The 1946 zoning code wasn't synchronized with the newly approved community plans. Every property in the city was now governed by two blueprints that were often markedly inconsistent with one another. It was largely left to the mayor and City Council to determine which document would apply to a proposed development.

Although Hamilton's plan offered the hope for balanced development, it was quickly scuttled by political realities. The pro-growth City Council, backed by regular infusions of campaign cash, refused to pass laws that would downzone real estate, as called for by the new law. As a result, the disparities between community-based planning and permissive zoning remained in place, and developers continued to win approval for projects that were often grossly out of proportion to the neighborhoods they impacted.

Unfortunately, the City Council was reluctant to update the code and approve new controls, despite state legislation that required them to do so. Thus, the mayor and City Council had unlimited discretion over development. As the city dragged its feet, new developments wreaked havoc. The citizens and planners who had painstakingly developed guidelines for future development felt their frustration turn to anger. The message was clear. If rational city planning was to take hold, citizens would have to rely on their own wits and legal resources.

Hundreds of ensuing land use battles were fought on a project-by-project basis across the city, and the deck was usually stacked against communities. Gail Goldberg, Mayor Antonio Villaraigosa's city Planning Director, summed it up years later when she told a gathering of city neighborhood leaders that in most cities, the value of a parcel of land is based on the underlying zoning. In Los Angeles, it's based on what a developer thinks he can have the zone changed to. It was easy to trace developer campaign contributions to elected officials who accommodated their requests. In recent years, this largesse hasn't been limited to campaign contributions. In 2020, the FBI indicted a number of city officials for allegedly accepting cash, in one case more than $1,000,000, for services rendered.

As I took office in 1975, the development process resembled a bazaar, where councilmembers, planning officials, developers, neighborhood activists and environmentalists haggled over the city's future. Let me be clear: I was no virgin when it came to political fundraising. I received contributions over the years from a wide array of donors, including developers. But I had no problem voting against a donor's project, and I often wouldn't accept contributions from a donor whose project I was inclined to support. I knew it would create an appearance of impropriety. As an anonymous City Hall lobbyist summed it up in a *Los Angeles Times* article: "Zev is the best example of one who takes [campaign] money with impunity and votes against you—with the compliments of the donor. Which is really a compliment to the son of a bitch." I wore that quote as a badge of honor.

In the city's land use wars, large and small projects were up for grabs, and whether they were approved or modified came down to a negotiation. I worked hard to get up to speed, reaching out to Hamilton and other experts. They obliged, offering to share their knowledge about the city and my district that otherwise would have taken years to learn.

My first foray into 5th district land use issues focused on placing forty-five-foot building height limits on many of the strip commercial streets such as Melrose and La Brea Avenues, and Beverly, Westwood, Pico, and Santa Monica Boulevards where they abutted low-rise residences. Joining with my colleagues, Marvin Braude and Joel Wachs, I also pushed for strict controls on hillside development, to protect them from destructive grading. We persuaded the council to pass a slope density formula that created an inverse relationship between the scale of development and the steepness of the hills. These, as it turned out, were the easy fights.

The Century City Plan

Some land use battles had been going on for years, long before I came onto the council. Plans to create a major urban center in Century City began in 1963 on the back lot of the Twentieth Century Fox Studios, just west of Beverly Hills. The property was sandwiched between Santa Monica and Pico Boulevards, and most had been sold off by Fox. Century City Inc., a subsidiary of the Alcoa Aluminum Corporation, became the largest owner of the remaining land.

Developers planned to build a massive commercial and residential mini-city on the site, based on the assumption that the proposed Beverly Hills Freeway would serve it. But that project was never built, due to intense opposition from Beverly Hills and other communities along the proposed route. By the mid-70s the freeway proposal was dead, but the Century City development plans were alive and well. The city of Beverly Hills and neighborhood associations legitimately feared that the area didn't have the capacity to absorb the impacts of such a plan. They feared that every street on the city's westside would choke on the traffic congestion generated by this new mega center.

This was the first major development controversy I faced, and it was a doozy. As I took my seat, Beverly Hills and several neighborhood groups filed a lawsuit against the City of Los Angeles, halting development on the massive lot. Unlike most land use controversies, however, all the parties, including the developer, wanted to negotiate an agreement. But finding a resolution was easier said than done. Beverly Hills demanded what amounted to a "no growth" solution that was dead on arrival. Commercial interests, especially Century City Inc., had a financial investment in this part of town from which they wouldn't just walk away. Residents of Cheviot Hills, an upper-middle-class neighborhood nestled between Century City and the Santa Monica Freeway, were concerned that their main residential street and access route to the freeway would become a perpetual parking lot. Other residents feared that high rise developments adjacent to their homes would put them in permanent shadow. I had the job of trying to square this circle. We all had one important advantage: The bulk of the land was owned by one company, making it easier to negotiate a responsible solution.

The planning process works best when competing interests come together in good faith, but even then it can take months or years to reach agreement.

I assigned my planning deputy, Howard Katz, to pull all of this together. It took several years, but we achieved a breakthrough, a rare win-win for all concerned. I should add that Howard achieved another breakthrough during this period: His office romance with Alisa Belinkoff, my environmental deputy, blossomed into marriage, a "development" we all endorsed.

The 1981 agreement we brokered reduced allowable development in Century City by more than two-thirds, which was itself a remarkable achievement. We also tackled the traffic issue head-on and addressed other environmental impacts. Typically, building development rights are based on the square footage of the underlying land, regardless of the building's use. But since traffic was the main issue in Century City, we decided to allocate development rights based on how many *vehicle trips* a building would generate. In short, if you chose to build a medical office building, a huge traffic generator, your building would be considerably smaller than a residential project that would produce a fraction of the traffic. The choice was up to you. We then agreed to cap the total number of vehicle trips that new development would generate in Century City, and each property owner within the plan area got a proportional allocation to which the owner would be entitled. It was a novel, common sense approach to planning and traffic regulation in Los Angeles that would be replicated years later on other major developments.

The plan also allowed for the construction of taller buildings in the center of Century City while limiting heights on its western edge, to protect the neighboring residential community. Twentieth Century Fox agreed to forfeit its commercial development rights on its studio lot in exchange for the right to build 2,400 residential units, a decision that was reversed a decade later in order to keep this major regional employer in the city. I pushed for the concentration of commercial uses in the northern half of the plan area, in anticipation that mass transit would one day come to Century City. I wanted that transit line—whenever it was built—to serve the maximum number of commuters, in what was sure to become one of the city's major job hubs. Little did I know that it would take four decades, but the Purple Line subway to Avenue of the Stars and Constellation Avenue in Century City was approved by the Metropolitan Transportation Authority before I left office in 2014. It is now under construction and due to open in the mid-2020s.

The bottom line is that we reached a deal in Century City after six years of difficult but good faith negotiations. Beverly Hills dropped its lawsuit, neighboring communities were largely satisfied, and the Gordian knot was cut. I had good reason to celebrate the agreement. But there was no time to rest on our laurels. New land use challenges were surfacing to the north and west, and even more complicated battles were about to begin.

Wilshire Boulevard and the Influence of Developer Money

The lore around City Hall is that councilmembers defer to each other on land use decisions in their districts. This unwritten rule is usually honored—except when it isn't. I learned that the hard way when deference was cast to the wind during a political war that erupted over development on Wilshire Boulevard in Westwood, a prime commercial and residential artery between Beverly Hills to the east and the San Diego Freeway to the west.

As the 1980s began, the development pressures on that part of Wilshire were enormous. A cluster of high-rise buildings—commercial and residential—was either in place on Wilshire Boulevard or in the pipeline when I took office. And the busy Wilshire corridor was already zoned for high density, high-rise development, as dense and as massive as any part of the city except for downtown.

This explosive growth inevitably transformed the area. Relatively affordable low-rise apartments were demolished to make room for luxury high-rise condominiums. Although I empathized with residents who opposed these projects, I couldn't stop all of them. Some were well underway. Some had a legal right to build based on existing zoning. My only hope was to propose a limited moratorium on high-rise construction, to give the city a chance to reassess the boulevard's future. The goal was simply to scale back the height of future condominium projects, not to radically decrease residential density. But my proposal failed by one vote. A majority of my colleagues succumbed to the influence of an array of influential lobbyists, allowing more luxury high rises to be built.

My intentions on the commercial parts of Wilshire Boulevard in Westwood, however, were different. I wanted the city to take dead aim at new office construction, because these projects were the single biggest traffic generators in this part of Los Angeles. In 1984, I proposed to slash future commercial development by 40 percent on Wilshire between Glendon and Veteran Avenues in the heart of Westwood, and this set the stage for a major political clash. Unlike Century City, where the landowners were cooperative in seeking a compromise, this was not the case with the half dozen owners who paid top dollar for their Wilshire Boulevard properties. They believed my plan would wipe out their investments and considered it a declaration of war. I ran headfirst into a buzz saw of political lobbying that made a mockery of the council's unwritten rule.

The proposal to slash commercial development initially got the support of the Los Angeles Planning Commission. It was led by Dan Garcia, a brilliant attorney with an unparalleled capacity to understand complex problems, and a public servant I greatly respected. His commission was the first stop on any zone or plan change in the city. In this case, commissioners determined that development along Wilshire had indeed become excessive. They agreed to a development moratorium that would give the city time to work out a more rational path forward. As the proposal moved to the City Council, I was hopeful it would enjoy smooth sailing. But I was thinking with my heart, not my head.

Developers planning massive commercial office buildings on Wilshire quickly amassed an army of influential City Hall lobbyists to defeat the moratorium. They included some of the most influential law firms in town as well as Philip Krakover, a former planner and, pound for pound, the most effective lobbyist of his time. He was a legend around the horseshoe until he died prematurely in 1987. When Phil was hired by a developer in my district, I knew I was in for a fight. As if that wasn't enough, property owners also hired individuals whom they thought brought "unique influence" to bear on specific councilmembers. We're talking about former staffers and political supporters who made a living as hired guns for precisely this purpose. The impact on my proposed moratorium was swift and deadly.

The first clue came when the council's Planning and Environment Committee voted down my proposal. Their rationale was that some land use issues had a "regional significance," thus superseding local concerns. No one was fooled for an instant. "Regional significance" was cynical shorthand for "extenuating political considerations." Indeed, the *Los Angeles Times* estimated that more than $35,000 in campaign contributions linked directly to developers impacted by the Wilshire moratorium were handed over to councilmembers' campaign coffers *while they were considering my proposal.* Today that would be equivalent to nearly $100,000. Shamelessly, the committee chairman, Howard Finn, proposed an alternative ordinance designed to kill the moratorium. Soon after, we learned that the "alternative" proposal was drafted by one of the developers' lawyers and approved by the committee without a single edit.

In the end, the council defeated the Wilshire moratorium on a 9–5 vote. I felt that I had been stabbed in the back. My colleagues let the Westwood community down. They also exposed a growing pattern of how the public's business got done in Los Angeles. Many voters increasingly believed that it wasn't the merits of a development that mattered, but whom the developer knew that dictated public policy and councilmembers' votes. For me, it was also personal. I was surprised by the opposition of Pat Russell, my good friend and political ally, whom I had supported in the bitter 1981 council presidency fight. I was also disappointed that Councilmember Peggy Stevenson, whom I routinely supported on difficult issues in her district, voted against the moratorium in mine.

I wasn't going to take this defeat lying down. I found a kindred spirit and ally in Councilmember Marvin Braude, who represented the Brentwood part of

Wilshire Boulevard, just west of the 405 freeway, as well as Encino and Tarzana in the San Fernando Valley. Marvin had lost his share of battles over growth as well, and we agreed that we had to send a message to our colleagues. As it turned out, Peggy Stevenson faced a stiff re-election challenge in 1985, and we decided that if a councilmember could violate the unwritten rule of deference to a colleague, we could ignore the maxim that members don't work to unseat each other at election time.

Stevenson had clearly begun to lose touch with her constituents and Michael Woo, a bright and ambitious young planner, launched a challenge to her in the municipal primary election. When he ran a close second to Stevenson, forcing a runoff eight weeks later, Braude and I stunned our colleagues by publicly endorsing him. And he won. Woo's victory should have been a wake-up call to City Hall, but our colleagues continued to green-light projects in our districts and beyond. At that point, Marvin and I agreed that we were past the point of trying to persuade our colleagues. It was time to appeal directly to Los Angeles voters.

Proposition U: The Nuclear Option

When you think about the issues that people discuss around the office water cooler, zoning isn't one of them. During the mid-1980s, however, traffic planning and zoning was arguably the talk of the town. Commercial growth was booming in areas where it wasn't expected. Although construction had visibly transformed downtown Los Angeles, high-rise growth between 1975 and 1985 grew at a three times greater rate in West Los Angeles, the South Bay, and the San Fernando Valley. These were more like suburban communities, portions of which were being rapidly transformed into high density centers. This wasn't just an abstract concern for neighborhood residents. If their daily commute was suddenly extended by an hour, or a permanent shadow was cast on their homes because of new development, they had every right to seek redress from city government.

It didn't take much insight to realize that slow growth sentiment was sweeping across Los Angeles. With the proper catalyst, it could become an unstoppable grassroots movement. So, in the spring of 1986, Braude and I met in his office for lunch and held what came to be known as the "Tuna Sandwich Summit." We were joined by our deputies, Cindy Miscikowski and Ginny Kruger. Both our districts had development crosses to bear. I had to contend with projects like the Beverly Center and the Westside Pavilion, both mega-shopping, dining, and entertainment destinations. Marvin was dealing with high rises on the Brentwood side of Wilshire, as well as a massive six-story structure on Ventura Boulevard in Encino, known as the Fujita building. Each of these projects was built in strict accordance with the existing zoning code, known as "by right" projects, and they became poster children for land use planning reform.

The Fujita building was particularly egregious. It bordered an entire block of modest, single-family homes with virtually no separation from its neighbors, not even an alley. Homeowners' lifetime investments plummeted in value when the new building cast a permanent shadow on the entire block. In the ensuing years, all the homes on the block were sold, demolished, and replaced with a block-long parking lot. This was a senseless tragedy, and yet it was perfectly legal. Once again, the city's zoning code failed to balance real estate interests with those of city residents.

It was clear to Marvin and me that we were being subjected to a war of attrition, unable to control this tsunami of development. Or could we? During our lunch I suggested that the time had come to use the nuclear option—to bypass the mayor and City Council and take our case directly to the voters. We agreed to launch an initiative for the November 1986 ballot that would cut in half the allowable square footage for new buildings on commercially zoned streets that served local neighborhoods.

And that's how Proposition U was born—officially titled the "Reasonable Limits on Commercial Buildings and Traffic Growth" initiative. Our aim was to redirect more intense commercial development into designated centers as the city's 1970s "Concept Los Angeles" directed, rather than to transform each of the city's neighborhoods into a regional center. We exempted from Prop U's control high-density centers such as downtown, mid-Wilshire, Koreatown, Hollywood, Van Nuys in the San Fernando Valley, and every redevelopment area in the city.

Thirty-seven years later, critics who weren't even born in 1986 claim that Proposition U is the cause of today's housing shortage. They are wrong. Proposition U did *not* reduce density on a single property that was zoned "residential." There were those who suggested that we include such a provision in our initiative, but we never considered it. Our beef was with commercial over-development on neighborhood-serving commercial streets, like Pico or Fairfax, not with residential development. Although commercial zoning allowed for residential uses, it was far more profitable to build retail or commercial projects than residential ones. That's why, to this day, there are few apartment buildings on commercially zoned streets. It is telling that neither the proponents nor the opponents of our ballot measure ever raised an issue over its impact on residential development.

Finally, to permit some future flexibility, Proposition U allowed future mayors and City Councils to modify the measure, without voter approval, but in compliance with environmental laws and legally required public hearings. A decade and half later, that's precisely what the mayor and City Council did, allowing significantly higher density for residential buildings but not commercial ones. To the extent that a one-paragraph initiative could be surgical and nuanced, this was it. In an analysis of the initiative, the *Los Angeles Times* got it right, even though it editorialized against our measure. Proposition U, the *Times* report said, didn't force voters to choose between growth or no-growth. It's "about where Los Angeles' intense commercial development should be allowed to take place, and how to go about it."

We had one final objective. It was our hope that Proposition U would change the culture that had turned City Hall into a development free for all. We believed that once the mayor and councilmembers heard from the voters, they would get the message that money shouldn't talk; people should. Not surprisingly, our colleagues hated what we did. I can hear their voices now: "This simply isn't done. It's an egregious violation of council etiquette, like campaigning for a colleague's defeat." The hypocrisy was breathtaking, but we paid it no mind. There was simply no way to achieve such sweeping reform using conventional legislative means.

Along with hundreds of neighborhood volunteers, Braude and I gathered the 100,000 signatures needed to qualify the measure, and we quickly won a spot on the ballot. Los Angeles residents would now have the opportunity to directly vote on growth policies affecting them. Critics took aim, arguing the measure would stifle commercial growth and impact the regional economy. Others said that it would disproportionately affect communities of color. These arguments rang hollow in every part of the city, despite the opposition of most of the City Council and tacit opposition from Mayor Tom Bradley.

We built a broad coalition of supporters from San Pedro in the south to Tujunga in the northeast, from South Los Angeles to the Westside, and from Boyle Heights east of downtown to Woodland Hills in the west San Fernando Valley. Voters were itching for a way to fight back, and we gave them a weapon with which to do so. Proposition U passed 69 percent to 31 percent. It was a landslide by anyone's definition, winning overwhelmingly in each of the city's 15 council districts. The voters agreed that although the city needed to grow, it had to do so while striving to protect its quality of life.

One of the collateral outcomes of Proposition U was the defeat of Pat Russell, then the Council President, six months later. A growing opposition to her mushroomed due to her pro-development policies in her southwest Los Angeles district. Coupled with her aggressive opposition to Proposition U, a political bullseye was tattooed on her incumbency from which she couldn't recover. Pat was defeated by a relatively wide margin in the 1987 city election.

That spring, in anticipation of this outcome, I went upstairs to John Ferraro's office to suggest that he run for Council President again. I added that "if you run, you will have my unconditional support." There was a six-year story behind that visit. In 1981, I was one of Pat Russell's strongest supporters in her challenge to Ferraro. Between 1981 and 1983, after he was forced out of his leadership post, John and I barely spoke a word to one another. "Hostile" would not begin to describe our relationship, and all of City Hall was aware of it.

However, that eventually changed. When a newspaper questioned Ferraro's integrity because he supported awarding a contract to a personal friend, the reporter asked me to comment on Ferraro's ethics. Both the reporter and Ferraro were surprised when I said that John and I had our differences, but one thing I would never do is question his integrity. My comments appeared in the article. That day, Ferraro and I found ourselves alone, shoulder to shoulder, in a City Hall elevator. He grudgingly thanked me for my statement. "Don't you think it's about time we bury the hatchet?" I asked. "You, me and our colleagues deserve better." He cracked a smile, and we began to gingerly rebuild mutual trust. It took a while, but it was that encounter in the elevator that led to my visit to his office years later. Ferraro was unanimously elected Council President on July 1, 1987, a position he held until his death in 2001. We remained frequent allies and personal friends until that fateful day.

Song Sung Blue on a Tennis Court

Not all land use disputes are settled with fierce legislative battles or political campaigns. One morning, I received a cryptic call from a representative of legendary singer-songwriter Neil Diamond. There seemed to be a minor zoning issue next to Diamond's mansion in Holmby Hills, an affluent enclave east of the UCLA campus. The singer's neighbor wanted to build a tennis court, but he needed a variance (permission) to encroach a small distance into his own side yard, not Diamond's. We were talking about inches, maybe a foot. Side yard variances are routinely granted with a neighbor's consent. But this wasn't any neighbor.

I met the singer at his home, to see why he objected. We sat in his breakfast nook, which was on the side of the house closest to his neighbor's proposed tennis court. Diamond was polite but intense. "I compose all my music right here," he said tapping the breakfast table. "The notion that I'd have to listen to tennis balls bouncing back and forth while I'm working is anathema to me. It will impact my creative juices."

I took a walk along the property line and frankly didn't see this as a huge issue. These homes were estates, and there was considerable distance between his house and the property line, let alone the proposed tennis court. But I believed him. Maybe I wanted to believe him, because Diamond is one of my all-time favorite singers. There isn't a song of his that I didn't love.

I told him that I would try to find a solution. I had recently met his neighbor at a charitable banquet, and I thought I could convince him to build the tennis court on the opposite side of his property, next to his other neighbor. "What happens when *she* complains to you," Diamond logically asked. I answered: "Your other neighbor is Marge Everett (owner of the Hollywood Park Racetrack), and she doesn't compose the music that America loves," I answered. "I don't care about her breakfast nook, but I do care about yours." Game, set, and match. To this day, I don't know what Diamond's neighbor ultimately did, but he didn't get the variance next to the singer's property.

UCLA's Expansion: Necessity Is the Mother of Invention

Sometimes, seemingly intractable problems are resolved by thinking outside the box and finding a solution. That was the case in the late 1980s, when UCLA needed to expand. One of the world's leading institutions of research and higher learning, UCLA was limited by the size of its campus. Although it was the largest employer and biggest traffic generator on the west side of Los Angeles, it was the second smallest campus in the University of California system. Only UC San Francisco, a medical school, had less acreage. But those geographic constraints weren't going to stop UCLA's Chancellor, Charles E. Young, one of the most exceptional leaders and public administrators with whom I ever had the privilege of working. He was on a mission to sustain UCLA's reputation as one of America's great universities, and he knew that it had to grow to remain at the cutting edge.

Accordingly, Young unveiled UCLA's Long-Range Development plan (LRDP) in 1989. It called for the addition of 4 million square feet of new building on the campus. When fully implemented, city planners estimated that the plan would add between 50,000–75,000 daily automobile trips to local streets that were already among the most congested in Southern California. I was between a rock and a hard place. Should the university expand so it could fulfill its mission? Or should it be restrained out of concern for the plan's traffic impacts? It looked like a lose-lose proposition, but I was determined to find a third way.

I called Chancellor Young and told him that his proposal had landed like a thud at City Hall, and with the university's immediate neighbors. It would generate more growth than the area could possibly absorb. He surprised me by challenging the city's traffic projections—arguing that the plan would add no more than 25,000 daily car trips, based on his staff's projections. I thought this was an absurd argument. Our own Century City Specific Plan had assumed that office space would generate 14 trips per 1,000 square feet, which in the UCLA plan's case would mean 56,000 daily trips. I jokingly replied, "Chuck, do you want me to answer that in writing, verbally, or by gesture?"

In reality, I had no leverage over the proposal. UCLA was on state-owned land, not subject to city's zoning laws. Nonetheless, Young was genuinely sensitive to the City's and community's concerns. He continued to engage me in a discussion over how we could resolve our differences. So, I suggested that he convene an all-hands meeting with our respective planners, traffic engineers, and lawyers. We would try to hash this out. He agreed, and the "summit" was set.

My goal was to give UCLA a green light, but with a couple of novel conditions. First, I proposed that the plan set a strict 25,000 daily vehicle trip cap on university-generated development, the precise number that the Chancellor had assured me would result from the LRDP. This concept was similar to the provisions of the Century City plan I negotiated a decade earlier. Second, I proposed that the university expand in four equal phases of 1 million square feet. If UCLA did not exceed the traffic cap at the end of the first phase, they would be allowed to proceed to the second phase, and so forth. If traffic blew past the cap, the university would be prohibited from expanding until it could bring its daily trip count below the cap.

We'd measure the amount of traffic entering the campus every October, UCLA's busiest month, and it would be easy to get an accurate count because there was a finite number of campus entrances and exits. My planners and traffic engineers loved the idea, but they questioned whether we could enforce this kind of a plan on state-owned property. I had a plan for that, too.

When we met in the chancellor's conference room on the second floor of Murphy Hall, our team was on one side and UCLA's was on the other. Young sat at the head of the table. I had not given him advance notice of my proposal. The university's group made their presentation first, repeating their claim that the plan would not increase traffic by more than 25,000 daily trips. When my turn came, I turned to Young and asked: "If your team is right about this, why don't we enter into an agreement to phase the plan?" I laid out my proposal, and Young immediately responded in a sentence that I'll never forget: "I think we can do that."

I was stunned, as was the chancellor's entire team. His traffic experts cautioned him that it was too risky to commit to my proposal. What if their projections were off and UCLA exceeded the cap, they asked? Young turned to them and said, "You guys have been telling me for months that we wouldn't generate more than 25,000 trips. We ought to be willing to put it in writing." I was floored. The chancellor was holding his team accountable for their assumptions, and he was doing it in front of us, on the record.

Then we moved on to the jurisdictional issue. "Chancellor," the university's general counsel said, "the Regents will never agree to this." He was right about that. So, I proposed that we enter into a memorandum of understanding (MOU) that would read like a contract, except for one clause. I proposed that the Regents be given the right, in their sole discretion, to abrogate the MOU if they found that doing so was in the best interest of the university. Of course, the Regents already had that authority. But I believed that if there was any UCLA project that was compelling enough to find its way onto the Regents' crowded agenda, it would be hard to oppose anyway. UCLA agreed to the proposal thanks to its Chancellor, and the Board of Regents of the University of California followed suit. Chuck Young was the leader of the university, and he wasn't afraid to lead. That's why he is in my pantheon of the extraordinary administrators.

Our deal turned out to be a smashing success. To comply with the traffic limits, the university dramatically expanded the number of student housing units on and near campus. As a result, what was once a commuter school for undergraduates became a predominantly residential campus. Thousands of students who once drove to school every day, like I did, now walked or used the university transit system to get to school. It was a profound and welcome change for UCLA, something that would have seemed inconceivable years earlier.

In the three decades since it was approved, traffic generated by UCLA has remained largely constant. Despite the robust expansion of the campus' infrastructure and the increase in its student body, it was generating approximately the same number of daily car trips in 2018 (the last count before the Covid pandemic) as it did in 1990. They have never come close to exceeding the cap. It's a remarkable achievement that I honestly never thought was possible.

This was a case where policy makers were willing to challenge institutional thinking. My idea was innovative, to be sure, but it would have been stillborn if Chancellor Young had dismissed it out of hand. Instead, he willed this agreement into being and directed his team to make it work. As a result, UCLA got its expansion, the university increased its student housing stock, Westwood was not inundated with more traffic, and we showed that town and gown problems plaguing universities across the country can be solved.

CHAPTER 12

The Mayor's Race
That Never Was

Several years after my election to the City Council, I was surprised by predictions in *New West* magazine, *Los Angeles Magazine*, and other publications that I would be a strong candidate to succeed Mayor Tom Bradley. Despite all the work and issues I took on in my first two years, the idea of running for mayor couldn't have been more remote. If I had any interest beyond the City Council, it was in running for Congress. Foreign policy and national issues had long been my primary interests, and if a chance arose to run for an open congressional seat, I would have jumped at the opportunity. But it was not to be. In the early years of my career, none of the city's incumbent Westside congressmen had any intention of giving up their seats. My council district was largely represented by the popular Congressman Henry Waxman, so any plans I might have had to go to Washington would have to wait.

Nonetheless, pundits continued to include my name among potential mayoral candidates, and I began to take the notion more seriously. The concept of being mayor of the nation's second largest city began to grow on me. Several members of the council, myself among them, began gearing up for a possible 1983 mayoral campaign. We did this in anticipation of a Bradley victory in the 1982 governor's race, which he was expected to win. When he narrowly lost to George Deukmejian in one of the most shocking upsets in California election history, those plans came to a grinding halt.

Five years later, however, there were signs that the mayor was losing his mojo. He came into office as a reformer, vowing to clean up the moral and political rot of the Sam Yorty years and to bring City Hall into the modern era. He kept those promises. But the fire seemed to go out of him after his second statewide loss for governor in 1986. He was becoming a tired, transactional mayor, increasingly on the wrong side of environmental and development battles. Los Angeles was moving in a new direction while Tom Bradley appeared to be stuck in neutral.

The most disturbing example of this surfaced on an environmental issue that he had made a centerpiece of his victorious 1973 campaign. Bradley had vowed to block Occidental Petroleum's plan to drill for oil along Pacific Coast Highway next to Pacific Palisades, a bucolic, affluent community overlooking the Pacific coastline. He voiced strong concerns that drilling in this seismically unstable terrain could trigger a catastrophic oil spill along the coast, one of the city's most precious environmental resources. In doing so Bradley took on the Occidental Oil Corporation and its powerful chairman, Dr. Armand Hammer. For twelve years the mayor kept his promise to block the drilling with his veto pen. Then he inexplicably changed his mind.

Days before the deadline to declare his candidacy for re-election in the 1985 mayor's race, I got a highly unusual weekend call at home from Bradley. He wanted to let me know that he had decided to reverse his position on Palisades oil drilling and would sign a pro-Occidental ordinance that had been narrowly approved by the City Council. He believed there were now enough safeguards in place to guard against any disasters. I was stunned, because this was one of the signature issues that helped him win his first mayoral election. And I certainly wasn't persuaded by his argument. The safeguards to which he referred were completely cosmetic and designed to give Bradley cover for his about-face.

In the spirit of full disclosure, I had voted to support the Oxy proposal at the onset of my City Council career. We were in the midst of an energy crisis in the mid-1970s, and I didn't believe that I could justify standing in the way of domestic oil production at a time when gasoline prices were rising and gas station lines were two hours long. But I had been wrong. The amount of oil that would be found in the Palisades and under Santa Monica Bay wouldn't make a dent in our domestic needs, and the risk-benefit ratio heavily tilted toward risk. By the time I got the weekend call from Bradley, I was a staunch opponent of Occidental's proposal and had voted against it.

Although I understood that elected officials had a right to change their minds, drilling opponents said that Bradley was essentially selling out the more than 55 million people who used the public beaches each year. The "No Oil" activists felt betrayed, because overnight their biggest City Hall ally became their arch enemy. Drilling foes, led by Robert Sulnick, urged me to enter the 1985 race against Bradley. I respectfully declined, but this reflected the level of their anger.

Indeed, the mayor's decision on Oxy signaled a disturbing change in his administration's values. He was grossly out of touch with public sentiment and the reform years seemed to be receding in the rear-view mirror. Amid these shifts in the political landscape, I began seriously considering a race for mayor in the 1989 election. Bradley may have been the ideal candidate to beat Yorty and usher in a more progressive, inclusive era at City Hall, but Los Angeles was now on the wrong course. It was time for a change, and I believed I could provide it. In April 1987, I decided to form an exploratory committee that would allow me to raise funds for a potential mayoral run. Still, I was under no illusion about the challenges I would face, especially if Bradley decided to run for re-election.

First, I respected the mayor and admired his personal journey, as did most Angelenos. I had no intention of demonizing him and would find it personally difficult and abhorrent to do so. My campaign would focus solely on the policies that differentiated us and the rudderless ship that City Hall was becoming. Moreover, I was keenly aware of the optics of a white, Jewish politician taking on an iconic Black political legend. I was determined that any campaign I ran would not be racially divisive. This was the last thing I wanted, or that Los Angeles needed. I was going to run a principled race, or I wouldn't run at all.

1987—The Battle Lines Form

If money is the mother's milk of politics, campaign fundraising is the castor oil—a foul but necessary evil. Nothing was drearier and more soul-sapping to me than the endless cycle of asking people for financial support. To complicate matters, the city's fundraising rules had radically changed. Prior to 1987, campaign contributions to candidates for city office were unlimited, but by the time I formed my committee, donor contributions were limited to $1,000. This would make it much harder to raise the money needed to run a citywide campaign.

Based on my projections, I needed at least $2.5 to $3 million just for the primary. To reach my goal I'd have to find upwards of 3,000 donors at $1,000 a piece, and far more if I was going to depend on smaller donors, which I fully intended to do. This was long before social media or PayPal. My efforts to grow my financial base would focus on personal solicitations, fundraisers in people's living rooms and word of mouth. There wasn't a week during this period when I didn't have four or five fundraisers somewhere in Los Angeles and an equal number of community events. I held "meet and greets" in every district in the city and garnered support from various ethnic groups and political persuasions. Although Bradley had to play by the same rules, he was the incumbent mayor and had a clear advantage. Still, thanks to my friends and supporters, and their friends, I was able to match him dollar for dollar over the next eighteen months.

It was a grueling undertaking. I found myself looking into people's eyes trying to see how many dollar signs I could count. Although I enjoyed promoting my policies, I wasn't comfortable promoting myself. Nonetheless, I hunkered down and did the best I could. Barbara, as in the past, was my most valuable political asset. As difficult as it was for me to walk into a room full of strangers, it was second nature to her. She was warm and open, and befriended people she didn't know with the ease of a knife cutting through butter.

All the while, I had a day job. I was part of the council's leadership by this point, and I had a district that was very demanding and deserving of my attention. I had two young children, too, and they also needed my time. Finally, I did need one or two moments a week just to breathe. One of my aides warned me that running for mayor of Los Angeles was the most difficult kind of campaign except for president, governor, or mayor of New York. Honestly, as I look back on this period, I don't know how I juggled all these responsibilities. I initially thought this would be my main hurdle in the race. But then the mayor who had seemed to be asleep at the switch suddenly woke up. Life got more complicated.

The Born-Again Slow-Grower

When I formed my exploratory committee, one of the key issues distinguishing me from Bradley was the city's growth and development policies. The landslide victory of Proposition U in 1986 reinforced that distinction, and the defeats of council incumbents Peggy Stevenson and Pat Russell were widely seen as canaries in the coal mine for the impending mayor's race. As Tom Bradley began revving up his bid for a fifth term, he hired a new team to reinvigorate his administration and his public image. He was preparing for a hotly contested race.

The mayor's campaign advisers knew he was vulnerable, so they devised what I believed was a two-pronged strategy. First, Bradley wanted to take a bite out of my electoral base, and he thought attacking my environmental credentials was the way to achieve this. Second, his team believed they could further erode my support by sowing anxiety that my challenge would be racially divisive, especially among liberal and Jewish voters.

We saw the first signs of his strategy to attack my environmental credentials when Proposition U was on the verge of approval. I had launched a plan to remedy lingering issues surrounding the development of the controversial Westside Pavilion shopping center that had opened in 1984 at Pico and Westwood Boulevards, just west of Century City. This was a mega-project that had been built "by right," in strict compliance with the existing zoning. Another developer had purchased property across the street from the Pavilion, where he wanted to build a new 300,000-square-foot retail center. This was the last thing the corner needed, given the impact the Pavilion already had on traffic and parking in the immediate area.

So, I approached Westfield, the Pavilion's owner, proposing that they purchase that property. I suggested they connect the two sides of the street with a pedestrian and vehicular bridge over Westwood Boulevard, allowing traffic to circulate within the center without clogging local streets. I also insisted that they build enough parking under the new site to make up for the shortfall created by their original development. This seemed like a Solomon-like solution to what had become a major problem. Westfield was ready to play, but the challenge was getting the neighboring developer to sell.

As it turned out, he had purchased his corner before our plans to launch Proposition U became public, and so he paid a pre-Proposition U price for the property. If approved by the voters, the new law would cut his development rights in half, making his project financially unsustainable. So both property owners realized there was a deal to be made. They negotiated for several months, and Westfield ended up owning both corners. The fat was in the fire.

Over the next eighteen months, Westfield sought city approval for the project I had proposed. The neighborhood largely supported it, realizing that we had all averted what might otherwise have been a disastrous development. Bradley's Planning Commission unanimously approved the project, but just as the City Council was preparing to give it the final nod Bradley scuttled our plans. He announced his opposition and vowed to veto the deal if the council approved it.

This was the first indication that he had any issues with my proposal. In fact, he had given every indication to Westfield that he supported it. The mayor cited the bridge as his reason, which was patently absurd. He knew that the bridge was the *raison d'etre* for the proposal in the first place. Bradley was clearly trying to put me on the defensive, and he was doing so in close collaboration with some of my district critics.

I remember my colleague, Marvin Braude, rising in a council debate to defend the bridge, saying: "It reminds me a lot of the Ponte Vecchio in Florence." I had no idea what he was talking about, and I quietly asked Joel Wachs, "What's the Ponte Vecchio?" He explained that it was a historic bridge in Florence, Italy, with quaint retail shops spanning the Arno River. The council approved my proposal, and the mayor kept his promise to veto it. His council allies saw to it that I didn't have the ten votes needed to override him, so I pulled the item from the agenda. I knew I would find a more propitious time to bring it back for a vote, and that happened the following year, when the project was finally approved with Bradley's support. I should note that, seventeen years later, Barbara and I visited Florence, and our first stop was the Ponte Vecchio. As I took in the scene,

I turned to her and said, tongue firmly in cheek, "This reminds me a lot of the Westside Pavilion."

This was one of many skirmishes the mayor and I had along the way, and it came with the territory. Some were good hits, and some were cheap shots, like the time Bradley held a press conference attacking a restaurant's permit to sell beer and wine. He scheduled it in my district on Yom Kippur, the holiest day on the Jewish calendar. He knew that I would be in the synagogue all day and would be prevented from responding in real time. So it went.

1988—The Lines of Division Grow Deeper

The second part of Bradley's strategy—sowing fear of a racially divisive campaign—fell into his team's lap on the night of Saturday January 31, 1988, in Westwood. The village, directly adjacent to the UCLA campus, had become a regional weekend attraction. Back then, its movie theaters were one of two places in Southern California where you could see a first-run film. Thousands of people flocked to this unique outdoor space. At my direction, the city banned weekend vehicular traffic in the village, transforming it into one giant and pleasant pedestrian festival. Without cars, the ambient noise level plummeted, and you could hear birds chirping and conversations taking place across the street.

In time, however, Westwood Village also began to attract opportunistic, violent street gangs. On this Saturday night, two rival gang members exchanged gunfire on Broxton Avenue in the heart of the village. One of the ricocheting bullets fatally struck Karen Toshima, a twenty-eight-year-old graphic artist, in the head. I coined a phrase for moments like this—a "there but for the grace of God it could have been me" crime. This wasn't a lover's quarrel that spun out of control; it was a random bullet that could have struck any one of us. Tragedies like this shake a community's confidence to its core, and Westwood was rocked by Karen Toshima's murder.

Elected officials have a duty at such moments to publicly express sorrow to the victim's family on behalf of the community, and to reassure the stricken residents of the adjacent neighborhoods. That's exactly what I did. I called a press conference with law enforcement officials on the following Monday to express the city's condolences and assure the public that the area was safe. This was the first crime of its kind that anyone could remember in Westwood. Since there had been no arrest in the case as the week began, the LAPD asked me to propose a financial reward leading to the apprehension and conviction of the suspect.

Of course, I obliged. No one should have expected anything less from an elected official. Then the fireworks began.

Councilmembers representing South Los Angeles questioned why a shooting in Westwood was getting special treatment. Well, it wasn't. Reward offers were commonplace in all districts, including South Los Angeles. Until now, no councilmember's request for a reward was ever questioned if it could help bring a perpetrator to justice. Now, none of that seemed to matter. The politics of race began dominating the Toshima case. Black community leaders, politicians, and clergy were up in arms. When I asked the LAPD to temporarily deploy more officers in the village on weekends, then-State Assemblywoman Maxine Waters and others who represented South Los Angeles charged that Westwood was getting special treatment and demanded higher levels of police protection for their districts as well. This was done. By now, however, it was clear that a council debate over the Westwood reward would erupt into a prolonged, racially divisive mess. So, in the interest of citywide harmony, I asked local merchants to raise funds for the reward instead, which they did. One week later the suspect was in custody.

I understood why Black leaders were upset that one murder in Westwood was getting so much attention. Back then, gang-related homicides averaged more than 400 annually in the city, most of them in communities of color. It was as though one gunshot victim in Westwood mattered while hundreds in South Los Angeles didn't. But it was precisely for this reason—that homicides in Westwood were so rare—that the media made a *cause célèbre* of the Toshima murder.

This tragedy demanded that the city come together, as we had done so many times before. But now we were divided. Police-community tensions, long-simmering institutional racism, and a high violent crime rate all converged, punctuated by a looming 1989 mayor's race. Ironically, a year later, after the passions of the mayoral contest subsided, a well-known restaurateur was murdered in a robbery, near Cedars Sinai Hospital on the Westside, adjacent to Beverly Hills. Once again, I offered a reward. This time, nobody objected.

Proposition O: Banning Coastal Oil Drilling

As the mayoral race came into sharper focus, Marvin Braude and I had some unfinished business to transact. He had spent nearly twenty years fighting Occidental Petroleum Corporation's scheme to drill next to an earthquake fault along the city's coastline. When Bradley reversed his position and approved the drilling in 1985, opponents went to court to block the project without success.

Our fortunes appeared to rise when drilling opponent Ruth Galanter defeated Oxy supporter Pat Russell in 1987. That gave our anti-drilling forces a slim 8–7 majority on the council, and we were buoyed by the prospects of finally voting to repeal the drilling project. But that would have been a pyrrhic victory. The mayor would have immediately vetoed the council action, and we didn't have the ten votes to override him.

Our options were exhausted—except for one. We could reprise our Proposition U success by appealing directly to Los Angeles voters to repeal the drilling ordinance, which they had the power to do. This wasn't a simple decision for me. On the one hand, I was gearing up for the mayor's race, and an anti-oil campaign would easily become a distraction. On the other hand, a winning campaign would kill a reckless project that threatened the Santa Monica Bay. It would further distinguish me from Bradley on the city's highest profile environmental issue. Many Angelenos remembered the 1969 Santa Barbara oil spill and they didn't want a sequel in their own backyard. Finally, a campaign against oil drilling would help me build an organization that could be folded into a mayoral campaign. So I went downstairs to Braude's second-floor City Hall office for another tuna sandwich summit.

I proposed that we launch an initiative to repeal the oil drilling ordinance. This would be a different kind of campaign than Proposition U, where we had little or no funded opposition. Occidental's chairman, Armand Hammer, had an ego too big for Mt. Rushmore, and he would spend whatever was required to defeat us. It would certainly be a David vs. Goliath struggle. "Let's do it," the normally taciturn Braude responded with enthusiasm. He turned to his Chief of Staff, Cindy Miscikowski, who had drafted the short paragraph that became Prop. U, and asked her to craft language for our new initiative. She completed the task that afternoon.

Next, we turned to the political consultants who ran the Proposition U effort, Michael Berman and Carl D 'Agostino. Both Michael and Carl were political veterans, long associated with campaigns for progressive and environmentalist Democratic candidates and officeholders. Michael got his start running Henry Waxman's first campaign for the State Assembly in 1968, and he was a computer mail guru without peer. Carl was a Democratic campaign expert and media consultant who most recently had been top aide to State Controller Ken Cory. BAD, as Berman and D'Agostino's firm came to be known, had been the most influential and effective Democratic campaign professionals in California for more than two decades. I had earlier approached Michael and Carl to run my mayor's campaign, which they were prepared to do once I pulled the trigger. But in the meantime, they were an invaluable resource on the Proposition U and

Occidental Oil campaigns. They also gave me counsel—sometimes solicited and sometimes not—on the mayoral sweepstakes. For now, however, we had an initiative to win, and they were all in.

The battle over Proposition O was an epic struggle, widely seen as a proxy for the mayor's race. Bradley's entire organization was hellbent on crushing the oil-drilling initiative. Our message was simple: it was irresponsible to drill for oil in a seismically active area as unstable as the Pacific Palisades, a stone's throw from the beaches and waters of Santa Monica Bay. This was the same argument that Tom Bradley had made in his 1973 mayoralty campaign.

City residents were generally in sync with our objective, and the Oxy campaign knew it. Their polling showed that voters, facing a simple up or down decision, would ban oil drilling in a heartbeat. So, the company hit on a different strategy. First, they qualified a competing initiative—Proposition P—that was virtually identical to ours, except that it *exempted* Oxy from the drilling ban. Then, they added a provision that would have earmarked some of the drilling royalties, if there were any, for parks, law enforcement, and public schools in low-income neighborhoods.

This was a cynical move designed to confuse and entice voters, and it made our task much more complicated. Just as important, Proposition P aimed to divide the city on racial grounds. Oxy's army of political consultants, flush with nearly a $9 million campaign war chest, descended on South and East Los Angeles. They cast the issue as one of privileged white neighborhoods putting their parochial interests ahead of parks, schools, and police funding for economically disadvantaged communities. The campaign threatened to turn ugly and fast.

Our main challenge was competing with Armand Hammer's bottomless pit of campaign money. Although we could never match him dollar for dollar, we needed several million dollars to get our message across. Marvin raised some money, but the lion's share came from Assemblyman Gray Davis, Congressman Mel Levine, and me. We transferred a sizable chunk of our campaign funds to the Proposition O campaign, raised the rest from contributors, and spent close to $3 million. What we lacked in funding we made up in community support and celebrities, including James Garner, Ted Danson, Chevy Chase, and Beau Bridges. They were all great spokesmen and validators for the cause.

Then, in July, tragedy struck. An Oxy oil rig in the North Sea blew up, killing 166 workers. It was the worst drilling disaster in history. Triggered by a gas leak, it could have happened at any oil rig, at any time. This is precisely what we were trying to prevent next to Santa Monica Bay. We turned to popular actor James Garner, whose wife, Lois, was one of the leading opponents of the drilling project, and asked him to film a TV ad. It proved to be the turning point of the contest. As the spot began, a fireball appeared on the screen and a voice said: "On July 5, 1988, Occidental Oil's Piper rig in the North Sea blew up, killing 166 people." Then the camera pivoted to Garner, sitting on a jetty at Will Rogers Beach across from the proposed drilling site. In a folksy but serious voice, he pointed to the proposed drill site and said: "I come from Oklahoma. Oil wells blow up there all the time. Now Occidental wants to put an oil rig right there, next to an earthquake fault. Vote No on P, Yes on O." Los Angeles residents took note.

The BAD Memos

The campaign seemed to be turning in our favor. But barely a month after the oil rig tragedy, I was shocked by a late afternoon call from a *Los Angeles Times* reporter. He wanted my reaction to two memos which had been prepared for me months earlier by BAD campaigns. The documents, which had been stolen and leaked to the newspaper, laid out Michael Berman's assessment of the upcoming mayor's race. I had not yet declared my candidacy, hired the firm, or solicited this analysis. But Michael took it upon himself to give me a brash, provocative, and cynical view of where he thought I stood. Michael was always blunt, and so were his memos.

In this case, most of his comments were brutally critical of me. I was spending too much time at City Hall. There was no need for me to attend every City Council meeting. I should spend all my time raising money, because "Jewish wealth in Los Angeles is endless." I should smile more, and so forth. He also wrote that I had fifty IQ points on Bradley and called environmentalists "tree huggers." For those who knew Michael, this was simply his way of getting the reader's attention.

When the memos became public, Bradley's campaign shifted into overdrive. They said the BAD comments were racist, as were the authors of the memos. Meanwhile, the *Times* had a field day with the story, as did radio and television news outlets. It dominated coverage for five consecutive days. I denounced the memos immediately, pointing out that they were unsolicited and certainly did not reflect my views. The comment about IQ's was ridiculous and insulting. But these were Michael's words, not mine.

I called Bradley, who was in Honolulu, to apologize, and to personally assure him the memos did *not* reflect my views of him. He was gracious and thanked me for the call. Minutes later, his office released a press release disclosing my phone call and calling on me to fire BAD from my campaign, even though

I hadn't hired them yet. To calm the furor, I said that they were no longer under consideration.

The following day, the Bradley team convened a meeting of prominent Jewish and Black leaders. They called on me and Bradley to sign a pledge not to run a racially divisive campaign. I refused to sign the document they drafted because it characterized Berman and D'Agostino as racists, which was patently untrue. How did they square this with the fact that BAD had done yeoman campaign work for Tom Bradley over the years—advising him on strategy, giving him caustic memos, and writing his campaign literature?

I decided to issue my own statement, saying: "I share in the desire that all political campaigns be conducted without regard to race or religion. In my more than thirteen years in public life I have fought hard to ensure that the conduct of political campaigns as well as the conduct of the affairs of government remain on a high moral and ethical plane and I will continue to do so."

As the controversy continued, I was heartened that Michael Jackson, the popular KABC radio talk-show host, blistered Bradley's chief of staff over his charge of racism in a live interview, one of several shows he devoted to the furor. At one point, Jackson read a line from the BAD memos describing the mayor's achievements: "Tom Bradley is the respected, admired leader of Los Angeles who quietly rebuilt downtown, the airport, brought the Olympics to Los Angeles, and led our city to a position of greatness." Jackson then asked, "This is racism?" Meanwhile, some of Los Angeles' most respected Black elected leaders vouched for Berman and D'Agostino on Jackson's broadcast, saying they had received equally irreverent memos from the firm during their own campaigns. Congressmen Mervyn Dymally and Julian Dixon and Assemblywoman Gwen Moore said they knew both men well, and that neither was racist.

Nevertheless, the memos threatened to capsize my nascent mayoral bid. In truth, these were the worst days of my political career. They can best be described by the feeling I had when I walked into Junior's Deli in Westwood for a breakfast meeting on the morning the Times broke the story. It seemed like every patron was reading the paper with my name plastered in a headline on the front page. I had the biggest pit in my stomach for days.

Finally, on the fourth day of the controversy, the other shoe dropped. The mayor's allies called a press conference demanding that Braude and I fire BAD from the Proposition O campaign. To do so at this critical juncture would have sunk the measure. I was so punch drunk from the week's events that I didn't know how to respond. Besides, this wasn't my decision alone to make, as Marvin Braude was a full partner in this enterprise. So, I went down to his office to advise him of what was happening.

"Marvin, I can't make an intelligent decision in my current state of mind," I said. "What do you want to do?" Braude was not a man prone to loud outbursts or impulsive decisions, and he was silent for a good minute. His analytical and contemplative demeanor sometimes drove me nuts. Then he turned to me and said: "Fuck 'em. We're not going to fire our consultants." I was relieved.

Election Night and Beyond

When the dust settled, Proposition O won a narrow 52–48 victory. Oxy's counter-measure, Proposition P, was trounced 65–35. Although we lost in South and East Los Angeles, the higher turnout in the Westside and Democratic parts of the San Fernando Valley pushed us over the top. It was a huge win for the environment, and a humiliating setback for Occidental Petroleum, Tom Bradley, and the City Council majority that approved the drilling. It also marked the second time in as many years that Los Angeles voters went over the heads of their elected representatives to approve an initiative that Braude and I put on the ballot.

Not surprisingly, pundits immediately focused on what it all meant for the 1989 mayor's race. Some observers suggested that any lingering fallout from the BAD memos had dissipated and wouldn't damage my mayoral campaign. I singled out Michael and Carl for praise during my remarks at the Prop O victory party, saying we were fortunate to have political consultants in our city who were in business to advance a genuine environmental agenda, instead of corporate priorities.

Looking back, I increasingly felt that I had been stampeded into severing my potential mayoral campaign ties with Michael and Carl, and this didn't feel right to me. True, their caustic and cynical style wasn't mine, and their words and metaphors were not part of my vocabulary. But the smoothly timed, well-orchestrated campaign against them and me shouldn't have been rewarded. The attack on BAD as racists was not just over the top, it was also pernicious.

When I went home after the victory celebration, I told Barbara that I had been reassessing my decision not to hire the BAD consultants. What did she think? "Why are you agonizing?" she answered. "They were wrongly demonized, and you shouldn't cave to the Bradley camp." This was politics pure and simple, she said. I never went wrong trusting Barbara's instincts or judgment. I decided to hire BAD as originally planned and let the chips fall where they may.

But first I had to make a fateful decision—to run or not. I had spent eighteen months laying the groundwork for a mayoral race and raised an impressive campaign war chest. I had traveled to every corner of the city in search of support. I was proud that, during more than thirteen years on the council, I had championed initiatives for a more livable Los Angeles, fighting for constitutional policing, civil liberties, and human rights. I helped keep the city solvent, and I had gained a reputation as a fiscally responsible progressive. As the deadline for a decision approached, however, I wondered if any of this had registered with city voters.

It wasn't an academic question, since I would have to give up my council seat to run. For all his setbacks, Bradley had politically revived himself in the previous eighteen months. He retained most of his personal popularity and was still widely respected. I could feel this in my gut, and I wanted to know exactly where I stood before crossing the bridge of no return. So, in mid-December I hired Arnie Steinberg, a capable pollster and Fairfax High alum, to survey city voters about a race pitting me against Bradley.

The results were extremely discouraging. If I ran, the survey concluded, Bradley would beat me 62 percent to 18 percent. Michael Berman, who didn't believe in polls, cautioned that a poll was just a snapshot in time, and it didn't reflect an issues-driven campaign in which I would go head-to-head with the mayor. He was right, but this snapshot showed I hadn't made enough progress to justify risking it all. Moreover, my decision wasn't going to be driven by numbers alone. If I entered the race, I had every reason to be concerned that it would turn racially divisive. Regardless of my aversion to that kind of a campaign, it would be thrust on me from the other side, as it already had been by the BAD memos, the Oxy campaign, and the Toshima murder.

It came down to a simple question: Would I rather remain a city councilman or be out of office? Likely, that was the choice I was making. I agonized over this through the holidays and discussed it at length with Barbara. As always, she said she would support whatever I decided to do. I went back and forth with Alisa, my Chief of Staff. On January 2, 1989, I went to the Michigan-USC Rose Bowl game with Ann Hollister, a trusted political confidante with a keen, analytical mind. Ann had worked in my council office, helped run the Proposition O campaign, and would have held a top job in my mayoral campaign. We talked it over for the umpteenth time, and at halftime I privately decided not to run. When I got home, I stood in my kitchen with Ann and Barbara and told them of my decision. I called Alisa to let her know, as well.

The about-face was emotionally wrenching, and it also posed an immense logistical challenge. My campaign had been wired to raise funds, deploy volunteers, produce TV spots, and send out campaign mailers. It was not designed to decommission itself on the eve of its launch. I had to immediately notify my team, my supporters, my staff, and the public. I successfully kept everything under wraps for four days, until a Friday January 5 press conference at City Hall, where I stood with Barbara and announced my decision.

Only a handful of my friends and supporters were privy to my thinking or to the poll I commissioned. When they heard my decision, many were deeply disappointed, and some were angry. I couldn't blame them. At the same time, I had to shift gears and run for re-election in my district. Several candidates had been preparing to run in anticipation of my vacating the seat, and they, too, were caught off guard. All but three of them deferred to me and suspended their campaigns when I filed for re-election.

Finally, as the law required, I had to return the lion's share of the $1.5 million I had raised for the mayoral contest. I vividly remember the scene at our campaign office with my fundraising staff on the floor, trying to match up thousands of thank you letters, envelopes, and refund checks. We were able to return 71 percent of each contribution we received, and many of my supporters were pleasantly surprised. Tom Jones, the former Chairman of Northrop Aircraft Corporation and a constituent, wrote: "Dear Zev. I have written checks to presidents, governors, senators, and mayors, and I have never received a penny back from any of them. Your check is so rare that I'm tempted to frame it and hang it up in my office."

As gut-wrenching as these last days were, the experience of this truncated campaign was rewarding. I met people in every community across the city, and many of them remain my friends to this day. I got to know Los Angeles in a more intimate and profound way than I would have otherwise. Crisscrossing the city for two years in search of support was a humbling but exhilarating experience for which I will always be grateful.

The loneliest day of my political life was the Saturday after my announcement. After years of a Grand Central Station-type tumult in our house, the phone didn't ring. Barbara was out with the kids, and I was alone with my thoughts. Then I got a call from Ginny Kruger, my trusted, long-time land use deputy. "Hi Zev," she said. "Larry and I were just thinking about you and wondering if you and Barbara would like to join us for dinner tonight."

The definition of a lonely, elected official is one who has nothing scheduled on a Saturday night—and my calendar that evening was as clear as an Alpine lake. I was thankful for the call and immediately accepted the invitation. There have been many acts of loving kindness shared with me and Barbara over the years, but this is one I'll never forget. When your fortunes are on the rise there is no shortage of people anxious to get on your calendar. When things aren't going so well, you find out who your friends are, and you hold them close. Ginny had the toughest job in my office, dealing with neighborhood groups and developers who were often at each other's throats, as well as hers. She performed the job with equanimity and grace, and it was those qualities that moved her to call me that morning.

People have asked me in the years since if I had any regrets in my public service career. Usually that's code for whether I regret my decision not to run for mayor in 1989. I do regret that I let down many of the people who supported and believed in me. They had backed me against an incumbent mayor who now would likely cruise to re-election, and they would be on the outside looking in. But I don't have any second thoughts about my decision. It was based on solid information I had available to me at the time, and it was the right decision for me and maybe for the city. The ensuing years have validated that. For those who continue to speculate on what might have been—well, that's pure speculation. I had to make a "go or no go" decision in early January, and I didn't have the benefit of hindsight. If there was a silver lining, it's that I would live to fight another day.

The 1989 Election We Didn't Expect

I didn't have much time for introspection in early January of 1989, because my campaign for re-election to the City Council took center stage. When it was all over, I won comfortably with 63 percent of the vote. The mayor drew what seemed to be only token opposition from Councilmember Nate Holden, who represented the mayor's old 10th district, and Baxter Ward, a former county supervisor and local television anchorman turned gadfly. The ensuing campaign proved the adage that in politics you've got to prepare for everything—especially the unexpected.

While the *Los Angeles Times* prepared to cover a ho-hum mayoral race, the *Herald Examiner*, its upstart rival, decided to play the role of the mayor's loyal opposition. Their reporters dug deep into his conduct in office, and they came up with a blockbuster that rocked his campaign. It turned out that Bradley had been paid $18,000 as an adviser to Far East Bank in 1988. In that capacity, it was alleged that he had instructed the City Treasurer to deposit $2 million dollars of city funds in that bank. If the allegation were true, it would be an actionable conflict of interest.

The smoking gun came in the form of City Treasurer Leonard Rittenberg's handwritten entry on the ledger recording the deposit. In the margin, in his handwriting, was the notation, "per the mayor." Although the note had been whited out, it was still legible when held up to a light. Rittenberg claimed that the mayor had never directed him to make the deposit, but he couldn't explain why he had written that note in the ledger. Bradley was now a weakened candidate, despite his denials of impropriety.

Then, on March 31, 1989, two weeks before Election Day, the *Los Angeles Times* published an investigative report that revealed Bradley was paid $24,000 annually to sit on the board of Valley Federal Savings and Loan, whose real estate subsidiary had been granted zone changes by the city on properties they owned and that financially benefited the bank. As a result of these scandals, Bradley barely avoided a runoff with Holden on Election Day, winning only 52 percent of the vote.

What wasn't known at the time was that the *Times* story on Valley Federal had been completed in August 1988, while it was publishing the BAD memo stories. It would have been a bombshell. However, the article was held for seven months by higher ups, and was only published after the Herald Examiner began to expose the Far East Bank scandal. At the very least, the Valley Federal revelation would have raised an ethical issue for Bradley and his campaign; at worst it could have raised legal conflict of interest problems. Without a doubt, it would have put Bradley on the defensive at the very moment that my mayoral ambitions were taking on water on the front pages of the *LA Times*. There is no telling how the dynamics of the mayor's race might have changed had this story not been held. But the *New York Times* reported that the LA paper's critics, including some of its staff members, speculated that the decision might have changed the city's political history. We will never know.

I had to laugh when, two days after the election, the *Los Angeles Times* exit polls showed I would have forced Bradley into a runoff had I entered the race. "If I had wings, I could fly," I told Barbara when I read the paper that morning. I couldn't have possibly known in January that the mayor would be engulfed by scandal three months later, and that voters would punish him with such a humiliating finish. Some pundits and supporters got revved up all over again, suggesting I made a fatal political mistake and would have been mayor had I stayed in the race. This, however, was a parlor game that pundits loved to play.

The day after my re-election I was back at work in City Hall. Although the daily routine around the horseshoe seemed the same, a closer look showed that Los Angeles was undergoing profound changes. The city was now a destination for hundreds of thousands of new immigrants from around the globe fleeing political instability and repression—the same circumstances that brought my parents to America six-and-a-half decades earlier.

This demographic transformation was bringing new energy and cultural vitality to Los Angeles, but it also contributed to a growing economic divide that would come to stress the city. As new immigrant communities arrived, they brushed up against established neighborhoods that were facing their own economic challenges, and in some cases the friction would generate violent conflict. All the while, police-community tensions were growing, and they would soon reach a crescendo. A perfect storm was gathering as the city entered the 1990s, and it was about to make landfall.

Shimon Soloveichik – My maternal
grandfather, a great thinker and
visionary–a man whom I would have loved
to meet more than any other ancestor.

Volko and Miriam Yaroslavsky – My paternal grandparents, who died during
World War II. Also in the photo are my aunts Rosa and Nura.
I am named after Volko, whose Hebrew name, Zev, means "Wolf."

Minna at 3 years old, with her mother,
Leah – My mother and maternal
grandmother.

Soloveichik, Minna, and my father, David Yaroslavsky, in 1933.

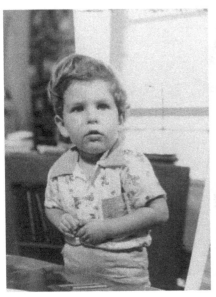

Me at four years old, in 1953.

My high school graduation picture –
Fairfax High School, 1967.

Minna Yaroslavsky – My mother,
the year before she died
at the age of 49.

My father, David Yaroslavsky, and
me on my wedding day to Barbara,
August 22, 1971.

Marching for Soviet Jews with U.S. Senator Alan Cranston and
Tom Bradley in 1969, following my return from the USSR.

Zev and Si Frumkin – my partner in the fight to free Soviet Jews. As close a friend as I ever had.

Zev and Barbara with lawn sign in 1975 –
Launching my first campaign for the Los Angeles City Council.

Zev and Mayor Tom Bradley – Being sworn into the Los Angeles City Council,
in 1975. The Mayor said, "Welcome to the establishment," and I answered:
"I may be part of the establishment, but the establishment is not part of me."

Talking with seniors about skyrocketing rents in 1978, at the Fairfax Senior Citizens Center.

Challenging LAPD chief Daryl Gates at a Los Angeles City Council Police Committee meeting in 1982.

The Pico-Robertson community meeting that I convened,
near the site where four innocent people had been randomly murdered in October, 1980.

1984 Olympics photo of the LA Coliseum – Joining with Councilman Bob Ronka
in the successful effort to protect L.A. taxpayers from runaway Olympics costs.
The result: the most profitable, privately-funded Olympics in history.

A classic example of overdevelopment encroaching on L.A.'s neighborhoods. It prompted my successful sponsorship of Proposition U in 1986, with Councilman Marvin Braude, to limit such development.

Holding an assault weapon – the City Council approved
my proposed ban on the sale of these weapons following the
fatal shooting of five children at a Stockton, California grade school in 1989.

Sammy's Camera on fire, walking distance from our Beverly-Fairfax home, during the 1992 Rodney King uprising. Unlike the 1965 Watts uprising, the fire spread well beyond South Los Angeles.

Emergency meeting in the Mayor's office two days after the 1994 Northridge earthquake. It seemed like the entire US government descended on Los Angeles (Left to right): Rep. Maxine Waters; Rodney Slater, head of the Federal Highway Administration; Rep. Norm Mineta, Chairman of the House Transportation Committee; Federico Pena, US Secretary of Transportation; Los Angeles Mayor Riordan; me; Henry Cisneros, Secretary of Housing and Urban Development; Los Angeles City Council President John Ferraro; and James Lee Witt, Director of FEMA.

My swearing in at the Los Angeles County Board of Supervisors in 1994.
A day later, Orange County declared bankruptcy.

With President Clinton on the tarmac at Santa Monica Airport in 1995 –
Announcing the historic deal to save L.A. County from fiscal collapse.

Greeting President Jiang Zemin of China in 1997 –
Only in America could an L.A.-born son of Jewish immigrants from
Ukraine meet the President of China and converse in Russian.

Justice for Janitors protest in downtown L.A.– I championed the cause of
the women and men who cleaned our work places after we went home to our families.

Completing the Orange Line in 2012 with Mayor Villaraigosa – an 18-mile, grade-separated busway traversing the San Fernando Valley. Over broad community opposition, I proposed what is now one of the most successful such projects in America.

Walt Disney Concert Hall – Frank Gehry's masterpiece, a glittering jewel and the home of the Los Angeles Philharmonic Orchestra. Photo: Adam Latham/LA Phil

Hollywood Bowl – We renovated the nation's most famous outdoor amphitheater, bringing it into the 21st century. Photo: Adam Latham/LA Phil

Conducting the LA Philharmonic in the *Star Spangled Banner* at the Hollywood Bowl – Classical music is my passion, and I had the privilege of performing with the orchestra on two occasions.

At a Board of Supervisors meeting, holding county bureaucrats accountable for the shameful record of protecting kids who were our responsibility. The stakes were too high for us to fail. (Left to right: staff members Alisa Belinkoff Katz, Lisa Mandel, Joel Sappell, and Joel Bellman).

A Los Angeles homeless encampment – One of America's greatest failures. Tens of thousands of Angelenos sleep in these ramshackle sites every night.

The Santa Monica Mountains National Recreation Area – the product of a decades-long crusade to create, expand, and protect America's largest urban national park.

My oldest granddaughter, Sadie, at the King Gillette Ranch – On my watch, we added 20,000 acres of the Santa Mountains to the public domain for all the future Sadies.

With protestors occupying the Maidan – Kyiv's main square – during the Orange Revolution, while monitoring Ukraine's historic 2004 presidential election.

Nigerian mothers carrying their children while standing in line for hours in brutal 100-degree heat, with humidity to match, to exercise their right to choose their president.

Me, Barbara, Mina, and David at my 2014 retirement ceremony at Disney Hall.

My sister, Shimona, and me. We shared a lot of happiness and heartbreaking sorrow.

My daughter and
family—Miriam
(in front), Dan, Mina &
Sadie (back row).

My son and family–
(L to R) Joshua, Katy,
Yael, Gabriel, & David.

Vacationing with Barbara
in the Dakotas in 2015,
after my retirement from
public service.

CHAPTER 13

Sudden Change

———

On a warm October afternoon in 1996, I watched the UCLA football team scrimmage at Spalding Field on campus, preparing for a game against the Cal Bears. The defensive and offensive teams were running pre-set drills when head coach Bob Toledo blew his whistle from the sidelines and shouted, "Sudden change!" There was chaos on the field. Players raced on and off, reacting to an unexpected game development, mimicking a change of possession. As I watched the scene unfold, I couldn't help but think that dealing with unexpected, destabilizing events is not limited to football games. It's part of everyday life, and that's certainly true in politics and government, where sudden change comes with the territory.

For me, the challenge was not so much the crisis itself, but how to respond to it. There were vivid examples in my early professional life—like the 1981 election of the City Council president, when Joel Wachs unexpectedly emerged as the body's leader. In an instant, City Hall's political status quo was upended. Or when my Chief of Staff reached me in Moscow to deliver stunning news: "The verdict just came down in the case you were sure we would win, and the judgment is for $3.2 million *against* the City." It happened big time when I learned that brutally candid memos written for my 1989 mayoral campaign had been stolen and leaked to the *Los Angeles Times*. In each case, it wasn't the sudden news that created the challenge as much as how I responded. Mismanaging a crisis is often worse than the crisis itself. That axiom was repeatedly affirmed throughout my career.

Nothing, however, prepared me or my colleagues for the unexpected changes that rocked Los Angeles during my last five years on the City Council, from 1990 to 1994. During this period, we grappled with two staggering crises: the 1992 civil unrest following the Rodney King verdicts and the 1994 Northridge earthquake. The city's resiliency was challenged as never before. Meanwhile, my political career was transformed by a door suddenly opening that I didn't expect. These were all adrenaline-filled moments, and I had to rise to the occasion. As British Prime Minister Benjamin Disraeli once noted, "Change is constant. Change is inevitable."

Reading the Tea Leaves

As the 1990s dawned, Los Angeles was hit by a national recession that impacted the southland more than any other part of the state. More than 500,000 non-agricultural jobs were lost statewide, nearly 85 percent of them in Southern California. Los Angeles County alone accounted for 63 percent of the state's job loss. Many of them were well-paying jobs in finance, defense, construction, and aerospace. Moreover, a decade of disinvestment in economically depressed communities by Republican administrations in Washington and Sacramento adversely impacted low and middle-income residents as well.

The downturn made a bad economic situation even worse in South Los Angeles. There, widespread unemployment increased, and the community experienced a huge exodus of manufacturing jobs. Its annual per capita income in 1990 was $7,600, some 52.6 percent lower than the countywide average, and unemployment among Black youths neared 24 percent. The area also suffered from a chronic shortage of commercial amenities, including supermarkets, drug stores, and department stores—the kind of businesses that most other communities took for granted. Although mom-and-pop outlets were disappearing across the southland, most South Los Angeles residents still depended on them, many of which were owned by Korean immigrant families. Most of the owners lived outside the area and employed few locals.

If this was the extent of the area's problems, it would have been a devastating picture. But South Los Angeles continued to be plagued by ugly tensions between residents and the LAPD, some twenty-six years after the Watts uprising in 1965. Many in the community viewed the police as a racially biased, occupying military force. In 1988, scores of officers searching for drugs and weapons virtually destroyed an apartment building at the corner of 39th Street and Dalton Ave. in South Los Angeles. They smashed furniture, kitchens, and bathrooms; punched holes in walls, destroyed toilets and wrote "LAPD Rules" graffiti on the walls. They rounded up dozens of residents, none of whom were ever convicted of a crime. What did they have to show for it? A few ounces of marijuana and less than an ounce of cocaine. Residents were furious at the appalling destruction, but even angrier when three officers charged with misdemeanor vandalism were acquitted.

These grievances continued to mount, fueled by traumatic memories of the police chokehold, arbitrary traffic stops, and the LAPD's use of excessive force, particularly against people of color. For many observers it was just a matter of time before South Los Angeles erupted. Then two seemingly unconnected events sparked an unprecedented social explosion.

Lighting the Fuse: Latasha Harlins

On a damp Saturday morning in March 1991, a fifteen-year-old Black girl named Latasha Harlins walked into Empire Liquor, a mom-and-pop store at the corner of Figueroa and 91st Street in South Los Angeles. She intended to buy a $1.79 container of orange juice. Harlins stuffed it into her backpack, with the top protruding, and walked to the counter with two dollars in her hand. Soon Ja Du, 51, the Korean-born clerk working in the store, suspected that the girl was going to steal the juice. Two eyewitnesses said Du cursed at Harlins, who insisted she was planning to pay for the drink. What happened next was tragic. Du reached across the counter and grabbed Harlins by her sweater, trying to pull the bottle out of her backpack. She fought back, punching Du in the face, causing her to fall to the floor. The owner got up and hurled a stool at Harlins and missed, falling to the floor again. Getting up a second time she drew a gun from under the counter and aimed it at the teenager. Harlins immediately placed the bottle of juice on the counter, turned her back and began walking away. But Du—holding the gun with two hands—fired at Harlins, who was three feet away, killing her with a shot to the back of the head. The dollar bills were still clutched in her hand as she lay dead on the floor.

Although the exact sequence of events, and the motivations of Du and Harlins, would be contested in a court of law, the underlying facts were beyond dispute. A security camera in the store had captured the incident, and the shocking events leading to Harlin's death were crystal clear. As news of the shooting spread, residents in the predominantly Black community were infuriated. In response, Korean shopkeepers said Du had ample reason to suspect criminal intent that day, given prior crimes committed against her family's store and other store owners. It was the latest manifestation of the racial and cultural gulf between the Black and Korean communities. Within days, a wave of demonstrations and boycotts aimed at Korean store owners spread across South Los Angeles. Mayor Tom Bradley and other city leaders pleaded for calm.

A jury convicted Du of voluntary manslaughter months later, and the verdict carried a maximum sentence of sixteen years in prison. But, in a decision that stunned the Black community and countless other Los Angeles residents, newly appointed Judge Joyce Karlin nullified the verdict. She said Du's actions, although violent, were driven by reasonable fears. "Did Mrs. Du react inappropriately?" she asked. "Absolutely. But was that reaction understandable? I think that it was." The judge said Du would suffer for her actions for the rest of her life and sentenced her to probation for five years, ordered her to do 400 hours of community service, and fined her $500. Apart from that, she was free to go.

The decision triggered a citywide uproar as a coalition of political, religious and community leaders demanded justice. To no avail.

Latasha Harlins' death would not be forgotten, and many believed that her killing and Karlin's verdict were principal contributing factors to the five days of unrest that ripped the city apart the following year. Her story was immortalized in pop culture by Tupac Shakur, who echoed community outrage and disbelief in his song *Hell Razor*, asking why Harlins had to die.

Texts, Lies, and Videotape

If the security camera recording of Harlin's death stunned the city, a home video shot thirteen days earlier in Lakeview Terrace, in the northeast San Fernando Valley, brought racial tensions in Los Angeles to a boiling point. Shortly after midnight on March 3, 1991, California Highway Patrol (CHP) officers attempted to stop a car speeding west on the Foothill Freeway in the northern part of the San Fernando Valley. The driver, a Black man, refused, and the incident quickly escalated into a high-speed pursuit. The CHP was soon joined in pursuit by several LAPD patrol cars and a department helicopter. They finally brought the vehicle to a stop in Lakeview Terrace, ordering two passengers and the driver to get out of the car and onto the ground. The driver's name was Rodney King.

His two passengers obeyed, but King initially refused to leave his car. When he finally complied, he was belligerent, and a CHP officer drew her gun. Ranking LAPD officer Stacey Koon then said that he and three of his officers, all white, would take over the arrest. Koon told his officers to subdue and handcuff King with a "swarm" tactic, in which they'd grab the suspect and overwhelm him with force. When King resisted, Koon twice directed the officers to Taser him, but King continued to stand. At one point he rushed the officers, leading them to wrongly conclude that he was under the influence of PCP. At that point, the officers began beating King with their batons, ultimately striking him fifty-six times, even after he had been pinned to the ground and ceased to offer any resistance. Medical evidence later indicated that he had fractures on his face, forehead lacerations, a fractured fibula, a broken cheekbone, and multiple bruises. Bound by handcuffs and cord cuffs, he was placed in an ambulance and taken to a nearby hospital.

King's later complaints that he had been beaten savagely and unnecessarily might have fallen on deaf ears by a police department that was known to cover up or minimize allegations of excessive force. True to form, the police report filed on the incident sought to justify the forceful response. The report had zero credibility, however, because of one extraordinary fact: Los Angeles resident George Holliday, who lived across the street, had made a home video of the incident. He offered the tape to the LAPD, but officers there were not initially interested in viewing it. He then gave it to television station KTLA, which aired the video. Holliday's footage went viral, sparking an uproar in Los Angeles and around the world.

The shocking tape—minus the opening thirteen seconds, which the television station cut because the footage was blurry—appeared to be an unambiguous portrait of police brutality. Reaction was swift, with nearly unanimous condemnation across the board. Even Police Chief Daryl Gates distanced himself from the four officers who arrested King, calling their actions a violation of accepted policy. Amid the growing controversy, charges against King were dropped and the District Attorney moved to indict officers Laurence Powell, Theodore Briseno, Stacy Koon, and Timothy Wind.

My heart sank as I watched the tape for the first time. For all the efforts that the Bradley administration, the City Council, and I had made to address excessive use of force, is this all we had accomplished? It felt like we had made no progress at all. The beating was a violation of King's constitutional rights, and the tape was an embarrassment to the city. I began to question whether *anything* could be done to transform the LAPD. Then things got worse.

Gates and other LAPD officials hoped to classify the incident as an isolated case of excessive force, but that became impossible when the department was hit with more unwelcome news. Since 1983, patrol officers routinely texted each other in their cars via Mobile Digital Terminals (MDT's). Detectives investigating the King beating checked out the messages sent by the four officers that night and came across jaw-dropping language. Less than an hour before King was stopped, Officer Powell had exchanged texts with Officer Corina Smith about a narcotics arrest she had made earlier in the Black community. Powell messaged her: "Sounds almost as exciting as our last call. It was right out of *Gorillas in the Mist*," referring to the title of a popular movie of the time.

When he read the message, Gates understood that Powell was comparing Black people to gorillas. The Chief immediately telephoned Mayor Bradley and members of the Police Commission to tell them about the message. The LAPD released the transcripts on March 18, three days after the officers were indicted. Soon after the messages were disclosed, Gates appeared before the City Council. His disturbing response to a point I made put the widening gulf between the LAPD and the public on full display:

ZEV: All of us have been stunned by what has happened, and I can't imagine that the chief or anybody else in the city would condone the kind of conversation that took place in Foothill Division that night. Blacks are not animals...they're not gorillas any more than any of us are. They're human beings. The first way to open the door to brutalizing people is to cheapen their worth as human beings. And when I read the transcripts of the conversation I was appalled. The ability to freely converse in racist terminology suggests a level of tolerance for that kind of discussion that is unacceptable by any standard of decency.

GATES: This is a department that this council has supported over and over again. This is a department that has supported you. Each of you. I will just tell you this: If you don't speak out on behalf of the men and women of the LAPD, if you don't do that at this crucial moment in our history, you'll have a department that is not going to be the kind of department that you want, the kind of department that people deserve.

As he had been so many times before, Gates was tone deaf—not only to how his comments landed in City Hall, but how they were received in the Black community and beyond. His attitude fueled demands that he resign. Few legal minds believed the city had a legal basis to fire him, because under the City Charter, Gates enjoyed virtual lifetime tenure. He could only be removed for cause, a high legal bar. The chief refused to even consider resignation.

The tide turned when Bradley appointed Warren Christopher, a prominent Los Angeles attorney, to head a commission examining the police department's culture and governance structure. Christopher, who would be appointed Secretary of State in President Bill Clinton's first administration less than two years hence, had a mandate to propose reforms. When the commission's report came out later in 1991, its central recommendation struck a nerve: The police chief needed to be accountable to the mayor, the police commission, and the public; and he or she should be limited to a maximum of two five-year terms. Bradley, pointedly referring to Gates, warned that no one should stand in the way of change. Soon afterwards the council put the reforms on the June 1992 ballot as Charter Amendment "F." The goal was to transform the LAPD from an insular police force into a department that partnered with and looked like the communities it served. Gates rightly saw it as a thumbs down on his job performance by the city's elite, but he was not about to throw in the towel.

Over the next few months he danced around the question of whether he would, or wouldn't, step down. At one point he said he planned to retire the following year. Later, he indicated he would only retire if Charter Amendment F passed. It was obvious that Gates could only be eased out of office with careful, backroom diplomacy, and those of us dealing with the issue realized that Council President John Ferraro was best positioned to convey such a message. He and Gates went back a long way, and John was one of the few political leaders from whom the Chief would take advice. I went up to Ferraro's office and encouraged him to try and quietly convince Gates to step down. In the ensuing weeks, John worked his magic with the help of Councilman Joel Wachs, often a department ally. They told the Chief that he should go out on his own terms and that he should do it sooner rather than later. It was time to leave with his dignity, such as it was, intact.

By April 1992, the expectation was that Gates would honor his pledge to step down. The trial of the four LAPD officers was nearing a conclusion and the case against them seemed airtight. The trial had been moved to Simi Valley in Ventura County, a mostly white and more conservative part of Southern California. Even so, millions of Angelenos, myself included, believed that the largely white jury would convict some, if not all the officers. The videotape provided incontrovertible evidence of officer brutality. A man on the ground had been beaten like an animal, and it didn't matter what he had done earlier in his life (King had a criminal record) or that he had initially rushed police officers before he was subdued.

Florence and Normandie

There were growing signs, however, that something was amiss in the courtroom. When three days passed without a verdict, some speculated that jurors had been swayed by the officers' argument that they were simply following department policy. Indeed, jurors later said the videotaped evidence did not by itself convince them that the officers were guilty. They concluded that the early, blurry portion of the footage—which most television viewers never saw—showed King charging at the officers, indicating they had a reasonable fear that he may have been on PCP, thus posing a serious threat to them. Others who saw the early portion of the footage had a different view, saying it showed King trying to flee the officers. However, what was indisputable to any reasonable observer was that the officers continued to beat King long after he ceased to resist.

When the verdicts were read at 3 p.m. on April 29, each of the officers was acquitted, although the jury hung on one count against Officer Powell. The city and the nation were stunned. No one would have predicted a complete prosecutorial shutout. No way! This view was widely held within city government, including in the LAPD, and it was a major contributing factor to their lack of preparedness once the verdicts were announced. The fact that Mayor Bradley and Chief Gates had not had a substantive conversation in more than a year also contributed to a complete system breakdown. The shock and betrayal were most viscerally felt in Los Angeles' Black community.

In the immediate aftermath, Mayor Bradley attended what was billed as a unity meeting to call for community peace at the First African Methodist Episcopal Church in the Crenshaw community in South Los Angeles. Rev. Cecil Murray was one of the most respected clergymen in the city, and his influential, politically engaged congregation was a familiar gathering place for political and community leaders. Bradley asked a cross section of the city's leaders to attend that evening, including me. When I arrived, I parked a few blocks away near Western Ave and Adams Blvd. A large crowd was gathered inside, and I was escorted to the stage where the elected officials were assembled. Although Bradley condemned the verdict, in my view he delivered an eloquent and tempered call for peace and unity. His critics saw it differently and blamed him for stoking tensions and contributing to the chaos that was developing outside as he spoke. I believed then and I believe now that his remarks struck an appropriate balance, given what happened in Simi Valley.

During the convocation, John North, a KABC Channel 7 reporter, asked me to come down from the stage for a live interview. While we were waiting to get the signal from the studio, I noticed a television monitor on the floor airing video of unrest in South Los Angeles. There were scenes of fires, looting and unruly crowds. "Why are you showing footage of the '65 Watts riots?" I asked North. He shot back: "That's not 1965; that's a live shot from our helicopter!" I was floored. Between the time I had arrived at First AME and this interview, a span of maybe an hour, the city had literally gone up in flames, and the uprising was just getting started. Most of us, including Bradley, had no idea what was unfolding just blocks away from the church.

The city was woefully unprepared. Political leaders were caught by surprise, and the LAPD had made only minimal contingency plans for this eventuality. There was no coherent strategy, a failure to deploy enough officers to quell spreading violence, and a failure to communicate with other law enforcement agencies. It was a collapse of responsibility across the board.

Bradley and Gates may have despised each other, but now their personal animus had put the entire city at risk. The flashpoint was the intersection of Florence and Normandie in South Los Angeles, where furious crowds were attacking innocent pedestrians and motorists, looting stores, and torching buildings. The spectacle was captured on live television, most notably the tragic attack on Reginald Denny, a white trucker who just happened to be driving through the wrong intersection at the wrong time. A group of thugs pulled him from his cab and savagely beat him within an inch of his life. The violence was appalling, but even worse was the fact that the LAPD was nowhere in sight. Minutes earlier, fearing that his men might be overwhelmed by hostile crowds and forced to open fire, the command officer in charge of the scene pulled his troops from the intersection. He left the area completely unprotected. It was a rout, and this time the LAPD was on the run.

If panicky residents and TV viewers wondered where the chief was when the violence erupted, the answer would have infuriated them. He was eighteen miles and worlds away from South Los Angeles. Ironically, Gates was in the affluent Brentwood neighborhood of West Los Angeles, raising funds to defeat Charter Amendment F, the measure enshrining the Christopher Commission reforms.

In the aftermath of the riots, another blue-ribbon panel led by former CIA and FBI director William Webster and former Newark Police Chief Hubert Williams, issued a scathing report on the department's lack of preparation for the Rodney King verdicts. "The city's standing emergency 'plan' was so general and unspecific, untested, unfamiliar to those who were later called upon to carry it out, and in large part nonresponsive to the nature of the civil disturbance that had occurred, that it proved to be essentially useless," the report concluded. As UCLA basketball coach John Wooden would often tell his players, "Failing to prepare is preparing to fail." And that is exactly what we had that night—a failure.

My experiences during those five days of rioting, death and destruction reinforced this conclusion. Minutes after the meeting at First AME Church ended, I began walking back to my car. Herb Wesson, then an aide to Councilman Nate Holden, rushed up to me and asked where I was going. When I told him that I was heading to my car, he said: "Councilman, you can't go out there by yourself."

I soon found out why. As I was escorted by several church deacons, I saw a neighborhood out of control. My car was unrecognizable when I reached it. Every window was smashed, and the interior had been stripped. Wesson arranged for me to get a ride home, and that's how the first night of the uprising ended for me.

The next day the city delivered a loaner car to my house, and I drove to City Hall for a briefing on the rapidly spreading unrest. A few hours later I got an urgent phone call—the kind you never forget. A neighbor called to tell me that Sammy's Camera Shop was on fire around the corner from our house, and that Barbara was in the middle of Beverly Boulevard directing traffic. I didn't doubt the story for a second, because it was just like her to take charge when chaos reigned. She helped keep traffic moving while a human chain aimed a heavy fire hose at the flames. It was an only-in-LA moment, with Orthodox Jews, Black people, Latinos, and Koreans fighting the fire in unison. About an hour after I arrived, a caravan of a half dozen police cars finally showed up, with shotguns protruding from the windows. Better late than never.

That night I went to the city's Emergency Operations Center, buried four stories under the City Hall East building, where the LAPD was holding its nightly staff briefing. Gates was sitting at the front of the room with his top commanders, and he looked visibly depressed, slumped with his head in his hands, staring vacuously into space. He didn't say a word as Deputy Chief Glenn Levant chaired the meeting.

At that moment, the department was wrestling with the problem of how to get food and gasoline to their officers in the riot zones. Neither was available in South Los Angeles because no one was open for business. The chief looked like a deer caught in the headlights, and I couldn't believe what I was watching. Finally, I leaned over to the mayor's aide, Anton Calleia, and whispered: "Why don't they have the officers drive across the LA River where businesses are still open, buy out the McDonalds outlets, refuel their cars at area gas stations, and bring back the receipts? We'll reimburse them when this whole mess is over." He passed the suggestion up to the dais. Problem solved.

All the while violence was spreading across the city. This was unlike the Watts uprising which was largely confined to South Los Angeles. At the next day's emergency City Council meeting, I was getting reports of fires and looting in Hollywood, Pico-Fairfax in mid-city, and even in the affluent Westwood community adjacent to UCLA. I walked over to Gates, who was seated at the witness table in the center of the Council chamber, and I privately suggested that he declare a dusk to dawn curfew. The Chief dismissed the idea out of hand. "If I do that, all of the restaurateurs in the city will go crazy," he said. I was incredulous. "Daryl, *no one* is going out to dinner in LA tonight," I replied. "You should impose a curfew until you can shut this chaos down." Later that day, Gates imposed the curfew. It struck me that things had reached a perilous state when someone like me was making tactical security recommendations to LAPD's police chief.

The rest of the story is well known. The National Guard, along with the LAPD, the County Sheriff's Department, and the California Highway Patrol, restored the peace after six days. The final toll was chilling. Fifty-eight people were dead, more than 2,500 were injured and 16,000 were arrested. More than 1,000 buildings had been destroyed, many of them owned by Korean merchants, resulting in more than $1 billion in damage. It was the deadliest and costliest civil unrest in American history.

In the years that followed, the city considered a flurry of ideas, programs, and strategies to prevent another societal breakdown of this magnitude. One of 1992's legacies that rose from the ashes was the unprecedented effort to reform the Los Angeles Police Department. However, after more than a quarter century, race relations and economic justice in Los Angeles remain a work in progress.

The End of an Era

Los Angeles would now face a new future, with new leaders. Voters overwhelmingly approved Charter Amendment F in 1992, ensuring that future chiefs of police would never again have unlimited tenure. Gates' successors would be held accountable for their job performance. Shocked and humiliated by his failure to lead, the Chief retired after fourteen years in the top job. Tom Bradley, clearly spent after five terms in office, decided not to seek a sixth.

His final term tainted his reputation, an unfortunate ending to a long and history-making career. Indeed, no mayor in the history of Los Angeles was more consequential than Tom Bradley. In the end, I considered it a privilege to serve with him. He opened City Hall to citizens who reflected the diversity of Los Angeles, appointing women and people of color to boards and commissions that historically were comprised of mostly white males. He could walk a mile in the shoes of every community in this city and felt at home in each of them. He presided over a remarkable transformation of America's second largest city, launching its first modern rail transit system. And, of course, any evaluation of Bradley would be incomplete without giving him the credit he is due for the 1984 Summer Olympics.

During the waning days of his administration, he initiated the implementation of the Christopher Commission recommendations, and he hired Willie Williams, the former head of the Philadelphia Police Department, to be the LAPD's first Black chief, replacing Gates. Although the mayor attempted to rebuild a physically and psychologically ravaged city as he was preparing to leave office, that task would largely be left to his successors.

Despite our rocky start in 1975, we became reliable allies. We collaborated to solve budgetary crises, correct law enforcement abuses, strategize on labor negotiations and partnered on a lengthy list of legislative initiatives. When we had differences neither of us let that get in the way of our relationship except, of course, during the eighteen months when we were on an electoral collision course. What I valued most about him as a politician is that when he gave me his word, I could bank on it. I reciprocated. This remains a rare quality among too many elected officials.

After the uprising, Rodney King filed a civil lawsuit seeking $10 million in damages from the city. The City Attorney, James Hahn, strongly recommended we settle with King for nearly $6 million. But the City Council was badly divided on the amount he should receive, some advocating as little as $1.25 million and some as much as $6 million. As Chairman of the Finance Committee, I was in the hot seat. I realized that this question could reopen old wounds, and that was the last thing the city needed. So I recommended that the case go to trial and let a jury decide. My colleagues overwhelmingly agreed. King won a $3.8 million judgment against the city. The United States Department of Justice subsequently filed separate criminal charges against the four officers. Two were found guilty of violating King's civil rights and sentenced to thirty months in federal prison.

Two days after the unrest ended, I was in the audience as Mikhail Gorbachev, former leader of the Soviet Union, addressed a luncheon of business and civic leaders on the top floor of the ARCO Towers downtown. When he took a few questions, someone asked his thoughts about what had just happened in Los Angeles. As he spoke, with a panoramic vista of the city behind him, we could still see smoke billowing from smoldering fires in various parts of the city. Gorbachev said the world was becoming a more complicated place, with racial and ethnic tensions spreading around the globe. "What you've experienced here," Gorbachev added presciently, "is only a sign of things to come."

Less than five years later the LAPD was rocked by a new scandal, inflaming community tensions once again. News reports and internal investigations revealed that the anti-gang unit in one of the department's divisions was a rat's nest of police abuse. Rampart Division, west of downtown, was in large part comprised of poor Central American immigrants, and it was ground zero for this law enforcement meltdown. More than seventy officers were initially targeted in a massive investigation that found police officers engaged in drug dealing, excessive use of force (including unprovoked shootings and beatings), a bank robbery, collaboration with criminal gangs, and the planting of false evidence on innocent community residents. The cover up that followed only added insult to injury.

The Rampart scandal led to the reversal of 106 prior criminal convictions and cost city taxpayers $70 million in legal settlements. Twenty-four officers were either fired, suspended, or were forced to resign. In the end, the city agreed to enter into a consent decree with the United States Justice Department, making the LAPD accountable not only to its own civilian authorities, but to a federal judge as well. The hammer had justifiably come down hard on the city. In short, as I said at the time, Rampart was an assault on democracy.

For those who toiled in the police reform vineyard, a depressing reality set in: An entrenched culture like the LAPD's could not be changed overnight. It would take years of hard, sustained effort to transform an institution that was long insulated from accountability. Such an organization couldn't be turned around on a dime. As a result, police reform in Los Angeles and, for that matter, across the nation continues to pose profound challenges.

The Northridge Earthquake

The city staggered out of 1992, exhausted but hoping to move on. A year later voters sent an emphatic message in the mayor's race when they elected Republican Richard Riordan, a prominent Los Angeles venture capitalist with deep pockets and even deeper ties to the city's elite. He won, easily defeating Democrat City Councilman Michael Woo. It spoke to the voters' state of mind that a city with an overwhelmingly Democratic electorate had backed the Republican Riordan in 1993. The last Republican elected mayor by Los Angeles voters was Norris Poulson in 1957. A majority believed the city was increasingly ungovernable and out of control. They responded favorably to Riordan's campaign slogan that he was "tough enough to turn LA around."

No one could have known that another devasting threat was just around the corner, a natural disaster that would literally rip parts of Los Angeles apart. The Northridge earthquake, with its epicenter in the northwest San Fernando Valley, shook the city to its core. Residents had every reason to wonder if their leaders would again fail the test of sudden change. This time, however, the story was different.

At 4:31 a.m. on January 17, 1994, I was awakened in our bedroom when the house began shaking. Dishes in the kitchen shattered as they hit the floor, and our daughter, Mina, ran from her bedroom into ours, diving under our bed covers. When Caltech seismologist Lucy Jones appeared on television to explain what was happening, we sat transfixed, hanging on every word. I called her "the seismologist psychologist," because she had a unique, calming influence on a city shaken by a seismic event. All the previous temblors I had experienced had a rolling motion, but this one was different. It felt as though nature had lifted our home up and then dropped it back on its foundation. It remains the most powerful quake I have ever experienced.

I made a quick check around the house to make sure everything was alright, then put on my clothes and drove to the nearby Park La Brea Towers to check on my mother-in-law. She came through the quake fine. Then I made my way to the San Fernando Valley, which was now a sizable part of my council district. There were scenes of heavy damage. The Ralph's Market at Hazeltine and Ventura Boulevard in Sherman Oaks was on fire. The parking garage at the Fashion Square shopping center, a few blocks away, had pancaked. Blocks of apartment houses between Kester and Sepulveda, north of Ventura Boulevard, were destroyed or seriously damaged. The quake that hit us that morning registered 6.7 on the Richter scale, a major event by any measure.

These were just the first powerful images of destruction that I witnessed. Turning around, I headed to City Hall to check in with the Emergency Operations Center, which had been a scene of dysfunction during the 1992 unrest. I wondered how well Los Angeles would respond this time. One of the first things I noticed was a huge pile of Styrofoam containers containing scrambled eggs, bacon, and wheat toast—all meant for emergency workers. They had been provided cost free by The Pantry, one of the city's best-known diners that just happened to be owned by Mayor Richard Riordan. When he awakened to the quake that morning, Riordan wanted to be sure that emergency personnel didn't go hungry. It was the first of many decisions he would make under fire, and the contrast between 1992 and 1994 couldn't have been more pronounced. Although tension permeated the EOC, it was operating smoothly, expeditiously, and effectively.

Riordan loathed bureaucratic handwringing and senseless delays. When he ordered his restaurant to deliver breakfast to the EOC, he didn't ask who was going to pay for it. Or where the purchase order was. Or whether we had competitively bid the contract. The mayor couldn't stomach red tape. One of the maxims he lived by, for better or worse, was: "It's easier to ask forgiveness than to ask permission." This guided every decision he made that morning, and it served the city well.

Riordan promised to get things done, and the earthquake offered the opportunity to demonstrate his ability to do so. As he drove his Ford Explorer in the pre-dawn darkness from his home in Brentwood, on the city's westside, to City Hall in downtown, he saw the bright headlights of a large truck rushing towards him on the Santa Monica Freeway. Swerving to avoid a collision, he slowed down, looked ahead, and noticed a section of the freeway was missing between La Cienega and Robertson Boulevard. It had totally collapsed. Hours later he and his aides began laying out a plan of action to rebuild key parts of the city's infrastructure, including five fallen freeway bridges.

The mayor ordered his department heads to chart detour routes for commuters, and he directed his staff to disregard the fact that some of the routes weren't even in his city. Describing his conversation with Robert Yates, the city's able Transportation Director, he wrote, "I stared at Bob for a long moment and then ordered him to take over the three intersections [in Culver City] in ten minutes. I gave him my home telephone number. 'If anybody complains, have them call me, and I'll ask for forgiveness.'"

Hours after the quake I was in Riordan's office when he got on the phone with the White House, seeking emergency funding and other support from President Bill Clinton. It was a chit he could easily call in. Although Clinton had endorsed Michael Woo, Riordan's opponent in the 1993 mayoral election, the President pointedly noted that this was not meant as a criticism of Riordan, whom he praised. Both Clinton and Riordan wanted to build a strong relationship with each other, and those ties were cemented in the quake's aftermath. This was leadership under fire, a complete reversal of the 1992 fiasco.

Riordan convinced the President to visit Los Angeles. When he arrived at Burbank Airport two days later, it seemed like the entire United States government disembarked with him from the plane. His entourage included Leon Panetta, the Director of the Office of Management and Budget; Henry Cisneros, Secretary of Housing and Urban Development; James Lee Witt, Director of the Federal Emergency Management Agency (FEMA); John Emerson, who had been Clinton's California campaign director and was now Deputy Director of Inter-Governmental Affairs at the White House (I called him Clinton's Governor-General for California because our State was one of his principal responsibilities); and many others. Riordan asked me to be part of his entourage, since much of the quake damage affected my council district. We had an all-hands-on-deck meeting in an airport hangar to brief the President on the damage and the region's needs.

We still didn't fully appreciate the scope of the disaster, however, until Clinton toured the scenes of destruction. He got a firsthand look when his motorcade stopped at the collapsed interchange at the junction of the Golden State and Simi Freeways. We traveled next to a devastated apartment building on Reseda Blvd. in Northridge. The President entered the apartment and commiserated with the tenants. It was vintage "I feel your pain" Clinton. Action soon followed, as FEMA centers sprang up across the southland, offering financial assistance to small businesses, homeowners, and renters.

Clinton and Riordan had similar motivations for their rapid response. The president was determined to oversee the Northridge earthquake more effectively than his predecessor, George H.W. Bush, had dealt with the devastation in southern Florida in the aftermath of Hurricane Andrew in 1992. Meanwhile, Riordan wanted his actions to stand in sharp contrast with the city's disastrous handling of the 1992 civil unrest. Governor Pete Wilson was also highly motivated. He cut red tape in launching the reconstruction of the Santa Monica Freeway, offering contractors financial bonuses if they finished the job ahead of schedule. The work was completed in a month; under normal circumstances it would have taken six to nine months.

There were daunting challenges everywhere we looked. Countless structures were in ruins, and 250 natural gas lines had ruptured, igniting dangerous fires all over town. More than three million residents lacked power, electrical transformers had burst into flames, and even streets were on fire. A 64-car freight train had derailed between Northridge and Chatsworth, and two of the main aqueducts bringing water to Los Angeles had fractured. All told, there would be 57 deaths and 8,700 people injured.

In my own district, large numbers of Sherman Oaks residents impacted by the earthquake were immigrants from Central America. Their apartment buildings, many of them built on loosely packed soils adjacent to the Los Angeles River, had suffered major damage. Many of these residents had been traumatized by prior quakes in their home countries and feared their apartments could not withstand an aftershock. Hundreds of them would camp out in area parks for days.

The Riordan Effect

Riordan's leadership spoke for itself. He could be brusque and autocratic, often acting impetuously. But he was a hard-ass who sometimes showed an empathetic side. We worked well together. Riordan could call on municipal powerbrokers to help him execute big projects. He could bring disparate leaders together and had a pipeline to the White House that bore fruit. In addition to earthquake recovery, he persuaded the Clinton Administration to help fund the Alameda Corridor project, a grade-separated rail line for shipping containers being transported from the Los Angeles and Long Beach harbors to the national rail network. At the time it was one of the most important infrastructure projects in the region, if not the nation.

For all his strengths, Riordan also had his quirky, unpredictable side. In 1994, we were engaged in a contentious labor negotiation with the union representing LAPD's rank and file officers. The city was smarting from a recessionary economy, the impacts of the civil unrest, the January 17 earthquake, and serious budget shortfalls. Nevertheless, management was offering a 6 percent pay raise over two years, while the union was demanding 9 percent. At the same time, all other city employees were getting a 2 percent raise. Neither side was willing to budge.

Riordan had taken a hard line on the negotiations, at one point saying, "...we cannot give in to demands that will essentially bankrupt the future of our city." Days later, under persistent public pressure from the police union, which had given him a key endorsement in his mayoral race, he flipped. In a secret meeting with union leaders at the Biltmore Hotel, he proposed a package that not only exceeded what the city had offered, but was more than what the union had demanded, giving them the equivalent of a 12 percent raise over 18 months.

Of course, the union was thrilled. I was beside myself. "Do you know what you just did?" I asked Riordan. "You just gave them more than they asked for, and it'll cost the city at least another $15 million—money we don't have in the budget." Riordan shrugged. "The extra money was for good will," he said. "Flighty" didn't begin to describe this about face. The council majority succumbed and voted for the deal, with Marvin Braude, Rita Walters, and me dissenting.

Tokyo, 4:00 a.m., December 2, 1993

As the year ended, I had no way of knowing that my own rendezvous with sudden change was just around the corner. When I began a fifth full term on the City Council, I knew that my years at City Hall would not last forever. Voters approved a charter amendment in 1993 imposing term limits on the city's elected officials, and I would have been forced to step down four years later. I began thinking about what I wanted to do with my future when lightning struck.

In November I traveled to South Korea and Japan with John Ferraro on a sister-city mission to Seoul, Pusan (Los Angeles's sister city), and Tokyo. I was jet-lagged for much of the trip and exhausted when we reached the last leg in Japan. Checking into Tokyo's Imperial Hotel late in the evening, I briefly turned on the television and then fell into a deep sleep. In fact, it was one of the best night's sleeps of my life, largely because the bed was the most comfortable I had ever experienced. I made a mental note to see if I could purchase one like it when I got home (I never did) and drifted off.

At approximately 4:00 a.m. I was awakened by the telephone. Who the hell is calling me at this hour, I wondered? I reached for the hotel phone and heard Alisa's voice, calling from Los Angeles. "I hope I didn't wake you," she said. "Are you kidding me?" I grumbled. She went on to tell me that Ed Edelman had just announced that he was not running for re-election to the Board of Supervisors the following year. He wanted to make sure that I knew about his decision. At that moment, with the rest of Tokyo still fast asleep, a bright new path had unexpectedly opened for me—one that would usher in the next stage of my political life. I told Alisa that I had to make one call, and if that went well, I was in. There was no way I would make a decision of this magnitude without con- sulting Barbara; her blessing was a prerequisite. I called her as soon as I hung up. Not surprisingly, she was enthusiastic and unconditionally supportive. So, I decided to cut short my Asian trip and return to Los Angeles immediately.

The next flight wouldn't be leaving until late afternoon, and the notion that I'd be sitting in a hotel room for twelve hours twiddling my thumbs was simply unacceptable. So, I began making calls to prospective supporters back home, where the business day was well underway. Political allies like Henry Waxman and Howard Berman came on board without hesitation. I called my key financial supporters to lock up their support, and reached out to colleagues on the City Council, who gave me strong endorsements on the spot, as did Mayor Riordan and former Mayor Bradley.

I made a special point of calling John Ferraro in his hotel room when the sun rose in Tokyo, three hours later. I had worked hard to restore a good personal and professional relationship with John and wanted him on my team. He couldn't have been more gracious and supportive. I continued contacting people back home until I headed to Narita Airport for a 4:00 p.m. flight to LAX. By the time I landed, I had pledges of support from more than 100 individuals, along with a whopping phone bill. Ferraro later joked that in all the time he had known me, he had never seen me run so hard and so fast for anything. If I hadn't found a flight, he said, I would have swum home across the Pacific.

I *was* excited because County Supervisor was a perfect job for me. Los Angeles was the largest county in the country, and the Board of Supervisors was its gov- erning body. Unlike the City Council, with fifteen discordant voices struggling to be heard and a mayor to contend with, the Board of Supervisors was *both* the executive and legislative branch of county government. There was no separation of powers, no real checks and balances. If I had a policy initiative to propose, all I had to do was round up two other votes and it would happen. Full stop. Every issue affecting our society crossed a county supervisor's desk on a daily basis. With its nearly ten million residents, Los Angeles County today would be the eleventh largest state in the union. It was one of the nation's largest urban labo- ratories where ideas could be tested, and solutions hatched to some of society's most vexing problems. This job was tailor made for a wonk like me.

Luckily, Edelman's Third District seat overlapped most of my political base in West Los Angeles and the southern San Fernando Valley. Voters in areas which were not in the overlap were nonetheless familiar with me. It wasn't as if I'd have to introduce myself to a whole new set of constituents. I couldn't have drawn a better supervisorial district to run in, and I was confident of my chances.

I announced my candidacy on December 8, 1993, just days after I returned from Japan. Although the press was filled with speculation about other candidates, I believed my strongest rivals would stand down once they did their own due diligence. That's exactly what happened. In announcing my candidacy, I pledged to shake up county government and make it more transparent, saying: "For too long county government has operated out of the spotlight, making decisions that would never have withstood public scrutiny had they been made in the open." I put special priority on reducing crime, reforming campaign finance laws, and ending fiscally irresponsible policies, adding: "We need a county government that holds itself accountable to the people, and that's why I'm running."

I started the race with enough funds to run a winning campaign. The election was anti-climactic, as I won nearly 70 percent of the vote in June, avoiding a November runoff. Los Angeles was preoccupied with serious issues that year, most notably earthquake recovery, and the lengthy hiatus between June and December, when I'd be sworn in, gave me a rare opportunity to bone up on county issues. I spent most of that interregnum finishing my duties as a city councilman and getting the equivalent of a Harvard education in health care finance. This turned out to be time very well spent. The issue was front and center from the moment I was sworn in as Supervisor.

I finished my duties as a councilman in a veritable sprint. Mayor Riordan generously hosted a going-away reception for me in the City Hall rotunda, and as I said goodbye, I reflected on the road I had traveled since entering the public arena in 1975. Although my core values remained unchanged, I was a changed man in many ways. I had become a consequential player in governing America's second largest city, a far cry from my Boyle Heights beginnings. I had come to know Los Angeles in all its complexity and diversity, in ways I could never have imagined when this journey began. My successful initiatives, and some gut-wrenching mistakes, honed my political and fiscal skills. They would serve me well in the years to come. And I was filled with gratitude for the constituents who had given me this singular opportunity. As I walked out of City Hall for the last time, I took a deep breath, amazed at it all, and feeling like the whole experience had gone by way too fast. But I was ready to take on the daunting challenges of making local government work in America's largest county.

Three things were clear as my new life began: The job of Supervisor would be more complex and challenging than anything I had tackled before; the stakes would be considerably higher; and my skills would now be challenged on a much bigger stage. It was a sudden change that filled me with anticipation and hope. But there was also a setback for our family.

A Painful Defeat, and a Life-Affirming Response

During my campaign for the Board of Supervisors, Barbara began to seriously consider running for my council seat. She would have made an excellent councilmember. She was a powerful force in many parts of our community—a member of our temple board, a passionate advocate of health care for all, a promoter of both our public school system and Jewish education, and much more. She had a robust rolodex, and was loved by so many whose lives she touched.

Although most people believed that her last name would be an asset, I felt it could also be a liability. To put it bluntly, I was worried that 5th district voters might not like the idea of their supervisor and councilmember sleeping in the same bed. But this was Barbara's career move, and her decision to make. So I gingerly raised the pros and cons, and left the final decision to her.

In July 1994, while David and I were on a vacation in Francois Lake, in the middle of British Columbia, I called Barbara to check in. She told me that she had decided to run. Despite my reservations, I was happy and excited for her. She went on to amass more than enough funds to mount a strong campaign, and she received many prominent endorsements, including Mayor Richard Riordan's.

Nonetheless, Barbara could not shake the mistaken perception that I had handpicked her to succeed me. Her two opponents were Roberta Weintraub, a former member of the Los Angeles Board of Education and Mike Feuer, the Executive Director of Bet Tzedek, a public interest legal services agency. Feuer fit the profile of the district, and if Barbara hadn't been a candidate I probably would have voted for him. Although Barbara was viewed as "Zev's candidate," Feuer was the community-based candidate, with no ties to the political establishment. He walked door-to-door soliciting votes and putting up lawn signs. Sound familiar? Mike and Barbara came in first and second in the primary, and he won the general election by more than 2 to 1.

Watching that campaign was one of the most painful experiences of my life. It was difficult to see the woman I loved lose in such a public fashion. But it didn't pain her as much as it did me. Barbara was the most resilient person I ever knew. She relished the opportunity to meet thousands of new people, and in the runoff election she came into her own as a public speaker—even against Feuer, an accomplished orator. People were impressed with her candor, authenticity, and humanity. When the election was over, Barbara was seen as public figure in her own right, not as "Zev's wife." It was a recognition she had been unfortunately denied in the campaign.

While many candidates would have gone into a fetal position after that loss, Barbara built on the experience and grew from it. A few years later, the Speaker of the California Assembly appointed her to the state's Medical Board, a position she held with distinction for thirteen years, three of them as its Chair. She was also tapped to serve on a number of city commissions and philanthropic boards. She became one of Los Angeles' most consequential and beloved civic leaders, while raising two children and putting up with me. I could not have been prouder of her.

CHAPTER 14

Designed Not to Govern

Beginning a new job is often full of challenges, but it's odd when one of them is struggling to tell people exactly what the job is. This was a problem I encountered in my duties as a Los Angeles county supervisor, not just in the first few months but over the next twenty years. People I met simply had no idea what the job of county supervisor entailed. If I had told them that I was a mayor, city councilman or congressman, they'd intuitively know. But telling people about my new post often drew the following response: "What do you supervise?" In truth, this confusion predated me.

In his 1961 memoir, *Thirty Explosive Years in Los Angeles County,* former County Supervisor John Anson Ford, who served from 1934 to 1958, conceded that few people understood the county or the five-member board that governed it. They didn't realize how much Los Angeles County had grown, the diversity of the board's duties, and that Los Angeles County had come to reflect the diversity of the nation as a whole, he wrote. Ford added that the county's unique division of powers and responsibilities, compared to most cities and the fifty states, was a "puzzling anomaly" that defied easy explanation.

Although I took office thirty-six years after Ford left the board, my challenge was identical. If I gave people a detailed explanation of the county's sprawling bureaucracy and its maze of departments, their eyes would glaze over. The nature of my work only began to sink in when I said I oversaw a $32 billion budget and over 100,000 employees. Then people began to understand.

The point was made unforgettably for me on February 27, 1983, when Queen Elizabeth II of England addressed the Los Angeles City Council, accompanied by her husband Prince Philip. Following her speech, the queen engaged me in a brief conversation about my studies in British Empire history. As something of an Anglophile, I was thrilled.

Afterwards, we all convened with hundreds of civic leaders at a reception for the royal couple at the Grand Hall of the Dorothy Chandler Pavilion, at the Los Angeles County Music Center. While everyone was fawning over the queen,

I noticed that Prince Phillip was standing alone on the side of the hall. So, I grabbed two of my colleagues and said, "Let's go keep the Duke of Edinburgh company." We walked over and introduced ourselves. "Your Royal Highness," I said, "I'm Councilman Yaroslavsky, and these are my colleagues, Joel Wachs and Hal Bernson." The prince looked puzzled. "Gentlemen, I've met the mayor, and I know who he is, and I've met the supervisors, though I don't know what they supervise," he said. "Now I'm meeting you councilors [sic]. I don't understand your system of government."

We proceeded to give him a short tutorial about the state-local government relationship. We explained that the state is divided into fifty-eight counties, all but one of which is governed by a five-member Board of Supervisors. Los Angeles was the largest of those counties, within which there were eighty-eight cities, of which the City of Los Angeles was only one. There were also specialized governmental units such as school, water, flood control, mosquito abatement, and transit districts that made up our governing constellation. I could see the growing exasperation in the prince's face. At that point he peered over his owlish glasses and, with a twinkle in his eye, pronounced, "I now understand the genius of your system—*it's designed not to govern.*"

This was a brilliant assessment. In a way, that is *precisely* what our state and local governments were designed to do—or not do. The structure took shape in the early 1900s when reformers, led by Governor Hiram Johnson, successfully convinced voters to approve sweeping changes to the State Constitution. They were determined to prevent an over-concentration of power in any one governmental jurisdiction, attempting to blunt the outsized influence that corporate interests, especially the railroads, had over public sector decision-making.

Among several key reforms, voters won broad powers of initiative and referendum, allowing them to take the legislative process into their own hands when their representatives failed to act or abused their powers. Citizens also won the right to remove incumbents from office through the recall process. The state constitution reinforced these "good government" reforms by making all local offices non-partisan, hoping to dilute the influence of partisan political machines. When I ran for the City Council and the Board of Supervisors, for example, my party affiliation did not appear on the ballot.

Today, California's counties and cities share their governing authority with a multitude of elected and appointed bodies. Public Schools in Los Angeles County are the responsibility of several dozen independent boards of education; regional transit is the responsibility of the Metropolitan Transportation

Authority (MTA); police and fire are largely the purview of cities; social services such as healthcare and public assistance (welfare) are a county responsibility, and so forth. Unlike New York City, where all of these responsibilities are vested in one government, our regional governance system is fundamentally decentralized. Prince Philip grasped this instantly.

I would spend the next two decades on the Board of Supervisors grappling with these contradictions and obstacles. But they were not insurmountable. The challenge for me was to make county government work despite these barriers. I would have to navigate that thicket of a Balkanized bureaucracy in order to accomplish anything. In the end, it all came down to leadership, and I was determined to lead.

Before I could begin, however, I needed to fully understand the beast I was about to confront. This was easier said than done. My first few months at the county were a period of acculturation and adjustment that I had not anticipated. It was also difficult for members of my staff who had come with me from City Hall. Back then we were used to serving our constituents on a person-to-person basis. Our phones rang all day long with citizens relating problems big and small. We had constant interactions with people over issues ranging from malfunctioning traffic signals to massive new developments threatening their neighborhoods. Cities were focused on issues that the middle class cares about, and many of our constituents made time to come to our offices, seek us out at community meetings and demand to be heard.

Life at the county couldn't have been more different. The first thing I noticed was a yawning silence that extended through the day. Few people called us with constituent problems. Was anybody out there? At the county I mainly got reports, audits, and data from several dozen departments. My four colleagues and I were called upon to make executive decisions on 100 or more agenda items at our weekly board meetings, all informed by the bureaucracy's reports. When I was asked about the difference between my old and new jobs, I'd answer that it was as though for twenty years I ran the busiest retail store in the chain. Then, because I did such a fantastic job, I was promoted to the corporate headquarters in remote Simi Valley. In other words, I was now far away from any daily contact with my clientele.

Whenever I walked down the eighth-floor corridor where our offices were located in the Hall of Administration, two blocks from City Hall, the lonely echo of my footsteps reminded me of the British House of Commons, which I had visited as a college student. I recalled the members of Parliament strolling the cavernous marble corridors of Westminster with their umbrellas tapping the floor, the echoes reverberating through the halls. On many days I could walk the eighth floor and never see another human being. Security guards prevented the general public from entering this inner sanctum without first being cleared by a board office. It was a profoundly eerie and unsettling change.

Even though my staff always understood that our county constituents were principally the under-served, we now viscerally felt it. We were responsible for people without health insurance, for abused children, families dependent on public financial assistance for their subsistence, the mentally ill, those incarcerated in county-run jails, and for young people in juvenile detention. We were society's safety net, and the bulk of our budget was focused on millions of vulnerable people. The challenge was how to best reach out and help them. We knew where our constituents lived, and we understood the existential problems they faced every day. But if they had a complaint, they wouldn't come to our office, or even call to register it. They were too busy working, too busy trying to make ends meet. And needless to say, many of them couldn't pronounce or spell "Yaroslavsky."

Beyond social services, we also provided municipal services to approximately 1.5 million people who lived in the county's unincorporated areas. These were communities that never became cities. Many chose to remain under county control because forming their own cities would have been prohibitively expensive. In these areas, numbering in the dozens, the Board of Supervisors assumed the role normally performed by a mayor and City Council—delivering police, fire, traffic, recreation, and other municipal services. The county also contracted out municipal services to many of its smaller cities, who chose not to provide them on their own. For example, when West Hollywood incorporated as a city in 1984, it decided not to form its own police department and, instead, paid the county to provide law enforcement services. About half of the county's eighty-eight cities contracted with the county Sheriffs', fire, animal care, and other departments for their services. This was a great deal for them, and a pet peeve of mine, because county government subsidized a significant part of the cost.

When I took office, Los Angeles County was extraordinarily diverse—racially, ethnically, and economically. Two of the supervisorial districts (the 1st and 2nd) had large Hispanic and Black populations, and residents of those areas were among the county's poorest. Two other districts were predominantly Anglo and more politically conservative (the 4th and the 5th). And then there was my district. Statistically, it was affluent, and its voters were predominantly Anglo. However, it had a growing immigrant population, mostly Hispanic, in the San Fernando Valley communities of Pacoima, Sylmar, Canoga Park, Reseda, North Hollywood, Van Nuys, Sun Valley, and North Hills. In addition, we had a large unincorporated area in the remote western part of the county. Both of these new constituencies were underserved, so I opened two fulltime district office to address their needs—an expanded office in Van Nuys, for county-dependent residents, and a newly built one in Calabasas, which served unincorporated areas in the Santa Monica Mountains, as well as the cities of Malibu, Calabasas, Agoura Hills, Westlake Village and Hidden Hills. Being indispensable to constituents had always been my hallmark, and we intended to continue that tradition.

Making Life-Saving Decisions

Clarifying our constituent mission, however, was just part of the puzzle. It was also crucial for me to understand how the day-to-day strategies of being a supervisor differed from City Hall. As a councilman I was one of fifteen members of a legislative body. Although I made a lot of decisions that affected my district, I wasn't the only person who made them. If I wanted to pass something ambitious and complex, like rent control, I'd need to get a majority of the council to agree, along with the mayor. Members of the council had to manage a maze of checks and balances. I brought a lot of these instincts to the county, but quickly learned that supervisors didn't spend a lot of time legislating. A rent control ordinance passed by the Board of Supervisors, for example, would only apply in the unincorporated areas, because the county was precluded from legislating for the 88 incorporated cities; only a city could pass laws within its jurisdiction.

Supervisors flexed different political muscles. We were principally an executive branch of government with no independently elected mayor to be a check on us. We were a five-headed executive that set policy and administered a vast bureaucracy. Each of us had broad powers, and no one person was in charge. Although we appointed a Chief Administrative Officer to run the county's day to day operations, he or she answered to the Board.

All of this came into sharp focus when I was talking to Alisa one morning about a major county issue that had just come up. "Let's schedule a hearing to discuss it," I told her. This is something we would routinely do in City Hall. She quickly disabused me of that idea. "You don't need to hold a hearing," Alisa said. "You and your colleagues are in charge here. Let's just figure out a solution, get the votes, and resolve the problem." It was an "aha" moment that helped shift us into gear.

The stakes were high. In the city, it wasn't an existential issue if we delayed trimming trees for a year. In the county, it was indisputably a matter of life and death if we closed a hospital, or ignored the abuse of defenseless children. How many kids would be taken away from their natural parents and placed in foster care, and how would it change the trajectory of their lives? If we shuttered a community clinic, how could we mitigate the impacts on access to health care? As a councilman I rarely lost sleep worrying about who would live and who would die. As a county supervisor I had more sleepless nights than I can remember. If I failed my county-dependent constituents, they could pay the ultimate price. It was a heavy burden, which I never fully appreciated until I retired twenty years later. Waking up a couple of weeks after leaving office, I felt like an immense weight had been lifted from my shoulders.

One of my most important initial responsibilities was hiring the best people to help implement my vision. Besides naming Alisa to be my chief of staff, I selected an experienced health policy wonk, Ron Hansen, to be my health services deputy. He was aided by a young and smart Elan Shultz, who went on to earn a Masters in Public Health and ultimately returned to the top health job in my office. I poached Marcus Allen, an experienced and able budget hand from the city, to be my finance deputy. When he left after a year to take another job, I replaced him with Richard Popper, one of the keenest financial minds, with one of the sharpest budget knives, in the business. I tapped Kevin Acebo, who had run my campaign, to oversee criminal justice. Vivian Rescalvo, Wendy Aron and Lisa Mandel were three stars who came on board over time to assume responsibility for gut-wrenching children's services issues. And I retained Ed Edelman's press deputy, Joel Bellman, who had an impeccable institutional memory.

I hired staff members with Sen. Henry Jackson's advice in mind—to surround myself with smart and able public servants. I treated them like a policy cabinet. We met every Monday at 9:00 a.m. to go over the board agenda and any other issues that we would face in the week ahead. After all, this was largely an executive job, and voters had a right to expect that we would execute what we proposed.

As I assumed my supervisorial post, I quoted the powerful words of British historian, Lord Thomas Macaulay, in my swearing-in speech: "No man is fit to govern great societies who hesitates about disobliging the few who have access to him for the sake of the many he will never see." I vowed that my team and I would be guided by those words. We would be laser-focused on the people we never see—the people who can't hire a lobbyist or lawyer; the constituents who can't take a day off work to find out what happened to their public assistance check; or the child who was beaten by a criminal parent or guardian.

Inauguration Day, December 5, 1994

I don't want to give the impression that our office was unprepared for the challenges that lay ahead. Far from it. On the day I was sworn in I delivered a speech that laid out my goals, and when I read it years later it seemed prescient—not just in the battles I fought, but in the intractability of the county's problems. Before an audience of nearly 1,000, I urged my colleagues to join with me in tearing down the barriers that separated county government from the people it served. It was time, I said, to overcome the mystique of the Board of Supervisors as a remote entity that few understood or knew how to approach.

I spoke about the need for comprehensive campaign finance reform law that minimized, or eliminated, the reliance on large campaign contributions. I called for expanded lobbying disclosure requirements, so that the public could know the extent to which influence is peddled in the Hall of Administration. I said we had to open up county government to the light of day. In fact, at my first meeting, I provided the third and deciding vote to televise board meetings—one of the last local elected bodies in Los Angeles County to do so.

I promised to address skyrocketing crime, to find alternatives to knee-jerk incarceration policies, and to improve the county's vast public health network. I pledged to address the vital importance of cultural facilities, the need to protect the county's vast wilderness and magnificent coastline, and the urgent challenge of reforming the Metropolitan Transportation Authority, which was riddled with bureaucratic incompetence, political corruption, and a culture of failure. I reserved most of my comments, however, for the county's precarious fiscal condition.

"Wall Street has lowered our bond rating twice in the last two years," I said. "Not only has this raised our cost of borrowed money, but it has been a vote of no confidence in our fiscal management from the people who know our books the best. This must stop, and the sooner the better. County government must live within its means by hiring only the most essential personnel (and) consolidating redundant agencies. This county could save tens of millions of dollars annually by being tough on itself."

I also noted that Los Angeles was heavily dependent on funding from federal and State governments. Since we were not complete masters of our financial destiny, it was crucial for us to tell our story more effectively in Washington, DC and Sacramento. If we were unable to deliver vital services to millions of people, it would be a social, economic, and political calamity.

The speech got a positive reception, and I was flattered when Mayor Riordan asked me to give him a personally signed copy. Swearing-in ceremonies are usually warm and gracious affairs, and many of my friends, family members (including my sister who flew in from Israel), and supporters came downtown for the occasion. We adjourned for lunch, and I expected the rest of the day to be taken up with the humdrum tasks of settling into our new offices. Then a bombshell hit. At 3 p.m., Orange County, our neighbor to the south, announced that it was going to file for bankruptcy the next morning. The financial and political worlds were in a state of shock. While it's one thing for an over-committed rural county to go belly up, it's earth-shattering news that California's quintessentially suburban, affluent, and mostly white county might be going broke.

Obvious questions followed: What did this mean for Orange County and, more importantly, what did it mean for Los Angeles? On one level, it was reassuring that their fiscal problems were vastly different from ours. They went bankrupt because their treasurer bet heavily on risky investments and lost. When the bottom fell out of the market they couldn't meet their financial obligations, so they had to declare bankruptcy to protect themselves from creditors.

We weren't threatened by bad investments, but Los Angeles had a major fiscal problem that had been festering for years, a ticking time bomb. The county was spending far more than it was taking in, to the tune of almost a billion dollars a year on a budget of what was then nearly $12 billion. This was an unsustainable structural deficit. Unlike the federal government, which had limitless borrowing capacity, we had to balance our budget every year as a matter of law. We couldn't perpetually go into debt to cover our operating expenses. Budgetary sleight of hand and short-term borrowing to mask overspending had been the rule, and it was an unacceptable strategy. Such a house of cards would inevitably collapse, jeopardizing vital services and causing the layoffs of thousands of employees. Nobody wanted this to happen, so it was imperative that the county change its culture in order to forestall such a bloodletting. At long last we would have to learn to live within our means. In the wake of the Orange County debacle, attention understandably shifted to Los Angeles and its spendthrift county government. We had our work cut out for us.

CHAPTER 15

The Crisis That Nearly Bankrupted the County

Prince Metternich, the nineteenth-century Austrian diplomat, once observed: "When France sneezes, the rest of Europe catches a cold." I'll take some liberties with Metternich's quote to fully convey the magnitude of the financial and health care crisis gripping Los Angeles in 1995: "When Los Angeles County sneezes, the rest of California catches a cold." This accurately describes the situation facing the body politic as I assumed my seat on the Board of Supervisors.

Indeed, Los Angeles was not just one of several thousand American counties. At nearly 10 million people, it was the largest county in the nation. Its geographic area—more than 4,000 square miles—was thirteen times the area covered by New York City's five boroughs. Our Department of Health Services (DHS), one of the county's largest departments, was a sprawling bureaucracy that included six public hospitals, a network of community health clinics and more than 26,000 employees.

Most important, the county's uninsured and under-insured population numbered nearly 2.5 million—by far the largest of any metropolitan region in the nation. If Los Angeles County's uninsured were its own county, it would have been America's third largest. Moreover, nearly 40 percent of all Californians who depended on government for social services like health and welfare lived in our county. In other words, we were too big to fail. This point was driven home during a meeting our board once had with former Senate Majority Leader Robert Dole of Kansas in his Capitol office. When my colleague, Yvonne Burke, cited the number of uninsured and under-insured people in our county, his jaw dropped. "Why, that's the entire population of my state," he declared. He appeared genuinely blown away.

This was the backdrop on January 19, 1995, when our board learned that Los Angeles County was on the verge of calamity. The lion's share of our $900 million budget deficit—$640 million—was in the Department of Health Services

(DHS). Taking an axe to the DHS budget had real-world consequences. It meant closing hospitals, trauma centers, and clinics. Hundreds of thousands of county residents would be denied access to vital hospital and clinical care. It would trigger a chain reaction causing the regional health care delivery system to crash. This was literally a matter of life and death.

A budget is not a document etched in stone; it's an annual spending and revenue *plan*. If a government agency plans to spend $100 million on a program, it better have a credible source of revenue to pay for it. Simply identifying funds that have little or no chance of materializing can quickly lead to a financial disaster. Elected officials need to be conscientious, disciplined, *and* honest on both the spending and revenue side of the ledger. It's a lot easier to spend than to collect, as the County found out the hard way in 1995.

Prior to my arrival at the Hall of Administration, the Board of Supervisors had adopted a $2.3 billion budget for the Department of Health Services. But it did so by claiming over $600 million in reimbursements for administrative and other costs—equating to more than 25 percent of its entire budget. The problem was that the bulk of the county's health budget was funded by federal authorities who did not agree with that claim. So, although the budget was balanced on paper, in reality it was total fiction.

Federal officials believed that the county was expecting reimbursements for federal program costs that were not eligible for such payments. Essentially, the Supervisors were risking the county's fiscal solvency on a hope that the new Clinton Administration would not allow the nation's second largest public health system to collapse. The county was also buying time in the hope that the Clinton health reform proposal, under consideration by Congress in 1994, would somehow address the county's fiscal crisis if and when it was approved. That proposal crashed and burned. So, while the impact of Orange County's fiscal fiasco was a stunning wake-up call, our dilemma was a nightmare all its own. We would spend much of the next two decades battling to right our ship.

As the end of the fiscal year approached on June 30, the county's Chief Administrative Officer, Sally Reed, informed the board that the federal government *would not* approve its $640 million request for Medi-Cal reimbursements. Reed was an able, but very conservative administrator, and she had a reputation among some of my colleagues of supporting draconian health cuts. She didn't support the need for a large county health system, especially hospitals, and she tried to convince the board that cuts were the only option. This was an odd belief in a county where nearly one in four residents had little or no health insurance.

At that moment, it appeared that the jig was up. We would now have to face the reality of cutting medical services and jobs to avert a total fiscal collapse—if that was even possible so late in the fiscal year. The news triggered an uproar, and few observers of county government expected a happy ending.

Steering Our Fiscal Ship

I didn't hold back when the Board of Supervisors faced this crisis in early 1995. "There's no excuse," I said, "for the Ponzi-like scheme we've been operating under. . .This should not come as a surprise to any of us that we're in this situation. This is not the first year the county has been spending well beyond its means. Today's discussion is the kind that should have taken place a long time ago." Not everyone on the board agreed. "This is a complete surprise," said an angry Supervisor Deane Dana. "I've never seen a complete turnaround of this magnitude."

Finding solutions would require a paradigm shift, not only by ending discredited budgetary practices, but by finding a more efficient way to deliver health services to our constituents. The board began exploring a variety of short-term actions to cut costs, including layoffs of county personnel. Under state law we had a legal mandate to balance our budget every year, and the longer we waited to remedy the situation, the more drastic the remedy would ultimately have to be.

In the Spring, Credit Suisse—one of several banks that guaranteed to investors that the county would honor its financial obligations—demanded to know how we planned to grapple with our nearly $1 billion deficit. They requested an emergency conference call with our Board of Supervisors at 10:00 a.m. on a Tuesday, the very day and time of our weekly meetings. When we suggested an alternate time, they refused. So, we recessed our board meeting and met in a windowless conference room behind the auditorium where we normally held public meetings, leaving bureaucrats and members of the public waiting.

The board and our CAO gathered around a speaker phone while our bankers gathered in Zurich, and it quickly became clear that this would not be a courtesy call. Credit-Suisse had done its homework on our budgetary woes, and they pressed us hard. What steps were we prepared to take to bring our spending into line with revenues? What were we going to do about employee salaries? How would we meet our responsibilities to fund the county's vast pension system, not just in 1995 but for decades to come? How many employees were we prepared to lay off? Which programs were going to be axed, and how soon? Then came the toughest question: How could we assure investors that this fiscal malfeasance would never occur again?

I would have been asking the same questions had I been sitting in Zurich. But I was in Los Angeles, and the questions I and my colleagues had were quite different: Would we be able to keep our emergency rooms and trauma centers open? Would they still be able to see children whose parents brought them to county-run emergency rooms with a high fever? Would we have enough doctors to treat the sick, or prescribe critically needed insulin for diabetics, or a technician to perform a chest x-ray or a mammogram?

This disaster had a human face, beyond dollars and cents. While Zurich was counting beans, my colleagues and I were thinking about people. In the end, Credit Suisse and other banks placed the county's credit under long-term review. It was a defining moment for this Board of Supervisors—the lighthouse by which we would steer our fiscal ship for the remainder of our county service. Each of us quietly vowed never to be put in this humiliating position again.

The County Appoints a Health Czar

The fallout from the Credit-Suisse encounter was swift and painful. In a report to the board, Reed outlined a series of budget cuts to close the deficit, and one of her suggestions was extreme. She proposed closing County-USC Medical Center, one of the largest publicly run hospitals in the United States and the anchor of the Los Angeles County health and trauma network. This hospital received 50 percent of all trauma cases in the county. The closure would save more than $300 million, Reed said, and the county had to be prepared to make such sacrifices. I knew that closing our flagship hospital would be a non-starter. So would Reed's alternative suggestion of shutting four other county-run hospitals in order to keep County-USC open. Either option would shred the safety net, disrupt health care for millions of people, and throw thousands of county employees out of work. Worst of all, the proposed closures could lead to a meltdown of the private hospital system, as well. Hospitals like Cedars-Sinai, UCLA Medical Center, Good Samaritan, and others would be overrun with demands they couldn't possibly accommodate. No hospital and no county resident, insured or uninsured, would be spared the consequences.

Newcomers can often look at government problems with fresh eyes, and that's what I tried to do. We needed to develop a new strategy to preserve our health system, but none of us had an answer and we knew it. My staff and I crafted a proposal to create a blue-ribbon task force of fiscal and health care experts. We'd give them thirty days to come up with both short and long-term solutions to address our crisis. I knew I could count on support from my Democratic colleagues, Gloria Molina, and Yvonne Braithwaite Burke, but I wanted a unanimous board to show a united front to Washington, Sacramento, and the public. This meant winning over the two Republicans, Mike Antonovich and Deane Dana. It wouldn't be easy, but I gave it a shot.

The Hall of Administration's eighth floor nurtured a strangely reclusive culture. Each supervisor was akin to an independent CEO, focused fulltime on running his or her district. Each of us was also one-fifth of the county's executive branch, since we didn't have an elected chief executive. We rarely got together outside of board meetings to discuss policy, or anything else for that matter. I was challenging these unwritten norms on the morning I walked over to Antonovich's office to pitch my idea to him. I had reached out in advance to Tom Silver, his highly intelligent and politically pragmatic Chief of Staff, to gauge his boss's possible reaction. He gave me good advice. "Talk to him like people talked to Reagan," Silver said. "Boil your pitch down to a few talking points. Make him feel like he's part of the solution." I did so and was gratified by Antonovich's reaction. He didn't need to be reminded that he had two of the county's six public hospitals in his district, and he knew how high the stakes were. He was on board. Next, we needed Dana's support. I approached Don Knabe, his chief of staff, who told me he would work on his boss, and he delivered. All of us believed that closing our hospitals for a short-term budget fix was a fool's errand—so we now had agreement on a plan to develop a plan.

The ease with which we reached this consensus underscored the gravity of the crisis, and it also demonstrated the advantage of having a non-partisan board. Our Democratic and Republican members didn't have to clear their positions with their respective party caucuses, because under the State Constitution local government is non-partisan. We don't run as Democrats or Republicans, so we don't need to cling to party identities. It's the way government should work. As New York City Mayor Fiorello La Guardia once said, "There is no Democratic or Republican way to pick up the garbage." He could have just as well have been speaking of health care.

After establishing the Health Crisis Task Force, we quickly appointed its five members. Molina appointed Jane Pisano, a USC vice-president; Burke appointed Ray Schultz, former head of UCLA's Medical Center; Dana appointed Tom Collins, CEO of Long Beach Memorial Hospital; Antonovich appointed Duffy Watson, CEO of Newhall Hospital; and I appointed Burt Margolin, a former Chair of the California State Assembly Health Committee and former chief of staff to Congressman Henry Waxman.

Burt was a master of the arcane world of health care finance. He had an impeccable strategic political mind as well as important relationships in Washington and Sacramento. His fellow panel members immediately chose him to chair the task force, and he was later given extraordinary but temporary powers as the county's unofficial "Health Czar." This meant he had wide latitude to negotiate directly with state and federal government officials on a plan to rescue our health system. The odds that this task force would come up with a fix were admittedly slim. A health industry official handicapped our chances as "much better than winning the lottery, but a little tougher than achieving peace in Bosnia."

Margolin made it clear from the beginning that he didn't come on the task force to shut down life-saving facilities. He was a reformer who blended a keen ability to push for change with a savvy, insider's sense of what was politically possible. When Reed and others argued that the only realistic solution was to close one or more county-run hospitals, Margolin's response was brief and to the point. "I want to change the premise of the debate," he said. "That's the only way we can realistically put a health network for millions of people back on track."

The creation of this task force, and the elevation of Margolin to "czar," was a pivotal moment. Until this point, efforts to plug the budget hole had deteriorated into a political free-for-all that was long on rhetoric but short on coherent solutions. The county needed one knowledgeable person to quarterback this effort. To its credit, the board willingly ceded some of its authority to prevent a moral and financial bankruptcy. Margolin was our czar.

Bill Clinton to the Rescue

Burt and his task force moved quickly to chart a new path forward. Under his plan, which the Board of Supervisors endorsed, we would try to convince the Clinton Administration to help us reconfigure the way we delivered health care services. The county's health system had been heavily based on hospital care. This was far costlier and less efficient than it should have been. Emergency rooms were often the only place where uninsured persons could find a doctor when they needed help, even for minor complaints. People with headaches and sprained ankles were seen in the same facilities that were treating strokes, heart attacks and gunshot wounds. As a result, our ERs were frequently overcrowded. It would have been far less expensive and more client-friendly if people were treated in community-based health clinics for relatively minor maladies.

It might seem obvious that we should simply have shifted more people to clinics, but federal rules did not provide reimbursement for such care. Although our hospitals were revenue centers, receiving huge Medicaid payments from the federal and state governments, the county's outpatient clinics got relatively little financial help. Unless this changed, there was no financial incentive for us to expand outpatient care. We aimed to change this system.

In July, Margolin and his task force proposed a plan that was one-part common sense and one-part Hail Mary pass. For our part, we would substantially expand the county's ambulatory (outpatient) care system to lessen the load on our overburdened hospital system. In return, we asked the federal government to let us use Medicaid dollars to pay for health services in our clinics. To accomplish this, we had to secure a Section 1115 waiver, a reference to a section of the federal code that authorizes demonstration projects—i.e., special programs allowing states to experiment with new ways of spending Medicaid funds. If it worked, it could be a national model. In addition, it would infuse new revenues into our system that could help plug the massive hole in our budget.

The unique—and controversial—element of our proposal was that the *county* was requesting the waiver, not the state. Federal authorities preferred to negotiate these agreements with states and then have them deal with their counties. The federal government hardly ever granted waivers directly to counties. However, Los Angeles County was bigger than most states, and we successfully made our case for our unique circumstance. Governor Pete Wilson's administration did not object, as long as we didn't demand state funds as part of the agreement. The state's Director of Health Services, Kim Belshe, came to Washington with our team and fully supported us when the time came to close the deal.

Margolin hoped that the Clinton administration would embrace our proposal because we weren't coming to Washington simply with our hand out. As he put it, the waiver would help Los Angeles "restructure its public health system over the next five years from a hospital-based enterprise to a more community clinic-based system that emphasizes primary and preventive care." We hoped to reshape an archaic health system into a twenty-first-century model for wellness.

Our congressional allies immediately endorsed the idea, but the initial reaction from federal Department of Health and Human Services bureaucrats was almost uniformly negative. They didn't appreciate the county laying the entire burden for its deficit on their doorstep. They believed that the State of California should bear some of this responsibility. California was stingy when it came to investing in the health safety net. Although we were in agreement with the Feds, the Wilson Administration was adamant about not contributing one cent to this deal. It was a very intricate political dance, and we were caught in the middle.

Thankfully, the final decision was not left to the bureaucrats. The 1996 presidential primary season would soon be heating up, and the last thing President

Clinton wanted was a total collapse of the Los Angeles County health system, along with the bankruptcy of the nation's largest county. Moreover, Clinton relished big, transformative reforms, and that is precisely what we were proposing. We thought we had a convincing case to make.

But there was a changing political landscape in Washington, DC. By 1995 Democrats had lost control of both houses of Congress, and newly empowered Republicans were in no mood to rescue urban, Democratic counties from financial disaster. We felt that the new Republican majority, led by Speaker Newt Gingrich, would not have been troubled at all if Los Angeles County imploded. It was a big roll of the dice.

On July 19, Molina and I flew to Washington to explain the existential crisis we faced and our proposed solutions. We met with California Senator Dianne Feinstein and Los Angeles Congressman Henry Waxman, both stalwart supporters of our county. We made the rounds with many members of the Los Angeles congressional delegation to plead our case, and we received staunch support from each of them.

Our most important meeting, however, was in the White House with Leon Panetta, the President's Chief of Staff. Molina and I, along with several members of our congressional delegation, met in Panetta's West Wing office for nearly an hour and a half. He was friendly and supportive. We asked that he agree in principle to work with us on a solution based on the Margolin framework that would be made public days later. Time was of the essence, because painful cuts would result if we couldn't reach a deal. Panetta was a former California Congressman and director of the Office of Management and Budget, and he understood the stakes. We agreed to set up a high-level working group whose goal was to reach an agreement. For the first time, we had real hope that there might be a rabbit in this hat.

The Tarmac at Santa Monica Airport

Over the summer, the White House and our county team hammered out the terms of a deal. On September 22, 1995, President Clinton announced the agreement on the Santa Monica Airport tarmac, joined by all five county supervisors. It was a dramatic moment, broadcast live on television and radio throughout Southern California. The agreement came ten days before we would have been forced to slash the health care safety net for millions of vulnerable county residents. The package also prevented the layoff of thousands of county health workers.

After months of uncertainty, the moment seemed surreal—and remarkable. The President led off the historic announcement by praising the plan's emphasis on ambulatory care. "This is a national issue," he said. "It's not a Los Angeles County issue. If it can be solved here with the restructuring, a lot of people all over America will be learning a lot from what you are doing."

Most significantly, a hidebound, financially hemorrhaging health care system was now going to be overhauled and stabilized. Getting to this point was not easy, I said, turning to the president, because "in order to remold steel, you have to turn the heat up…hot enough so that it is pliable. The heat has been turned up on the Los Angeles County health system now, to the point where it can be remolded in a more effective, more efficient way that better serves our public."

There were great sighs of relief at the County Hall of Administration the next morning. The key outlines of the deal had been struck less than three months after the formation of the health care crisis task force. It was an extraordinary achievement. Yet nothing is ever simple in life or politics. My colleague, Yvonne Burke, voiced a note of caution that proved to be prescient: "It's very encouraging, let's hope everything holds together," she said. "I won't be totally relieved until the money is here in our hands."

Sure enough, in the following months the bloom was off the rose. All our discussions had assumed a five-year agreement, and so did our financial projections. This was standard procedure. But federal negotiators suddenly threw us a curve. They approved only one year, and refused to even consider granting the remaining four years until all the details of the first-year funding package were settled. It appeared that the bureaucrats wanted to just give us enough money to get them through the Presidential election year, but no more.

We fired back, saying it would be impossible to make meaningful, long-term plans—let alone adopt responsible budgets—unless the full five-year funding was assured. It seemed like we were back at square one. So, on March 4, 1996, Molina, Burke, and I again flew back to Washington, DC to urge Panetta to honor the original promise. We received that assurance, a full six months after the waiver was first announced. "We've got a deal," I told reporters, emerging from our final meetings at the White House.

Success has a thousand parents, and we had our share: President Clinton and his team, including his able senior advisor and my longtime friend John Emerson, who more than once got our negotiations back on track; our congressional delegation, especially Senator Dianne Feinstein and Congressman Henry Waxman; organized labor, especially the Service Employees International Union (SEIU); and a united Board of Supervisors that had worked as well together as at any time in my twenty years on the board. But singular credit goes to Margolin, without whom none of this could have been possible.

The Second Medicaid Waiver

The smart money was that Los Angeles would easily secure an extension of its five-year Medicaid waiver when the deal expired in 2000. We had made a good faith effort to reform the county's health system, and the political stars seemed to be in alignment once again. The Clinton Administration was still in power, and we believed they would extend this much needed partnership.

So much for conventional wisdom. What should have been a painless process became unexpectedly contentious as the year began, and fears grew that we again would face the calamity we had dodged five years earlier. The county got flak from federal health care officials who were not pleased with the progress we had made toward the waiver's goals. In our defense, we had reduced the number of beds budgeted for hospital care and increased the total number of Los Angeles County outpatient clinics from 39 to 170. We were able to do this through an innovative private/public partnership with non-profit clinics that served residents in every part of our sprawling county. But we had failed to meet every benchmark spelled out in the original agreement. Moreover, federal officials were rightly miffed that Sacramento, now flush with budget surpluses, was reticent to contribute money to the second rescue package for Los Angeles. An extension was now in doubt.

Again, I flew back to Washington with my colleagues, Molina and Burke, to argue our case. We were told that the federal government was not going to give us an unconditional extension, and there were rumblings that they wanted to cancel the waiver entirely. We were able to convince the administration to phase out the original waiver over time. This wasn't what we had hoped for, but it was better than an abrupt termination of the agreement that would have sent our county into a financial tailspin. Still, we remained at loggerheads with the Administration. The county believed it needed a $975 million infusion, while the federal government had dug in its heels at a little more than $800 million.

As the expiration date of the first waiver neared, I began calling allies in Washington to see what could be done, and I struck gold with Senator Feinstein. She had a fundraiser scheduled in Beverly Hills at which President Clinton would be the headliner, and she offered to arrange a face-to-face meeting for the two of us. I could make one last pitch to get the waiver extension back on track.

After consulting with our county officials, I was authorized to split the difference at just shy of $900 million.

Getting to Know Bill Clinton

Although Clinton was going to be mobbed that afternoon at the fundraiser, I didn't come at him out of nowhere. And the back story shows the importance of relationships in politics. We had met eight years earlier at LAPD Commission President Stanley Sheinbaum's home in Brentwood, where then-Governor Clinton was staying during a Los Angeles visit. While Sheinbaum and I were discussing police department matters, Clinton returned from a jog on San Vicente Blvd. I was a dedicated runner myself, and we spent a few minutes comparing notes. The two of us quickly hit it off; I promised to send him a book about marathoning, and he promised to keep in touch.

Eight months later I was in New York City to attend the Democratic National Convention. As I jogged through Central Park one morning, I noticed a police presence up ahead with lights flashing and a large group of people in tow. On a wild hunch I thought it might be Clinton out for a run. I made my way to the scene where I saw Clinton, surrounded by a phalanx of Secret Service agents who prevented me from approaching. So, to get his attention, I shouted: "Governor, it's Zev Yaroslavsky."

He immediately turned to me and told the agents to let me through. "Zev, I see you're still running," he said, and then offered to give me a ride back to my hotel in his motorcade. He sat up front, and I sat in the back of his limousine. There I was, in a car with the next President of the United States for forty minutes (even motorcades fight traffic in Manhattan). We talked about a variety of issues, and he graciously made sure I had seats that night at the convention to hear my former aide, Bob Hattoy, deliver a powerful convention speech on behalf of AIDS research funding.

I reconnected with Clinton over the years, most notably in the aftermath of the 1994 Northridge earthquake, when he brought an entourage with him to tour the damage in the San Fernando Valley. I previously met with him in the Oval Office in June 1993, when I brought my eleven-year old son David to have lunch in the West Wing with my friend and presidential assistant John Emerson. Presidential Press Secretary Dee Dee Myers saw us and invited us to watch the President speak with our space shuttle astronauts who were circling the globe in space. David and the president had a good chat, and I got a few words in, as well. Most notably, my colleagues and I were with him at the Santa Monica Airport to announce the waiver agreement. This was the backdrop to our meeting on June 24, 2000, six days before the expiration of the waiver. Feinstein escorted me to the President, reminded him of why I was there, and left us alone to talk.

"So, Zev, I understand we have some issues," he said. I explained that the federal government had offered $823 million, and we had demanded $150 million more. I told the president that we needed at least $900 million to make the deal work. I asked, "couldn't we split the difference?" He replied, "So you're telling me that if we get up to $900 million, we could wrap this up?" "Exactly," I said, handing him a memo that I had asked Margolin to prepare. "OK, thanks, I got ya," he replied. Thirty-six hours later our county staff in Washington got a call from an administration official saying that the proposal I gave the President had broken the logjam and we now had a deal. In a surprise, the negotiations also produced a contribution of $300 million from a less resistant State of California, under the leadership of its Democratic Governor, Gray Davis. The total package came to $1.2 billion, and we had dodged another bullet.

Big Tobacco to the Rescue

The waivers didn't completely solve the health department's fiscal problems, but they did stop the bleeding. Where we once faced a nearly three quarters of a billion-dollar deficit in 1995, we were $100–200 million in the red by 2002. This gap was more of a rounding error than a crisis in the world of big government budgets, yet it was still unsettling that we couldn't balance our books. We were always one change of administration—one shift in national economic circumstances—away from returning to the financial brink. This weighed heavily on me and my colleagues, and I was always looking for new sources of revenue that would stabilize our fiscal condition.

One such source turned out to be the tobacco industry. For me, this was personal. I was seven years old the first time I purchased a package of cigarettes. I went to the Reyes grocery store on Soto and Barlow Streets in Boyle Heights, around the corner from our apartment, and told Mrs. Reyes that my father had sent me to buy a package of Old Gold cigarettes. It was a lie. Neither of my parents were smokers. But I wanted a pack of Old Gold's in the worst way, because one of my favorite television programs was Sam Levinson's "Two for the Money," a quiz show sponsored by that cigarette brand. Mrs. Reyes obliged, and I took the pack into our back yard on Breed Street, lit the cigarette and took a puff. What followed was not pretty. I started coughing uncontrollably, got nauseous and vomited. I was hardly old enough to light a match, let alone smoke a cigarette.

The day after I graduated high school, I became a two pack a day smoker. I was addicted to this pernicious habit for the next twelve years. Smoking caused my blood pressure and heart rate to go up and my quality of life to decline. I smoked in classrooms, libraries, restaurants, and even in the City Council chambers, where several of us filled ashtrays with dozens of butts during our long sessions.

I knew this habit was a killer. I had been educated about the dangers of tobacco and tried to quit smoking on several occasions, without success. Then I watched as my colleague, John Ferraro, recovered from heart bypass surgery. I watched as one of our closest friends, Barbara's roommate during my college years, contracted lung cancer and was given little chance to live. Neither one of them was a smoker. I asked myself, how long could I dodge a life-threatening illness if I let this habit control me?

Then, on May 21, 1979, I came down with a cold and I couldn't smoke without choking. That day I decided to break the habit once and for all. I took it one day at a time, using every trick in the book to stay on the wagon. The one that worked best was taking my pulse. It turned out that after I quit smoking, my heart rate dropped from ninety to seventy beats per minute. Whenever I had the urge to light up, I'd calculate how much harder my heart would have to work in an hour, a day, a month, and a year. By the time I figured out that my heart would beat 10.5 million times more annually if I resumed smoking, I lost the urge. I quit cold turkey and haven't lit a cigarette since.

Smoking was a public health crisis fueled by an industry that profited by addicting users, especially young people, to its product. The more I learned about the problem—especially from my friend, Congressman Henry Waxman— the angrier I got. Even before I quit, I had joined with Marvin Braude, the "no smoking" leader on the City Council, to pass ordinances banning smoking in Los Angeles restaurants, supermarkets, elevators, and eventually at parks and beaches. Now, as a county supervisor, I had an opportunity to help make the tobacco industry pay for the costs they had imposed on society, and I wasn't going to squander it.

In the mid-1990s several states filed lawsuits against "big tobacco," the five largest tobacco companies, seeking billions of dollars in damages to compensate their public health systems for the costs of treating tobacco-related diseases. As these legal actions moved forward in 1996, I proposed that the Board of Supervisors file its own lawsuit. After all, we were the nation's largest county, and we spent at least $300 million annually on cancer, heart disease, asthma and other illnesses related to tobacco use. I argued that we should join the national lawsuit as a standalone county, given our size and the magnitude of our damages.

The county's legal team gave us the green light to proceed, and a subsequent court decision upheld our right to do so.

In the summer of 1998, before the issue even came to trial, "big tobacco" sued for peace. They negotiated a $300-billion settlement with all 50 states, and in the negotiations that ensued, Los Angeles County received $2.8 billion over twenty-five years—approximately $112 million annually. Our health system got its first check two years later, a huge victory, even though it didn't fully compensate us for our costs. Health advocates thought we didn't drive a hard enough bargain, but I said at the time, "It's hard to walk away from that [money] if you're Los Angeles County, and you remember what it was like in 1995, when we weren't sure we could keep our health clinics open." That pretty much summed it up. We took the bird in the hand.

The Trauma Tax

Despite this bonanza, the county health budget was still financially under water in the spring of 2002. Every year we had to find a way to balance our health department budget. I was at my wit's end, wondering if there was anything more we could do as a board to break this cycle. On a morning jog through Hancock Park, where I did some of my best thinking, I came up with an idea.

When I got into the office, I gathered Alisa Katz, Margolin and my finance staff, along with David Janssen, our very able Chief Administrative Officer. I told them I wanted to propose putting a tax on the November ballot to raise enough money to end the perpetual health department deficit. "Now tell, me, what's wrong with that idea?" I asked. No one said a word. I could feel their juices flowing. I was especially focused on Janssen's reaction, not just because I trusted his judgment, but because my colleagues relied on his recommendations as well. He liked the idea. After years of playing defense, we would now be going on offense.

The measure would offer county voters the opportunity to solve our decade-long fiscal crisis. Our pitch would focus on one principal issue: We had to protect our emergency rooms and trauma centers, which were extremely expensive to operate and had been steadily declining in number. As our team started to see the possibilities, I asked how much we would need to raise each year to permanently close the funding gap. "If we could get around $200 million a year, it would really make a difference," Janssen said. I asked his folks and mine to pencil out a proposed measure, and then I would make a political judgment of how much we'd ask the public to pay.

When I approached my colleagues for their support, I immediately received it from Gloria Molina and Yvonne Burke. Like me, they wanted to be pro-active for a change. We couldn't be faulted for trying, even though a tax earmarked for a social service had never been approved by county voters. I now had enough votes to place a measure on the ballot, but getting voter approval would be a heavy lift. Under Proposition 13, any tax of this kind required approval by two-thirds of the voters. I asked my polling firm, Fairbank, Maslin and Maullin, to measure public sentiment for such a tax. "You're right on the cusp at 66 percent," John Fairbank told me. "With a well-funded campaign, it's possible to eke out a win." We were encouraged.

I decided to propose a "parcel tax" of three cents per square foot on all residential, commercial, and industrial buildings in the county. This was a modest charge that would cost the average homeowner $42 per year. The good news was that Measure B, as it came to be known, would generate $168 million annually in county funds. Under federal rules, those funds would be matched by an equal amount of federal and state dollars, bringing the total new funding to $340 million annually, with cost-of-living adjustments built in. If approved, this would be a game changer.

Our campaign message was clear and direct: Los Angeles County used to have twenty-two trauma centers, now it only had thirteen, and more were threatened with closure. This wasn't hyperbole. As my five-year old grandson would say, "It's for real." I crisscrossed the county, delivering an urgent message at town hall meetings and chamber of commerce luncheons: "All of us are just one heart attack away from needing an emergency room, and one drunk driver away from needing a trauma center. Consider this a supplement to your health insurance policy." I felt like we were getting traction.

Just as important, the Service Employees International Union (SEIU), which represented thousands of county health care workers, stepped up big time. The stakes for their members were huge, so they did something I would have never expected nor counseled. They mortgaged their headquarters building to the tune of $1.5 million and contributed all of it to our campaign. Rick Taylor, an early chief of staff of mine who left to become a successful campaign consultant, produced what in my opinion was one of the best television ads in my lifetime.

The ad shows an ambulance rushing an injured child to a trauma center. The paramedic calls into the hospital base station to tell them he's on the way. He's told that there is no room at the emergency room, and he's directed to the nearest available facility. The paramedic tells the hospital that it's just too far away. The boy's mother has a look of panic on her grief-stricken face, and then resignation. The ad then ends with our tag line: "Los Angeles County used to have twenty-two trauma centers, now it only has thirteen, and more are threatened with closure. Vote for Measure B because you never know when you'll need a trauma center." It is one of the most powerful television ads I have ever seen, and I still get goose bumps when I think about it. I have no doubt that without it, Measure B would not have passed.

In mid-October, our pollster started tracking voter support for Measure B on a nightly basis, and we were still hovering right at 66 percent. Fairbank told me the polling showed that 45 percent of Republican women were undecided. If we could convince even a modest percentage of them to come our way, it would tip the balance in our favor. He asked if I knew anyone whose endorsement could move Republican women voters. I came up with one idea—Marge Hearn, the widow of Chick Hearn, the legendary radio and television voice of the Los Angeles Lakers basketball team.

Hearn, who had died earlier that summer at the age of eighty-five after falling on his patio in Tarzana, was exceedingly popular among Southern California residents—especially among the working class, blue collar, and Republican voters we needed to sway. When he lay in a coma at the Northridge Hospital trauma center for three days, news of his condition was covered around the clock by every television station in town. If the President of the United States had been in a local hospital, he wouldn't have received more coverage in the Los Angeles media market.

When Chick died, every Laker fan felt they had lost a family member. I called Tim Leiweke, who ran AEG (the Anschutz Entertainment Group), which owned Staples Center where the Lakers played. I asked if he would call Marge and broach the idea of her signing a post card supporting Measure B. "Give me a couple of hours," he said. He called me back to tell me she was on board.

I drafted the text of a post card that we sent to 400,000 Republican households throughout the county. The text, in part, read: "When my husband, Chick Hearn, fell on our patio last summer, we were fortunate that we had a trauma center nearby. Not everyone is so lucky. Los Angeles County used to have twenty-two trauma centers; now we have only thirteen and more are threatened with closure. Take it from me, you never know when you'll need a trauma center. Vote Yes on Measure B." Days after the card hit the mailboxes, Fairbank called to tell me that Republican women *and* men were now breaking decidedly in our favor. It worked.

We caught one last "break," if you can call it that, on the Sunday before the election. An early morning fog bank hit the south end of the Harbor Freeway, causing a hundred-car pileup. Dozens of motorists were hospitalized and nine of them were transferred to trauma centers. I was home that afternoon watching the NFL game of the week, and during halftime the network switched to Long Beach Memorial Hospital, one of the county's thirteen remaining trauma centers, for an update. The Chief of Emergency Medicine was briefing the media about the accident and the hospitals to which the victims had been transported throughout the county. He told the press that we didn't have enough nearby trauma centers to treat all the critically injured, adding: "And that's why we need people to vote for Measure B on Tuesday." Maybe there is a God, I thought.

Measure B won with 73.8 percent of the vote, one of my most satisfying achievements as a public official. It was a longshot, but as I frequently remind myself, "Wayne Gretzky didn't make 100 percent of the shots he didn't take." Molina, Burke, and I took our shot, and we scored. SEIU risked their building and saved our health system in the process. Rick Taylor saved his best work for his most consequential effort, for which he was minimally compensated. Our pollster gave us impeccably accurate data. And the voters of Los Angeles County responded. Health officials would tell me years later that Measure B was the one thing that ended our perpetual health department deficit. We were no longer as dependent on the whims of Washington; we could leverage the funds generated by this voter-approved tax to permanently bring our health budget into the black.

A Philosophy Backed up by Discipline

I remember stories my parents used to tell me of how the experience of the Depression was seared in their psyche. Frugality, value shopping, and the sin of leaving food on one's plate—these were lessons they learned and passed on to me and my sister. It's not an exaggeration to describe the impact of the 1995 fiscal crisis on County government's psyche in similar terms.

If fiscal responsibility had been empty rhetoric in the Hall of Administration before 1995, it was now a philosophy, backed up by a discipline to match. Members of the Board of Supervisors, our CAO David Janssen, and many of our department heads were psychologically changed. We all realized how close we had come to bankruptcy, and it wasn't lost on us that not one member of the Orange County Board of Supervisors ever got elected to another office after *they* declared bankruptcy.

Our county was now fiscally stable compared to other local governments, especially the City of Los Angeles, where layoffs and furloughs were *de rigueur.* When I left office on December 1, 2014, our health budget had a $400 million surplus—something that no one could have imagined twenty years earlier.

The county's overall budget remained balanced, even during the Great Recession of 2009. While other jurisdictions were struggling to keep their heads above water, our Wall Street bond ratings steadily rose to the highest possible level. It was a vote of confidence in the Board's fiscal management.

Crises pose tough choices, and politicians are too often averse to making them. I've learned through experience that the longer one delays making a difficult decision, the more difficult that decision will be when it is inevitably made. My colleagues and I took that lesson to heart, made some tough decisions, and took calculated risks. As a result, we prevented the bankruptcy of America's largest county. That's the way government ought to work.

CHAPTER 16

The Transit Revolution

For all its natural beauty, glorious weather, dynamic economy and cultural and sports attractions, few things define Los Angeles as much as automobile traffic. The simple act of getting around—to work, the supermarket, a kid's soccer game—is colored by a question that haunts every resident: What's the traffic like, and how long will it take me to get where I'm going?

We all have a horror story about congestion. Mine unfolded years ago on a Monday night. I left an event in Santa Monica, where I had just cut the ribbon on a new housing project for mentally ill homeless women. I had one more appearance that evening, at 7:15 p.m. in Beverly Hills. I began driving to the event at 6:30 p.m. thinking I'd have more than enough time to reach my destination, about four miles away. Fifty minutes later I was still west of the 405 Freeway, approximately *one mile* into my trip. Realizing I'd never get to Beverly Hills in time, I gave up and headed home. The entire eleven-mile trip ultimately took me one hour and forty-one minutes. I could have jogged it faster.

Months later I recounted the story to *Los Angeles Times* columnist Steve Lopez, who was writing about mounting traffic woes on the city's west side. I told him that after this experience I asked Liz Rangel, my secretary, not to schedule me for any events west of the 405, unless I was out of there before 2:30 p.m. or after 8:00 p.m. The story got a lot of attention and people flooded me with their own congestion nightmares. Every resident of Los Angeles saw him or herself as a traffic engineer, and they all had ideas for reducing traffic—from the sublime to the ridiculous. I tossed my own into the hopper, including turning Olympic and Pico Boulevards, both heavily traveled crosstown thoroughfares, into one-way streets, but I couldn't get the city to go along.

Grappling with transportation has been a dominant concern in Los Angeles for nearly a century. Beyond the drain of time spent behind the wheel, it has profound social impacts, including the cohesion of family life and the health of one's state of mind. Traffic was an urgent concern for me, since I represented one of the most congested areas in Southern California. Over the years there had been myriad efforts to fund and construct new transportation systems in Los Angeles County. They were unsuccessful at first, but they eventually gained momentum. I played a role in getting some of these proposals off the ground, and halting others that were transparently unwise. Today, the continuing effort to expand Los Angeles' transit networks has become the largest, most sustained public works project of its kind in the United States. Critics may still joke about the region as a smog-choked, freeway-centric world, but that reality is changing.

Railroads, Red Cars, and Freeways: A History Lesson

It surprises many to learn that long before freeways blanketed the southland, Los Angeles' transportation was based on railroads and streetcars. The city's growth took off in the late nineteenth century when intercontinental railroads connected Los Angeles with the east coast and midwestern states. As the population spread beyond the downtown core, real estate developers financed the construction of electric rail lines connecting travelers with growing suburban neighborhoods. The rail links to these new subdivisions were prime selling points for new home-buyers. The trolley system, with its busy Red and Yellow cars, shouldered the burden of getting Angelenos to and from their destinations. But all that began to change as the automobile became more affordable and ubiquitous.

By the time World War II ended, millions of people had moved into the area and automobiles were essential for day-to-day travel. They were a faster and more convenient alternative to commuter rail and street cars. As the region grew, planners began green-lighting the first freeways in Southern California. Line by line the street cars disappeared, and the final route shut down in 1961. Except for local and long-haul bus service, there was no viable option to the automobile. Newly built freeways became instant parking lots and air pollution grew to unhealthful levels. All the while, real estate developers continued to subdivide relatively inexpensive land in the San Gabriel and San Fernando valleys and beyond. They built tens of thousands of Southern California's iconic middle-class homes with backyards, and some with swimming pools.

This development pattern—building out, not up—was largely served by the county's expanding freeway system. But it also defined a resurgent mass transit system that political leaders began building in later decades, essentially a light rail system that ironically mimicked the old Red and Yellow line corridors. This was the only way to build transit for a region that was so spread out. Los Angeles simply didn't have the density of jobs and population to warrant spending hundreds of millions of dollars per mile on a vast network of subways.

To illustrate this, imagine drawing a circle with a seven-mile radius on a map of Paris with its center at the Eiffel Tower. Most of Paris would land inside the circle. But if you drew the same circle on a map of Los Angeles, with the center at City Hall, the overwhelming majority of the population would live outside the circle. Put simply, subways in Paris, Hong Kong, and New York reach far more people per linear mile than in Los Angeles. This cried out for a hybrid of mass transit options, something that many politicians found hard to swallow.

When Tom Bradley ran for mayor in 1973, he campaigned on a promise to break ground on a subway system within eighteen months. But he ran head-long into fiscal realities and sub-regional infighting, and he couldn't fulfill his commitment for nearly two decades. Ballot proposals to raise sales taxes for transit had failed in the 1960s, and Bradley's 1974 bid for a sales tax increase was also defeated. The issue percolated for six more years until the mayor and Los Angeles County Supervisor Kenneth Hahn teamed up in 1980 to propose a half-cent sales tax increase, this time to fund specific routes, with construction deadlines. Proposition A, as the measure was known, passed with 54 percent of the vote. With revenues finally in hand, planning began on what would become the Blue Line, a light rail connecting downtowns Los Angeles with downtown Long Beach, the second largest city in the county. Plans were also launched for the Red Line subway, that would eventually connect downtown with the San Fernando Valley. In ensuing years, three more half-cent sales taxes—Proposition C (1990), R (2008), and M (2016) were approved by county voters. Slowly but surely, the Los Angeles transit revolution had begun.

Methane, Megadeals, and Mismanagement

Although both new projects initially enjoyed broad support, the Red Line was soon caught up in controversy. In May 1985, a powerful explosion rocked the Ross Dress for Less store on Third Street, just east of Fairfax Ave. The blast was triggered by a spark that ignited a pocket of methane gas leaking into the store's basement, and the resulting fireball decimated the structure. It also cast a pall on plans to build a subway nearby, underneath what is known as the Miracle Mile portion of Wilshire Blvd. and under Fairfax Avenue. Both areas sat on a major methane gas field.

Congressman Henry Waxman, who represented the area, had long harbored concerns that the subway would spawn gentrification and completely change the character of the Beverly-Fairfax neighborhood. This was a personal issue for him, as well as a policy concern. In his first campaign for the State Assembly in 1968, he walked door-to-door in that area, and the residents delivered for him.

They remained the backbone of his political base when he ran for congress. He was protective of this part of his district, which was one of the centers of Los Angeles Jewish life, and he feared that its senior citizen population would be displaced by new development spawned by the subway. He was also convinced that the community's mom-and-pop stores would not survive in the new-look neighborhood of glass-walled office buildings and shops envisioned by transportation planners. Henry wanted none of that.

Now, in the aftermath of the Fairfax explosion, Waxman sponsored legislation banning the use of any federal transit funds to build a subway in the area's high-risk methane zone—a circle approximately four miles in diameter, with the explosion site at its center. Since the affected area was mostly in his Congressional district, his colleagues deferred to him. Although Waxman's fear of gentrification was legitimate, even prescient, I believed his proposal was an over-reaction and said so at the time. There were methane gas pockets throughout the city, and no one could remember a comparable methane explosion during decades of underground construction. Moreover, safety concerns could be mitigated. But Waxman remained firm. The ban was approved by Congress and signed into law by President Ronald Reagan.

Suddenly, the Fairfax portion of the subway that had been in the works for years was a non-starter. Instead, alternate plans were made to tunnel through Hollywood and then on to the San Fernando Valley. Construction began in 1986 on the Red Line's first leg from Union Station to 7th St. and Alvarado Blvd., a distance of 4 miles. Building began that same year on the light rail line between downtown and Long Beach, the first leg of which opened in 1990. Three years later, just months before Bradley left office, he celebrated the opening of the subway's first leg. Its terminus happened to be across the street from Langer's Deli, a landmark and personal favorite of mine, that was struggling to stay in business. A few days after the 1993 opening, I took members of my City Hall staff on a subway ride to the deli and treated them to its signature pastrami sandwich. When we arrived, there was a line of people all the way around the block waiting to get in, and I remember joking with owner Norm Langer that it was worth $1.2 billion to keep his deli in business. Langer's got a shot in the arm and is still going strong.

But trouble was lurking on the horizon. The two agencies that shared responsibilities for transit in Los Angeles—the Los Angeles County Transportation Commission and the Southern California Rapid Transit District—had been fighting embarrassing turf wars for years, and State legislators finally ran out of patience. They passed legislation authored by San Fernando Valley Assemblyman Richard Katz, merging the two agencies and creating the

Metropolitan Transportation Authority (MTA). Like many mergers, however, this one was awkward. The MTA quickly bogged down in a new morass of political infighting and institutional rivalries. It was almost impossible to administer the new agency without stepping on land mines, and corruption soon reared its head as well.

Some of the agency's routing decisions made no sense at all. The new Green Line along the Century Freeway, which stretched twenty miles from Norwalk in the southeast part of Los Angeles County to El Segundo, near the Pacific Ocean, bypassed Los Angeles International Airport. To this day I call the project "the Moses Line," because one can see the Promised Land from the route but can't enter it. Another boneheaded decision was to bypass the Hollywood Bowl on the Red Line's route into the San Fernando Valley. The world-renowned amphitheater attracts thousands of people most summer nights. But it could also do double-duty for transit purposes, with a huge parking lot that commuters could use during the day and throughout the Bowl's nine-month offseason.

All five Los Angeles county supervisors served on the newly formed MTA board, and the transportation issues that I had periodically spoken about as a councilman were now part of my daily responsibilities. This was the unsettled climate at the MTA when I became a member of its Board of Directors in 1995.

Cracking Down on the MTA: Proposition A

The challenges facing us were rooted in the governance structure of the new authority. Along with the five county supervisors, the MTA's thirteen voting members included the mayor of Los Angeles and three of his appointees, and four members representing the county's smaller cities. From the outset there were bitter parochial battles over how and where transit funds should be invested. These fights usually erupted between the City of Los Angeles and suburban communities in the region, especially in the San Gabriel Valley.

A key problem was that many areas, and the politicians who represented them, wanted a gleaming a new underground rail system. But this was financially impossible. Subways, which cost $300 million per mile to build at that time, had to be reserved for the region's densest centers and corridors. They were not political rewards to be handed out on demand. Unfortunately, the MTA Board majority had great difficulty saying "no" to projects, regardless of the cost. The new agency was starting to remind me a lot of county government—it was committing to spend money it didn't have. Put bluntly, the newly constituted MTA was cruising toward bankruptcy. The agency was already spending nearly one-third of its $1.2 billion operating budget on debt service. Now the board was voting to incur even more debt to build new lines that the agency could not afford.

It didn't help that the Red Line also became the subject of jokes on late night television. When a tunneling disaster created a massive sinkhole in Hollywood in 1995, there were jokes about "the sinkhole that ate Hollywood Blvd." But it was no laughing matter to me. On a visit to the site, Los Angeles City Councilmember Jackie Goldberg and I were nearly swallowed up by the hole. We furiously back-pedaled as a sizable portion of the boulevard gave way beneath our feet and barely avoided disappearing into the abyss.

To his credit, Mayor Riordan brought in corporate turnaround specialist Julian Burke in 1997 to impose discipline on the beleaguered MTA. His first order of business was to propose cutbacks in the capital program in order to get the agency's fiscal house in order. But Burke's recommendations met with resistance, because the board lacked the discipline to prevent the MTA's financial implosion. In a nutshell, there was more political remuneration in cutting ribbons on new and expensive rail lines than in cutting spending. Clearly, stronger medicine was needed.

As a result, I made one of the most painful political decisions in my career. I launched a 1998 ballot measure—Proposition A—that prohibited the MTA from spending *any* of its sales tax revenues on new subway construction. This meant that both the Eastside and Westside subway projects would be stopped in their tracks. In the case of the Eastside, a light rail project was ultimately built at a fraction of a subway's cost. As for the Westside project, the MTA had proposed building a subway under Pico Blvd., one mile south of Wilshire, to avoid the methane gas zone. It would have been a colossal mistake to build it through that corridor, which had minimal density. My view was that if Proposition A passed, it would force the MTA, and ultimately Congress, to revisit the safety issue as well as the federal funding ban on tunneling in the methane zone.

Admittedly, I was taking a two-by-four to the agency in order to force it to make tough decisions about where to invest its scarce funds. I was a subway *supporter*, yet I was proposing a more conservative budgetary approach than most of my transit allies. If the MTA's reckless spending didn't stop, the county's transit agency wouldn't have enough money to operate effectively. To be sure, this wasn't Boston's "Big Dig," which ran up more than $10 billion in cost overruns. But the county was well on its way to a fiscal train wreck if the profligate spending wasn't stopped. Proposition A won an overwhelming victory with 68.1 percent of the vote, rolling up huge majorities in every part of the county.

The voters' verdict was a wake-up call for an agency that had become a national embarrassment, and it had the desired result. The tough love that the ballot measure meted out forced board members and agency staff to rein in their spending aspirations. Transportation engineers now had a mandate to plan less expensive modes of transportation, including light rail and busways that could move tens of thousands of people far more economically than subways. The MTA board grudgingly went along. Consequently, the agency slowly began resuscitating its reputation. Although its public approval rating was only 31 percent in 2000, nearly a decade later it had doubled to 61 percent. The agency had gained the confidence of county voters, and was now poised to launch a dramatic expansion of the regional transit system.

The Courage to Try Simple Solutions: The Orange Line

The following year, 1999, I was part of a delegation that visited Curitiba, Brazil, to observe a cutting-edge bus rapid transit system. The brainchild of Jaime Lerner, an architect and urban planner-turned-mayor and governor, the system featured five major street corridors, all reserved exclusively for buses. Our delegation, led by Mayor Riordan, also included Supervisor Yvonne Burke and State Assembly Majority Leader Robert Hertzberg. I brought with me my able transportation deputy, Samantha Bricker. She started working with me as a fifteen-year-old intern and now directs the multi-billion-dollar capital program at LAX. I knew that if I got any ideas on this trip that could be applicable back home, she would be the one to convert them into reality. She would also be my agent in negotiating with stakeholders and running interference in the MTA bureaucracy.

Seeing the Brazilian bus system in action made a huge impression on me. I knew immediately that this model could be easily replicated across the San Fernando Valley, linking the North Hollywood subway station in the east with Warner Center, a major employment hub, in the west. The MTA owned an abandoned fourteen-mile-long railroad right of way across the valley that was once part of the Red Car system, and it would be perfect for the line I had in mind.

My idea was to pave the right of way with concrete and asphalt—like a highway—and run articulated buses (two buses hooked together) on this exclusive guideway, carrying up to 100 passengers at a time. Unlike the cost of a subway ($300 million per mile), or a light rail line ($75 million per mile), this project would cost less than $15 million per mile to build. Of course, I would face local opposition and legal challenges. For years, residents and their representatives opposed the concept of such a line. My constituents liked things the way they were. But county taxpayer funds had already been used to purchase this real estate for transit. Where others saw abandoned train tracks, I envisioned a light rail on rubber tires, whisking tens of thousands of daily commuters across the valley.

On the flight home from Brazil, I drew a diagram of the proposed valley system on the back of a cocktail napkin and showed it to Hertzberg, my airline seat mate. He loved it. Back in Los Angeles, I asked Bricker to engage MTA staff to conduct a cost analysis for the project. They came back with a cost estimate of approximately $300 million. The price tag was daunting, but we already had $200 million in the MTA budget for cross-valley transit, and all we needed was another $100 million. Then I got a call from Hertzberg, who was sitting in the Governor's office in Sacramento. He asked if we could use an additional $100 million for transit. "Are you joking?" I asked. Governor Gray Davis had a robust surplus in his State budget, Hertzberg said, and he was looking for ways to spend it on one-time projects. He wanted Los Angeles to benefit from part of the largesse, and the majority leader seized the opportunity. Yes, I told him, the money would close the financial gap for the busway across the valley. And that's how the Orange Line, as it came to be known, was fully funded.

Of course, it wouldn't have been Los Angeles if obstacles didn't surface. First, we had to get the project approved by the MTA Board. There were two competing routes. The one I favored traveled along the entire abandoned railroad right of way, including along Chandler Blvd. Meanwhile, I was encountering strong opposition from community groups, from one end of the Valley to the other. In the east, there were concerns about how the guideway would be landscaped. In the west, equestrians, who had been using the abandoned right of way as their own private bridle trail wanted to keep it that way. Many of the residents were concerned about potential noise and traffic problems.

All these complaints paled compared to the hostile reaction I got from one of the city's largest Orthodox Jewish synagogues, Shaarei Tzedek Congregation. It was located on Chandler Blvd., adjacent to the proposed busway. Congregants were incensed about the project and at one point I became *persona non grata* in that community. They staged a protest rally of over 1,000 residents against the project, and I bore the brunt of their ire. Adinah Solomon, my long-time field deputy, called me from the rally and was distraught. She had volunteered to take part of her Sunday to observe the event. "They hate you," she said. "If you were here they would hang you." Adinah, who was beloved by everybody and had been with me from the beginning, felt she had let me down. But I quickly disabused her of that notion. We were all in this together.

So why were emotions running high? The synagogue's leader, Rabbi Marvin Sugarman, was a Talmudic scholar whom I knew well, and for whom I had immense respect. Right off the bat he told me that construction of the Orange Line busway, would be a disaster. Mystified, I asked him to explain. He said that his temple was on the south side of Chandler Blvd., and although half of his congregants lived on the south side, the other half lived on the north side. On the Sabbath, all his congregants walked to religious services. He argued that those who lived on the northern side of the boulevard would be taking their lives into their hands crossing the right of way, as buses whipped by at thirty-five miles per hour. He feared that half of his members would be forced to quit the congregation, which meant the synagogue would implode.

I would never endorse a project that forced a synagogue, church, or mosque to close. So, as a confidence-building measure, I proposed that we put a crosswalk right in front of his synagogue, enabling congregants to safely cross the busway. The rabbi said it would be too dangerous for them to cross without a signal. OK, I said, we'd install a pedestrian signal that congregants could activate by pushing a button—turning the light red for the buses. "Ah," the Rabbi answered. "You know that on the Sabbath my congregants are prohibited from activating electricity." Of course I knew that, explaining that we would install a Sabbatical light at the crosswalk. It would be programed to turn red automatically between sundown on Friday through Saturday night, just like the system devised by the city's Chief Traffic Engineer in the mid-1970s for orthodox Jews in the Fairfax neighborhood.

I thought we had finally put the Rabbi's concerns to rest, but he couldn't take "yes" for an answer. Regardless, this is how I dealt with all the concerns that arose along the fourteen-mile corridor. I engaged the public, listened to their concerns, and tried to take them off the table one by one. In the end, the MTA board approved the Chandler alignment by one vote.

People eventually made peace with the Orange Line, and it became one of the biggest success stories of the Los Angeles transit revolution. When it opened in 2005, we expected 7,000 daily riders; we had 14,600 on day one. Ten years later, the number had soared to more than 33,000. People were voting with their feet. Indeed, the Orange Line was more than a transit system—it was also a recreation and beautification project. We built bike and walking/jogging paths parallel to the busway and landscaped it with a variety of trees and flowers. As a bonus, the busway came in under budget—a rarity at the MTA.

When I first discussed this idea with Jaime Lerner, he spoke to me like a teacher to a student. "Have the courage to try simple solutions," he said. That statement impacted me as much as any seven words ever uttered in the public policy realm. So often, solutions to complex problems can be found hiding in plain sight, and this was a perfect example of that.

By the time the line opened, Rabbi Sugarman had retired and moved to Jerusalem. But he came back to Los Angeles for a visit just as the busway opened. When I ran into him at a banquet, I asked if he had seen the Orange Line in operation. He said he had. "How do you like it?" I asked. "The Orange Line—what's not to like?" he replied. I loved it and jokingly told Rick Thorpe, the CEO of the project, that he should put a picture of Rabbi Sugarman on every billboard in the San Fernando Valley and plaster that quote beneath it.

On the first day of operations a woman came up to me, hugged me, kissed me, and thanked me. She explained that she lived in Van Nuys and commuted on public transportation to her Long Beach job, forty miles away. Before the Orange Line, her trip took two hours and fifteen minutes each way. Now, the same trip was taking an hour and a half. We had restored seven and a half hours a week to her life—the equivalent of an entire workday. She could now spend more time with her children, read a book, or do whatever she pleased. Our encounter was a reminder that transit projects are built for people, not for real estate developers or construction contractors. Today, riders cross the valley in forty-two minutes, which is faster than most car trips on the Ventura Freeway during the work day. The line carries more people than some of the region's light rail lines and is considered the most successful busway in the United States.

The Expo Line: Times Change

Years before I joined the MTA board, transit officials purchased another abandoned railroad right of way. At the time, no one could have guessed that this acquisition would pave the way for construction of a desperately needed and historic transit line, the first to serve traffic-choked West Los Angeles since the abandonment of that Red Car line more than a half century earlier. The corridor in question paralleled Exposition Blvd., extending from just south of downtown on the east, to Santa Monica on the west.

A grassroots movement had formed to turn this right of way into a light rail line, and it was a great idea. But in the late 1980s there was no source of funding to design or build the project. Moreover, the plan drew strong opposition from Cheviot Hills residents, who feared the so-called Expo Line would have a negative impact on their upper middle-class community. I had reservations about the route as well, but for different reasons. I thought commuters would be better served by an alternate route that would reach far more people, including the densely populated community of Palms, as well as Culver City's business district and its motion picture studios. It was all moot, however, when the project was shelved in 1989 for lack of funding.

Plans for the Expo Line sprang back to life a little over a decade later, when funds previously earmarked for the Red Line subway became available for the first phase of this project, which would run from downtown Los Angeles to the eastern edge of Culver City, halfway to the ocean. It would serve the University of Southern California, the Los Angeles Coliseum, and several museums in Exposition Park, south of downtown. Few questioned the need for the new line in one of the city's most congested corridors, and the state legislature established the Exposition Light Rail Construction Authority to manage the project. I became a member of its board and one of the project's chief advocates.

MTA wanted to build the line at ground level, although it would have overpasses at major intersections along the route. This proposal, however, sparked strong opposition from Steve Sample, USC's respected president. Sample loved the fact that Metro would have two stops adjacent to the university, but he hated the idea that the line wouldn't be built as a subway. He insisted that we build the USC segment underground at an additional cost of $120 million. Asked why, he said "every rail line in America has a right side and a wrong side of the tracks," which he felt would adversely impact his campus. Incredulous, I asked, "Tell me, which side would be the right side, and which would be the wrong side of the tracks? With USC on one side and the Natural History Museum, the California Science Center, the African American Museum, and the Coliseum on the other, there would be no 'wrong side.'" Sample remained unmoved.

As members of the Construction Authority, Supervisor Yvonne Burke and I began to worry that this dispute would cause irreversible delays and jeopardize the entire project. We tried to reason with Sample, pointing out that similar light rail lines had worked successfully, including in Pasadena (where he lived), Salt Lake City and San Francisco. There was no "wrong side" in these communities. In fact, the Salt Lake City light rail line ran at ground level right through the campus of the University of Utah. I asked him, "Don't you think UCLA would love to have a light rail serving its campus?" He snapped back, "Then put it out there, but not here." Burke and I finally offered to tunnel under Exposition Boulevard—but only if the university would pay for the added $120 million cost. At this point USC's Board of Trustees came to the rescue. Key members saw our proposed project as an amenity, rather than a threat, and they weren't about to raise the money needed to meet Sample's demand. The issue died without a whimper.

A decade later, as the first phase of the Expo Line was under construction, we turned our attention to planning the second phase—from Culver City to the Santa Monica Pier. This turned out to be a bit more complicated than we anticipated. I asked Vivian Rescalvo, my former children's service deputy who was now my transit deputy, to help navigate this thicket. During our evaluation of alternative routes, it became clear that the route I favored back in the 1980s was unfeasible (it would have gone west on Venice Blvd. and north on Sepulveda Blvd, reconnecting with the Exposition right of way). The Sepulveda route would have required the demolition of hundreds of apartments, a non-starter for me, and it would be cost-prohibitive. So, I supported the only other alternative, which was to follow the original Expo Line right of way adjacent to Cheviot Hills.

When I announced my position, I took considerable heat from some of my former Cheviot Hills constituents at a public meeting. They were irate. They read a letter I had sent them in 1988 making my arguments for the alternative route. Now, they said, I was going back on my word. My response was simple and direct: "The world has changed since 1988." I was stunned by the applause of the several hundred people in attendance, who outnumbered the opponents from whom I even won some grudging respect.

Although some branded me a hypocrite for changing my position, I recalled Ralph Waldo Emerson's famous observation: "A foolish consistency is the hobgoblin of little minds." There is a difference between taking principled stands as a public official and clinging to a position regardless of changing circumstances. Times had certainly changed in West Los Angeles. Traffic congestion was at an all-time high, and even most Cheviot Hills residents now supported the route adjacent to their neighborhood. There was only one way we had found to get this project from downtown to Santa Monica, and it was time to be on our way.

The first leg of the Expo line reached Culver City in 2012, and the second leg opened to Santa Monica in 2016, on time and under budget. Riders would now be able to travel from downtown Los Angeles to Santa Monica without the hassles and aggravation of traffic congestion. At the same time, we were connecting passengers to an emerging transit network crisscrossing the county. Angelenos could not only travel from Santa Monica to Culver City; they could go downtown, transfer to Pasadena on the Gold Line, or to Long Beach on the Blue Line, or to the San Fernando Valley on the Red Line. Truly, the system was becoming a whole that was bigger than the sum of its parts.

Initial estimates were that the Expo Line would carry 75,000 riders a day by 2030, but three years after it opened its ridership was already more than 60,000 a day and growing. There was one final bit of good news: At a key juncture along the route, Expo Line cars glided parallel to the Santa Monica Freeway, in plain sight of commuters hopelessly stuck in traffic. It was better than any billboard we could have imagined.

Politics, Demographics, and Policy: The Advent of Measure R

By 2005 the MTA had opened the Orange Line, the Pasadena Gold Line, the Red Line subway to North Hollywood, and the Green Line light rail on the Century Freeway. The agency had also broken ground on the Eastside Gold Line light rail project, which would connect the predominately Latino communities of Boyle Heights and East Los Angeles to the region's emerging transit network.

When Tom Bradley launched the region's transit revolution in 1973, Los Angeles was predominantly white and middle class. The voters were even whiter and more affluent. That changed dramatically in the decades that followed. As a result of changes in the nation's immigration laws, coupled with economic opportunity and political upheaval in their countries of origin, hundreds of thousands of immigrants, especially Latinos and Asian-Pacific Islanders, made Southern California their new home. By the turn of the current century, Latinos had become a distinct plurality of the population, Asian and Pacific Islanders were growing at an even faster pace, and whites were becoming a minority.

This dynamic also impacted Los Angeles politics. In 2005, city voters elected Antonio Villaraigosa to the mayor's office, the first Latino to hold that post since the nineteenth century. Reflecting this new demographic reality, the City Council and other elected bodies were steadily diversifying racially and ethnically, including the MTA board. Many of the new residents were disproportionately low income and transit-dependent. As a result, there was a growing constituency for an expanded public transit system, and it was willing to pay for it. This presented an unprecedented opportunity.

With the 2008 presidential election approaching, a group of MTA board members—including Villaraigosa, former Assemblyman Richard Katz, Supervisor Yvonne Burke, and me—concluded that the time was right to put a new sales tax increase for transit on the county ballot. The goal was to accelerate construction, and secure long-term funding, for projects that were nothing more than plans on a shelf to that point.

We reasoned that turnout in the November election would be higher than usual, boosting the tax increase's chance for passage. The proposal we drafted called for a half-cent sales tax increase generating nearly $40 billion over thirty years for mass transit, highway construction, and street repair projects. It would cement the county's commitment to enlightened transportation policies, and lock in a source of local revenues that could be used to qualify for matching federal transit funds.

Not surprisingly, we faced a tough battle. First, Proposition 13 required us to get approval from two-thirds of the voters. That would have been hard enough under the best of circumstances, but there was still little or no consensus about transit policy in the county—a 4,058-square mile area stretching from Lancaster in the Mojave Desert in the north, to Long Beach on the border of Orange County in the south. Still, the payoff would be worth the effort. Flush with new revenues, we could green-light several long-overdue mass transit projects.

One of the motivating factors behind this initiative was Mayor Villaraigosa's 2005 campaign promise to build a "subway to the sea." Like me, he understood that the route *had* to run under Wilshire Boulevard. It was a linear center that needed to be the backbone of the Westside mass transit system. However, Congressman Henry Waxman's 1985 legislation banning the use of federal funds for a subway under Wilshire was a hurdle that needed to be cleared. So, Villaraigosa approached Waxman and offered to empanel three experts who would re-examine the safety of tunneling in the methane gas zone and present their findings to the Congressman. He agreed. The panel, including one member appointed by Waxman, unanimously concluded that tunneling could be done safely. Waxman accepted the conclusion, introduced a bill in Congress to rescind his earlier legislation, and it was approved and signed into law in 2007 by President George W. Bush.

Backers of what became Measure R drafted the ballot proposal, taking into consideration the views of competing stake holders; transit vs. highway advocates; bus vs. rail proponents; and eighty-eight cities that made up the county. We were buoyed by early public opinion polls showing that we were sitting right at the two-thirds mark. But the fight was far from over. State legislation was needed to authorize a measure to raise the sales tax, and the MTA board had to ultimately vote to place it on the ballot. Assemblyman Mike Feuer authored the bill and tenaciously navigated the treacherous minefield known as the Sacramento legislative process. The measure itself would repeal the prohibition on the use of sales tax revenues for subways that I had authored a decade earlier. Vivian Rescalvo, my deputy, collaborated with Richard Katz and Villaraigosa's staff to minimize stakeholder political opposition, and to get the seven board votes necessary to put the measure on the ballot. We succeeded with one vote to spare. I was cautiously optimistic that the measure would pass.

Then the Great Recession struck. In the summer of 2008, the US economy cratered, along with the public's confidence in it. Measure R suddenly seemed like a crazy idea. The notion that we might get a two-thirds vote for a tax increase at a moment of economic panic struck me as delusional. I was blunt about this, telling Villaraigosa that we might be kidding ourselves. So, I suggested it would be prudent to commission one more poll to measure public support. This was the least we could do before approaching supporters for the $4 million our campaign would cost. Villaraigosa and Richard Katz agreed, and the results were remarkably encouraging. They showed us still at 66 percent, just shy of the required two-thirds. With a strong campaign, we could get over the hump. It was a gut check decision, but we trusted our polls. "You live by the sword, you die by the sword," we concluded, and the campaign began.

We hit voters with television ads and targeted mailers. On television we displayed a countywide map showing all the transit lines that the tax measure would fund. Our mailers were targeted locally, detailing what the measure would do for residents in each part of the county. Opponents, meanwhile, couldn't muster a meaningful campaign. Everything broke our way, and Measure R passed with 67.9 percent of the vote. It was a testament to how frustrated county residents were about traffic. They had voted to tax themselves in the midst of economic uncertainty unparalleled since the Great Depression.

We did especially well in traffic-plagued communities on the Westside and San Fernando Valley, as well as among transit dependent voters in Central, East and South Los Angeles. Without a doubt, the heavy minority voter turnout generated by Barack Obama's historic election made the difference. Almost 80 percent of those voters supported Measure R. Villaraigosa deserves credit for his vision, leadership, and courage. He had a lot to gain, but the most to lose by leading this campaign. Measure R was his finest hour as mayor, and he earned renewed respect from me.

The victory paved the way for an even greater success eight years later, when voters enacted another half-cent sales tax, Measure M, building on Measure R and more than doubling funding for an ever-expanding regional transit network. Today, twenty percent of the sales tax revenues collected in Los Angeles County are earmarked for transit. No other transit agency in the nation comes close to this level of local taxpayer support. As a result, Los Angeles is being transformed. A city and county whose transit system was once a laughingstock is now the national leader. Where the map once displayed a maze of inter-connecting freeways, it now shows a network of color-coded subway, light rail, and bus rapid transit lines, with more to come.

The subway may not reach the sea, but it will get to the West L.A. Veterans Administration, serving the Miracle Mile, Beverly Hills, Westwood, and UCLA along the way. To the east, light rail is planned for the southern portion of the

San Gabriel Valley to complement the Gold Line on its north side running from Pasadena to Claremont. A light rail project serving the Santa Ana Freeway corridor in the southeast county is on the drawing boards as well. The Crenshaw light rail project, now under construction, will finally connect LAX to the region's transit network. The airport is also building a transformational people mover, which will connect its terminals to the transit system for the first time.

In the aftermath of Measures R and M, it appeared as though our region was irreversibly committed to giving the public an alternative to the automobile. Scholars and policy makers wondered whether Los Angeles could ever become a transit-oriented city. To do so would require Angelenos to make huge changes in their daily commuter habits. But make no mistake, the train had left the station.

CHAPTER 17

Arts and Culture:
Los Angeles' Golden Age

———————

As the sun rose on 1995, Los Angeles was in a funk. The scars of the Rodney King uprising remained fresh, and memories of the Northridge earthquake still rattled the region. Although the nation was beginning an economic recovery, county officials were wrestling with a deepening budgetary crisis as Orange County's bankruptcy cast a pall over local government finance throughout California. What unwelcome news would hit us next?

For me, the answer came in a late 1995 meeting with Sally Reed, the county's Chief Administrative Officer. Never one to mince words, she told me there was a disaster brewing over the long-stalled project to build a new symphony hall on county-owned land across the street from the Los Angeles County Music Center. Although Mrs. Lillian Disney (Walt's widow) had made a generous $50 million lead gift to build a new home for the Los Angeles Philharmonic, the campaign to raise the remaining funds had faltered. The county was committed to building a $100 million underground garage as part of that deal. It raised the funds by issuing construction bonds that would be paid off with parking revenues generated by concert patrons. Now, it looked like there would be no concert hall and, thus, no revenues to pay off the bonds for the garage which by now had been built. Under those circumstances, the County's general fund would have to cover the cost of the garage, which was never part of the original deal. Reed said it was time to pull the plug on Disney Hall and find another use for the land that would generate enough revenue to retire the debt.

Looking back, I'm struck by how immediate and visceral my response was. This was the *last* thing the county should do, I answered. The nation saw Los Angeles as a victim of catastrophes, both natural and man-made. If we folded our cards now, we'd be showing the world that we couldn't marshal the resources for a major civic project—the biggest since the 1984 Olympics.

I had no idea how my colleagues would react to Reed's suggestion. But as the supervisor representing Los Angeles County's third district, I inherited a formidable legacy of support for the arts from my predecessors, especially John Anson Ford and Ed Edelman. Even though I didn't focus on culture as a public policy issue early in my career, I now eagerly embraced the county's mantle for the arts.

We had a lot to lose by terminating the Disney Hall project, and I told Reed in the strongest possible terms that doing so was out of the question. She backed off and never formally raised the possibility again. But I wasn't alone with her in my office that morning. There were ghosts in the room watching over me, and I keenly felt their presence. If I had said yes to Reed, they would have rolled over in their graves. My mother most of all.

Minna Yaroslavsky had lived and breathed classical music. On a summer night in 1943 she attended the Hollywood Bowl concert where Sergei Rachmaninov conducted *and* performed his renowned Second Piano Concerto. The highlight of the evening came when my mother went to the stage door and waited for Rachmaninov to emerge. When he exited, she greeted him in her elegant Russian. He gallantly kissed her hand and thanked her. It became a fabled moment in our family lore. At home, my mother religiously listened to Los Angeles classical music radio station KFAC and made sure I could hear it throughout the house. I grew up listening more to Brahms and Beethoven than to rock and roll, and my mother insisted I take piano lessons to nurture my appreciation for the classical music art form.

This passion for music ran in our family. My great uncle, George Koukly, was a professional musician who played the string bass with impresario Sol Hurok's orchestras. He traveled the country accompanying the likes of the Bolshoi and Royal Ballets. Less than five feet in stature, Koukly played the bass, one of the tallest instruments in the orchestra. He took me to performances whenever he visited Los Angeles and sat me down with him in the orchestra pit at the old Philharmonic and Shrine Auditoriums, allowing me to turn the pages of his musical score. He introduced me to megastars like Dame Margot Fonteyn and Rudolph Nureyev, and he had a profound influence on my love for classical music and ballet. I had other mentors as well, including Robert Williams and Robert Zarlenga, my Bancroft Junior High orchestra teachers who convinced me to play the oboe. I felt the presence of these folks and others when I pointedly said "no" to Reed's proposal to kill the concert hall project.

My love for music wasn't just a childhood passion. As an adult, I regularly attended concerts at the Music Center and the iconic Hollywood Bowl. I watched and learned from my City Council seatmate, Joel Wachs, for whom the arts was a signature issue. He was a driving force in the establishment of the Museum of Contemporary Art (MOCA) on Grand Ave. "People don't come to New York City for the crime and graffiti," he'd say. "They come for the museums, the concerts and the Broadway shows." Upon joining the Board of Supervisors, I was ready to play a role in advancing and expanding public support for the arts.

Disney Hall: Building the Future

The county had a pivotal mandate when it came to the arts. It owned and operated virtually all the Southland's major publicly owned cultural facilities, including the Los Angeles County Museum of Art (LACMA), the Music Center, the Hollywood Bowl, the John Anson Ford Theatre, and the Natural History Museum. As the new Third District Supervisor, I was stepping into some big shoes. Ford, who served on the Board of Supervisors from 1934 to 1958, was a progressive trailblazer who marshalled political and financial support for the Hollywood Bowl, and laid the groundwork for the construction of the Music Center on Bunker Hill in downtown.

Ed Edelman, my immediate predecessor, served from 1974 to 1994. He negotiated a landmark deal with LACMA, establishing a guaranteed level of annual funding from the county's coffers that is unprecedented among publicly owned museums in the United States. He also helped secure the land on which Disney Hall would be built, and launched the first upgrade of the Hollywood Bowl in two generations. Third district supervisors traditionally took a lead role in cultural issues, in part because the district was home to some of the county's most prominent cultural institutions. But Edelman and I were additionally motivated by our personal love for the arts.

Due to an earlier redrawing of supervisorial district lines in 1991, the Disney Hall site was no longer in the Third District when I arrived on the board. But I took an abiding interest in pushing for the creation of what would become an architectural and acoustical masterpiece. Frank Gehry's design for the hall was bold and imaginative, and if we could pull it off it would be a lasting achievement for Los Angeles.

Were there roadblocks? Of course. Construction costs were woefully underestimated, and the eventual price tag would swell to more than $284 million. It was unclear in the beginning whether the funds to build the hall would or could be raised, given the failure of previous efforts. The picture began to brighten one day when I got a phone call from Mayor Riordan's Chief of Staff, Bill Ouchi, several months after my meeting with Reed. He wanted to know if the County would welcome the mayor's involvement in breathing life back into the project. I enthusiastically endorsed the idea, knowing Riordan's deep connections to the city's philanthropic community. But I also recommended that the mayor approach my colleague, Gloria Molina who represented downtown, to get her support. Approaching her would be more than a simple act of political courtesy. With her approval, we would have clear sailing; without it, we would be dead in the water. The mayor called a meeting in his City Hall office to which he invited me, Molina, businessman/philanthropist Eli Broad, and several others to discuss the path forward. I was gratified that Gloria not only endorsed this unified approach but agreed that I represent the Board of Supervisors on the Walt Disney Concert Hall Committee that would oversee construction.

This was the beginning of the effort to get Disney Hall back on track. Riordan knew that a successful completion would benefit all concerned: The County, the City, and the Los Angeles Philharmonic. It would also be a dramatic boost to the region's self-confidence. He turned to Broad for the philanthropic heavy lifting and asked him to serve as Chair of the concert hall committee. Broad was a well-known, civically active billionaire who was also a major patron of the arts. He would eventually build "The Broad," his own contemporary art museum on Grand Ave. across from Disney Hall, and the Broad Contemporary Museum at LACMA. He had a deep appreciation and understanding for culture and its importance to Los Angeles. Andrea Van de Kamp, Chairwoman of the Music Center Board, and a member of the Walt Disney Company's Board of Directors, completed the troika that led our team. She, too, played a consequential role in the historic fundraising effort, including securing $30 million from the Walt Disney Company. They got to work quickly and effectively.

Some may ask why a new concert hall was necessary in the first place. Didn't Los Angeles already have a distinguished music center, just across the street from the proposed concert hall? To be sure, the Dorothy Chandler Pavilion was an outstanding, all-purpose theater, but it was not the best place to hear a classical music concert. It had 3,200 seats, way too many to fill night after night, and its acoustics did not convey the full range of sound that an orchestra as good as the Los Angeles Philharmonic could produce. The design and acoustical engineering of the new hall would finally give its musicians a hall to match their talent.

Unfortunately, there was initial tension between Broad and Gehry. They had a history that wasn't going to be easy to navigate, stemming from a dispute over the construction of Broad's Brentwood home, which Gehry originally designed. This rancor threatened to torpedo the Disney Hall project from the outset. In fact, when our committee and Gehry's team met for the first time in the architect's office, it was like a Soviet-American summit meeting. Frank and his team were on one side of the table, with Broad and our folks on the other. Tensions escalated quickly as Eli and Frank exchanged words, and decorum took a holiday. At one point, one of Gehry's partners had to restrain him from walking out of his own conference room, grabbing him by the belt loop of his pants and sitting him down. "Calm down, Frank," he said. "Let's play this out and see what happens." It is a testament to both strong-willed men that they found a way to bury the hatchet and allow their considerable civic pride to prevail.

By 1997 the county had a new CAO, David Janssen, who was an enthusiastic supporter of the project. Janssen was a regular presence at the Disney Hall Committee meetings, and he formed a strong alliance with the rest of the group. On occasion, if the construction project had a cash flow problem, he deferred deadlines until private fundraising could catch up. He was key to keeping the project moving and ensured that the County did not get in the way of its completion. Soon the money began arriving in big chunks. Corporate and civic leaders, culture philanthropists, and others kicked in nearly $200 million. All told, the Disney family was in for $90 million, and the Walt Disney Company donated another $30 million to build the Roy and Edna Disney/CalArts Theater (REDCAT) into the hall's structure. As it turned out, sixty-one companies and individuals gave $1 million or more, along with the state, the county and the city's Community Redevelopment Agency.

Construction began in 2000 and as the building began to take shape, Disney Hall's angular, jutting girders atop Bunker Hill drew thousands of curious onlookers. Long before opening night, it was one of the most talked-about structures in the world. In 1997 I travelled to Bilbao, Spain, at Gehry's invitation, for the opening of the Guggenheim Museum which he designed. Sheathed in titanium, it reflected light differently from a variety of angles at various times of the day. Overnight, it transformed a backwater industrial town in Spain's Basque region into a cultural tourist destination. I was confident that Disney Hall would have a similar impact on Los Angeles when it opened its doors. I wasn't disappointed. With its twisting, shimmering surface of stainless steel, Disney Hall marked a "riotous rebirth of downtown Los Angeles," according to the *New York Times*. The hall's principal acoustical engineer, Yasuhisa Toyota, had allowed the LA Philharmonic to be heard in all its glory.

The Disney Hall project took me to many parts of the world during this period. In 1998 I flew to Salzburg, Austria, to solicit a major eight-figure donation for the hall from a prospective donor. Barbara accompanied me (at our own expense), and I told her that we would either come back with the project's largest donation or, at least, have a great visit to Salzburg and its music festival (we did). One of the trip's most memorable experiences took place when our hosts,

Joseph and Brig Troy, invited us to attend a five-and-a-half-hour performance of Wagner's opera, Parsifal, starring Placido Domingo. We had just flown from Los Angeles to Munich, rented a car for a two-hour drive to Salzburg, and changed clothes to be ready for a 5:30 p.m. curtain. Wagner was not Barbara's favorite composer, and we were both jetlagged. When the performance was over, Joe invited us backstage to meet Placido. As the great tenor came out of his dressing room, he heaved a big sigh and said, "You don't know what it's like to stand there and sing for five and a half hours." To which Barbara responded, "You don't know what it's like to sit there and listen for five and a half hours." There wasn't a hole in Austria big enough for me to crawl into, but that was Barbara. Fortunately, Placido had a sense of humor—or deep empathy.

Another trip took me to Sapporo, Japan, to experience the Kitara concert Hall. It had been acoustically engineered by Yasuhisa Toyota, who was doing the same for the Disney project. The group included Toyota, Philharmonic Music Director Esa-Pekka Salonen, Los Angeles Philharmonic President Deborah Borda, *Los Angeles Times* music critic Mark Swed, and me. It was an ear-opening three-day trip. No matter where I sat in that hall, I felt like I was sitting in the best seat in the house. The professionals took copious notes as I took it all in. It was a transformative moment that confirmed for me that we were on the right track.

When Disney Hall was nearly complete, I asked Borda if I could go on stage with my recorder, a woodwind instrument that I have played around with most of my life. I wanted to play a tune and hear what it sounded like in the new venue, and she obliged. So, I took Ginny Kruger, then my arts deputy, on stage with me and played "Danny Boy." The hall's acoustics even made me sound decent, a tall order indeed.

Toyota once told me that acoustics is a science *and* an art. No matter how carefully one engineers a concert hall, you never know for sure how it will sound until the first notes are played. So, as I walked into the second half of the orchestra's first rehearsal in the hall, I spotted Toyota and asked, "How does it sound?" He smiled and said, "You listen and let me know what you think." The smile told me everything I needed to know. He had previously explained that the measure of acoustical success would be how well you could hear the low notes on the musical spectrum. As I listened to the orchestra play, my eyes welled up with tears. Every note—from the lowest to the highest—was clearly audible from the first row to the last.

Walt Disney Concert Hall opened in the fall of 2003, and the celebration stretched over three nights. That same week I was engaged in a contentious negotiation to end a month-long bus strike in our county. My "good fortune" landed me as chair of the Metropolitan Transportation Authority during the crisis, and we were negotiating with the transit unions in my office conference room, one block away from the opening night festivities. We laid out some negotiating positions fifteen minutes before the concert's start, and then I asked that we reconvene at 11:00 p.m. to discuss them further. I arrived at Disney Hall just in the nick of time, and as I walked down the red carpet, I was alone. Barbara was already seated inside, while I was peppered with questions from the press about the status of the strike. "We're still negotiating," I said, "and we'll be negotiating after the concert as well." But for the next three hours, I was going to celebrate one of Los Angeles' greatest cultural achievements. I was thrilled that we had finally reached this moment, savoring music by Mozart, Stravinsky, and Charles Ives. It had been a long journey, and I was one of a handful of people who knew how close we had come to having nothing to celebrate.

Today, nearly two decades later, hundreds of thousands of music lovers attend concerts at Disney Hall every year. It is the envy of cities around the globe, and the Los Angeles Philharmonic, now under the direction of Gustavo Dudamel, is widely recognized as the nation's most daring and accomplished orchestra. Building the hall was a textbook example of vision and teamwork. It was constructed in the aftermath of one of the worst periods in Los Angeles history. Civil unrest, a destructive earthquake, fires, floods, and a deep economic recession made this project's completion highly improbable. For the first time in a generation, we demonstrated that the county could still do big ambitious things against long odds. The civic leadership got together and said, "enough is enough."

Restoring Gems: The Hollywood Bowl and the Ford

If the construction of Disney Hall was a big step into the future, the efforts I spearheaded to revitalize the Hollywood Bowl and John Anson Ford Theatres were case studies of historical restoration and preservation. The challenges of preserving landmark cultural venues are no less important than the herculean efforts to build new ones.

In the case of the Hollywood Bowl, the tell-tale signs of neglect were not so obvious. The nation's most prominent outdoor amphitheater had been so successful that most people simply assumed it would last forever. Los Angeles audiences have enjoyed the beautiful and distinctive site on summer evenings, ever since a ramshackle version of the iconic structure opened in 1922 in its natural bowl-shaped setting. With its gleaming white shell and seating for nearly 18,000 people, the Bowl has been the summer home of the Los Angeles Philharmonic for a century.

It is one of the few major American orchestras whose winter and summer homes are located in the same city.

The venue has hosted a steady stream of A-list classical, pop, rock, jazz, and new age music under the stars through the years, and millions have flocked to see and hear them. Until the Covid pandemic hit in 2020, people enjoyed outstanding music, at still affordable prices, every summer. Neither the Great Depression nor World War II could shut it down. When my parents took visitors on a tour of Los Angeles, the Bowl was always one of the four sites on the tour. They particularly enjoyed taking Israeli friends there, suggesting that their ancient Roman amphitheaters had nothing on the Hollywood Bowl.

By 1996, however, the structure was showing disturbing signs of age. Ernest Fleischman, the former President of the Los Angeles Philharmonic, came to see me immediately when he learned that I was developing a ballot measure to fund the construction and restoration of county and municipal parks and recreation facilities, a category which included the Bowl. He made a persuasive case that the theater would likely not survive another generation unless its decline was reversed. The most troubling problem was that asbestos was leaking onto the shell-shaped stage, as well as into the Bowl's administrative offices below it. If we didn't act, we could be endangering the wellbeing of performers and staff. I was certain that Cal/OSHA, the state's occupational hazard agency, would eventually shut the place down. The estimated cost of the shell's demolition and replacement was $18 million, a bargain by any measure.

Championing the Bowl was not a hard decision for me, given its legendary status and my family's personal history with it. I told Fleischman that I was all in. What would my musical mentors have said if I had done otherwise? Voters eventually gave strong approval to the funding measure, after a campaign in which my message was simple: Do we want this Bowl to be like the Roman Colosseum, a museum piece where people would point and say, "here some of the great musical compositions in the history of mankind were once performed?" Or do we want it to be a living, breathing state of the art venue for the performing arts for generations to come?

We made additional investments in subsequent years, replacing every seat in the amphitheater and each of the fifty-year-old picnic tables. The County also upgraded the sound system and installed four large LED video screens, which democratized the Bowl experience. Now, whether patrons spend $200 or one dollar for a concert ticket—I insisted that we not raise the prices on the least expensive seats—they can share in the intimacy of a performance as never before. Finally, in perhaps the most popular improvement of them all, we expanded the overcrowded restrooms.

When the Board renewed its long-term contract with the Los Angeles Philharmonic to operate the Bowl in 2003, we ensured that it would continue to have a summer home unmatched by any other American orchestra. The 30-year lease also gave the Philharmonic the right to book highly lucrative rock concerts. This dependable source of revenue made the Philharmonic one of the nation's most well-endowed symphony orchestras.

In both the Disney Hall and Hollywood Bowl projects, it helped to have Borda at the helm of the orchestra. Los Angeles had wooed her away from the New York Philharmonic in a brilliant coup in 2000, and she quickly established herself as a visionary, rigorous, and fiscally prudent leader. When Fleischman urged her to pursue a talented young conductor named Gustavo Dudamel, she mounted a full-court press to bring him to Los Angeles. Deborah and I worked closely together on numerous Philharmonic initiatives, and it would be an understatement to call her one of the most impressive cultural arts administrators in the nation.

Borda also made possible one of the more memorable nights of my life, when she asked if I would narrate Aaron Copland's "Lincoln Portrait" at the Bowl. The historic 1942 piece by one of America's greatest composers—a symphonic homage to our 16th president—always had a special place in my heart, and Borda knew it. Copland's stirring music, and the accompanying text, focused on justice, democracy, and moral leadership. The concert would be held on September 11, 2012, eleven years after that dreadful day in our nation's history. I was in Washington, DC that day and will never forgot visiting the Lincoln Memorial late that night. It was still standing while the Pentagon burned. Of course, I accepted Borda's invitation to speak some of the very words that were etched in the shrine's marble, accompanied by the Philharmonic on the Bowl stage.

I knew I'd be humbly joining an extraordinary list of Americans who had narrated the piece, so my first objective was to do no harm. Beyond that, I wanted my narration to match the shifting, nuanced tempos of Copland's glorious, fifteen-minute composition. I have read music since I was young, and I spent hours perfecting my timing so that Lincoln's words would be spoken precisely where Copland had intended. I prepared as though for a test at Juilliard. In a review of the performance, *Los Angeles Times* music critic, Mark Swed, praised my delivery *and* noted that my "musical timing was expert." Mission accomplished!

The Hollywood Bowl project was a labor of love. Restoring the John Anson Ford Theater in the Cahuenga Pass, on the other hand, was more like a rescue mission. Originally a wooden structure, it burned down in 1929 and was rebuilt in solid concrete. For forty years, the 1,200-seat outdoor theater was the home of "The Pilgrimage Play," a New Testament-based story about the life of Jesus.

Patrons were transported to another part of the world, and to another millennium, as they entered the venue with architecture mimicking the walls of Jerusalem's old city. When the Pilgrimage Play ran its course, my predecessor, Ed Edelman, led an effort to repurpose the theater for locally based productions that reflected the diversity of Los Angeles and showcased some of its emerging artists. The transformation was successful. But the facility, nestled in a canyon across the Hollywood Freeway from the Bowl, had fallen into a state of profound disrepair. Many believed it wasn't worth saving. The Ford had been damaged by floods and landslides, plagued by exposed and faulty electrical wiring, and cursed by Rube Goldberg fixes over the years. It's a miracle that the place had survived at all.

Before I left office, the County commissioned Brenda Levin, an historical preservation architect extraordinaire, to create a master plan to renovate and upgrade the Ford and its campus. We launched what became a $70 million campaign to bring the venue into the twenty-first century. When the theater reopened in July 2016, the slopes behind the stage were stabilized, the exterior was completely rebuilt, the acoustics were markedly improved, a modern lighting and drainage system was installed, the seats were replaced, the off-center stage was repositioned, and new dressing rooms replaced the inadequate old ones. In short, an eighty-five-year-old crumbling facility was now as state-of-the art as it could be. Nevertheless, the project significantly exceeded its original budget for a variety of reasons, and I credit my successor, Supervisor Sheila Kuehl, for securing the additional funds to get it across the finish line. In 2019, Kuehl persuaded the Los Angeles Philharmonic to take over management of the theater, a wise decision that strategically positions it for greatness.

As I prepared to leave the Board of Supervisors, the Philharmonic's Board of Directors surprised me by naming the main gate to the Hollywood Bowl in my honor. Borda called it "The Great Gate of Zev," a variation on Mussorgsky's "Great Gate of Kyiv" from his classic masterpiece, "Pictures at an Exhibition," and one of my favorite pieces of music. I was overcome with emotion at the event commemorating the naming. What were the odds, I wondered, that a kid like me from Boyle Heights would rise to a position where I could help expand the cultural footprint of our county? I thought of my parents, my great uncle, my music teachers, and the community in which I was raised. All of them led me to the gate that day.

Every Great Metropolis Needs a Great Museum

I used to tell audiences that although I don't remember anything from my high school trigonometry class, I do remember my eighth-grade music appreciation class. There, I began to hone my love for classical music. Unfortunately, I couldn't say the same about the fine arts. I never took an art appreciation class in school, and never quite connected with paintings and sculpture in the same way as classical music, ballet, and opera. But I made it my business to learn as much as I could about our county's art collection when I joined the Board of Supervisors and became a steward of the Los Angeles County Museum of Art (LACMA). My education began on a rainy afternoon in 1996, when I visited the museum and its new President, Andrea Rich, who had been a friend for many years.

What I saw was a prominent museum—the largest of its kind in the western United States—with a visibly deteriorating physical plant. The buildings had been constructed in the 1960s, when LACMA opened on its Wilshire Blvd. site, so they weren't ancient. But the first thing I noticed were the buckets of water in the basement's corridors. They were filled with rainwater pouring down from the roof three floors above. There were priceless works of art between the roof and the basement, so this wasn't just a structural problem; it was an existential threat to the institution's most valuable assets. To complicate matters, the museum's budget was out of whack, and this posed another problem.

Rich, who had been UCLA's Executive Vice-Chancellor under Chancellor Charles Young, was a smart and tough administrator who made the trains run on time. A relentless budget hawk who did not suffer fools, she was chosen to whip LACMA into shape. Not an easy task. Rich first had to balance the institution's bloated budget and bring its spending into line with revenues. She didn't waste any time getting to work and, in the process, she stepped on some toes on the Board of Directors and among the curators. But Andrea understood that if the institution financially imploded, nothing else really mattered. Beyond the need for immediate repairs, the museum's campus had expanded one building at a time over the years, with little or no regard for its overall coherence. Balancing the budget while simultaneously rebuilding the site was an extraordinary challenge.

Eli Broad, perhaps the most influential member of the museum board of directors at the time, led an effort to rethink the LACMA campus. The plan was to replace the four worn and dysfunctional buildings with one large new building. An architectural competition was held, and Dutch architect Rem Koolhaas won the commission. Broad insisted that the philanthropic community partner with county government to fund this endeavor. He rightly believed that a civic project of this magnitude should have broad civic participation. Given the recession of the early 2000s, however, the county was in no position to fund a museum replacement project, and the LACMA board did not appear to have the capacity to do so either.

As a result, in 2002 I came up with an idea to launch a private fundraising campaign for this and other county cultural institutions. I proposed a $250 million general obligation bond, the proceeds of which would only be spent if they were matched by private contributions. Broad and other cultural leaders loved the idea, and they stepped up to support it financially. However, under California law, the bond had to be approved by a whopping two-thirds of the voters, and we fell short on election day, winning only 62 percent of the votes. Anywhere else in the country this would have been a landslide victory, but not in California. With insufficient funding, the LACMA plan died on the vine.

In the aftermath, Broad decided to fund a new pavilion on the museum campus, now known as the Broad Contemporary Art Museum (BCAM). Many hoped it would house his extensive contemporary art collection, but instead he eventually chose to build and self-finance his own museum, "The Broad," across from Disney Hall and the Museum of Contemporary Art (MOCA) on Grand Ave. in downtown. He had long hoped to turn Grand Ave. into a cultural promenade, and he eventually did. Today, his fingerprints are all over MOCA, Disney Hall, the Los Angeles Unified School District's high school for the arts at Sunset and Grand and, of course, "The Broad." Eli's contributions to the county are indisputable. His legacy is permanently enshrined in Los Angeles' cultural landscape.

There was one unexpected benefit from the failed bond measure. I had long believed that the San Fernando Valley could sustain its own performing arts center. The Valley was not a cultural wasteland, as some believed, and its residents deserved to enjoy a first-rate cultural experience without having to drive all the way to downtown. I called Jolene Koester, the President of California State University, Northridge (CSUN), and asked her if she would be interested in building a performing arts center on her campus. To sweeten the pot, I told her that I would include $15 million in our bond measure for that purpose. I cautioned her that she'd only get the money if the bond passed, and if she matched the proceeds with private donations. She immediately jumped on board and started soliciting some of CSUN's biggest donors for the match.

Koester was a persuasive fundraiser, as any university president must be these days. When our measure failed, she wouldn't let the CSUN Performing Arts Center die. She continued to raise funds, including a major gift from former California Lt. Governor and music executive Mike Curb, and she simply willed the project into existence. Today the Performing Arts Center is a strikingly beautiful edifice, one of the San Fernando Valley's crown jewels. It's known as the Soraya, named for Soraya Nazarian, whose family made a major sustaining gift to the theater several years after it opened.

Meanwhile, the need to revitalize LACMA grew more urgent. The museum took a big step in 2006, when it hired Michael Govan as its new CEO. He was a boyishly handsome leader who combined boundless vision with superb organizational skills. Where others saw challenges and obstacles, Govan saw opportunities. He had been wooed away from his position as the head of the Dia Art Foundation in New York, where, among other things, he transformed an abandoned factory in the town of Beacon, New York into a vibrant new museum housing contemporary art exhibits. Govan had previously worked at the Guggenheim Museum, where he oversaw the construction of Frank Gehry's Bilbao project. The LACMA search committee was impressed by his ability to think outside the box and to make things happen, and so was I.

Govan could see that the Los Angeles arts scene was rising like a rocket, and he relished the opportunity to harness that energy. His biggest challenge was conceiving a plan for the museum's replacement and winning support from Los Angeles' considerable philanthropic community. We didn't have to wait long to see him put his plans in action. Govan helped the museum raise more than $251 million in his first three years on the job. At the same time, he built consensus for the transformation of the LACMA campus, a new blueprint created by architect Peter Zumthor. Like the previous Koolhaas plan, LACMA's existing buildings would be replaced by a single new building. However, because two new pavilions had been built on the campus in the intervening years, the only way to accommodate a new building would be to cantilever over the world-famous La Brea Tar Pits, an active ice age fossil excavation site. Scientists raised strenuous objections to this option, so another configuration had to be found. Zumthor and Govan's solution was to construct a curving building, bridging Wilshire Boulevard, connecting the original campus to a large piece of property owned by LACMA across the street. The design was met with praise and criticism. Without a doubt, it took some getting used to.

Moving the Great Boulder

Govan was the personification of "outside-the-box" thinking. To illustrate this, consider the story of Michael Heizer's massive 340-ton granite boulder and its dramatic 11-night trip from a Riverside County quarry to LACMA on Wilshire and Fairfax. Heizer, a land artist, had gained notoriety for a series of outdoor art installations, most notably "City"—an ambitious constellation of geometric shapes, rectangles, triangles, parallelograms, and some indescribable optical illusions erected on an isolated site in Lincoln County, Nevada, 100 miles due north of Las Vegas. It's not the end of the world, but you can see it from there.

Govan told me about "Levitated Mass," a Heizer idea to suspend a giant boulder over a walkway on the LACMA campus, beneath which visitors would pass, experiencing an illusion that the rock was levitating over them. It sounded crazy and compelling. The real fun began when Heizer finally found the stone he was looking for. "We've got to transport that boulder from Riverside County to the Miracle Mile, and it's going to be difficult," Govan said, with extraordinary understatement. "We need permission from four counties and twenty-two cities."

This struck me as nearly impossible. Any one of those jurisdictions could kill the project by denying a permit allowing a 100-yard-long flatbed truck to carry a 340-ton rock over its asphalt streets. Good luck with that, I thought. Undeterred, Govan traveled to City Halls and prowled county Halls of Administration seeking permits, like a political candidate soliciting votes. I relied heavily on one of my deputies, Maria Chong-Castillo, to help him navigate this unprecedented political thicket. She had worked for me almost since the day I was first elected in 1975, and I depended on her for all things related to public works and construction. Maria worked the phones with city managers along the route, and she covered herself in glory. LACMA finally got all the approvals it needed, with key help from my colleague, Don Knabe. Govan confidently expected that the boulder's trip across Southern California would be one huge regional block party. And it was.

I was still skeptical, asking "Who's going to come out at 2 a.m. to watch a truck with a big rock rolling through their community?" Well, it showed how much I knew. Each night thousands of people turned out to watch this spectacle. When the boulder finally arrived on the Miracle Mile, the assembled crowd reminded me of the Tournament of Roses Parade in Pasadena. The spectators were four or five deep along Wilshire Blvd. It was a tribute to Heizer's and Govan's ability to see things the rest of us couldn't. The entire project was privately financed to the tune of over $9 million, thanks to Govan's Midas touch. Today, "Levitated Mass" is one of the most intriguing attractions on the LACMA campus, drawing tens of thousands of admirers every year.

Govan's reputation as a miracle worker was growing, and he made believers of his board members, many of whom he had recruited since arriving in Los Angeles. He also made believers of the Board of Supervisors who were impressed by the momentum he was building at the Museum. We were all committed to his larger vision, and we wanted to help him succeed.

Meanwhile, philanthropists Stuart and Lynda Resnick funded a second pavilion on the campus, significantly expanding the museum's exhibition space. The new Reznik and Broad pavilions solved one of the main problems with the earlier Koolhaas plan. Now, LACMA wouldn't have to completely shut down for several years while the new building was constructed; some of its art still could be exhibited in the new pavilions.

The Board of Supervisors eventually committed $125 million toward the $650 million project, a match of approximately one dollar of public money for every four dollars of private philanthropy. This was a great deal for the county because the public would own a new museum at a fraction of the cost to build it. Govan called it a milestone for Los Angeles, and he was correct. As I write, the old LACMA property is a construction site and the new project has broken ground, despite continued sniping about its design.

Saving the Los Angeles Opera

The Los Angeles Opera is one of the nation's leading opera companies, delivering stellar performances with some of the world's greatest singers. Founded in 1986 and guided for thirty-four years by international opera star, Placido Domingo, it became one of the county's most acclaimed cultural institutions. Few people remember, however, that in 2010 the Los Angeles Opera was nearly bankrupted. The Board of Supervisors played a crucial role in saving the company.

Once again this was a case of how my personal history impacted an important policy decision. My son, David, had competed on his Monroe High School academic decathlon team, and one of the subjects he was required to master was opera. I came to love the sounds of Verdi, Puccini, and others drifting from his bedroom every evening as he prepared for the competition. Soon, much to my surprise, I was listening more to arias than cable news at night. When our Los Angeles Opera company fell on tough times, I couldn't look the other way. I couldn't let David down.

The problem surfaced when the opera announced an ambitious plan to perform Richard Wagner's epic Ring Cycle, consisting of four lengthy, German-language operatic dramas. This would not only be a local event of enormous proportions, it would also attract opera lovers from around the world. Ring groupies typically travel thousands of miles to experience this operatic spectacle wherever it's performed, and the financial prospectus for the Los Angeles production assumed significant ticket revenues from out-of-town visitors. But then the Great Recession hit in 2008. International travel came to a standstill over-night, blowing a $14 million hole in the "Ring's" $32 million budget. Suddenly the LA Opera was staring down the barrel of financial ruin.

Marc Stern, a business and civic leader, was Chairman of the Board of the Opera and its greatest benefactor. He came to me with a proposal. "I'm not asking the County for money," he said, "But we have a bank willing to loan us the money we need on condition that we find a guarantor of the loan. Do you think the County would be willing to be that guarantor?" This was an unprecedented request. The County had never put its full faith and credit behind one of the Music Center's resi-dent companies, even to save it from bankruptcy. It would be a heavy political lift. Stern assured me that he had the donors lined up to repay the loan, but the money would only be available over the next several years. "I can assure you the loan will be repaid," he said. I asked Stern to show me the list of donors from whom he received commitments, and he obliged. It was a credible list of some of Los Angeles' most philanthropic patrons, and I was convinced. Now I had to convince my colleagues.

As difficult as it was to break with precedent, I argued that failing to act would be a disaster. The opera was the Dorothy Chandler Pavilion's main tenant, and we owned the Chandler. If the opera went out of business, the Music Center's largest theater would be dark most of the year. This would have serious eco-nomic consequences for the county treasury, for our cultural landscape, and the self-confidence of our community. Shuttering one of the nation's premier opera companies was simply not an option. Three of my four colleagues—Gloria Molina, Don Knabe, and Mark Ridley-Thomas—were convinced, and in one of the most important cultural decisions the board ever made, we approved the loan guarantee that saved the company.

The loan was paid off in 2012, one year early, and opera officials came to our supervisors' meeting to present a mock check to mark the occasion. You could have written an opera based on this story. Once again, a champion had stepped up in the person of Marc Stern. When soldiers are in a bunker taking incoming fire, the bonds forged are everlasting. Marc and I got to know one another in the bunker during this saga, and our friendship was cemented then and there. He is an angel in the city of angels.

The Golden Age of the Arts

Los Angeles had become one of the world's great cultural hubs by the time I left office in 2014. In the space of twenty years, a stunning array of cul-tural institutions were built or renovated mostly with private funds. The list included Disney Hall, the Hollywood Bowl, the John Anson Ford Theatre, the San Fernando Valley Performing Arts Center (the Soraya), LACMA, the Natural History Museum, The Broad Museum, the Broad Stage in Santa Monica, the Getty Center in Brentwood, the Getty Villa in Pacific Palisades, and the Colburn School and Conservatory of Music, and the list goes on. It would have been a great achievement if only two of them had been completed during this span. But they were all built, and more. No metropolitan area in history can point to the development of so much cultural infrastructure as was built in Los Angeles in those two decades. For arts and culture in our region, it was the golden age.

Today the arts in Los Angeles employ more people than the defense industry. They provide jobs in radio, television, music, film, digital platforms, visual arts, and theatre. Los Angeles has more museums per capita than any other US city, and more festivals than anywhere in the world, representing more than 100 distinct nationalities and communities. We are the largest commercial book market in the United States, and before the Covid pandemic we presented more theatrical productions—an average of 1,500 annually—than any other city in the world. We are now one of the world's great cultural centers. This is where young, cutting-edge artists want to be, because here they're judged on their imagination, creativity, and originality, not on their pedigree or social connections.

It's no wonder that cultural tourism has become a powerful force in our economy. Prior to the pandemic, 2.58 million people visited the region each year for its cultural attractions, generating more than $1.1 billion in economic activity beyond what they spent directly at arts institutions. In short, the cultural arts are an industry that creates jobs, leaves no toxic residue, creates no air or water pollution, and nominally impacts traffic in our region. Above all, it fosters understanding across racial and ethnic lines, especially important in a region as diverse as Los Angeles.

As I left office, I thought about why I've had a passionate love affair with the arts. I realized that, although every other facet of life moves at warp speed, the arts are rooted in repose and move at a contemplative pace. You can't appreciate Beethoven's Fifth Symphony with the attention span of a tweeter, and there is no substitute for sitting through an entire Verdi opera. Most of my life I've moved from crisis to crisis, from issue to issue. I've longed for and cherished those moments when I could just slow down and take life in. The arts give us all these moments, and more. I was blessed to be able to help extend that opportunity to millions of others.

The transformation of the Los Angeles' cultural landscape is the product of a committed civic leadership, an enlightened community, and political leaders who understand its importance to a diverse, international metropolis. I was surprised and humbled one Sunday morning when I opened my newspaper to read that *Los Angeles Times* music critic, Mark Swed, had cited my advocacy for the arts as I left the public stage: "It would be hard to find another major politician anywhere in the entire country with Yaroslavsky's record for outright arts support and achievement."

As I hope I've made clear, this was a labor of love.

CHAPTER 18

God Isn't Making Mountains Anymore

It is a story as old as the hills. A prominent Los Angeles developer unveils a controversial project in the heart of the Santa Monica Mountains, but runs into stiff resistance from homeowners and activists. The proposal triggers heated public hearings—with appearances by Hollywood celebrities—and finally winds up in the courts, where opponents kill it with legal delays and other roadblocks. But their rival plan to create a public park on the site also dies a slow death, and as the dust settles, both sides vow to fight another day.

Although it sounds contemporary, the year was 1928 and real estate mogul Alphonzo Bell, Sr.—whose name graced communities like Bel-Air, Bell Canyon, Bell Gardens, and Bell, California—had launched a campaign to turn what is now Topanga Canyon State Park into a limestone quarry. His doomed project, between Pacific Palisades and unincorporated Topanga, is long forgotten, but it had one distinction: It was one of the first documented clashes between developers and conservationists in the region's sprawling mountain ranges, and a precursor of even bigger battles to come.

Indeed, although the Santa Monica Mountains were largely the domain of wealthy landowners through the 1930s, the area began changing dramatically in the 1940s and 1950s. Developers, spurred on by rising land values and boosted by powerful new earth-moving machinery, descended on the bucolic landscape and eventually built massive communities in once-pristine settings, carving out entirely new cities. The relentless development seemed unstoppable, because the Los Angeles County Board of Supervisors and the Los Angeles City Council had never met a development they didn't like.

By the mid-1960s, however, a coalition of homeowners and environmentalists had seen enough and rose in opposition to destructive, unchecked development. In time, their resistance morphed into a political movement, culminating in the creation of the Santa Monica Mountains National Recreation

Area (SMMNRA) in 1978. Although the recreation area was part of a larger bill authored by Congressman Phil Burton, the SMMNRA portion of the bill was crafted by Congressman Anthony Beilenson who represented the area. A year later the state legislature, led by California State Assemblyman Howard Berman, established the Santa Monica Mountains Conservancy, with the goal of acquiring as much of the mountains for parkland as possible.

Creating a national park and expanding publicly owned open space was challenging, because the Santa Monica Mountains was a hodgepodge of acreage—some in public hands and some in private ownership. To expand public ownership, the government had to either buy the land or convince property owners to dedicate their land to permanent open space. The latter was most often done as part of a development deal, where the government would green light the construction of a house, or a small number of houses, on a small portion of a 50-acre piece of land, in exchange for a donation of the remaining property to a public agency.

Preserving this rich environmental resource was not just a policy objective for me. It was personal. I vividly remember summers with my family at the Habonim camp in Green Valley, just north of Saugus. It was where I saw my first rattlesnake, my first deer. I spent years hiking the mountain trails of Griffith Park, a 3,000-acre swath of land in what is now the heart of the city, gifted by Griffith J. Griffith to Los Angeles in 1896. Neither he nor the City could have imagined in the late nineteenth century how central that park would become to this region. It was the only wilderness accessible to me, one of the few places where I could see stars deep into the heavens at night. I was a city kid, and it filled my senses.

Decades earlier, when Bell's Topanga Canyon scheme ignited controversy, Sylvia Morrison, a wealthy Pacific Palisades homeowner, spoke words of opposition that ring true today: "Beauty is our greatest asset in this district," she told the city's Planning Commission, "and our heritage of the hills must not be wasted." With the creation of the National Recreation Area and the Conservancy, Los Angeles finally had the tools to honor the shared values that linked generations of mountain activists. The area was within an hour's drive of 15 million people, and in my inaugural speech to the Board of Supervisors I said protecting the mountains of western Los Angeles County for future generations would be one of my top priorities. I intended to keep that promise—but doing so would be a challenging task.

One of the biggest hurdles I faced, at least initially, was winning the trust of people who had lived in the mountains for years and had been fighting irresponsible development long before I came to the board. Some of them were wary of me, a newcomer who lived in the heart of the city, and it was hard to blame them. They felt perpetually under siege, given the county's relentless opposition to wilderness preservation. In the mountains, actions spoke louder than words, and the people I represented knew the difference.

"God Isn't Making Mountains Anymore"

Some twenty years after the creation of the SMMNRA, Beilenson reflected on the bitter development battles that had become a way of life in the Santa Monica Mountains. "We've got about 10 million people in the county who've got almost no park land at all," he said in an oral history. "If the county had done what it should have done, perhaps it wouldn't have been necessary for the federal government to step in." Beilenson was right. The county's kneejerk support for development projects in the Santa Monicas was legion, and there was a sense that no one in authority cared.

This attitude began to change somewhat in the early '90s. A lawsuit by the Mexican American Legal Defense Fund led to the redrawing of supervisorial district lines in order to create a majority Latino district. As a result, in 1991 Gloria Molina was elected to the Board, making her the county's first Latina Supervisor. She was the antithesis of the person she had replaced, Pete Schabarum, who was pro-development in the extreme. Molina had the guts to stand up to real estate interests, as did Supervisor Yvonne Braithwaite Burke, who was elected a year later. Along with Ed Edelman, they formed a pro-environment majority. When I replaced Ed in 1994, that majority remained intact.

Soon after Molina joined the Board, she cast the deciding vote to place Proposition A, a $540 million park funding measure, on the ballot. Spearheaded by Edelman, county voters overwhelmingly approved it. Proposition A provided funding for urban parks and recreational facilities, as well as for land acquisition in the mountains surrounding metropolitan Los Angeles. It was a game changer that continues to make it financially possible to save our most ecologically significant lands.

During the six-month interval between my election to the board and taking the oath of office, I thought long and hard about the Santa Monica Mountains. This was one of the most ecologically rich and diverse areas adjacent to any metropolitan region in the nation. It had everything: High coastal mountains, deep canyons, creeks, waterfalls, oak groves, wildlife, the Pacific Ocean, multiple climates, and sheer beauty. It would be my mission to preserve this place so that future generations could enjoy it, too.

I had honed my land use skills on the City Council and embraced a mantra that would serve me well in future development battles within the county: Terrain should dictate development, not the other way around. Just as I had no patience with developers who pushed for high-rise buildings in quiet city neighborhoods, I was determined to change the county culture that approved sawed off mountain ridges and destroyed priceless wilderness to turn a profit. Although I respected the right of landowners to develop their real estate responsibly, they would no longer have carte blanche to decimate what nature had created millions of years earlier. As I said at the time, quoting an old environmental slogan, "God isn't making mountains anymore."

The Canary in the Coal Mine

My goal from the beginning was to acquire as much land for the public as possible and make it part of the expanding Santa Monica Mountains park system. That took money, and there wasn't enough of it to buy every desirable piece of open space. Instead, we needed to prioritize the resource value of parcels before we purchased them. This was too important a matter to leave to guesswork, so I asked the Santa Monica Conservancy and its dynamic director, Joe Edmiston, for assistance. He and his team developed a comprehensive memorandum for me—a parcel by parcel assessment—to ensure that the open space we purchased would have the highest ecological value. When it was completed, I called it my "Acquisition Bible" and kept it handy in my desk drawer.

As for those properties that didn't make the cut, they were still worth protecting. The county had the power to enact and enforce zoning regulations in the unincorporated parts of the mountains, in order to preserve the natural environment. As a councilman I had dealt with zoning issues in the hills above West Los Angeles, where pristine land bordered urban and suburban communities. But I never dealt with proposals that would have transformed beautiful wilderness into San Fernando Valley-type subdivisions—where homes and shopping centers would replace vast acres of hills, mountains, chaparral, and oak groves. In the first half of my City Council career, I was forced to make compromises with a council that was often partial to the real estate industry. Now, on the Board of Supervisors, I had more power to assert my will. I recalled Lyndon Johnson's 1965 speech to Congress, in which he said that he never dreamed he would have the chance to exercise the power that was now his. "But now I do have that chance," he said, [and] "I mean to use it." Well, I meant to use mine as well.

The unincorporated part of the mountains—where the county controlled land use decisions—had two sections: the North Area (21,000 acres) and the Coastal Zone (51,000 acres). I first turned my attention to the North Area that extended from the City of Los Angeles' western border to the Ventura County line, generally north of the Santa Monicas' highest ridgeline.

Although the Board of Supervisors adopted regulations governing the North Area in the early 1980s, supervisors routinely changed or ignored them. They approved numerous housing developments that flagrantly exceeded zoning guidelines. These developments forever transformed the Conejo Valley and its pristine landscape in the heart of the mountains into the suburban communities of Calabasas, Agoura Hills, and Westlake Village. Those decisions, in turn, reawakened an open space movement whose foot soldiers organized angry protests and filed lawsuits aimed at forcing the County to respect its own rules.

As I arrived on the scene, the North Area was akin to the wild west of land use. Mountains were graded and degraded; oak groves hundreds of years old were being bulldozed, and the County treated rules as suggestions, not red lines. I was determined to change that. Over several years, we approved zoning controls that reduced allowable densities, closed development loopholes, strictly limited destructive grading, and forever protected the ridgelines from being touched by a single bulldozer. I must credit my crack staff—especially Laura Shell, Ginny Kruger, and Ben Saltsman—who gained the confidence of most of the area's residents, even those who did not necessarily agree with every outcome. Based on four decades in this line of work, I learned that when elected officials and their staff treat citizens with respect, they will usually reciprocate. They will respect the process if they feel their points of view are seriously considered. Ginny, Laura, and Ben were good listeners and skilled negotiators. All the while Alisa Katz, my Chief of Staff, administered the county's park fund budget with an eye towards buying ecologically desirable properties before they were developed. We had a talented team.

When the Board finally approved our North Area plan in October 2000, it was the proverbial canary in the coalmine. We showed that it was politically possible to change the decades-old culture of the growth machine, and to draw a line in the sand before all was destroyed. We sent a message that responsible land use rules were the new normal, and we expected them to be religiously enforced. Protecting the second area under our jurisdiction, the mountains' Coastal Zone, was no less urgent. But it would have to wait for more than a decade.

The Gold Standard of Acquisitions

Going forward, we had funds to help us acquire highly valued lands. Both Proposition A (1992), and a subsequent Proposition A (1996) which I authored, generated a stream of revenues allowing us to dramatically expand the area's national and state park footprint. Esther Feldman, who ran the Los Angeles office of the Trust for Public Land, skillfully strategized and helped guide these measures to success. But money itself was not enough.

Acquiring land in the Santa Monica Mountains often resembled a high-stakes poker game, where skill and strategy counted just as much. I held some cards—tens of millions of dollars earmarked for land acquisitions—while landowners had theirs, the price at which they'd be willing to sell. It was all about timing, value, and resources, overlaid with the "Acquisition Bible" the Conservancy had prepared for me. During a strong economy, the cost of land could be prohibitive; during a down economy, some landowners were eager to sell at bargain prices.

Some negotiations went smoothly. For years, we had our eyes on a spectacularly beautiful 750-acre property owned by filmmaker James Cameron ("Titanic" and "Avatar") and his wife, Suzy. There had been a proposal to build several homes on the land, a project that would have graded the natural terrain beyond recognition. But the environmentally conscious Camerons ultimately agreed to sell the property to the Conservancy for $12 million, a very fair price. Funds from the state and the county's Proposition A funds largely paid for this acquisition. Beyond the sheer beauty of the land, the acquisition closed a critical gap in the Coastal Slope Trail, which connects the Pacific Palisades with Ventura County. It's a gem of a wilderness route where hikers can traverse dozens of miles of trails and never see urban Los Angeles.

On other occasions, persistence paid dividends. Firehouse Hill, a parcel of several hundred acres, was a stunning gateway to the Santa Monica Mountains for motorists driving west on the Ventura Freeway. As people entered the national recreation area, they'd see a panoramic view of the hills, dotted with groves of oak trees, some of them hundreds of years old. This land was a prime target for acquisition, but the owner stubbornly insisted that he was going to grade the hell out of it and build a seventy-home subdivision on the site. He was so sure of himself, he invited me to take a drive with him on the property in his jeep. At one point, as he was describing his plan, I stopped him: "I think you've made a huge mistake bringing me up here," I said. "Now that I've seen it, I believe this property should be part of the park system. It should never be developed." I asked if he would be willing to negotiate a sale, but he declined.

This owner's appeal to me was one for the books: He said the proceeds from the development was going to be a Bar Mitzvah gift for his son, a nice little inheritance. Seriously. I couldn't help but recall that my most precious Bar Mitzvah gift was a prayer book from my family and a telegram from my aunts in the Soviet Union. The notion that I was going to let this man destroy untouched wilderness for his son's Bar Mitzvah was insulting on many levels.

Lightning struck soon after, and the property fell into bankruptcy. Eventually Fred Sands, a prominent Los Angeles realtor and a constituent, purchased the land. He had an equally improbable plan to build a 250,000 square foot shopping center on the site. That, too, was a non-starter, which probably didn't surprise him. I had known Fred for many years, and we kept talking about his selling the property to us, which he didn't rule out. Persistence paid off, and we began a conversation about a sale of this stunningly beautiful gateway to the Santa Monicas. I asked Joe Edmiston, the Conservancy's executive director, to negotiate the deal. We finally bought the land for $6.75 million. It was worth every penny.

There were also times when I paid a price for being too tough. We had our eyes on a breathtaking piece of property in the mountains above Pepperdine University, near the Malibu coast. The land, owned by the Adamson family, was one of the first real estate holdings in the post-Spanish land grant era. It looked like Shangri-La—a plateau 1,500 feet above sea level, surrounded by peaks offering spectacular views of Santa Monica Bay. The family was willing to sell for $6 million, but based on our appraisals I didn't believe it was worth more than $5 million and stood firm. When the dust settled, businessman Michael Milken bought the property, proposing to build a baccalaureate high school along with several homes for its teachers and staff. Although the idea may have been noble, I and county staff strongly believed that the construction would excessively disfigure the site. His plan triggered clashes with the county that persisted after I left office. When I asked Milken if a purchase was possible, he said he wouldn't sell for less than $20 million, a price that was out of the question. In this case, I had made the wrong call in not accepting Adamson's offer.

Some negotiations could take several years to complete, but nothing compared to the nearly thirty-year battle over the King Gillette property, one of the most stunning sites in the heart of the Santa Monicas. The razor scion built an iconic home with, what else, a razor blade-shaped swimming pool on a ranch at the corner of Las Virgenes Canyon Road and Mulholland Highway. He ultimately lost the 800-acre property during the Depression, after which it was owned by a Hollywood mogul and two religious orders. In the mid-1970s, it became a prime but elusive candidate for public acquisition. The California Department of Parks and Recreation began efforts to acquire the site in 1976, but plans fell through when Soka Gakkai/Nichiren Shoshu of America, a Buddhist religious order based in Japan, outbid them for the property in 1986. For a decade or more, they established and operated a university for some 500 students on the site. All the while, public agencies made aggressive but unsuccessful efforts to purchase the property for the expanding park system.

When I arrived at the Board of Supervisors, the Mountains Recreation and Conservation Authority (MRCA), a companion agency to Conservancy, was embroiled in a lawsuit attempting to acquire the site by eminent domain. Relations between the two sides had soured, marked by profound mutual distrust. I was determined to turn over a new leaf and agreed to meet with Soka officials after I took office at the county. Although nothing fundamental had changed, the personal dynamic was different. I realized that we had to show the owners respect, not contempt, and they were visibly relieved that they could hold civilized conversations with me. Meanwhile, the MRCA and Soka settled their eminent domain lawsuit, with the courts giving their blessing to an acquisition.

Now it was only a matter of price. But it soon became apparent that the MRCA had badly overplayed its hand. Although it offered to pay $20 million to buy the property, Soka officials insisted their land was worth much more. A court would now have to rule on the purchase price. Then, unbelievably, the Conservancy revealed that it actually did not have the money to complete the deal at practically *any* price. The agency would have gone bankrupt if they had been forced to purchase the property.

This was more than a money problem. All of us who represented the area had backed the Conservancy's lawsuit, assuming they had the funds to close a deal. When it turned out that they didn't, we had egg on our faces. Park acquisition advocates now focused their attention on the area's elected officials—hoping we would secure the tens of millions of public dollars needed to make a deal. But we didn't have that kind of money at the time either, and we were not happy campers. The angriest person of all was Tony Beilenson, a normally quiet and cerebral man who represented the area in Congress.

Tony asked me to set up a meeting with him and the Conservancy's Joe Edmiston, so we could hash out this fiasco. When it came to land acquisitions in these parts, Edmiston was part poker player, part magician, and part real estate maven. But he proved he was human when this purchase collapsed.

We got together in my office on the morning of October 3, 1995. Beilenson immediately confronted Joe about this turn of events. Edmiston told us that he understood why we would think we had been played, but he respectfully disagreed. He said he had reason to believe that funds would be forthcoming from the State for the acquisition, but the funds did not materialize. For all the years I knew Beilenson, I had never seen him lose his cool, but there's a first time for everything. He was infuriated. The two men began shouting at each other when my secretary, Liz, walked in the door. "I just wanted to tell you that they're about to announce the verdict in the O.J. [Simpson] case," she said, bringing a momentary halt to the verbal fisticuffs. We turned on the television, watched the jaw-dropping verdict and began processing it when Beilenson abruptly broke the mood. "OK, ok, ok, that's over, let's get back to what we're here to talk about," he snapped, and the arguments resumed.

When it became clear that public agencies didn't have the money to purchase its property, Soka unveiled plans to expand its university to 5,000 students on the property, a dramatic expansion. At that point, long-simmering community opposition to the project erupted into a political donnybrook, with the Board of Supervisors having to decide on the new plan. The Soka battle would be grueling and intense, likened by one observer to the Santa Monica Mountains' equivalent of thermo-nuclear war. It was a story that had everything—grassroots mobilization, legal wheeling and dealing, subterfuge, intrigue, and high-powered political lobbying. Soka had friends on my board, so this was going to be a difficult minefield to navigate.

Ultimately, we negotiated a compromise in 1996. Soka agreed to preserve most of its undeveloped land in its natural state, and the county approved a plan allowing the school to increase its enrollment from 500 to 650, a net increase of only 150 students. In any other community, this would have been a smashing political and environmental victory. But this being the Santa Monica Mountains, it was only the end of the beginning. Environmentalists quickly filed a lawsuit challenging the new plan. The county won in the lower court but lost on appeal, sending everyone back to square one.

Our level of frustration was enormous. But this, as it turned out, was a fortuitous development. Soka had opened a second campus in Orange County, and the growing costs of operating both sites, in addition to Japan's tanking economy, caused them to reconsider their future in the Santa Monica Mountains. In 2004, I got an astonishing call out of nowhere from Mark Armbruster, an attorney representing Soka. I had known Armbruster since his days as a deputy to Councilman Joel Wachs in City Hall, and we had a good relationship. He asked if Los Angeles County would be interested in buying the site. This was a surprise, since Soka had refused to consider a sale of their property after the conservancy debacle. I asked Armbruster, "Are you personally curious, or are you bringing me a message from your client?" He responded, "I'm speaking for my client." I asked him to set up a meeting with Soka's top decisionmaker, and it became clear that they were serious.

The poker game had changed in a heartbeat. I began calling my partners in the federal and State governments to give them the news. By this time, more State and local funds had become available for a purchase of the site, but we would have to move quickly to negotiate a price. There could be no repeat of the earlier debacle. We quickly scheduled a meeting of what can only be described as the Santa Monica Mountains version of a United Jewish Appeal fundraising meeting. In an extraordinary convocation, National Park Service representatives and elected officials sat around a table in the Agoura Hills office of State Assembly member Fran Pavley. We all checked our governmental seals at the door and focused on the only question that mattered: How much would the Soka property cost, and how much could each of our agencies contribute? Eleven different funders—mostly public agencies—committed to contributing a total $35 million, the agreed-upon sales price. The two principal contributors were the State of California and the County of Los Angeles. It was the gold standard of acquisitions, and good government in action.

Today the King Gillette property houses the Santa Monica Mountains National Recreation Area Visitors Center, and it's fittingly named for Congressman Beilenson. Even though Edmiston's negotiating tactics ruffled feathers, his legacy as a visionary and pragmatic leader was secure. On the morning we announced the deal, he spoke for all of us at a press conference when he said: "We stand here today to say to you that this land, this earth, now belongs to the people."

The Last Piece of the Puzzle

On April 1, 2012, Peter Douglas died after a lengthy battle with cancer, and the California coast lost one of its biggest champions. The longtime Executive Director of the California Coastal Commission, he was an outspoken advocate for protecting the State's 1,100-mile shoreline, its greatest ecological treasure. He played a leading role in writing the 1972 ballot measure that eventually led to the creation of the agency, and he helped draft the California Coastal Act. I respected him so much that when Governor Pete Wilson's appointees on the Coastal Commission once moved to fire him, I prevailed upon the Board of Supervisors to join thousands of protests across the state demanding that the panel reconsider, which they did. When Peter died, activists knew he would be hard to replace. Indeed, a Coastal Commissioner observed that with Douglas' death, the only decisions left for the commission to make would be to choose the color of the cement used to pave over what's left of this beautiful natural resource.

Amid this pessimism, I saw opportunity. We now had a chance to fill in the last piece of the Santa Monica Mountains puzzle, approving a Local Coastal Plan (LCP) that would protect the area against rampant development. It was one of the last remaining sections of the California coast that had no LCP—meaning that the Santa Monicas were governed by land use policies that clashed with ecological values. Although the end of my time in office was approaching, we had a chance—one final chance—to protect the stunning beauty of our beaches and mountains for generations to come.

But it would be a daunting task. Here's why: In the Santa Monica Mountains, the county's portion of California's coastal zone is several miles wide, stretching from Malibu's inland border to the mountains' highest ridgelines. The Coastal Commission governs development in this area, and it requires both the local governing body—a City Council or Board of Supervisors—and the Commission to approve an LCP. Once approved, the plan ideally reflects a unified consensus between State and local governments about what can be built and where. Without an LCP, there is likely to be perpetual conflict between State and local agencies. Since an LCP had never been approved for the 81 square mile area of the Santa Monicas, conflict between the state and county was all too often the norm. The result was that real estate interests navigated the mine field of government agencies, too often to their advantage.

For years, getting such a plan approved was elusive. Two efforts had been made—one in 1986 and one in 2006—but the county and Coastal Commission could never agree on the plan's provisions. In the mid-1980s, the Board of Supervisors had a decidedly Republican, pro-development majority, and two of its members were outspoken supporters of real estate development in the mountains—the bigger the better. Environmental protection was not as high a high priority for them. The 2006 effort to pass a plan happened on my watch, but it never got out of the starter's gate. And that's where Peter Douglas comes in.

As much as I respected him, Douglas was also a nemesis. Our conflict grew out of a section of the Coastal Act that mandates strong protections for "Environmentally Sensitive Habitat Areas" (ESHA). Bear with me: These include "plant or animal life or their habitats [which] are either rare or especially valuable because of their special nature or role in an eco-system and which could be easily disturbed or degraded by human activities and developments." Put simply, this broad, sweeping language gave the coastal commission the power to restrict or prevent development in order to protect ESHA-designated sites.

Douglas' controversial approach to land use regulation in the Santa Monicas was to declare nearly *every* single, square foot of the mountains ESHA. This was absurd on its face, because not every part of the mountains was ecologically sensitive. Some areas had been degraded or disturbed decades earlier; some were already developed with homes, golf courses and even a university. Some had never been sensitive habitat to begin with. I told Douglas that when you declare everything to be ESHA, then nothing is ESHA. Doing so actually made it more difficult to protect parcels that *were truly* ecologically sensitive.

This was not just a philosophical argument. The United States constitution requires government to compensate a property owner if its regulations make it impossible for the owner to salvage any value from a property. It's called "inverse condemnation," or a "taking." The State of California could not prevent development on all parcels in the mountains, because it could not possibly afford to compensate all its property owners for their economic loss.

Douglas, however, had a "Plan B." To avoid an unconstitutional "taking" of unaffordable property—whether it was a massive new subdivision or an additional bedroom to a house—he proposed that the Coastal Commission impose a "mitigation" fee on the owner. This, Douglas argued, would compensate for the environmental impact of a project in exchange for allowing it to proceed. To me, this felt more like a shakedown than sound environmental policy.

I made a herculean effort to convince Douglas to open his mind to a more scientific and less transactional approach, but he wasn't moved. He had forced the city of Malibu to accept this approach when developing its own LCP, and he would not consider treating the county's unincorporated area differently. If I brought an alternative proposal to the Coastal Commission, he warned, "It will be dead on arrival." So, I put our 2006 proposal for an LCP on the back burner.

Douglas's death marked the end of an era, and all of us who knew him were deeply saddened. But I also hoped that his successor, Dr. Charles Lester, would be willing to consider a different approach. I didn't know Lester, and he didn't know me. He had been Douglas's second in command, as well as a scientist and an academic. So, I made an appointment to meet with him at the county's offices in Marina Del Rey to assess his openness to an alternative approach. I brought along my crack land use deputy, Ben Saltsman, and County Planning Director Richard Bruckner, while Lester brought his deputy, Jack Ainsworth.

I began by telling Lester that if I were in his shoes, I wouldn't trust Los Angeles County either, given the historic animosity between the two agencies. But I asked him to look at my land use record at the county, and to wipe the slate clean. We had acquired close to 20,000 acres of land, much of them in the Coastal Zone. We had slashed development rights in other parts of the Santa Monicas—notably in the North Area—to levels that no one could ever imagine. In addition, we had virtually eliminated the rapacious grading and ridgeline development that had destroyed so much of the area's ecology. I told Lester that what I had done over nearly two decades would be the template for what I wanted to do in the Coastal Zone, and that I was willing to do whatever was necessary to get an LCP approved in the two years I had left in office. There was only one caveat: I wasn't going to lift a finger to do this unless I knew that he would keep an open mind on the ESHA issue.

In that spirit, I offered an alternative plan: We would carefully evaluate every one of the 51,000-acres in the Santa Monica Mountains part of the coastal zone, to determine which properties were truly ecologically sensitive. We then would *prohibit development* in those areas. I was prepared to commit $2 million in county funds to purchase privately owned parcels if it became necessary to purchase ESHA where a credible development was proposed. As for the remaining sites, we would draft the most protective zoning controls we could, to minimize environmental damage. When the meeting ended, there were no "dead on arrival" declarations. He told me he wanted to think about it.

Lester got back to me a couple of weeks later. He said he'd like to see if we could work together to develop a plan. This was a huge breakthrough. We could now enter negotiations and build the coalition we'd need to get an LCP approved. I asked Saltsman to quarterback the county's effort going forward, because he was politically smart and an exceptionally gifted negotiator. His job was to come up with a strategy and act as my representative in the LCP negotiations with every stakeholder group. He had a partner in our County Planning Director Richard Bruckner, who often played bad cop to Ben's good cop. During this battle it was common for Ben to be out four nights a week, being part negotiator, part psychologist, and part enforcer. He gained the confidence of virtually every player in this drama, and he did it all while attending law school at night, graduating first in his class. I get exhausted just thinking about it.

This effort consumed a disproportionate amount of my time during my last two years in office, and it was no wonder. We were mounting something akin to a military campaign—storming beachheads, battling to win hearts and minds, and engaging in hand-to-hand political combat to forge a consensus. The initiation of the LCP started with the Board of Supervisors adopting the plan's framework on a 4 to 1 vote. But the outcome would be in doubt until the very last vote nearly two years later. The challenge would be to unify disparate interest groups in the spirit of compromise, with the objective of producing an historic environmental achievement.

The Battle Begins

To fully appreciate this, it helps to know the cast of characters: There were the residents, who wanted to protect their homes, their views, and the quality of life that beckoned them to the mountains in the first place. There were the environmentalists who recognized that if we got this right, we could save the Santa Monica Mountains, one of California's most unique and threatened ecological gems. There were specific advocacy groups, some focused on cleaning up the pollution in the Santa Monica Bay, others on the mountain terrain or the preservation of oak groves and wildlife migration routes, and still others on restoring life to mountain creeks. There were the equestrians who had been a part of the mountains' culture for more than a century. There were developers who were at odds with just about everyone, and they had considerable political influence in the decision-making bodies of government. There was a Board of Supervisors whose members were divided on the plan's vision. Finally, there were the Coastal Commissioners, who were also divided on what a plan should look like. They would be the ultimate arbiters of what passed muster.

The political landscape was as rugged as the mountains themselves. And the only way these seemingly irreconcilable parties could come to together was if they compromised in the interest of passing a plan that was more important than their individual differences. The clock was ticking on my final two years and, if we failed, an opportunity like this might not present itself for another generation. From experience, I knew that nothing focused one's attention like a deadline.

Collisions between policy and politics were inevitable. For example, the differences between equestrians and Heal the Bay activists seemed insurmountable, and it took an intricate, three-way compromise to finally resolve them. The Commission was concerned that dozens of owners had allowed horse waste to spread beyond their property lines. The law required them to make costly physical improvements and pay hefty fines. The equestrians demanded complete amnesty, but the Commission would not even entertain the idea.

To complicate matters, the members of Heal the Bay—whose *raison d'etre* was to eradicate pollution in the Santa Monica Bay—wanted to crack down on horse owners as well. They argued correctly that a significant portion of the bay's pollution stemmed from horse feces that flowed into mountain creeks and ended up in the ocean. They insisted that equestrians "clean up the horse manure" before it caused any more damage. The politics were treacherous, because equestrians had friends on the Board of Supervisors, while Heal the Bay had allies on the Coastal Commission. Each side had leverage over the other; each had the power to torpedo the LCP. And it didn't help that the horse owners were wrongly convinced I wanted to kick them out of the Santa Monicas. The standoff called for compromise, and that's where our office played a crucial role.

First, I had to convince Heal the Bay that throwing the book at the horse owners was a political non-starter. If we treated equestrians like pariahs, they wouldn't get two votes on the Board of Supervisors, including my own. On the other hand, I had to convince the equestrians that allowing their violators to remain scofflaws was unacceptable. When we came to the first hearing in April 2014 in Santa Barbara, it was clear that the commissioners wanted *all* the horse violations cleared up immediately—a decision that ultimately would have sunk the LCP. Both sides were unhappy, and pandemonium erupted in the hearing room.

I could see the whole plan slipping away, so I stood up and asked the commissioners if I could be heard. I urged them to take a deep breath before voting and then made a case for the horse owners. I argued that we needed to find a resolution that fell somewhere between the "death penalty" and complete amnesty. There was much more at stake in this plan than horse manure. "Give us the time to work out a middle ground that's acceptable to you, your staff and the stakeholder community," I said, proposing that we set aside the amnesty issue and leave it for a subsequent hearing.

The commission agreed, and in the ensuing weeks we negotiated intensely with all the parties and came to a last-minute agreement. Under the arrangement, horse owners agreed to make improvements to their property to comply with the law. In return, they'd get a reasonable amount of time to pay off their fines. When the dust settled, the equestrians cautiously agreed to the deal, Heal the Bay accepted the compromise, and the Coastal Commission was satisfied.

But we still weren't out of the woods. Heal the Bay had additional concerns. For years, they had criticized the proliferation of vineyards in the mountains. Some people didn't understand their opposition, and I didn't initially warm to their position myself. But facts were facts. Vineyards didn't just provide bucolic scenery or a glass of cabernet. They also degraded the environment, with hillside grading and terracing that damaged the mountains' natural contours and indigenous vegetation. The pesticides they used found their way into the creeks that native wildlife drank from, and their residue ultimately polluted the Santa Monica Bay and its beaches.

I decided to support a ban on future vineyards in the area, arguing that we don't plant vineyards in Yosemite or Sequoia National Parks, so let's not do it in the Santa Monica National Recreation Area either. This was a case where policy and political considerations coincided. I needed Heal the Bay standing shoulder to shoulder with me when I brought the plan to the Coastal Commission. Without their support I might not get the commission's approval. A vineyard ban would be a huge win and make it possible for them to support the horse keeping compromise. It was also the right policy for the Santa Monica Mountains.

There were other issues that required painstaking negotiations, and we traversed those minefields with care. In the end, we got it right. As Saltsman told me, the key to our coalition-building efforts was listening in incredible depth to what people had to say. "It meant going out every day and night and meeting with every constituent who sought us out in good faith," he said. "It meant going door to door, sometimes staying up all night, to make new allies."

As our first important Coastal Commission meeting approached, I took an entire day to personally call or visit each one of its twelve members. Saltsman worked the phones and even flew with me to various parts of California to make our case. These overtures are known as *ex parte* communications, which commissioners are required to disclose at the beginning of each meeting. On the day of the vote, each commissioner announced the time and date that I had called and what we discussed. The repetitious reports by one member after another were almost humorous, causing the commission chair to note dryly, "it seems that Supervisor Yaroslavsky was busy on the phone that day."

On April 10, 2014, after an extensive and detailed staff presentation, a long public hearing and a robust discussion, the California Coastal Commission unanimously voted to approve the Land Use component of the LCP. The equestrian issue was deferred to a subsequent commission meeting. We were overjoyed. Our euphoria, however, was short lived. Developers, who found it hard to argue that the mountains needed more subdivisions, suddenly joined forces with grape growers who were battling the vineyard ban. Both groups hoped their last-minute alliance would be enough to kill the plan when the commission considered the implementation plan at a subsequent meeting. The vote to *implement* our proposal would come three months later. In July, they unanimously approved that plan, including the vineyard ban and the equestrian compromise we had agreed to days before.

When we had first started crafting the plan, the idea that we'd get a unanimous vote from the Coastal Commission on something this complex and historically elusive would have been a pipe dream. Now, there was only one more hurdle to clear. The Board of Supervisors had to ratify the Coastal Commission's action.

Not surprisingly, our opponents ramped up their efforts in the weeks leading up to the August 26 board vote. Spurred on by real estate interests, some horse owners were getting cold feet, suggesting they were not as happy with the plan as they initially were.

I had every reason to believe that Ruth Gerson, the leader of the equestrian community, backed our plan, but just to make sure I asked her to write a letter to the Board affirming her support. Without her endorsement, I was afraid we would lose a key board vote. She found one excuse after another, telling me why she hadn't done it. "The fax machine was broken, my horse was sick, I was pre-occupied," she said. When I persisted, she finally said, "I'll do it, but you must promise me that you'll come to our next equestrian day and ride a horse." This was a big ask, because when I was a kid a horse threw me, and I hadn't mounted one since. Nevertheless, we all had sacrifices to make, so I agreed. A true *quid pro quo*. When I eventually got on a horse at the equestrian day, I looked like a natural—until it took one step. At that point I said, "I rode the horse, and I'm getting off the damn thing." Promise made, promise kept!

In the final hours before the Board's vote, real estate interests solidified their alliance with vineyard owners, and they were buoyed by the fact that only four Supervisors were scheduled to be present for the decisive meeting—Gloria Molina, Mike Antonovich, Don Knabe, and myself. The fifth, Mark Ridley-Thomas, scheduled himself to be absent that day. Under Board rules, we needed the votes of three of the four supervisors present to pass the plan. Molina backed my efforts from the beginning, but Antonovich was a saboteur, trying to kill it at every turn. I would have to rely on Knabe, who would normally have been inclined to support a less restrictive plan. He represented the other half of the county's coastline and knew how challenging it was to get an LCP through the process. Without his support, all our work would be in vain. The day before the vote, I walked into Don's office next door to mine, and I made an impassioned pitch. He didn't give me a commitment on the spot, and I didn't expect him to. But Knabe and I had a great relationship, and I was hopeful he wouldn't let me down.

The next day, after a lengthy public hearing, the Board finally prepared to vote. Antonovich, carrying the developers' water, moved to amend the plan by removing the vineyard ban, an action that if approved would have sent us all back to drawing board. Knabe seconded the vineyard motion, and more than a hundred LCP supporters in the Board hearing room gasped. They could count the votes and were convinced that even though the amendment wouldn't pass, Knabe's support of it meant he would probably vote against the plan, thus sinking it. I was less concerned. When the roll was called, the vote was 2–2, with Molina and I voting "no." Needing three votes, the amendment failed.

Now we moved to the final vote on the plan. As the roll was called, I voted "yes." Antonovich voted "no." Molina voted "yes." And then Knabe's name was called. You could hear a pin drop. The fate of a two-year, painstaking battle to preserve and protect the coastal mountains of western Los Angeles County hung in the balance. Knabe paused and then said, "yes."

Passage of the Santa Monica Mountains Local Coastal Plan was one of my proudest accomplishments in public office. As my twenty-year career on the Board of Supervisors ended, our team had spearheaded the acquisition of more than 20,000 new acres for public parkland in these mountains, and we had relentlessly protected the lands that remained in private hands. It was a remarkable achievement made possible by thousands of people, some of whom are no longer with us. All of them helped us save one of our nation's great natural resources.

A few weeks before I left office, I took my nearly four-year-old granddaughter, Sadie, to the King Gillette Ranch for a short hike. As we walked the grounds, Sadie was enchanted by the high mountains and deep valleys; the ducks quacking and the frogs croaking. I could see the wonderment in her eyes. It wasn't lost on me that the investment of time and resources so many of us had made in preserving the Santa Monicas was for all the Sadie's who would come along in future generations. They would be able to experience nature in all of its glory, just like we and our ancestors did.

The media doesn't always grasp a moment like this, but *Los Angeles Times* columnist Jim Newton got it: "Yaroslavsky and his staff worked for more than a decade to get to this point, and some of the activists were involved just as long," he wrote. "Ten years of sometimes contentious and tedious meetings, way outside the limelight, have produced something profound."

CHAPTER 19

Confronting the Homeless Crisis

When President John F. Kennedy launched his plans to land a man on the moon in 1962, he said: "We don't do this and the other things because they are easy. We do them because they are hard." The decision to tackle big challenges can be a bracing, life-altering moment for those who enter the public arena, and their motivations range from the highest levels of human aspiration to the daily push and pull of politics. But sometimes the decision springs from something more visceral and personal, something closer to home.

For me it happened on a summer night in 2002, when I got a call from my daughter, Mina, who was pursuing a master's degree in Public Policy at the Kennedy School of Government at Harvard. On her summer break, interning for the City of Oakland, she called to describe an encounter she had that afternoon with a homeless man on Telegraph Avenue in Berkeley. "I saw him sitting on a curb, so I sat down next to him and engaged him in conversation for about twenty minutes," she told me. Preparing to leave, she pulled a couple of dollars from her purse. The man stopped her. "I don't want your money," he said. "You've given me something far more important. You've given me your time and your respect." Then she added, "Dad, while we were sitting there, a couple hundred people walked by us and not one of them bothered to make eye contact with either one of us."

I was jarred by that observation. During my daily life, I didn't make eye contact with homeless people either. Despite my self-professed concern, I had never locked eyes with the homeless man who camped on the Melrose Avenue off-ramp of the Hollywood Freeway that I sometimes used when driving home from downtown. I realized that whenever I made eye contact with people who needed help, I couldn't turn my back on them. I had to do something. The one thing I couldn't do is pretend they didn't exist. If I didn't make eye contact, on the other hand—well, out of sight, out of mind.

Mina's story was a metaphor for the way American society historically dealt with homelessness. We refused to make eye contact with this brand of human suffering. Elected leaders from the White House to City Halls around the country routinely avoided talking about the homeless, hoping they might just disappear. Local governments sequestered them in places like Skid Row in Los Angeles, the Bowery in New York, or the Tenderloin in San Francisco. I had never made the issue one of my top concerns but now, unexpectedly, that had changed.

In the crass world of politics, it is axiomatic that if you launch an initiative, it pays to be around when you finish the job. This is the metric by which most politicians—and constituents—measure success. If you propose to build a senior citizen center or a transit line, you want to complete it before your next election so you can add it to your resume of achievements. Seen in this light, tackling homelessness may be a noble objective but it's like shoveling sand against the tide. It's not a politically remunerative cause. The homeless crisis was not created overnight, and it's not going to be solved overnight either. The list of political leaders who have been advised that they could never solve the problem no matter how hard they tried is a mile long. Making it a *cause célèbre* could be a political liability, because it would likely end in perceived failure. That's one of the reasons why this shameful situation went unaddressed for decades in the richest nation on earth.

A History of Neglect and Dysfunction

The growth of homelessness in Los Angeles, and the story of my office's efforts to make a dent in this intractable problem, is at once sad and hopeful. Los Angeles has had its own unique experience with homelessness—and understanding that history can tell us much about the appalling social conditions we face today.

The problem stretches back more than 100 years, dating from the completion of the trans-continental railroad link to the city in 1876. Hundreds of unemployed men who had once worked on the project began congregating in an area east of the railroad terminus that became known as "Skid Row." Some of these inhabitants were substance abusers, some had physical or mental health issues, and still others were simply down on their luck. Over the years, the fifty-one-square block area was packed with seedy, tenement hotels and beleaguered people who were the forerunners of today's homeless.

Their numbers exploded in the 1970s after then-California Governor Ronald Reagan signed the Lanterman-Petris-Short Act, a law that de-institutionalized many people with mental health challenges. Many professionals believed they could be better treated in outpatient settings, but some individuals fell through the cracks and wound up on the streets. Soon, they were joined by waves of homeless veterans returning from the Vietnam War and other individuals who increasingly found themselves on the wrong side of a growing economic divide. In 1976, Mayor Tom Bradley's administration adopted the "Containment Policy," which "encouraged" homeless persons to take up residence on Skid Row. The initiative was principally designed to keep the homeless away from a rapidly redeveloping downtown. The policy was widely seen as a failure.

Three decades later, growing pressures to gentrify and develop the downtown area, plus a push by the city itself, forced thousands of homeless out of Skid Row. They dispersed throughout Los Angeles and began living in tents under freeway overpasses, in public parks and on sidewalks. The new enclaves popped up in neighborhoods far from downtown—in the San Fernando and San Gabriel Valleys, the Westside, Koreatown, South Los Angeles, Hollywood, and Venice. Suddenly, homelessness became a part of daily life in myriad Southern California communities, and no one could ignore it. When the city settled a lawsuit in 2006, upholding the legal right of homeless people to sleep on the sidewalks, the proliferation of tent communities accelerated.

By 2020 there were more than 66,000 homeless in Los Angeles County on any given night—a 12.7 percent rise over the previous year—with thousands more living in cars. Meanwhile, tens of thousands of tenants were only one eviction notice away from losing their homes. Contrary to public perception, the vast majority were not from out-of-state seeking shelter in our communities. They were sons and daughters of Southern California.

Although the number of homeless as a *percentage* of the Los Angeles population did not significantly increase over the years, their sheer numbers did and began impacting neighborhoods that had never experienced homeless persons before. As a result, the issue became a priority concern for the public and its political representatives, eclipsing crime and traffic in most public opinion surveys. When a councilman representing the affluent Pacific Palisades gets calls that there are homeless encampments in their local park, it's not just a policy question; it becomes an existential electoral issue.

Given this history of institutional avoidance and failure, I had no illusions about the challenges I faced when I decided to do something about homelessness. Even though some of the social and economic issues were clearly beyond anyone's control, government dysfunction and neglect at all levels had exacerbated these long-simmering social problems. There was enough blame to go around.

From a fiscal policy point of view, the federal government didn't help. In 1986, Congress enacted President Reagan's tax reform legislation that made afford- able new rental housing development far less attractive to investors. There were other factors, too. On again-off again recessions and the savings and loan scan- dal contributed to economic uncertainty. The net effect was that between 1986 and 1991, apartment construction plummeted by 75 percent nationally, and Los Angeles wasn't spared. When construction finally picked up again it was largely focused on the high-end market. Moreover, multiple national administrations, both Democratic and Republican, cut low and moderate-income housing subsi- dies, which in the ensuing years took a toll on the affordable rental housing supply. At that time, for every twenty Los Angeles residents seeking a subsidized housing unit, only one succeeded. Those odds only worsened in the years that followed.

For its part, state government made it far more difficult for cities and coun- ties to address the prohibitive cost of rental housing. The legislature pre-empted local governments from enacting tougher tenant rights laws that would have protected the rapidly dwindling supply of affordable housing. Mayors, boards of supervisors, and City Councils had their hands tied as rents escalated and incomes didn't.

In Los Angeles, local officials were AWOL on a host of other issues that con- tributed to the rent burden and homelessness. Over the decades, the demolition of rent-controlled apartments continued, forcing low-income tenants to seek housing at market rent levels, a price they could not possibly afford. Local offi- cials also stood by as affordable apartments were converted to short-term rentals, through services like Airbnb, which removed as many as 20,000 units from the rental housing market in the City of Los Angeles alone. It's no surprise that one of the fastest growing demographics in Los Angeles' homeless population consisted of renters who had been evicted and could not afford replacement rents.

Today, Los Angeles has two housing economies—one for the free market and a separate one for persons on the lower half of the income spectrum. Market rate apartments are being built at a record pace. In 2018, the city approved more new rental units than in any year since 1981, but few of them were affordable to low and moderate-income residents. Some of this new construction came at the expense of older affordable units that were demolished to make room for them.

In 2020, monthly median rent in Los Angeles County was nearly $2,000. If a family with an annual household income of $30,000 or less (18 percent of county households in 2020) could find an apartment at $1,300/month (65 percent of the median), it would need to spend at least half of its income just for housing. That would leave less than $15,000 for all its other needs—food, clothing, medical, utilities, transportation, and emergencies for an entire year.

For them, the economic stress was even worse, and some of them became homeless. This math was simple and devastating.

In short, we don't have an acute shortage of market rate housing today in Los Angeles. What we have is a crisis-level shortage of *affordable* housing that is worsening every day. A 2022 countywide survey that I directed at the UCLA-Luskin School of Public Affairs found that nearly one in four Los Angeles County residents went to bed at night fearing that they might lose their housing *and* become homeless as a result.

The Birth of Project 50

My homeless initiative in Los Angeles County began with small steps. In 2005 I hired an indefatigable deputy to focus on homelessness. Flora Gil Krisiloff bore in on the problem in a vast county bureaucracy where no one department was responsible and accountable for this issue. She immersed herself in homeless policy, quickly becoming a driving force in the county family. She also forged a strong working relationship with Phil Mangano, Executive Director of the US Inter-Agency Council on Homelessness in Washington, DC.

When I traveled to New York in 2007 for my son David's law school graduation, I asked Flora if there was anyone worth meeting there who had successfully tackled homelessness. She suggested I connect with Roseanne Haggerty, a respected community development activist and MacArthur Fellowship recipient. Haggerty had founded "Common Ground," a program that housed hundreds of Manhattan's homeless in the Times Square Hotel on 43rd St. Formerly a men's hotel, it had become a notoriously dangerous site nicknamed "Homeless Hell." It was a dumping ground for the city's most intractable cases and a sewer of drug-dealing, prostitution, and violence.

Haggerty vowed to change all that. She eventually transformed the site into what is known as a permanent supportive housing project. Her efforts were boosted by a blend of federal and non-profit funding, and guided by a radically new, but disarmingly simple, approach to dealing with the problem. She unconditionally offered safe and secure housing units to homeless persons—no questions asked. Stating the obvious, she told me that "if we want to end homelessness, we first have to provide homeless persons with a home." This "Housing First" approach operated on the notion that people needed the security of a place to live, before they'd be psychologically prepared to accept social services that addressed the problems that made them homeless in the first place. Establishing trust between her agency and her clients was a prerequisite to success.

I set aside an hour to meet with Haggerty but ended up spending half a day. It was an education and a half. I toured the repurposed Times Square Hotel, now a poster child for "permanent supportive housing." We walked through the neighborhood and met with people whose lives she had changed. The results spoke for themselves. After several years, Haggerty's program had reduced homelessness by 87 percent in one of the world's most infamous twenty-block areas. I wondered if her approach could work in Los Angeles. Her answer was an unequivocal "yes." In fact, she offered to convene a symposium in Los Angeles, with officials who had successfully addressed homelessness in cities across the nation. Haggerty only asked that I bring our team to such a meeting to learn and exchange ideas on how to change the homelessness paradigm in our city. I was all in.

We gathered in the fall of 2007 at the Los Angeles County Hall of Administration, and I immediately sensed a new energy among our professional staff. They showed an enthusiasm I hadn't seen before, and a belief that they could make real headway. I could feel my own creative juices flowing, too. The sense of possibility was palpable. As the meeting ended, I asked our visiting experts where they thought we should start. Some of them had visited Skid Row the night before, and what they saw informed their response. "Unless you solve homelessness on Skid Row," one of them said, "you won't solve it countywide." They believed this downtown enclave was the core of the region's problem, spinning off homelessness to the rest of the county.

As a first step, they recommended that we identify the 50 most vulnerable homeless people on Skid Row—those most likely to die within the next year if they remained on the streets—and provide them with a housing unit. We agreed and made plans to conduct a census of every homeless person living in the area. This would not just be a head count but an interview as well. We needed to determine how long people had been living on the streets and what maladies they had, including health, mental health, and substance abuse problems. Once we got our target group into housing, we would offer them a range of services aimed at addressing those issues. It was a noble effort, but there were numerous obstacles.

First, there was a problem of perception. Public fatigue and anger over homelessness was pervasive, and the last thing Angelenos wanted to hear in late 2007 was yet another politician promising to cure an unsolvable problem with a costly new program. At times like these, I invoke one of my fundamental political axioms: When you propose something revolutionary, call it a "pilot project." Since a pilot is not necessarily permanent, it can overcome the institutional defensiveness—and public skepticism—that innovative ideas spawn. If an experiment succeeds, we can build on its success. If it it's a flop, we can pull the plug and go back to square one. After all, it was only a "pilot." That's how I unveiled our effort, which we dubbed "Project 50."

We conducted our Skid Row census in early December 2007, just weeks after the conference. When it was completed, we had identified 470 individuals living on the streets there, a significantly lower number than any of us expected. Our team was encouraged. It's hard to get your arms around an effort to house tens of thousands of homeless persons. By contrast, housing 50 or even 500 seemed manageable. We set out to answer three questions: Could we successfully house the most vulnerable homeless in a "housing first" program and keep them in the program? Would it be cost-effective? And, if we were successful, could we scale the program to ultimately house the 25,000 chronically homeless people in our county?

Drafting such a plan is one thing but executing it is another. Homeless persons do not typically trust government or authority figures. Even when they are unconditionally offered a housing unit, they're more likely to decline than accept, at first. In New York, I asked Haggerty how she dealt with that phenomenon. "We never give up on any person," she said. "We never take 'no' for an answer." That's how we recruited candidates for the Los Angeles program.

Once a homeless person accepted a housing unit, we offered him or her a broad array of services. If they had mental health issues, we provided a psychiatrist or psychologist. If they had physical health problems, we got them into one of our county clinics for treatment and medication. If they were addicted to drugs or alcohol, we got them into a rehabilitation program. First, however, we had to place them in housing, and we found a partner in the Skid Row Housing Trust, a homeless housing provider in downtown. Thanks to them, we were able to enroll 75 homeless persons in the initial pilot. The goal was to get participants settled as quickly as possible, and then begin the long, difficult journey of reintegrating them into society.

Project 50 was a success. After two and a half years, over 90 percent of our clients remained in the program. Only two people dropped out—one died, and the other returned to his country of origin. Just as remarkable, a county analysis found that it was actually *cheaper* to house the homeless and provide them with services than to leave them on the streets to fend for themselves. The pilot cost us $3.04 million, while the cost of doing nothing would have been approximately $3.28 million. The costs were offset by savings generated because participants were no longer cycling in and out of hospital emergency rooms, shelters, and jails. At bottom, Project 50 demonstrated that housing the homeless and providing them with social services was not only morally right, but fiscally sustainable.

One of the principal reasons for our success was the collaborative working relationship we established among twenty-four public and private agencies, a rarity in the splintered, siloed world of Los Angeles City and County government. In doing so, we turned an innovative concept into a working reality. Project 50 exploded the myth that the hardcore homeless on Skid Row couldn't be helped.

Battling Roadblocks

There were cynics, of course, who continued to believe that it was wrong for the county to house drug addicts and alcohol-dependent homeless people with taxpayer funds. Conservative Supervisor Mike Antonovich was a principal proponent of this view. I had faith, however, that if Mike could see this program in action, even *he* could change his mind. One day, when he made a disparaging remark about Project 50 at our Board meeting, I asked him to come with me to one of our permanent housing sites and judge the program for himself. To his credit, he agreed. As luck would have it, when we arrived a group of clients was singing "Happy Birthday" to one of the formerly homeless clients. Antonovich asked whose birthday it was, and one of them responded: "I'm celebrating two years of sobriety, so we're having a party." It was an "aha" moment for Mike that I wouldn't have had the chutzpah to script. Although he didn't become a supporter of our program, he never publicly criticized it again. Sometimes, even small steps can represent a victory.

With this successful "pilot program" under our belt, the next logical step was to ramp up from seventy-five clients to 500, and ultimately to 5,000 and beyond. We would now be able to justify expanding this homeless strategy to areas beyond Skid Row. We knew what worked, and all we had to do was summon the will to do it. Then I ran into a brick wall.

When the County's chief executive office and I recommended expanding the pilot to 500 clients, I couldn't get one other member of the Board of Supervisors to support it. Some members thought it was too expensive, even though the analysis demonstrated otherwise. Some didn't want taxpayer money to be used to house people with addictions, even though a program like ours was the only way to effectively treat homeless drug and alcohol dependency. And there was the pettiness and jealousy that too often infect politicians and their staffs. There were also institutional rivalries. The county's temporary homeless shelter agencies wanted funding from the Project 50 expansion, even though they did not provide permanent housing, or services to break the homeless cycle. Some of them simply gave the homeless a cot and a roof over their head for the night. I referred to them as the "Shelter Industrial Complex," but they were influential with my colleagues and some county bureaucrats.

One of my greatest disappointments as a supervisor was my inability to overcome these barriers and expand Project 50 countywide. Over time, we could have housed and served the needs of thousands of homeless men, women, and children. Instead, Los Angeles lost nearly a decade of valuable time during which the problem grew so pervasively that no one could ignore it any longer. In 2016 and 2017, city and county voters overwhelmingly approved a $1.2 billion bond and a sales tax increase to build housing and provide services for the homeless, a measure of the public's frustration with the issue.

Despite these setbacks, I wasn't going to be deterred. With comparatively meager resources I decided to at least expand Project 50 in my Supervisorial district—in Venice, Santa Monica, Hollywood and Van Nuys—and the results continued to be remarkable. We were able to approve and build close to 750 permanent supportive housing units. A key source of new housing turned out to be motels and old hotels. In many cases they had become hotbeds of prostitution and drug use, much like the Times Square Hotel in New York used to be. It was relatively easy and inexpensive to transform them into homeless housing. Moreover, we encountered practically no neighborhood opposition to these projects, a collateral surprise. Neighbors preferred a supervised housing program for the chronically mentally ill homeless to a seedy, crime-ridden motel near their homes.

My principal partner in this effort was "Step up on Second," a Santa Monica based non-profit homeless housing provider. Step Up had pioneered the hotel/motel conversion concept in Los Angeles, for which it received national recognition. On one occasion, former President Bill Clinton and Los Angeles Laker star Kobe Bryant appeared at a fundraiser for a Step Up project at an abandoned hotel in Hollywood. I found another partner in the non-profit Los Angeles Family Housing Corporation. This agency had the courage to adopt permanent supportive housing as its model, unlike so many other organizations that were still stuck in the temporary shelter paradigm. It is now one of the most successful non-profits in the homeless housing arena. All told, we put a very modest dent in the homeless challenge.

Where Do We Go from Here?

In October 2016, two years out of office, I paid a visit to Miguel Santana, then the Chief Administrative Officer for the City of Los Angeles. He previously had overseen homeless policy as one of the county's Deputy Chief Executive Officers. The city had placed a $1.2 billion bond measure on the November ballot to target homelessness, and it seemed headed for approval. I suggested to Santana that Los Angeles move quickly to buy or lease motels across the city with the bond proceeds. As we had done earlier in my district, the city easily could turn these facilities into permanent supportive homeless housing. Santana agreed, but even he couldn't get the city's lawyers and bureaucrats out of their own way. Inertia can be a powerful force, and the idea languished.

The situation changed completely when the 2020 Covid-19 pandemic descended upon California. Governor Gavin Newson launched "Project Room Key," a program to acquire or lease hotels and motels for homeless housing. And he earmarked $1 billion in the State budget to pay for it. He expanded that program, now called "Project Home Key," to include services as well as housing. There was an urgency to getting the unhoused into housing because of the fear of the virus's spread in the many encampments around the state. There was also a sense of urgency among city officials. They, too, began leasing up motel and hotel rooms by the thousands. What a difference a crisis makes. This could have been launched years ago, but it took Covid-19 to motivate officialdom. Time will tell whether the state and local governments demonstrate the capacity and political will to scale this program to a level that makes more than a dent on the numbers of homeless on our streets.

Looking ahead, we need to be prepared for a long haul. This problem won't be solved overnight. So, in the short term, rapid housing, using the hotel/motel model and other innovative approaches combined with supportive services, can be an effective bridge to permanent housing. The city and county should not take their foot off the gas pedal once the coronavirus pandemic ends.

Second, a partnership between the federal, state, and local government in solving homelessness is imperative. No city or county can solve this problem alone. The federal government must get off the dime and invest in *affordable* housing, through direct appropriations and tax credits. The State of California has passed dozens of bills to boost development of market rate housing, but it has done little to protect or expand affordable housing for low and moderate-income persons. Going forward, *all new housing* projects must include a meaningful set-aside for low and moderate-income tenants. Failure to do so will only exacerbate the homeless crisis.

Third, the City and County should agree on the joint appointment of a homeless/housing czar—an official who can move homeless housing projects through the bureaucracy at a rapid clip. For those who argue that politicians will never relinquish authority to an appointed official, they should look to the example of the 1995 Board of Supervisors when it appointed a powerful health czar—Burt Margolin—to help avert a County bankruptcy. Politicians will cede authority when their own political survival is at stake. Homelessness is now the number-one political issue in Los Angeles. This issue dominated the 2022 Los Angeles municipal election, and it will make or break political careers in the years ahead.

On December 12, 2022, in her first act as the newly elected mayor of Los Angeles, Karen Bass declared a "state of emergency" over the crisis of the unhoused. This gave her considerable authority in siting and expediting construction of homeless housing within the city limits. More importantly, this decision put the mayor front and center in addressing this crisis—something that none of her predecessors chose to do—and in doing so, she was willing to be held accountable for the results of her efforts. It's a courageous decision, and it's the right one. If she succeeds, it will be an historic and overdue achievement.

Fourth, we must address the economic divide in Southern California and across the nation. Wages are not keeping pace with the cost of living, especially housing prices. Until Angelenos' incomes *and* benefits rise, a significant percentage of them will be consigned to a precarious economic existence, and too many will land on the streets. Growing the incomes of our workers is an important part of the solution to this mother of all social problems.

Finally, the county needs a major governance overhaul. It is incomprehensible that a county as large as Los Angeles has no elected executive who is electorally accountable to all ten million of its residents. It desperately needs one! Functionally, the current five-member board model puts no one in charge, and the consequences are often costly. This is plainly evident in dealing with the tens of thousands of unhoused persons on the streets and sidewalks of the Southern California region.

Homelessness is the moral challenge of our time. It demands the urgency of the Manhattan Project and the precision of our space program. When I think about the task ahead of us, I am reminded of the first-century Jewish sage, Rabbi Tarfon, who left us these words: "You are not obliged to complete the work, but neither are you free to desist from it." That was good advice 2,000 years ago—and it's good advice today.

CHAPTER 20

Tragedy and Resurrection at MLK Hospital

———

It was a tragedy that stunned the world. When Edith Rodriguez arrived at the emergency room of Martin Luther King Jr./King Drew Medical Center on May 9, 2007, the forty-three-year-old mother of three complained of intense abdominal pain. As she sat in a waiting room chair, Rodriguez suddenly fell to the floor and a security camera captured an appalling scene: Patients looked on quietly while hospital employees ignored her cries for help. Nurses went about their business and a janitor cleaned up around her, oblivious to her suffering. In a span of forty-five minutes, she died from a perforated bowel. The grainy video went viral and showed a stunning lack of humanity in a county-run hospital serving one of Los Angeles' poorest communities. But the real tragedy was that Rodriguez's ordeal, however shocking, was not a one-off. The horrific indifference that killed her was a bureaucratic, political, and medical train wreck, decades in the making.

Although horror stories of botched care were nothing new at MLK, Rodriguez's death proved to be the straw that broke the camel's back. When the hospital failed to pass a crucial certification test several months later, the federal government finally pulled the plug, announcing that it would withhold more than $200 million in annual funding, or half of MLK's annual budget. At that point, the Board of Supervisors had no choice but to close the facility. The decision must have seemed like a no-brainer to an outsider. Although the hospital's defenders claimed it acted properly in *most* patient cases, this was hardly reassuring. Medical care is not baseball. Batting .750 in the big leagues will get you into the Hall of Fame, but it's totally unacceptable in a critical care hospital. The troubled institution—one of five county-owned hospitals—had run out of time and excuses.

Still, our decision to close MLK was anything but simple. In truth, it was one of the most personally gut-wrenching decisions I ever had to make as county supervisor. When it comes to life-saving care, we fully expect all employees to maintain the highest standards, regardless of who their patients are or where they live. However, MLK was not like any other hospital in Los Angeles, and therein lay the heart of the problem.

Rising from the Ashes

Soon after the Watts Rebellion ended in the summer of 1965, California Governor Pat Brown appointed former CIA Director John A. McCone to head a commission that would identify the root causes of the civil unrest and offer possible responses. The eight-member panel found that the lack of decent, accessible medical care in South Los Angeles was at the top of the list. There were no major hospitals or emergency rooms in the area. Residents typically were transported as far as County/USC Medical Center in Boyle Heights, fifteen miles away, for trauma and other emergency medical services. This was intolerable, because in medical emergencies every minute can be the difference between life and death. Indeed, people in South Los Angeles did die for lack of timely care.

The McCone Commission recommended that a modern, fully equipped medical center be constructed in the area, and Supervisor Kenneth Hahn, who had represented this part of the county since 1952, led the effort to get it done. When it opened in 1972, King/Drew was a state-of-the-art facility that addressed the needs of one of the nation's most medically underserved communities. Residents in South Los Angeles died of heart disease, stroke, lung cancer and diabetes at a higher rate than in any other part of the county. It quickly became clear, however, that MLK would be more than a hospital. Overnight the 394-bed facility became a source of pride in the predominantly Black community. It was a symbol of social investment and economic recovery in one of the nation's most impoverished areas. The new medical center generated thousands of critical local jobs that were as important to local powerbrokers as the services it provided. After years of feeling marginalized and overlooked, the people of South Los Angeles began to believe that for the first time the government was paying attention to their needs.

It was not unusual for the county's hospitals to develop strong ties to the communities they served. Although they were technically accountable to the Department of Health Services (DHS) headquarters in downtown Los Angeles, the real decision-making power was centered in the facilities themselves. They were typically run more like franchises than extensions of a cohesively run health department, and this model was taken to an extreme at King/Drew. From the start, the hospital and its community were joined at the hip. Community leaders, including politically powerful unions, influenced and in some cases dictated staffing decisions. MLK didn't just reflect the community; it seemed to be run by the community. This dynamic too often caused legitimate criticism to be swept aside, and quality health care suffered as a result. Eventually stories began surfacing about shocking incompetence at the hospital.

In 1989, a jaw-dropping series by *Los Angeles Times* investigative reporter Claire Spiegel laid bare an institution where appalling lapses in standards and procedures were the norm. There were stories of routine surgeries that led to unnecessary patient deaths, reports of filthy conditions in the emergency room, and cases where senior attending physicians slept on the job and ignored their responsibility to supervise young resident doctors. There were reports about gravely injured patients who waited for hours in the Level One Trauma Center, because neurosurgeons were not on the premises or available to treat them within twenty minutes of arrival, as required by Los Angeles County regulations. Most critically, the newspaper found that "disproportionate numbers of patients are dying at MLK compared to the county's two other major acute care public hospitals." The stories also found that, when it came to deaths of elderly patients, King was among the worst 50 hospitals in the nation. When critics demanded that doctors and administrators be held responsible for these failures, the community circled the wagons to defend them. Any serious attempt to discipline or remove workers who performed poorly ran into a brick wall of resistance.

At the same time, one can't discuss MLK Hospital without acknowledging the horrific, continuing legacy of racism in America. The hospital was born out of the Watts uprising and named for the iconic Black leader of the American civil rights movement. That was testament enough to the primacy of this institution in South Los Angeles. Community leaders and health care advocates deeply resented downtown's "meddling" in this institution. Any effort to hold the hospital accountable for day-to-day performance sparked angry protests. This charged atmosphere caused county officials to tread gingerly.

Many of the area's political leaders who might have been concerned about MLK were reluctant to weigh in. It was risky, if not politically suicidal, to question its quality of care. When shortcomings were revealed, the response often was that the county had not allocated enough money to the hospital.

Members of the Board of Supervisors were also hesitant to enter the fray. They religiously observed a rule that one must never intervene in the politics of another member's district. For years Supervisor Kenneth Hahn's staunch defense of the hospital kept critics at bay. However, MLK's problems eventually became impossible to ignore. In 1989, increasingly critical evaluations by government regulators led to a federal threat to withhold millions of dollars in Medicaid reimbursements from the hospital.

Although the board fired William Delgardo, who had been the hospital's chief administrator for fourteen years, this didn't silence Hahn. Despite his failing health, he showed up at the tumultuous board meeting where Delgardo's fate was decided, and he angrily reaffirmed his support for the chief. At the emotional community rally protesting the move, a member of the hospital's community advisory board said that Martin Luther King's name alone guaranteed the hospital would not be treated fairly, adding that there was no good reason to fire Delgardo.

Enough Blame to Go Around

Even with new administrators in charge, the hospital's problems continued. As I joined the board in 1994, they seemed more insurmountable than ever. Officials at DHS headquarters in downtown were more frequently on top of conditions at Olive View Hospital in the San Fernando Valley and County/USC Medical Center in Boyle Heights. But they either didn't have a clue about day-to-day problems at MLK, or were reluctant to do much about them. When negative stories appeared in the press, they often told me that they were reading about it for the first time like everybody else.

The hospital's troubles grew more pronounced in 2004, when federal officials determined that MLK had fallen out of compliance with Medicaid standards. They warned that the hospital had to radically improve its operations or face possible closure. Over the next three years, MLK was buffeted by additional critical reviews from government regulators and peer group evaluations. Local leaders once again fought to protect the now 450-bed hospital that also had a trauma center, a neo-natal intensive care unit and other services. But community protests that worked in the past were now falling on deaf ears. The hospital was living on borrowed time.

These problems worsened when the *Los Angeles Times* trained its sights on the hospital yet again, uncovering fresh horror stories. In a blistering Pulitzer Prize-winning series, the Times documented skyrocketing payments to malpractice victims and patients dying from drug overdoses, left to perish in their own vomit. Hospital personnel were using stun guns to subdue disorderly psychiatric patients. And it laid to rest the complaint that the hospital was financially shortchanged by the county. Supervisors, it turned out, spent far more at MLK, per capita, than at other public hospitals. Again, the *Times* concluded that this was one of the worst hospitals in California, and perhaps the nation.

The most stinging criticism, however, was leveled at the Board of Supervisors. Board members, the Times wrote, had more power than anyone to improve conditions at the hospital, but they failed to do so. Amid these appalling stories my colleague, Supervisor Gloria Molina, said that the board should be collectively embarrassed by its failure to improve conditions at MLK. This was a discouraging admission for a member of "what is, by some measures, the most powerful local body in the United States," the *Times* noted.

For the next three years, the board mounted a last-ditch effort to keep MLK open while trying to reform its operations. But this was like asking Los Angeles drivers to simultaneously switch from driving on the right side of the road to the left side without crashing. As improbable of success that this strategy was, my colleagues and I could not in good conscience simply shut the hospital down without making every effort to fix it. We took aggressive, expensive, and deeply unpopular steps to decompress the hospital's operations and relieve day-to-day pressures on its staff.

Amid intense opposition, we closed the trauma center, which demanded more of the hospital than it could manage. We shuttered the neo-natal intensive care unit and eventually reduced the number of inpatient beds to a meager 48. Recognizing that new blood was needed to oversee the hospital, we placed it under the administrative direction of UCLA-Harbor Medical Center, located several miles away in Torrance. We spent tens of millions of dollars on consultants and beefed-up efforts to discipline employees, clashing with unions who defended their members. The sad truth, however, was that none of these efforts stemmed the hospital's decline, let alone reversed it. We were fighting an unwinnable battle.

Indeed, the board faced angry crowds at special public hearings that it was required to hold before reducing medical services. We wanted to keep as much of the hospital open as we responsibly could, because we couldn't ignore how service cutbacks, or closure, would impact the 50,000 patients who annually came to the hospital's emergency room. Although the ER was meant to deal with critical, life-threatening emergencies, it also treated patients with ear infections, the flu, and other non-critical ailments. The ER was the provider of last resort because, unlike private clinics or doctors, federal law required it to treat *any* patient who walked through its doors for *any* reason. This was a byproduct of our dysfunctional national health system, where tens of millions of people did not have insurance or a medical home.

The bill finally came due on August 10, 2007, when the federal government said it would no longer provide funding for MLK's hospital operations—principally Medicaid and Medicare reimbursements—amounting to approximately half of the hospital's revenues. Herb Kuhn, acting deputy administrator for the US Centers of Medicare and Medical Services said a crucial federal inspection found that "conditions at the facility have placed the health and safety of patients at risk." It was not the first time that federal officials made such a determination, but previously they were reluctant to pull the funding plug because of political pressure from the county and the community. This time, however, they were appalled when the problems in the hospital metastasized, as shown by the Edith Rodriguez tragedy. Their patience had finally run out. Federal regulators canceled the federal contract with MLK, pulled its funding and forced us to close the hospital for good.

In the aftermath, critics charged that we had waited too long to act. The danger signs had been apparent for years, they said, and we were asleep at the switch. These criticisms were justified, but if we had closed the hospital three years earlier, we would have heard different criticisms: Why didn't you try to fix it while keeping it open? Where will our residents go in a medical emergency? Why lay off 1,600 employees without a fight? There were no easy answers, only hard choices. But our Board did wait too long—decades too long—to hold the hospital accountable for the quality of its performance.

King Drew Medical Center was a key link in the chain of county health care, and its closure threatened to create problems for private and public hospitals throughout the region. After the shutdown, we took immediate steps to restore the medical safety net that had suddenly vanished for South Los Angeles residents. Most patients would be transferred to nearby St. Francis Hospital, a privately owned non-profit facility. Ambulance crews transferred emergency cases to the other available hospitals. We opened an additional fifty-two beds at Rancho Los Amigos National Rehabilitation Center in Downey and twenty beds at Harbor-UCLA Medical Center in Torrance, hoping that these efforts would provide short-term relief while we worked on a long-term solution.

I felt a profound sense of failure through it all, and still do. The ultimate responsibility for the MLK fiasco lay with the entire Board of Supervisors, including me. We had severed the medical lifeline to a community that deserved better. Local elected officials, community stakeholders, clergy and organized labor also bore responsibility for the debacle. For more than three decades they decided that defending an appalling status quo was more important than improving quality hospital care in the community they served. But make no mistake: This was a County failure—and the Board of Supervisors was its governing body. This is another example of where the county could have benefited from an elected county mayor. Anyone holding that office never would have allowed the hospital to deteriorate, knowing that he or she would be held principally accountable for such a calamitous result.

Rising from the Ashes Once Again

On the day after MLK closed, I drove to South Los Angeles with Carol Kim, my health deputy, and visited the hospital to see how the skeleton staff was functioning. The reaction we got was chilly, to say the least. Workers knew who I was and were not happy to see me on the premises. There was an angry look on their faces, as if to say, "What the hell are *you* doing here?" I thought to myself, "I should have been here thirteen years ago." A while later we headed for St. Francis' Hospital, about a mile away, where the reaction could not have been more different. Receptionists greeted us warmly and asked if we wanted to meet with the administrator. We were invited to take a tour and made to feel welcome. It was a metaphor for the whole saga. An old, embittered order was dying, while a new, more hopeful medical landscape was taking shape.

As we left St. Francis, I asked Kim if she had ever seen the world-famous Watts Towers, which were nearby. She hadn't, so I offered to take her to see one of Los Angeles' artistic treasures. A local resident came up to me as we walked through the towers and asked, "Aren't you Supervisor Yaroslavsky?" I said I was, and she erupted in fury. "You should never have shut down our hospital," the woman said. "Shame on you and shame on the other board members. You're a bunch of racists." I said I was sorry she felt that way, and that we had tried to save the hospital. "Yeah?" she answered. "You didn't do shit." At that point, an angry crowd started to gather, and we politely left the scene. It was a painful exchange, but I didn't take it personally. I completely understood the resident's rage and her sense of betrayal. She was speaking for tens of thousands of others as well. It was *our* job not to fail her, and we fell terribly short.

As we drove back to the office, I decided that I couldn't just walk away from this disaster. There had to be a way to restore decent medical care to this underserved community. We needed to establish a new hospital on this South Los Angeles campus—one that ensured excellence and had zero tolerance for incompetence. There were a variety of ideas bandied about, but they were all dead ends. I first called the Dean of the USC Medical School and asked if he would be interested in partnering with us, but he and the university wouldn't touch MLK with a ten-foot pole. Private hospitals were similarly uninterested because of the economics and the politics. If the county chose to reopen MLK on its own, we would be faced with the same problems that doomed it in the first place. Our decentralized governing structure would be a barrier to transparency and accountability. Civil service regulations and union rules would have forced us to rehire problem employees, in addition to the good ones. The cycle would begin all over again.

Nine months after the hospital closed, I came up with what I thought was the ideal solution. In an op-ed for the *Los Angeles Times*, I proposed a partnership between the University of California and Los Angeles County. The UC medical system was a powerful statewide public institution that shared the county's mission to serve the poor and indigent. It was not simply motivated by profit or beholden to private investors. If one of the nation's most prestigious public universities wouldn't partner with the nation's largest county to resurrect a critically needed hospital, who would?

To make the idea work, I believed the county and its Board of Supervisors would have to cede day-to-day management responsibility for the new hospital to an autonomous governing board. Federal and state funds that had flowed to the county for the shuttered MLK Hospital would have to be allocated directly to the new entity. For its part, the University of California would be responsible for medical staffing. Just as important, the new facility would not be encumbered by the county's civil service rules. New administrators wouldn't be forced to hire back old employees, and the relationship between the County and the new MLK would be at arm's length.

I believed this model was the only one with any prospect of success, and I was gratified that it got an immediate response. I received a call from Gov. Arnold Schwarzenegger's office on the morning my column was published. "The Governor just read your proposal, and he would like to meet with you to discuss it," an aide said. Supervisor Yvonne Burke, who represented South Los Angeles, traveled with me to the Governor's Santa Monica office to meet with him and Kim Belshe, his Secretary of Health and Human Services. Schwarzenegger liked to get big things done. "Action, action," was his signature exhortation in his thick Austrian accent. He wanted action on this plan, and he turned to Belshe, directing her to get it done. She was a smart, budget-conscious cabinet officer and urged the Governor to proceed cautiously. To be honest, if I had been in her shoes, I would have counseled him the same way. Schwarzenegger, however, would not be deterred. "We need action, we need action," he kept saying, and the plan slowly became a reality. The Governor cleared the political path, and the Board of Regents of the University of California eventually agreed to partner with the county.

And that, in a nutshell, is how King/Drew Medical Center rose from the ashes. Mark Ridley-Thomas, who succeeded Burke on the Board of Supervisors, oversaw the development of an entirely new campus on the MLK site. It now includes a hospital, an emergency room, an outpatient clinic, and a wellness center. The new facility is run by a non-profit entity and governed by a seven-person board of directors. UCLA provides physicians and medical expertise. Although the 131-bed hospital is smaller than its predecessor, it has plenty of room to grow. And, though the campus still lacks a trauma center that, too, may be in its future.

Ever since the MLK Hospital scandal erupted, I've asked myself how it could have been averted. The debacle was triggered by a perfect storm of Los Angeles' crippling racial legacy, a corrupted organizational culture and, most importantly, a failed county governance structure. In any organization, responsibility ultimately rests with its leader. But in our County the "leader" is a five-member Board of Supervisors that is too often paralyzed by political indecision and a dysfunctional, fiefdom culture. In short, it was ill-equipped to prevent a crisis of this magnitude. Once again, the Duke of Edinburgh's words come to mind: In the case of MLK Hospital, Los Angeles County was "designed not to govern." And its most vulnerable residents paid the price.

CHAPTER 21

Every Cause
Needs a Champion

On the morning the Orange Line Busway opened in 2005, project manager Rick Thorpe put his arm on my shoulder and thanked me for taking the lead on that effort. I appreciated his compliment but said it had truly been a team effort. "No," he answered. "Every project needs a champion, and you were the Orange Line's."

His words didn't initially register with me, but over time I realized there was something to what he said. Although this may sound like a cliché, political leaders are supposed to *lead*. They can lend their credibility and spend accumulated political capital to pursue and implement intelligent policies. Like many of my colleagues, I took ownership of some specific causes along the way. Sometimes I did so on my own initiative, and sometimes events forced my hand. In each case, these were the causes that spoke volumes about what made me tick.

The Gun Show Ban

Amid the never-ending carnage of gun violence in America, it's not surprising that efforts to ban the sale and use of deadly weapons frequently gather speed in the wake of horrific attacks on innocent people. That was certainly the case in 1989, when a white supremacist shot and killed five Southeast Asian children and wounded dozens of other people with a semi-automatic rifle at an elementary school in Stockton, California. At the time, Los Angeles was reeling from a gang-related shooting spree that had killed 257 people the previous year. Too much of that violence had been perpetrated with semi-automatic guns. The school massacre was too much to bear. But in the face of a formidable lobbying effort by the National Rifle Association, efforts to ban these guns had stalled in the state legislature.

I was disgusted. Enough was enough. So, I sponsored a measure banning the sale, possession, and use of semi-automatic weapons in the City of Los Angeles. It sailed through the council on a 12–0 vote and Mayor Tom Bradley signed the legislation into law. Soon after, Sacramento legislators finally approved a state-wide measure banning these guns, a law that had been languishing in legislative neverland for what felt like an eternity.

This was just the beginning of my involvement with the issue. When I moved to the Board of Supervisors, I won passage of a measure banning the sale of so-called junk guns—cheap, easily accessible weapons—in the county's unincorporated areas. But Los Angeles County was still being ravaged by gun violence. Semi-automatics were not only the weapons of choice for gang members; they were also being used in robberies and hate crimes. This was the case in 1997, when a wild, nationally televised shootout between bank robbers and the LAPD erupted in North Hollywood. Two of the illegal weapons used in that melee were purchased at the Great Western Gun Show, which was held four times a year at the Los Angeles County Fairgrounds in Pomona. Two years later, a white supremacist seriously wounded five children at the North Valley Jewish Community Center in Mission Hills and killed a US Postal Service worker later that afternoon in a nearby suburb. He used automatic weapons traced to a gun show in the State of Washington.

The Great Western Gun Show in Los Angeles was the nation's largest. Billed as a memorabilia and Wild West exhibition, it was also a hotbed of unmonitored sales of banned weapons that took place in the light of day. The event was nominally regulated by the Federal Bureau of Alcohol, Tobacco and Firearms, but it typically drew more than 50,000 visitors per day, and was not effectively policed. Customers flocked to the event from all over the region to buy machine guns, automatic and semi-automatic weapons, hand grenades, and bazookas. They took advantage of legal loopholes to avoid background checks. It was also a place where individuals felt comfortable hawking piles of racist and antisemitic literature. It was a disgrace.

I had been through enough civil liberties wars to know that free speech protections barred us from cracking down on offensive, bigoted publications. We would also be on shaky ground if we pushed for a county measure singling out this gun show at this location. Courts had ruled that such action would be an unconstitutional restriction of "commercial speech." I finally hit on an approach that County attorneys were confident would pass constitutional muster. I proposed that we ban gun sales of *any* kind on *all* county-owned property. I introduced the legislation in 1999, ten years after my city assault weapon ban.

Critics, including the NRA and the Great Western show owners, immediately attacked my proposal. They argued that we were simply trying to shut down the gun show and put them out of business. But they were wrong. Under my proposed ordinance the event could still *display* antique and collector guns, which Great Western said was their principal objective. They just couldn't sell any functional guns. It was hardly a stunt, as owners suggested. The gun show brought in an estimated $1 million per year in rent to our fairgrounds, so cancelling it outright would have financial consequences. I believed strongly, however, that the county shouldn't be making money from gun sales. How could we credibly speak about the horror of semi-automatic weapons on our streets while our fairgrounds pocketed huge rents from the nation's biggest gun bazaar?

The measure was approved on a 3–2 vote, with Gloria Molina and Yvonne Burke joining me. Opponents argued that the underground market for such guns was widespread, stretching far beyond the boundaries of California, so there was no way to meaningfully reduce the inventory. It didn't matter. I knew that even if our legislation saved one life, it was worth every penny the Fairgrounds lost.

Gun advocates promptly sued the County, but the effective date of the law was delayed by an injunction while the courts addressed its constitutionality. Ultimately the California Supreme Court upheld our law. They ruled that the County had a right to prohibit the sale of guns on its own property. At that point, the Great Western Gun Show folded its tent and moved to Las Vegas.

It's been more than twenty years since that battle, and the carnage from gun violence continues to mount in our nation. We have a long way to go before military style weapons are banned and gun show loopholes are plugged. These measures have broad support across our country, and Congress should seize every opportunity to erase them from our daily lives. Unfortunately, our leaders in Washington rarely miss an opportunity to miss an opportunity when it comes to ending the epidemic of gun violence that has turned our streets, schools, nightclubs, and houses of worship into killing zones. But at least we would make a difference, small as it may have been, in Los Angeles.

The Cross, the County Seal, and the Constitution

As a child growing up in Boyle Heights, I could see City Hall and its 27-story tower from our apartment on Breed Street. It was the tallest building in Los Angeles in the late 1950s, dominating the Civic Center skyline and beyond. During the Christmas and Easter seasons, we could see it lit up at night with a Latin Cross, the universal symbol of Christianity. I remember asking my dad, "Why is there a cross on City

Hall and not a Star of David?" I don't remember his answer. He probably didn't feel like explaining the Bill of Rights to a seven-year-old—or the tower's geometric limitations. Still, I wondered why my city chose to favor one religion over others.

As an adult, I had no problem articulating these concerns. City Hall was supposed to represent all of us, not just one group. The first amendment and myriad Supreme Court decisions, made that clear. When I joined the City Council in 1975, plaintiffs filed a lawsuit challenging the constitutionality of the City Hall cross. The City argued that it was not motivated by religion, but simply by a desire to celebrate the holiday spirit. The State Supreme Court didn't buy it and ruled that the cross could no longer appear on the seat of Los Angeles city government.

Just before I joined the Board of Supervisors, Yvonne Burke launched a similar effort to remove the image of the Latin cross from Los Angeles County's official seal, where it had been displayed since 1957. The county seal was ubiquitous. It appeared on vehicles, documents, and buildings. It contained an assortment of icons: The Hollywood Bowl representing arts and culture; a star representing the motion picture industry; an oil derrick representing the region's oil rich history; a cow symbolizing the dairy industry; and the Roman goddess Pomona representing agriculture. Finally, there was the Latin cross. County documents stated clearly that it represented *religion*. Burke cited court rulings that prohibited such displays, but she eventually withdrew her initiative amid a backlash from hundreds of Christian clergy and a lack of support from a majority of her colleagues.

For years, I stared at that seal knowing that it was unconstitutional. Many non-Christian county employees—Muslims, Jews, Hindus, and Buddhists—asked me to do something about it, but I chose not to initiate what I knew would be a divisive debate. In 2004, however, the ACLU resurrected the issue by giving the Board an ultimatum: Either remove the cross from the seal or be sued. Now, the issue had landed squarely in our lap. Meeting in closed session the County Counsel, Ray Fortner, advised us that our official seal was unconstitutional, and that we would lose if the issue went to trial. Adding insult to injury, he told us we would be forced to pay the ACLU's legal fees, as well as our own, when we lost. Burke, Molina, and I voted to settle the matter and remove the cross from the seal. When we announced our decision in public session, the fight got ugly.

Religious leaders blasted our action and insisted that we fight the ACLU in court. They disingenuously argued that the cross didn't represent religion, or even Christianity. Rather, they said, it was placed on the seal to represent the historical role that the Franciscan missionaries played in the settlement of our county. Aside from being patently untrue, that rationale was an insult to the Indigenous population that called Southern California home long before the first missionary showed up. The ruthless treatment to which they were subjected was a matter of public record. Nevertheless, we agreed to address the missionaries' role in the history of our region by replacing the cross with a likeness of the San Gabriel Mission, the first in Los Angeles County. To recognize its original inhabitants, we removed the goddess Pomona and replaced her with the likeness of an Indigenous woman. I thought we had settled the matter.

But the opposition grew more intense. Right-wing talk show hosts, including Bill O'Reilly, Dennis Prager and others declared war on us. They urged cross supporters to show up at the Board's next meeting and make themselves heard. More than 2,000 angry and hysterical citizens descended on the Hall of Administration that week. They crammed into our hearing room, which held 800 people, and we had to provide additional rooms for the overflow crowd. The raw language of the nearly 8-hour hearing moved Yvonne Burke to say that the protesters had whipped themselves into a "religious frenzy." She added that the atmosphere was "as close to the Inquisition as we've seen."

The protestors expected me, a Jew, to oppose the cross. But it was viewed as an act of betrayal by Burke and Molina, who were Christian. For them, it was a far more courageous stand than it was for me. Still, I came in for my share of attacks. Talk radio blasted my motives, and our office switchboard was flooded with thousands of irate callers. At one point, Liz Rangel, my secretary, walked into my office and told me that the secretaries in our front office were having a challenging time with all the calls. I assumed that she was referring to the call load, but she wasn't. "They don't agree with your position, and they're finding it difficult to explain a position that they don't agree with," she explained. I felt terrible that I had put my staff in that position. I went up front, sat at an empty desk with a telephone, and began answering calls. I was within earshot of the secretaries, so they could hear my explanation to the callers.

The very first call I answered was from a hostile San Fernando Valley constituent. "This is Supervisor Yaroslavsky," I said. She didn't believe it was me. "I want to speak to *the* Supervisor," she responded. "This is *the* Supervisor," I said. The caller then explained that she was calling about the cross matter—but first she wanted me to know that she was an Armenian Christian who had taken my mother's Hebrew class at Los Angeles City College in the mid-1950s. I was floored. She proceeded to tell me what a wonderful woman my mother was, and that it was the best class she ever took. She then gave me her pitch on why the cross should remain on the seal, and I gave her my pitch in return.

She was about to hang up when I asked if I could pose a question to her. "Why would an Armenian Christian like you take Hebrew in college?" She explained that she was raised at home speaking Armenian and wanted to learn another complicated language. "You chose the right one," I said. We parted on extremely friendly and respectful terms. I spent the entire day fielding calls, and I enjoyed every minute. It was like walking precincts again. When the day was over, Liz took me aside to say that the secretaries appreciated what I did. I told her that I was happy to take a small part of the load off their backs. "No, that's not it," she again explained. "They now fully understand your position, and they agree with you." That, alone, was worth a day on the phones.

Other episodes were not so polite. Pat Boone criticized the Board of Supervisors majority during remarks at a Pepperdine University event, and Prager, whom I had known since 1969, regularly attacked the board's decision on his syndicated program. Bill O'Reilly insisted that I come on his nationally televised Fox television talk show—the most watched on that network—but I declined. His producers made several attempts to get me to agree, assuring me that I would be treated fairly. "What a deal," Joel Bellman, my press deputy, told them. "It ain't happening." I was booed at the July 4 parade in Pacific Palisades, my favorite parade of the year, and the mail and calls I got were vile. Still, that was nothing compared to what my two colleagues had to endure from their clergy and constituents.

The one interview I agreed to do on a conservative talk-show was with Hugh Hewitt. He was a friend and had frequently interviewed me on KCET Public Television's "Life and Times" program, an influential weekly news round up. I had respect for Hugh as a journalist. When he asked if I'd go on his show, I told him I would, knowing he would treat me fairly. He did. During the interview, he said many of those protesting felt I was hostile to Christianity. "Hugh," I said, "we replaced the cross with the San Gabriel Mission, not with a delicatessen. How hostile could I be?" We both chuckled, and he thanked me for the interview.

The most moving moment of the whole saga came when I was at home, responding to angry e-mails at 1:00 a.m. I saw a message pop up in my inbox from Andy Benton, the President of the Church of Christ affiliated Pepperdine University. We had bonded in 1995, during one of many wildfires that threatened the campus, and I held my breath as I opened his message. "I just want you to know that as a Christian and as a lawyer, I think you did the right thing," he wrote. "I don't believe in quixotic battles." Few messages I've ever received meant more to me than that one. We weathered the storm, and the county had a new seal that would pass constitutional muster.

The battle, however, was not over. Ten years later, in 2014, the Board voted to restore the cross to the seal by a 3–2 vote. This time the ACLU filed its promised lawsuit. Mark Ridley-Thomas, who had replaced Yvonne Burke in the intervening decade, delivered the pivotal third vote to bring the cross back. When the federal court trial concluded, Federal Judge Christina Snyder issued a blistering ruling against the County. Restoring the cross to the seal, she said, "places the county's power, prestige, and purse behind a single religion—Christianity. . ."

Many people, including friends who agreed with my position, wondered why I cared so much about this issue. Didn't I have more important things to do with my time? That was the gist of an email I got from former Los Angeles City Councilman Arthur K. Snyder, from whom I hadn't heard in years. He advised me to drop the matter because it was politically dangerous. In truth, a poll revealed that a two-to-one majority of my district's voters wanted the cross kept on the seal. "Art," I wrote, "there's one thing you don't understand about me. I'm willing to lose an election over this. I take seriously my oath to 'preserve, protect, and defend' the constitution, and that's what I intend to do."

As I have long believed, the key question is not which positions politicians will support or oppose. It's the issues they're willing to lose their office over in the name of principles that matter. James Hahn—the son of legendary LA County Supervisor Kenneth Hahn, and the fortieth mayor of Los Angeles— learned this the hard way. Hahn, who succeeded Richard Riordan in office, was elected in 2001 with strong support from Black voters in South Los Angeles and white voters in the suburban San Fernando Valley. But he lost the support of Black voters when, in the aftermath of the Rampart police scandal, he refused to reappoint LAPD Chief Bernard Parks, a veteran Black leader of the department. Similarly, the mayor alienated Valley voters in November 2001, when he campaigned against and helped defeat a ballot proposal that would have allowed the Valley to secede from Los Angeles in order to form a separate city.

I believe history will look kindly on his decision to hire William Bratton to be the new LAPD Chief. Bratton, the former head of the police departments in New York City and Boston, took on the challenge of changing the deeply entrenched culture that led to the scandals that plagued LA's police force. Indisputably, that is still a work in progress. Similarly, Hahn believed it was important for Los Angeles to remain intact as a city, and not splinter apart. He believed he was doing the right thing in both cases, and he was well aware of the risks. In the end, he paid the ultimate political price for both decisions, losing his re-election in 2005 to Antonio Villaraigosa.

In my case, the county seal battle was about much more than the Latin cross. The Bill of Rights was designed to protect our nation from the tyranny of the majority. Upholding the Constitution is often politically difficult, precisely because doing so can often offend that majority. Nonetheless, that is the oath we were sworn to uphold. A governmental body that arrogantly picks and chooses the constitutional provisions it will uphold is no different than the monarchies our founders were determined to put on history's ash heap.

As we found out in the aftermath of the 2020 presidential election, the Constitutional oath is a public servant's duty and the underpinning of our democracy. Any politician who is hesitant about fulfilling that oath should go into another line of work.

Saving the Veterans Administration

For decades, real estate developers had set their sights on the West Los Angeles Veterans Administration property on Wilshire Boulevard. Nestled between Westwood and Brentwood, the land included nearly 400 acres of some of the most valuable real estate in the United States. The original owners had donated the site to the United States in the late nineteenth century, as a place to heal the physical and psychological wounds that military veterans incurred defending our nation. The first people to be served there were veterans of the Civil War, but now, more than a century later, a new war was about to engulf the property.

Starting in the 1980s, two presidential administrations wanted to declare the property "surplus" and sell it to real estate speculators. They could have cared less about the purpose of this sanctuary in the middle of our city. When the Reagan Administration began exploring ways to sell off 109 acres of the V.A., it set off a political firestorm. The notion that massive commercial development would occur at the expense of our veterans triggered intense opposition. US Senator Alan Cranston won approval in 1988 for legislation that stopped the scheme dead in its tracks.

Years later, shortly after President George W. Bush was inaugurated, the plan reared its ugly head again. This time, stewards of the property floated the idea of issuing long-term leases for commercial development that would amount to *two* new Century Cities. I was appalled, and I tried to convince lower-level V.A. officials to abandon the plan. Getting nowhere, I asked for an appointment with President Bush's first V.A. Secretary, Anthony Principi. My plan was to make an impassioned, personal appeal to him. He was a Vietnam War vet and had a reputation for caring about our men and women in uniform. If I didn't succeed, I was at least hoping to buy time to develop an alternative political strategy. Principi agreed to meet with me in Washington on September 12, 2001.

Three staff members—Alisa Katz, Laura Shell, and Brence Culp—accompanied me on what would be a pivotal meeting. We flew to Washington on the morning of September 10 and arrived in the capital in the early evening hours. We grabbed dinner and called it a night. The next day I was scheduled to meet with Senator Dianne Feinstein and Congressman Henry Waxman, who represented the V.A. property. They had been helpful to me and the county on many issues, and I wanted to brief them on my upcoming meeting the following day with Principi. I went up to my hotel room, reviewed my talking points and hit the sack.

At around 6:30 a.m. on the morning of September 11, I went out for a long jog. When I returned to my room at about 8:50, I turned on the "Today" Show and was stunned to see one of New York City's World Trade Center towers in flames. Then another plane crashed into the second tower, a third into an empty field in central Pennsylvania, and a fourth into the Pentagon, less than three miles from my hotel room. Had I run across the Memorial Bridge that morning, as I had originally planned, I would have seen the entire disaster at the Pentagon unfold before my eyes.

My staff members came up to my room to confer. Not surprisingly, all of my appointments on Capitol Hill were cancelled. In fact, every appointment I had during my scheduled two-day visit was cancelled—except for the one with Secretary Principi. His assistant called me late that Tuesday morning and said, "I've checked with the Secretary, and he has cancelled all his meetings, except for yours. He wants to meet with you at the appointed time—1:30 p.m. tomorrow." I was incredulous. If there ever was a good excuse to cancel a meeting, this was it, but Principi wanted to go ahead. I didn't know whether that was a good sign or not.

When we arrived at V.A. headquarters a few blocks from the White House, we went right to Principi's office on the top floor of the building. He greeted us cordially and then invited us to look out his window, which had an unobstructed view of the Pentagon. Plumes of smoke were still rising from the crash site, twenty-eight hours after the attack. We were speechless, more like traumatized. Given the circumstances, I felt that my reason for being there was profoundly trivial. But the Secretary kept the appointment, and I told him how grateful I was for that.

I made my case for the V.A. to scuttle plans to privatize its West Los Angeles campus. It was not as though the need for its services had waned. Indeed, given the events of the previous day, they would likely be needed for generations to come. More than 1 million veterans lived within fifty miles of the site, more than in 42 other states combined. They were served by a major hospital and many other social services, and the need for this complex was indisputable. Principi listened politely, even carefully, but he didn't budge.

Sensing that I wasn't getting anywhere, I shifted to Plan B. I asked the Secretary if he would put the plan on hold, so he might come to Los Angeles and meet with community stakeholders before he made a final decision. I was pleasantly surprised when he agreed. Two months later we met at the V.A. headquarters in Brentwood. The Secretary heard from our Congressional representatives, community and business leaders, residents, and above all, veterans. We were all of one mind, and Principi was apparently moved. He gave us his word that he would take the privatization plan off the table and would not resurrect any version of it without discussing it with us first. We had dodged a bullet.

When we finally returned to Los Angeles on Friday September 14, I was startled by the sight of 100 or more people lined up around a block in Hollywood— all waiting to get into the AAA Banner store. Every one of them had come to buy an American flag. For one fleeting moment our nation was united, and partisanship was cast aside. I was moved to tears.

Five and one-half years later—ironically during Memorial Day weekend of 2007—I learned that the Bush administration was taking another crack at the privatization plan. This time it looked more serious. Principi had left his post at the end of Bush's first term in 2005 and James Nicholson, a Colorado real estate developer and former chair of the Republican National Committee, had taken his place. He did not feel bound by Principi's promise to us in 2001 and was moving quickly to make this valuable real estate available for private development. Undoubtedly, a long list of real estate developers would be lined up to develop the land on some of the most valuable acreage in the nation. The Office of Management and Budget valued the property at $4 billion, and their plan was to allow as much as 7.2 million square feet of new building, mostly commercial office space. The threat to the V.A. had never been greater.

Los Angeles Times columnist Steve Lopez captured our sentiment when he suggested in his column that it was too much to expect the V.A. to protect medical services for soldiers returning from Iraq and Afghanistan, given its dollars-driven decision on the West LA property. What in the world, he asked, was the V.A. thinking?

I decided that our only hope was to exercise the nuclear option, and that meant securing an act of Congress to block this scheme. The problem was that President Bush would veto any stand-alone bill. But I had an idea. A few years earlier I had read "Charlie Wilson's War," a book that chronicled an east Texas Congressman's crusade to fund surface-to-air missiles for the *mujahedeen*, who would use them to shoot down Soviet helicopters that propelled their invasion of Afghanistan. Wilson used his perch on the Appropriations Committee to pay for armaments that even the Reagan Administration didn't ask for.

Intrigued that this might work in our case, I called my friend, Congressman Howard Berman. Based on what I had read, I wanted to clearly understand the congressional rules. Was it true that any piece of legislation that may have even a remote impact on the federal budget could be inserted into a comprehensive appropriations bill? "Yes," he answered, "all you need is someone on the Appropriations Committee to insert it." The implication was clear. President Bush could easily veto a stand-alone bill, but if that same language was slipped into an appropriations bill, he'd be forced to choose between signing or vetoing the entire bill. That's because the President doesn't have the luxury of a line item veto like governors and mayors do. Berman understood where I was headed and told me that my strategy was sound.

As it turned out, Senator Dianne Feinstein served on the Senate Appropriations Committee. I flew to Washington to meet with her, and she agreed to carry the legislation. All she needed was the right appropriations bill. She found a good one in May 2007—the bill to fund the Iraq War. Feinstein inserted our language into the Senate version of the bill. Meanwhile, Congressman Henry Waxman, who did not serve on the House Appropriations Committee, asked one of his colleagues on the panel to insert the same language into the House version of the bill. If both versions of the bill contained our language, it would be a done deal.

At the last minute, however, I was told that Bush's chief of staff, Josh Bolten, called key House Democrats and warned them that if the West Los Angeles V.A. language was included in the War bill, the President would veto the whole damn thing. For reasons I will never understand, the House conferees blinked and took the language out. Feinstein's Chief of Staff, Christopher Thompson, called me that evening to let me know what happened and that Feinstein was angry about it. She promised that she would look for the next appropriation vehicle, and insert our language in it.

As always, Feinstein was good to her word. But it took an intricate parliamentary dance to save the day. On September 5, 2007, the United States Senate debated an omnibus appropriations bill to keep the entire government running. The bill contained our language, but a last-minute amendment by Senator Jim DeMint (R-South Carolina) sought to remove it from the bill. Feinstein moved to table the amendment (effectively killing it) and as that motion was debated, my staff and I sat in my office and watched the proceedings on CSPAN. As the roll was called, Feinstein positioned herself next to the well on the Senate floor where every Senator goes to announce his or her vote. I could see her busily pigeon-holing some of her colleagues. When the vote was tabulated, she won by a lopsided 66–25 margin. Significantly, twenty-two of the votes to table came from her Republican colleagues. Several weeks later, President Bush had no choice but to sign the omnibus bill with our language in it. The V.A. was saved.

The next morning, I called Congressman Berman to thank him for his invaluable guidance throughout this process. "You know," he told me, "there are members of Congress who have been here for twenty years and haven't had a bill signed by the President. You're not even a member of Congress, and you have." I asked if he knew Charlie Wilson and, if he did, to please thank him for helping to save the West Los Angeles Veterans Administration.

Justice for Janitors

My workdays in the county were long, and it wasn't uncommon for me to be the last one to leave my office. As I left, the janitors who cleaned our offices were just coming to work, and it always weighed on me that while I was on my way home to see Barbara and the kids, Alma, the eighth-floor janitor at the Hall of Administration, wasn't going home to see hers. I wondered when she was able to see her family. Over the years, I engaged her in conversation about everything from A to Z. Sadly, in my last year in office, she contracted an aggressive form of cancer, and the prognosis wasn't good. All of us on the eighth floor raised some funds to make sure her family had the resources needed to take care of her everyday needs. Finally, after a valiant battle, she succumbed.

Over the course of forty years I felt a kinship with people like Alma and thousands of other janitors across Los Angeles. They worked long hours sweeping floors and cleaning toilets after the rest of us had gone home. Although Alma was a county employee with county benefits and union protections, thousands of janitors working in privately owned buildings were not so lucky. They had no health benefits, no paid sick or vacation time. As newly arrived immigrants, some of them undocumented, they had no leverage over the landlords who paid their paltry wages. Many of them held down two or three jobs.

When Los Angeles janitors launched a major campaign in the late 1980s to fight for union representation, I immediately joined with them. The fact that they earned less per hour than workers who cleaned animal cages at the zoo was a moral outrage. The cost of raising their pay above minimum wage would have been chump change to the companies who owned or managed high-rise office buildings in downtown or Century City. They could have easily afforded to do so but stubbornly refused.

The battle reached a new level in 1990 when the Service Employees International Union (SEIU) jumped into the fray. They launched an effort to organize the janitors and asked me to be one of their political champions. They said they needed someone who could speak credibly—and bluntly—to Los

Angeles building owners about the need to recognize the janitor's union, and I was happy to oblige. Things got bloody in June of that year when SEIU organizers led a march from Roxbury Park in Beverly Hills to the Twin Towers in Century City, where Tom Bradley and I were waiting to speak. As the marchers peacefully crossed into Los Angeles, the LAPD was waiting in riot gear and began mercilessly beating them. There were dozens of injuries, forty arrests and a lot of blood in the streets. I flashed back to my college days—especially to the disastrous 1967 anti-war demonstration against LBJ that took place a block away.

To no one's surprise, the union sued the City. The LAPD bore significant liability for its violent and unnecessary reaction. Although the City Council was initially divided about approving a financial settlement, the City Attorney—citing damaging video evidence of the LAPD's tactics—told the council that the cost would be far greater if the case ever went to a jury trial.

I did not hold back when it came my turn to speak to my colleagues. I told them that these janitors had launched a peaceful protest in pursuit of a living wage, and they had the crap beaten out of them by the LAPD. I said they deserved to be compensated for what happened and maybe, just maybe, this would prevent such a shameful police response from happening again. We settled the case for more than $2 million, and it was a bargain.

Soon afterwards SEIU chose labor activist, Mike Garcia, to lead the union. We became political allies as well as good friends. He and his organizers targeted one building after another with highly visible informational picket lines, while I spoke frankly to the owners behind closed doors. Many of them were my constituents, and some were even my supporters. I warned them that their appalling treatment of the janitors would come back to haunt them. Some of the owners were worried about breaking ranks with their fellow landlords if they succumbed to union demands. "Paying a decent wage is going to cost 1 percent at most, so don't tell me you can't afford that," I said. I told them to raise their tenants' rents if they had to, and not to worry about breaking ranks with other owners. "Sooner or later, you're all going to be picketed," I said. "We're hanging together on this."

The protests continued throughout the decade, culminating in a general strike of janitors in 2000 at more than 500 work sites. During that action I took to the op-ed pages of the *Los Angeles Times* and wrote that "Los Angeles cannot survive half rich and half poor. Our society will be judged," I wrote, "by how we treat our most vulnerable members, and by whether we value them not just as workers, but as human beings."

Justice for Janitors began making real progress, winning higher wages and health benefits, paid sick leave, and paid vacations, and I credit Garcia for that progress. Unlike a police or fire union that had considerable leverage over management, the Justice for Janitors campaign had nothing but the moral high ground. It was up to the rest of us, who had political influence, to persuade their employers. Indeed, the support of public officials was critical to the janitors' cause because management would ultimately have to answer to them.

Fighting side by side with Garcia was a natural outgrowth of my upbringing. I had parents who lived their lives pursuing justice. My father fought for the very issues that Garcia and his union were fighting for. Mike and I had another thing in common: We both had Type 2 diabetes and often compared notes on our conditions, trying to boost each other's confidence. Sadly, diabetes got the best of him, and he died in 2017. His funeral at the Cathedral of Our Lady of the Angels drew a large crowd of politicians, labor leaders and janitors. As I was walking out, the union's president took me aside and said: "Mike never forgot what you did for us, and neither will we."

In truth, the janitors gave more to me than I ever gave them. Our alliance gave me a sense of added purpose, both personally and politically. I viscerally feel the pain of growing income inequality. It is a crippling social crisis that affects every aspect of life in the southland and across the nation. Sub-minimal incomes are a barrier to affordable housing, quality health care, and a quality education. We ignore this economic divide at our own peril.

The good news is that each of us can play a role in making this a more just and compassionate society. But we have to stand up for those with no voice, and to fight for their rights. At some point in our lives, each of us must look in the mirror and ask: "What are the causes we are prepared to champion?"

CHAPTER 22

Witness to History

In April 1990 I got a phone call from an old friend, Ken Wollack, who was then the Executive Vice-President of the National Democratic Institute (NDI). Ken and I met during the McGovern for President campaign in 1972 and had remained good friends ever since. Now he was working for a new non-governmental organization that nurtured emerging democracies around the globe. They focused on election observation, citizen participation, political party development, and governance. Ken got right to the point: "How would you like to go to Romania next month?" I thought this was some kind of joke and said, "Romania? What the hell for?" As it turned out, the Balkan nation would be holding its first election since the fall of Nicolae Ceausescu, a despot who for decades ran the country with an iron fist. NDI was invited by the new interim government to send an observation team to monitor the election, and Ken wanted me to be part of the delegation.

My juices were flowing as I listened to the pitch. In truth, my life-long interest in foreign affairs had never waned. I watched in astonishment as the Berlin Wall came down in November 1989, and as democratic movements began sweeping across eastern and central Europe. Working with NDI would be a singular opportunity to play a bit role in the democratization of a former eastern bloc dictatorship—something I never dreamed I would witness. Without even checking my schedule I told Wollack, "Sign me up." That's the way my three-decade affiliation with NDI began.

I had no way of knowing at the time that I would travel around the globe monitoring elections, conducting seminars on local governance, and helping to build democratic institutions in Eastern Europe, Africa, Latin America, and Asia. I would be both a participant in and a witness to history. The missions in which I participated were exhilarating, and in some cases life changing. To be sure, this wasn't part of my job description as a councilman, but I had been tapped for this work precisely *because* of my political and local government experience. And let me say at the outset that there were no luxurious accommodations or financial perks. You haven't really lived until you've walked in ankle-deep mud down a country road at the onset of a Ukrainian spring.

I am a firm believer that elected officials at all levels should get out of their own zip codes and see the world. Los Angeles had become an international city, and its elected officials and citizenry would be better served if their representatives had some direct understanding of what made the rest of the world tick. I wanted to put my skills to effective use in the interest of democracy, and I knew I would learn a lot in the process. So I jumped when opportunity knocked.

Romania, Romania

I arrived in Bucharest, the Romanian capital, in late May of 1990. The guide-books called it the Paris of the Balkans, and I understood why when I took a walk through the central part of the city. The architecture of the older buildings had a Parisian flair, and the streets were lined with thousands of trees. I took an immediate liking to the city, even though it suffered from long-deferred maintenance. Clearly, the government hadn't invested in what made Bucharest special. Except, that is, for the Casa Populi, a larger-than-life palace on a hill that Ceausescu had built as a tribute to himself. It was visible from virtually every part of town, and to the public it symbolized the regime's warped and corrupt priorities.

Ceausescu was a diabolical leader who fostered paranoia and ruled through intimidation. When I talked to local officials and ordinary citizens, I was struck that they all believed the government could hear—literally—every word that passed between us. Even in the countryside, Romanians were convinced that the secret police were listening. They believed every room in their apartment was bugged and that their neighbors were government agents who reported on their comings and goings. Of course, it was impossible for any government to be so omnipresent—or so competent—but Ceausescu wanted people to fear that this was the case. In this fraught environment, Romania was about to experience its first brush with modern democracy.

The way NDI conducted its election observations fascinated me. First, our 30-person delegation spent two days in the capital being briefed by political parties, civil society, and the press. Then we met with the presidential candidates, including interim President Ion Iliescu. He was an old Communist apparatchik who suddenly found himself in charge after the revolution that toppled Ceausescu. Iliescu was the favorite to win because he was the only credible candidate. His main opponent was the leader of the so-called Peasant Party, who had returned from exile in Paris, where he lived in comfort off the Champs

Elysees. He was hardly what the Romanian people were looking for in the leader of the *Peasant* party.

After these initial briefings, the delegation was divided into 15 teams of two members each, plus an interpreter and a driver. We were deployed to 15 different provinces around the country, where we engaged in intense discussions with local politicians, civil society, and the press. We asked all of them what we should expect, where did they think there would be problems, and what should we be on the lookout for. I was deployed to Timis Province in western Transylvania, bordering on the former Yugoslavia. Timisoara was the provincial capital and cradle of the rebellion that ultimately toppled Ceausescu. My partner was Lottie Shackleford, the first woman mayor of Little Rock, Arkansas, a vice-chair of the Democratic National Committee, and an emerging national Black political leader. We had met in prior years during our involvement in the National League of Cities.

The night before the election, Lottie and I sat down in our hotel restaurant and mapped out a plan for the next day. We selected the first polling place where we'd monitor its opening, ensure that the ballots and booths were in place, and see if the new Romanian election laws were followed. Throughout the day we'd travel to dozens of polling stations, talking to officials and voters to determine how things were going. It became a trip into the heart of the Transylvanian countryside, a place where chickens, geese, and cows roamed through little villages, like a scene from "Fiddler on the Roof." At day's end, we selected a polling place to watch, to ensure that all the ballots were accurately counted, secured, and delivered to the provincial tabulation center.

Lottie and I made a great pair—a Black woman from Little Rock and a Jewish guy from Beverly-Fairfax. We brought our own political and lived experience to bear on the election observation process. For a nation that had not conducted a "free" election in decades, Timisoara had executed the technical voting mechanics remarkably well. With a few exceptions, the Romanian election was uneventful, and not surprisingly Iliescu won the election in a landslide. However, our delegation's fact-finding report ultimately pointed out that an election is more than what happens on Election Day. The lack of a credible political opposition and the government's control of the media had pre-determined the outcome.

What I remember most was the robust political atmosphere in Bucharest and Timisoara. Demonstrations in the main squares of both cities were tumultuous. For the first time, tens of thousands of young Romanians felt free to rally around democratic principles without fear of retribution. We saw banners in Opera Square in Timisoara, which read "Jos Communismu" (Down with Communism). Peasants in the countryside, their faces hardened by decades of poverty and oppression, stood in line to cast their votes. The air was full of possibility, even though voters had just elected a former Communist. A nation that once banned open campaigning and free speech was now tiptoeing its way to a new political normal.

A year or so later, President Iliescu made a visit to Los Angeles, and the Romanian Consul-General asked me to attend a reception in his honor. I prepared a proclamation of welcome and brought it with me to the Century Plaza Hotel. When I arrived, the last thing I wanted was a photo with him because in my mind there was a question about his political legitimacy. So, I made a few generic welcoming remarks and then stood far enough away so that photographers couldn't get the two of us in the same frame. Then Iliescu came to the podium, put his arm around me and pulled me next to him. "I want to thank my old friend, Zev Yaroslavsky," he said. "We met in Bucharest and have known each other ever since." So much for my logistical skills.

Romanian foreign policy at the time was truly complicated. Although the nation was technically part of the Soviet bloc, it didn't always fall in line with Moscow. When the Soviets organized a boycott of the 1984 Olympics in Los Angeles, Romania boycotted the boycott. In fact, one of the most moving moments of the Games occurred at the opening ceremonies when the Romanian team entered the Coliseum. The athletes received the loudest standing ovation of any country, except for the United States; it was Los Angeles' gesture of gratitude to the Romanian team for bucking the Soviets.

The Jewish community of Romania had a rich and long history, so before I left for home, I paid a visit to the nation's legendary Chief Rabbi Moses Rosen at Bucharest's historic and beautiful Central Synagogue. I was joined by Norm Ornstein of the American Enterprise Institute, who was also a member of our delegation. Rabbi Rosen welcomed us into his study and proclaimed, "I don't know if you have any questions, but I have all the answers." For the next hour, he regaled us with a history of the Romanian Jewish community and his role in leading it. Rosen was often criticized for maintaining a relationship with Ceausescu. Indeed, he was at best agnostic about where the 1989 revolution would lead. But he had his reasons. The Chief Rabbi walked a tight rope—more like a minefield—in representing the interests of his flock, many of whom luckily avoided extermination by the Nazis as World War II wound down. From 1967–1989 his relationship with Ceausescu helped open the doors for Jewish emigration from Romania, a nation that was still plagued by a legacy of antisemitism. Over 100,000 Jews were permitted to leave for Israel in exchange for a substantial ransom, in part because Rosen had a relationship with the Romanian leader, tenuous as it was.

The day I left Bucharest, I went shopping to bring back souvenirs for my family and staff. I walked for two miles up one side of Bucharest's main boulevard, and down the other. I couldn't find a single souvenir worth purchasing, but I did see a suit for sale in a store window for the equivalent of $5. I didn't buy it. On my way home, I overnighted in Paris before catching a morning flight to LAX. During the night I found a mini-can of Diet Coke in the hotel's wet bar that also sold for $5. Who knew that in 1990 you could buy a suit in post-Soviet Europe for the same price as a can of soda in France? This was a metaphor for the economic challenges facing the former Soviet bloc, and how they navigated them would help determine whether their experiment in democracy would succeed.

The Soviet Union Dissolves

NDI asked me to make two trips to Russia the following year. The first was to Moscow and Leningrad in May 1991, and the second, in October, was to Moscow and St. Petersburg. A lot would change in Russia during the five months separating these trips, and not just the name of its second largest city. An attempted coup against President Mikhail Gorbachev in August failed, and Russians took to the streets, blocking revisionist attempts to reinstall the Communist regime. The Soviet Union as we knew it dissolved.

On my first trip that year, I was part of a delegation that was asked to conduct two-day seminars on local government finance for newly elected local officials. NDI believed that change would have to begin at the local level for democratic principles to take hold. They weren't wrong, but this was easier said than done. We focused on helping these officials develop basic governing skills in a democratic environment—something they were experiencing for the first time.

Our delegation included Wollack, Mike McFaul, who would become the US Ambassador to Moscow two decades later, David Aaron, the former Deputy National Security Advisor to President Jimmy Carter, Mayor Tom Volgy of Tucson, Arizona, along with me and two NDI staff. From the outset there was a gulf between our delegation and the Russian councilmembers. I knew little about the finances of Soviet cities, where they got their resources, or how they forecast revenues from year to year. My audiences were equally mystified by our political and economic system, which mandated transparency in its financial dealings.

Before I left for Moscow, I asked my old friend, Si Frumkin, to translate an eight-page summary of the Los Angeles City budget into Russian, including pie charts and graphs. I brought copies with me so I could share some of the tools of our trade. Still, how do you discuss financial forecasting and taxation with people whose system never required either at the local level? Soviet-era economic plans were more political fiction than credible budget documents. We were speaking Greek to them, and they to us.

Translation from English to Russian was also an issue, even with highly competent simultaneous interpreters. The night before our first seminar, an official from the American embassy gave us some pointers. "Don't use idioms when you speak, because they don't translate the way you intend," he said. "For example, I once gave a speech here on partisan politics in the United States, and I was forty-five minutes into my talk before I realized they were translating 'partisan' to mean those who fought heroically against the Nazis during World War II. Naturally, they were puzzled." Given that, I wondered, how they would translate "balanced budgets," or "progressive taxation"? I took the embassy official's advice to heart, as much as I could.

As an aside, I always found that being able to speak to people in a common language was a huge asset. Whether it was in Hebrew that I spoke at home growing up, or Spanish that I learned in high school, or Russian that I studied at UCLA—it fostered a connection that was more difficult to achieve through an interpreter.

My most memorable example of this was when the President of China, Jiang Zemin, arrived in LA on an official visit in 1997. I was asked to be part of the greeting party. I noted in his biography that Jiang studied in the USSR for five years as a young man and spoke fluent Russian. When he descended from his aircraft he approached me, and we shook hands. I asked him in Russian, "*Govorite po Russki?*" (Do you speak Russian?). He incredulously responded in Russian, "*You* speak Russian?" A minute-long conversation ensued. I saw him several times during his three-day visit, and each time we had pleasant talks in our common language. At a civic banquet closing his trip, he walked down the double-decked dais and toasted the dignitaries in Chinese. But when he came to me, he declared with a big smile, "Nazdrovia," Russian for "to your health." Only in America could an LA-born son of Jewish immigrants from Ukraine meet the President of China and converse in Russian. When we speak the same language, it changes the character of the conversation—and maybe the quality of a relationship.

When our budget workshop with the Moscow officials commenced, we immediately ran into trouble through our interpreter. It was clear that our hosts were struggling to understand what we were saying, so we opened the floor to questions. Maybe this would help us clarify the confusion. It didn't. The first question blew my mind. "Mr. Yaroslavsky," Moscow Councilman Alexander Plokhin asked, "When municipal properties get distributed to city officials, how do you prevent the mayor from taking all of it?" I was stumped. The best I could do was explain that in America public assets can't be transferred to *any* official, even to the mayor or city councilmember. The Russians looked more confused than ever.

It was only two years later that I understood the question. Tom Bradley had invited Moscow's mayor, Yuri Luzhkov, to Los Angeles for an official visit. He asked me to attend their press conference, which I was pleased to do. One reporter posed the following question to Luzhkov: "Mr. Mayor, how would you compare your job to that of our own mayor?" I thought that was an odd question. How would our visitor have any way of comparing the two jobs? But Luzhkov rose to the occasion. "I imagine that when Mayor Bradley goes to bed at night, he worries about the crime rate in the city, the condition of his streets, traffic congestion, and those kinds of things," he said, as though he was a Los Angeles City Hall veteran. "When I go to bed at night, I worry about whether beef shipments from Kazakhstan's cattle ranches will arrive in the morning, because the city owns all the butcher shops. I worry about whether the flour will arrive on time from Ukrainian wheat fields, because the city owns all the bakeries. If the shipments are late I, as Mayor, will have tens of thousands of angry citizens on my back."

Suddenly, I realized what those questions in Moscow were all about. When the Soviet system collapsed, all the enterprises owned by the Communist government were up for grabs, and the mayors were best positioned to seize them. Entire industries—hydroelectric power plants, oil refineries, truck factories and the like—became the property of those who happened to be in the right place at the right time, and who were shrewd enough to seize the opportunity. Many of the Russians who became rich "oligarchs" didn't earn their way into wealth; it virtually fell into their lap. Most of them ran those enterprises, and they simply transitioned from Communists to private entrepreneurs.

Years later I met one of these oligarchs, and I summoned the courage to ask him how he became one. He told me that his father had run a hydro-electric power plant in Siberia, and when the government collapsed, he moved quickly to take it over. The son later leveraged that asset to buy a major oil company, and the rest was history. Transparency meant one thing in the United States, and quite another in the former USSR. No wonder the Moscow city councilmen were resentful and jealous. They weren't getting any of the action.

We found similar unrest in Leningrad. Their mayor, Anatoly Sobchak, was a proponent of democratic reform. When Mikhail Gorbachev was kidnapped in the summer of 1991, Sobchak publicly stood up to the attempted coup, organizing a protest demonstration with hundreds of thousands of people in the city's main square. McFaul, our future ambassador to Moscow, advanced our Russian trip, and his counterparts in Leningrad were two young apparatchiks—an ambitious deputy mayor named Vladimir Putin and his deputy Igor Sechin. Putin, of course, became President of the Russian Federation less than a decade later, while Sechin became the CEO of Rosneft, Russia's biggest oil company. It's good to have "friends" in high places.

I was honored when Wollack asked me to join him in speaking to the Leningrad City Council on behalf of our delegation. Who could have predicted that the grandson of a Leningrader, and a former Soviet Jewry activist, would find himself on the rostrum speaking to this 500-member body? As I stepped to the microphone, chills ran down my spine. I tried to connect with the audience by recounting my grandmother's history in their city. "She lived here and survived the Great Patriotic War (as the Russians referred to World War II)," I said. "And she is buried here in your great city."

As I stood before an audience that resembled a joint session of Congress, I sensed that I wasn't connecting with them. Each councilmember sat grim-faced and unmoved. I said to myself, "This shit isn't working, so I better try something else." I did an awkward segue: "I bring you greetings from your sister city, Los Angeles, California." Suddenly, the entire body stood up in unison and applauded robotically, as the North Koreans do at a party congress. I did my best not to burst out laughing. I spoke for a few minutes about the political transition they were going through and that we were honored to be a part of this historical transformation. "Democracy is hard work," I said. "Where I'm from, we are still trying to perfect it after more than 200 years." Then I sat back down next to Wollack. "I can't believe this," I whispered to him. "Nobody in America gives a damn about sister cities, and here it gets a standing ovation?" We both began to chuckle like two kids in a Sunday school class who couldn't control themselves. Fortunately, we managed to avert an international incident.

On our last night in Leningrad we went to a nightclub for dinner and a musical performance. At one point Ken stepped away from our table and when he returned, he told us that there was a casino in the back of the showroom. We had some avid blackjack players in our delegation, including me, and we made a beeline for the casino, taking seats at the table. As I entered, I exchanged a $10 bill for 400 Rubles, a much better exchange rate than I could have received on the street. At that moment, I should have known that I would never see the money again. The dealer made up her rules as she went along. When she had an "18" she drew a card, coincidentally, a deuce. When she and I both had "20," she swept up my rubles into her money belt. No casino in the world would have done either one of those things. When I protested to the pit boss, he simply said, "Russian rules." David Aaron, who was sitting next to me, leaned over, and whispered,

"This is exactly how they negotiated the SALT II Treaty." Ten minutes later, my 400 rubles were gone.

Ukraine: A Time of Ferment

I made several more trips in the early 1990s to Russia and Ukraine under the auspices of NDI, and it gave me an opportunity to travel to places that in Soviet days were off-limits to Americans. The Communist system had collapsed, almost overnight. There were no rules, and everyone was out for him or herself. Wealth was concentrated in a small percentage of the population while everyone else was struggling and the infrastructure was crumbling. Driving on post-Soviet roads was like skiing on a slalom course; we swerved to avoid enormous potholes. Many of the roads in country towns were unpaved, posing serious driving challenges at the end of winter, when the snow began to melt, and the frost began to thaw.

Medium-sized cities, like my mother's Ukrainian hometown of Poltava, had no heating until November 1. Unfortunately, I came there for a visit in October 1993, ten days before the heat was turned on, by which time the temperature was already well below freezing. I slept in every piece of clothing I brought with me. Residents of small towns and villages had no running water, and they could only get it by pumping from outdoor wells. Food, coal, sugar, and other living necessities were rationed; there were few telephones and no bathrooms, only outdoor outhouses. The one thing they had in abundance was electricity. Most of the residences had two rooms—a bedroom that also served as a living room, and a kitchen with a coal burning stove. In many ways, the former Soviet Union felt like an underdeveloped country with a hydrogen bomb.

The natives were restless. During a 1993 trip into the Ukrainian countryside, we were having a pleasant enough conversation with our driver, an employee of the city of Kyiv. At one point I asked him how democracy felt after years of Soviet rule. His demeanor immediately changed. "This democracy, it's all bullshit!" he said. "Before, we had no crime, no worries. Now I take *this* with me wherever I go," pulling a machete from beneath his seat. "*I* have to protect myself now. It's a disaster." I felt like I was in the nineteenth-century American West.

There was a poignant moment in March of that year which I'll never forget. One of Kyiv's top city administrators invited our group to dinner at her apartment. After the meal I asked how she got involved in the democracy movement in her homeland. She said that the breakdown in the public's trust of the previous regime had begun years before, during the 1986 meltdown of the Chernobyl nuclear reactor. It started with women—specifically, mothers. She spoke bitterly of officials who had told them that everything was under control when evidence to the contrary was all around them. Their children were getting sick, even dying, she said. Babies were born with deformities downwind of the accident. Mothers like her didn't believe a word they were being told. "When your kids are suffering because of government lies, it's a declaration of war," she said. These fearless women were among the first to reveal the chinks in the Soviet armor, and they would stop at nothing to protect their young. As she explained, once you lose confidence in your government over one thing, you begin to question everything. "We are not going back," she declared. Nearly three decades later, that resolve suggests why the Ukrainian resistance to Putin's unprovoked invasion seems unbreakable.

The 2004 Ukrainian presidential election carried echoes of that outrage. I was asked to be part of an NDI team to monitor the contest on December 26. We were deployed to Cherkassy province along the Dnieper River, a three-and-a-half-hour drive from Kyiv. This election was a redo of one held a month earlier, where the coal miners' union from the Donbas region of eastern Ukraine traveled the breadth of the country stuffing ballot boxes in support of pro-Russian Prime Minister Viktor Yanukovych. The Ukrainian Supreme Court invalidated that election, and reform candidate Victor Yushchenko prevailed the second time around. This came to be known as the "Orange Revolution." The resilience of the Ukrainian people came through loud and clear.

Even though corruption was not limited to one party, the nation's passion for mastering its own destiny was deeply imbedded in its citizens. Tens of thousands of protestors occupied the Maidan, Kyiv's main square, until a fair election was completed. They were prepared to put their bodies in the way of the armored vehicles that threatened to roll into the square to disperse the protestors. Our government, in the person of our ambassador, played a key role in averting a blood bath.

The Russian government, led by Vladimir Putin, was aggressively meddling in Ukrainian domestic politics. Presidential elections there were not only contests between two political parties, but between Russian imperial ambitions and Ukrainian aspirations for independence. This feeling was palpable across Ukraine. Tensions erupted into conflict when the Russians decided to invade and occupy the resource rich Donbas region that resulted in a long simmering war between the two countries. Then, in 2022, Putin launched a massive invasion of Ukraine, determined to replace its democratically elected government with a Russian-friendly regime.

Many observers were surprised at the level of Ukrainian resistance and the ineffectiveness of the supposedly superior Russian military. Although the jury is still out on whether the Ukrainians can sustain their resistance, I wasn't surprised by their courage and toughness. I could see it in their yearning for independence and freedom. I saw it in the looks on the faces of young men who occupied the Maidan and on their huge signs which read, "POKA," Ukrainian for "It's time."

The Ukrainians are a proud and complicated people, with a long and troubled history. As I write in early 2023, it's impossible to predict how their latest chapter will end. Russia and the West will have a lot to say about the outcome. But, as we have seen, anyone who underestimates Ukrainians' resolve, does so at their own peril. They will have something to say about their own fate, as well.

I often joke that I didn't do a good job promoting democracy in the former Soviet Union. In truth this part of the world has never experienced sustained democracy, and it's naïve to expect these systems to turn on a dime. As we have recently witnessed, even nations where democracy has taken root for over 100 years are being tested as never before. So why would we expect a better result where authoritarian regimes have been in place for most of the last 1,000 years?

Unforgettable Moments in Russia and Ukraine

On these NDI missions, I made memorable side trips to visit my mother's and father's birthplaces in Ukraine. I already knew my mother's address, 67 Pushkin Street in Poltava. It was written on the postcard my grandfather had sent her from the 1911 Zionist Congress in Basle as a keepsake when she was two years old. I found it easy to locate the house, which had remained largely unchanged since pre-revolutionary days. When I arrived, I was trembling with excitement (it was also twenty degrees and windy). I had two cameras dangling from my neck, one still and one video. I was determined to document this moment for my sister and my children. I picked up some tree branches and a hand full of dirt from the property to bring home. I felt like Neil Armstrong and Buzz Aldrin must have felt when they landed on the moon, rummaging for rocks to bring back to earth.

As I walked around the property, three elderly women standing nearby voiced suspicion of my activity. So I walked over and explained in my broken Russian why I was there. Their demeanor immediately changed. We had a conversation about the history of the neighborhood, and they assured me that my grandfather's house pre-dated World War I. This is where Shimon Soloveichik taught a new generation of Jewish students, the place where my mother played as a little girl. I couldn't wait to tell my family.

On another trip I visited my father's birthplace in Belaya Tserkov, a small city about fifty miles southwest of Kyiv. The winding Ros River ran through the heart of the town, framing a bucolic scene like something out of the Shenandoah River valley. The name of the city means "White Church," and there is one in the center of town. I walked over to it and found a statue of Yaroslav the Wise, a tenth-century figure who is credited with the unification of the principalities of Novgorod and Kyiv. I stood in front of old Yaroslav and had my photograph taken for posterity.

I also took one good look around and privately expressed my gratitude to my dad, who at the age of eighteen had the guts to pack his bags and head for America. As President-elect Ronald Reagan told our City Council on January 13, 1981, it's the ones with "derring-do" who come to our shores. From my biased point of view, my parents' birthplaces were good places to be *from*. Visiting the world of my ancestors was a transcendental experience, a chance to commune with them and see where and how they lived. As it turned out, I was a witness not only to world history, but to my own as well.

Two final encounters left memorable impressions. On my way back to my hotel after an early dinner in Kyiv, I came upon the Kyiv Opera House where I had seen the opera "Taras Bulba" with my father in 1968, on my first trip to the USSR. Out of curiosity, I walked up the steps to see what was playing that night. The main door was slightly ajar, and an elderly ticket-taker saw me. "Please, come in," she said. Frankly, I was bushed and in no mood to see Donizetti's "Lucia di Lammermoor" that evening. "No, please come in," she insisted. "We won't charge you. There are empty seats on the main floor, and we can't stand to see them go to waste."

Fearing it would be an insult to do otherwise, I obliged and watched a remarkable performance. One of the lead singers got sick, and the understudy only knew her role in Ukrainian. The audience and I were one of a handful of people in history to hear a version of this opera where the male lead professed his love in Italian, while the woman sang of hers in Ukrainian. Donizetti would have rolled over in his grave. As for the free tickets, I wondered whether such a thing could ever happen at the Los Angeles County Music Center. Would an usher ever tell me to please come in, we have empty orchestra seats, and we can't stand to see them go to waste? We all know the answer to that question.

Finally, on one of my trips to Moscow I visited the Novodevichy Cemetery, where many of the Soviet Union's historical figures are buried. Tombstones in Russian cemeteries are often sculpted works of art, and I was advised to see them if I had the time. I arrived just before closing time when dusk was settling in on a chilly October day. An octogenarian woman was sweeping the pathways with a well-worn broom, as I stared at a marble likeness of opera singer Feodor Chaliapin, a famous basso profundo. "Ah, Chaliapin," she passionately proclaimed in Russian as she approached me. "He had such a wonderful voice and sang such beautiful songs." I didn't know much about Chaliapin, but this babushka educated me in a hurry. These two stories are what I love most about people in that part of the world. No matter their social status, they are steeped in the arts, and they embrace them. It's not just part of their culture, it's in their DNA.

Mexico, Nigeria, and Beyond

In the years to come, NDI asked me to join teams monitoring elections in Mexico, Nigeria, and other countries. The 2000 Mexican presidential election was a contest that would topple the Institutional Revolutionary Party (PRI), ending its seventy-one-year rule. I was deployed to the city of Morelia, the capital of the state of Michoacan. The government was determined to run a competent and honest election, and they spent $70 million to do it. Exit polls conducted by an independent election commission were released as soon as the polls closed, to discourage any vote count manipulation.

The main challenge to the PRI came from the National Action Party (PAN) and its leader Vicente Fox, a private businessman who was then Governor of the state of Guanajuato. We met with Fox a few days before the election. He was a charismatic man who spoke fluent English. Fox told us his message was "change"; that it was time to remove a regime which had been in power for seven decades. Mexicans agreed, and he won a historic victory.

Later, in 2011 and 2015, I joined observation teams for the Nigerian national elections. I was excited because I had earned my master's degree in British Empire History and was well-schooled in the British influence in West Africa. Back at UCLA, I never imagined that I would one day be standing at the junction of the Niger and Benue Rivers, the Mississippi and Missouri Rivers of West Africa. But there I was.

Nigeria is the richest country in Africa, thanks to its oil, but that wealth is concentrated in a small number of people. The rest of the nation lives in desperate poverty. They are geographically and religiously divided—Muslims populating the northern part of the country, and Christians dominating the south. These divisions understandably manifest in the political sphere, as well. The elections were unlike any I had monitored. Most polling stations were outdoors, because there weren't enough indoor facilities sufficiently large to accommodate the voters. All day long, men and women stood in long lines to cast their ballots in unbearably high temperatures with humidity to match. I run four miles a day, but I was physically exhausted by 10:00 a.m. Nigerian voters, however, were patiently *standing* in line well into the afternoon, waiting for their turn to cast votes. I'll never forget the sight of three women carrying babies on their backs in sacks, as they stood in line under a brutal sun. That's how committed they were to making democracy work.

NDI missions also took me to Turkey and the Republic of Georgia, but a 1998 trip to Bosnia-Herzegovina left an especially vivid impression. I arrived in Sarajevo with my Chief of Staff, Alisa Katz, three years after the Dayton Accords ended a genocidal civil war driven by old ethnic hatreds. It had devastated the region. In Sarajevo, where the 1984 Winter Olympics were held, casualties numbered over 100,000, mostly Bosnian civilians. Makeshift cemeteries could be found on street corners everywhere, and countless buildings had been destroyed by Serbian artillery.

The tragedy was brought home when our team met with thirty representatives of civil society in Mostar. The city was made up of Croatians and Muslims, and they had been at war with one another. Our hosts introduced themselves to us around the table. The first one, Irina, said, "My mother is Croatian, and my father is Muslim. I love them both very much, but they can't live together anymore. Religion takes precedence over love." And so it went as each participant introduced themselves with the same story. It was a heartbreaking moment. Against all odds, the young, pragmatic idealists at our table were trying to re-establish a *civil society* in their city. All I could think was how easy it is for hatred hundreds of years in the making to rear its ugly head—and eviscerate any semblance of humanity.

Cuba and Human Rights

In March 2003, Barbara and I joined up with a USC sponsored visit to Cuba. My main purpose was to meet Oswaldo Paya, the leader of Cuba's human rights movement known as the Varela Project. I arranged to meet him at his home, in the poorest part of Havana. Three friends accompanied me—David Abel, publisher of the respected Planning Report, a Los Angeles newsletter, Pasadena Mayor Bill Bogard, and Pasadena Councilmember Steve Madison. The four of us hired a driver to take us to our 5:00 p.m. appointment and then back to our hotel. When we arrived, Paya's wife greeted us and said that Oswaldo would arrive shortly. Then a man came to the house and told Mrs. Paya that all her husband's disciples around the country had been arrested, and that Paya himself would be late in arriving. We waited as long as we could, but after an hour we had to leave. I left a note for Paya on our way out.

When we returned to the United States, I wrote a blistering letter to Fidel Castro, demanding the release of all these political prisoners. A few weeks later, one of my colleagues, Supervisor Don Knabe, traveled to Cuba. He met with officials of the United States legation in Havana, and one of them asked, "You're not going to do something stupid like your colleague, Zev Yaroslavsky, did while *you're* here, are you?" I was astonished that my visit to Paya's home had gotten on our diplomats' radar screen. It also dawned on me how close I may have come to becoming a long-term guest of the Cuban government.

Paya died in 2012, when his car careened off the road and smashed into a tree. Although the government called it an accident, Cuban witnesses said another vehicle had deliberately hit his car, driving it off the road, and Paya's followers blamed his death on the Castro regime. It was a stunning loss for Cuba's fledgling democracy movement, and a reminder of how dangerous it can be for people of courage to stand up, speak out, and fight for democracy.

Nothing angered me more over the years than dictatorial regimes that brutally suppressed dissent. And nothing has inspired me more than human rights activists around the world, and here at home, who risked everything to speak truth to power. They are the true heroes on the front lines of history. Since my college days, I felt an obligation to travel around the world to meet with dissidents, build their morale, and report on their struggles. After all, had my parents met and remained in the USSR rather than New York, I might have been one of them.

CHAPTER 23

Who Could Have Imagined?

After UCLA basketball coach John Wooden's wife, Nell, died many years ago, I learned that he wrote a letter to her once a week and put it on her pillow. I thought that was an odd thing to do, but after Barbara died I completely understood it. The letters were his way of communicating his love for her, and keeping her memory alive. Although I haven't written Barbara any letters, I periodically talk to her side of our bed at night. I bring her up to date on our kids and grandkids, and I tell her how much I miss her and love her.

Several months after I lost Barbara, my son, David, sent me an email reflecting the deep sorrow, the wrenching loss we all felt. He shared thoughts that deeply touched me: "She knew how much you loved her, and there was nothing that could have made her happier than to know that. Her life with you was unlike anything she could have imagined. So full, so filled with acts of love and kindness."

Indeed, who could have imagined this life? As I prepared to leave public office toward the end of 2014, I was full of thoughts and memories of the road the two of us had traveled together. When Barbara stood next to me as I took my first oath of office, we could not have imagined how the next forty years would transform our lives.

In the years that followed I made my share of mistakes, and I learned from them. As Mark Twain observed, "Good judgment is the result of experience and experience the result of bad judgment." I left office with a reservoir of both. I didn't have an agenda for my first year on the City Council. But by the time I took my seat on the Board of Supervisors, I had a clear-headed and ambitious bucket list of objectives. When I left the Hall of Administration twenty years later, I accomplished what I set out to achieve, and then some. I was able to walk out before having to be carried out.

In an editorial, the *Los Angeles Times* wrote that I had "evolved from an upstart and slightly unkempt anti-Soviet activist to a master of both the budget process and the quotable one-liner. Despite his long tenure in City Hall, he retained some of his anti-establishment cantankerousness." I was heartened by that last sentence, because I held fast to my 1975 promise that "I may be part of the establishment, but *the establishment is not part of me.*" I never let the trappings of office define me. I had very few personal effects hanging on the walls of my office because I always viewed myself as a renter, not an owner.

Indeed, I was ready to say goodbye when the time came. The crowd that gathered for my retirement gala at Walt Disney Concert Hall gave me a memorable send-off. Barbara, Mina, David, and I sat in the front row as colleagues regaled us with tributes, music, song, and comedy. I even received a surprise video message from Vin Scully—the Dodgers' Hall of Fame broadcaster and a Los Angeles icon—whose job I not so secretly coveted. Vin acknowledged this, and suggested that perhaps now was the right time to transition to a broadcasting job with the Dodgers. He gave me some sobering advice:

> I decided that I would grab the bull by the horns and talk to Zev about a career in broadcasting now that he's out of the city. My first thought was, and I explained it to him carefully, that he'd probably have to start in a lower classification of the minor leagues in order to work his way up to the big leagues. The Dodgers have a team in Class A. That's about the lowest classification in the minor leagues. The team is in Michigan, and its name is the Great Lakes Loons. I thought if there's an opening with the Loons, that might be a good place to start.

Scully's video brought the house down. Mina and David had the unenviable task of following him, but they rose to the occasion, as they always do. They introduced me with a short trip down our family's memory lane. When I got up to say goodbye, I told the audience that my greatest wish was to live long enough to see how my own children turned out—something my own parents were not able to do. That wish came true.

Mina, then thirty-seven, became an art therapist, after a short stint working in San Francisco's city-county government. She received her undergraduate degree from the University of California, San Diego, a master's degree from the Kennedy School of Government at Harvard, and another master's degree from Notre Dame de Namur University in Belmont, California. She is now a community leader in Northern California in her own right. She is politically active and serves on the boards of her temple and her daughters' school. Her husband, Dan, is a gifted and successful high-tech consultant whom I have on speed dial whenever my computer crashes. Mina and Dan are exceptional parents to our first two grandchildren, Sadie and Miriam.

David, then thirty-two, became the first attorney in our family, after receiving his B.A. from the University of California and a law degree from N.Y.U. For five years he was in private practice, where he met his wife, Katy. He then moved to the Los Angeles County District Attorney's office, where he was a prosecutor for five years. On January 2, 2019, one week after Barbara's passing, Governor Jerry Brown appointed David to the Superior Court bench where he currently serves as a judge. In 2022, after working in the private, non-profit, and government sectors, Katy was elected to the Los Angeles City Council's Fifth District—the same one to which I was elected forty-seven years earlier. David and Katy are the loving parents of three children—Gabriel, Joshua, and Yael, who bears Barbara's Hebrew name and vibrant blue eyes.

When it comes to our kids, and their families, I draw on Shimon Soloveichik's words, with a slight twist: "A father and father-in-law's soul lives in his children and their spouses." Both our children and their families have made Barbara and me exceedingly proud. They have followed in the Soloveichik tradition of idealism, ethics, and taking on causes bigger than themselves. Their namesakes, my parents, also would have been proud to see them grow and blossom into the people they have become. And I'd like to think that Barbara and I had a bit to do with their interest in public service and *tikkun olam*—Hebrew for repairing the world.

The single most important person in my life, however, was Barbara, my first and only love. Nothing I accomplished would have been possible without her optimism, her impeccable political instincts and, above all, her unconditional love. Public life is full of obstacles, but they are far easier to navigate when the relationship with your life partner is rock solid and mutually trusting. We had all of that and more.

In my eulogy for Barbara, I said that "I came to realize that as beautiful as she was on the outside, Barbara was far more beautiful on the inside...She loved people, she loved to love people, she engaged people, she embraced people, and she took care of people, often at her own expense." At the onset of our relationship, she promised to love me forever if I let her, and she more than kept that promise. She made my life worth living.

On the eve of Thanksgiving 2014, I sat in my empty office, packing up the last odds and ends I was taking with me. I penned my last official letter to Marc Stern, chair of the Los Angeles Opera, expressing gratitude for our partnership and friendship. I hugged every member of my staff, especially my trusted executive assistant Liz Rangel. All of them had been like family to me. I did all I could to hold back the tears, but I couldn't. I would miss them. Then I told Alisa Katz, my long time Chief of Staff, that I was ready to leave. At about 5:00 p.m. the two of us walked out the front door of our eighth-floor office that for twenty years had been the eye of the storm. It was a bittersweet moment. We stopped, took a selfie, and never looked back.

After a six-month hiatus, I accepted an offer from UCLA's Chancellor Gene Block to return to my alma mater to teach Los Angeles History and Public Policy. Alisa joined as my partner in this enterprise we call the "Los Angeles Initiative." We also direct an annual countywide survey—the UCLA- Luskin Quality of Life Index—that tracks how county residents rate their lives in our region. I have received immense satisfaction collaborating with smart colleagues and eager students, who are determined to make their own contribution to society. Until the Covid pandemic, I continued working with NDI to monitor elections in emerging democracies, although I sometimes wonder if it's a little presumptuous of us to export democracy given our own troubled democracy. From time to time I weigh in on a variety of local issues on television, with articles, research papers, and speeches, and I also serve on a number of non-profit boards.

I have been lucky to lead a rich and rewarding life. During my years of service, I've met the President of China and the Queen of England; Prime Ministers of Israel and the King of Jordan; European leaders, and several Presidents of the United States. But just as important, I have worked with janitors fighting for a living wage, citizens battling for civil rights and liberties, and homeless persons in desperate need of supportive housing. To quote Lord Thomas Macaulay once more, this was work done on behalf of "the many we never see." It is principally to them that I have dedicated my life, and it has been a privilege.

Epilogue

If there is one message I hoped to convey in these pages, it is that we can make local government work. Indeed, some of the most far-reaching public policy initiatives of our time have been championed by a growing cadre of visionary and smart local leaders around the world. They've refused to wait for their national leaders to address issues such as climate change, racial justice, ethnic tensions, and growing income inequality. During my four-decade public service career, I challenged myself to tackle big problems, despite our government's structural weaknesses. There were moments in my journey when conventional wisdom dictated that some problems were simply beyond our capacity to solve. But I wouldn't be deterred.

I heard this when Los Angeles County was on the verge of bankruptcy, when a catastrophic earthquake ravaged our city, and when a tax rebellion threatened our ability to deliver services to our residents. I heard it when we protected low and fixed-income renters from losing their apartments because of skyrocketing rents. We were scoffed at by detractors who believed that our government and civic leadership had lost its capacity to complete transformative projects, such as a modern rapid transit system and the building of new cultural institutions. I was warned that it was politically dangerous for public officials to demand constitutional policing from intransigent law enforcement agencies. Critics said our campaign to protect neighborhoods from commercial overdevelopment was a fool's errand, and that in a county known for its explosive growth, we could not find a way to preserve its majestic mountains and iconic coastline.

All these naysayers were proved wrong. We showed that local government *can* work with the right kind of leadership. But our work is far from done. Widening income disparities, an acute shortage of affordable housing, growing homelessness, failing public education, and racial bigotry's crippling legacy remain the unfinished business of our society, not just in Los Angeles but across our nation. And now we have a new challenge: Preserving our nation's democracy and its institutions.

In my farewell address at Disney Hall in 2014, I told the audience that our county, with its five-member board, was the worst from of government I could think of—unless you're one of the five. No rational person would design such a governing structure for a $40 billion corporation with 110,000 employees.

If there's one thing I would change if I could, it would be to create an elected executive for Los Angeles County—putting one person in charge of this gargantuan organization and holding him or her accountable for running it. But just because the design is flawed doesn't mean we can't find a way to get important things done.

I signed up for a life in public service because of an almost evangelical belief that I could make the system work for the people I was elected to represent. And I wanted that work to be consequential. This is the highest calling in a democracy. The public has a right to expect its leaders to summon the courage to tackle intractable problems. They should also expect their leaders to take calculated risks in doing so, regardless of the odds. As a nation and as a community, we must find and elect such people—leaders with character and integrity. They are the ones who will shepherd our democracy into the future. If we fail, we do so at our own peril. As Cicero wrote two millennia ago, "The good of the people is the greatest law." After forty years in public service, I believe this must be more than a hope. It's an imperative.

Acknowledgments

This book has been a seven year project. I intended it to be a history as much as a memoir, and as a result it was as much a research project as it was telling my story. In the course of this saga, I had the help from a broad cross section of public servants (present and past), academics, political activists, friends, and family. I wish to acknowledge them, because without them this book would not have been completed.

UCLA Professor **Stephen Aron**; **Aileen Adams**; **Alessandra Anzani**; **Wayne Avrashow**; L.A. County Supervisor **Kathryn Barger**; L.A. Mayor **Karen Bass**; **Alisa Belinkoff Katz**, my long-time Chief of Staff and UCLA colleague; **Joel Bellman**, my press deputy of twenty years and institutional memory; **Miriam Rosenblum Benjamin**; **Sheldon Benjamin**; **Carol Biondi**; **Dan Bressler**, my lifesaving high tech guru and terrific son-in-law; **Mina Yaroslavsky Bressler**, my cherished daughter and sounding board; **Matthew Charlton**; **Maria Chong-Castillo**, my longest serving staff member and dedicated public servant; **James Conlon**, Music Director of the L.A. Opera and international conductor; **Geoffrey Cowan**; **Kim Ennis**; **Heidi Evans**, an early press deputy and great friend; **Terry Friedman**, former California State Assemblyman, retired Superior Court Judge, and eagle-eyed editor; **Josh Getlin**, my co-author and friend without whom none of this would have been possible; **Annie Gilbar**; **Cliff Gilbert-Lurie**; **Leslie Gilbert-Lurie**, a dear friend whose finger prints are all over this book thanks to her rigorous edit of every page in it; **Karlene Goller**; former Congresswoman Jane Harman; **Ann Hollister**, a decades-long friend and political advisor; **David Israel**; **Howard Katz**, an early Chief of Staff and good friend; **Becca Kearns**; Professor **Shaul Kelner**; **Ginny Kruger**, my dear friend and loyal deputy for three and one-half decades; **Shimona Yaroslavsky Kushner**, my loving, big sister and editor extraordinaire; **Lennie Laguire**, my former communications deputy who gave me pivotal advice at a critical point in this project; Jared **Levine; Susan Levinson**, the best transcriber I ever worked with; **Lisa Mandel**, my former child-welfare deputy; U.S. District Court Judge (Ret.) **Nora Manella**; **Burt Margolin**, former California State Assemblyman who made an invaluable contribution to Chapter 15; **Paul Maslin**; **Mike McFaul**, former U.S. Ambassador to Russia; **Cindy Miscikowski**, former L.A. City Councilmember and comrade in arms; UCLA Professor **David Myers**, my colleague, whose constructive advice was on point and without whom this book would never have gotten published; UCLA Professor **Victor Narro**; **Kira Nemirovsky**; **Jim Newton**, former *Los Angeles Times* journalist, author, and colleague, whose advice has been invaluable; U.S. Senator **Alex Padilla**; **Liz Rangel**, my executive secretary, who knows more about me than I do; **Vivian Rescalvo**, my former transportation deputy; **Connie Rice**, civil rights attorney, author, and dear friend; **Tim Rutten**, former *Los Angeles Times* journalist who gave me sound advice and who sadly died in 2022; **Ben Saltsman**, my former land use deputy; **Miguel Santana**, former City of L.A. Chief Administrative Officer, now President and CEO of the Weingart Foundation, and a consequential civic leader; **Joel Sappell**, former *Los Angeles Times* investigative reporter, later my communications director and friend of four decades; **Laura Shell**, my former land use deputy and County Planning Commissioner; **Elan Shultz**, my trusted health deputy who distinguished himself in challenging times; **Chad Smith**, President of the L.A. Philharmonic; **Adam Sonenshein**; **Raphe Sonenshein**, Director of the Pat Brown Institute, Cal. State University; **Yolanda Valadez**, one of my secretaries who had no idea how critical she would be to his book; **David Yaroslavsky**, my son, who like his sister, is a shrewd sounding board on all things; and Councilwoman **Katy Yaroslavsky**, my daughter-in-law who now holds the seat that launched my political career.

To each and every one of these individuals, I owe a great debt of gratitude.

Source Endnotes

Introduction

P. 3——— "We do not display greatness…" – *Penseés*, Section VI, by Blaise Pascal, 1660

P. 5——— "There are 14 or 15 million…" – President John F. Kennedy address to United Auto Workers Convention, May 8, 1962

Chapter 1

P. 8———…a tribute book that chronicled his life… – *Life's Furrows, Shimon Soloveichik: Life and Letters,* 1952

P. 10———…in the anthology of essays… – *Life's Furrows, Shimon Soloveichik: Life and Letters,* 1952

P. 10——— "He was influenced by…" – *Life's Furrows, Shimon Soloveichik: Life and Letters,* 1952

P. 11——— "When detractors…" – *Life's Furrows, Shimon Soloveichik: Life and Letters,* 1952

P. 12——— "I can still see…." – *Life's Furrows, Shimon Soloveichik: Life and Letters,* 1952

P. 15——— "His years in Los Angeles…" – *Life's Furrows, Shimon Soloveichik: Life and Letters,* 1952.

Chapter 2

P. 22——— "It was a place where…." — Gustavo Arellano, *LA Taco,* July 30, 2018

Chapter 3

P. 39——— "If an individual wants…." – Sidney Blumenthal, *The Guardian,* Nov. 7, 2003

Chapter 4

P. 49——— "If I've lost Cronkite…" – *Washington Post* May 25, 2018

P. 51——— "The policeman." – Witcover, Jules, *The Year the Dream Died*

Chapter 5

P. 59———As author, Yossi… – Yossi Klein Halevy Interview in documentary film, *Refusenik, 2007*

P. 64———A *Los Angeles Times* survey showed… – *Los Angeles. Times,* Aug. 24, 1973

P. 65———…our protest was splashed… – *Los Angeles Times,* Dec. 18, 1973

Chapter 6

P. 74———…nearly 50 percent of… – Braun and Company Records, California State Archives

P. 84———…and when the Los Angeles Times endorsed her…" – *Los Angeles Times,* May 22, 1975

P. 89———That picture ran… – *Los Angeles Times,* May 29, 1975

Chapter 7

P. 97———"I would much rather celebrate…" – *L.A. Weekly,* Feb. 28, 2013

P. 99———"The legislature's leading crusader…" – *Los Angeles. Times,* Jan. 29, 1992

P. 100———"The Chargers could be here…" – Conan O'Brien Monologue, Feb. 17, 2015, *Newsmax*

P. 100———"…the project caused…" – *The Santa Monica Freeway Diamond Lanes: Evaluation Overview,* – U.S. Department of Transportation, 1997

P. 101———"agency's press releases…" – Joan Didion, *White Album,* 1979, "Bureaucrats, p. 82"

P. 101———"The Diamond Lane is…." – *Los Angeles Times,* March 31, 1976

P. 105———According to a 2016 report…. – Padma Nagappan, "How Water Use Has Declined with Population Growth," *The New Humanitarian,* Nov. 8, 2016

P. 106———"…a key Los Angeles City Council Committee" – *Los Angeles Times,* Sept. 2, 1977

P. 107———…endorsement of the *Los Angeles Times* – *Los Angeles Times,* Oct. 23, 1978

P. 108———"…people ought to vote for it." – *Los Angeles Times,* Oct. 31, 1978

Chapter 8

P. 114———…a painful but survivable hit… – *California and the American Tax Revolt: Proposition 13 Five Years Later, Los Angeles Times,* June 1983

P. 118———"…I do not know what we are going to do…" – *What History Tells Us About Rent Control in Los Angeles,* UCLA Luskin Center for History and Policy, October 2018

P. 121———"What Los Angeles has…." – "The Impact of Rent Control on the Los Angeles Housing Market," RAND, August 1981

Chapter 9

P. 126————"...creates a real threat..." – *Washington Post*, Dec. 13, 1977

P. 128————"...innocents abroad..." – *Los Angeles Times*, May 20, 1978

P. 130————Ueberroth succeeded... – *Lessons Learned from the 1984 Olympic Games*, Zev Yaroslavsky, Alisa Belinkoff Katz, Caitlin Parker Aug. 25,2015; a project of the UCLA Dept. of History

P. 131————"Even I was one of..." – Peter Ueberroth, *Made in America: His Own* Story, 1985, p. 28

Chapter 10

P. 135————Author Carey McWilliams... – *Southern California: An Island on the Land*, 1973, p. 291

P. 138————With Mayor Tom Bradley's blessing... – *Los Angeles Times*, April 11, 1975

P. 140————"...wide of the mark" *Los Angeles Times*, April 4, 1980

P. 140————"...PDID files...secretly stored in the home garage..." – *Los Angeles Times*, Jan. 7, 1983

P. 143————"We are going to be soliciting..." – *Los Angeles Times*, June 4, 1994

P. 147————"We may be finding...." – *Los Angeles Times*, May 8, 1982

Chapter 11

P. 153————"Zev is the best example of...." – *Los Angeles Times*, Nov. 6, 1979

P. 157————...more than $35,000 in campaign contributions... – *Los Angeles Times*, Oct. 31, 1984

P. 160————In an analysis of... – *Los Angeles Times*, Oct. 12, 1986

Chapter 12

P. 180————But the *New York Times* reported... – *New York Times*, Aug. 10, 1989

P. 180————I had to laugh when.... – *Los Angeles Times*, April 16, 1989

Chapter 13

P. 182————"Change is constant, change is inevitable" – Benjamin Disraeli, Speech on Reform Bill of 1867

P. 184————"Did Mrs. Du react inappropriately?" – *Los Angeles Times*, Nov. 16, 1991

P. 186————"*Gorillas in the Mist*" – *Los Angeles Times*, March 19, 1991

P. 187————"All of us have been stunned" –Los Angeles City Council proceeding, March 20, 1991

P. 190————"The city's standing emergency 'plan'…" – "The City in Crisis" report by William H. Webster and Hubert Williams

P. 190————"Failing to prepare is preparing to fail" – Andy Hill with John Wooden, *Be Quick, but Don't Hurry*, 2001, p. 156

P. 193————"What you've experienced here…" – Mikhail Gorbachev speech at a civic luncheon at ARCO Towers, May 1, 1992

P. 196————"I stared at Bob…" – Richard Riordan, *The Mayor*, 2014, p. 9

P. 198————…offering a 6 percent pay raise… – *Los Angeles Times*, June 3, 1994

p. 198————"…we cannot give in to demands…" – *Los Angeles Times*, June 15, 1994

P. 198————…the equivalent of a 12 percent raise…" – *Los Angeles Times*, June 28, 1994

P. 200————"For too long county government…" – *Los Angeles Times*, Dec. 8, 1993

Chapter 14

P. 203————"A puzzling anomaly" – John Anson Ford, *Thirty Explosive Years in Los Angeles County*, p. 16

P. 208————"No man is fit to govern" – Lord Thomas Macaulay, nineteenth-century British Historian

P. 209————"Wall Street has lowered our bond rating…" – Zev Yaroslavsky Board of Supervisors Inaugural Address, Dec. 5, 1994

Chapter 15

P. 211————"When France sneezes" – Prince Klemens von Metternich, 1830

P. 213————"This is a complete surprise" – *Los Angeles Times*, Jan. 20, 1995

P. 216————"Much better than winning the lottery" – *Los Angeles Times*, September 20, 1995

P. 219————"This is a national issue" – *Los Angeles Times*, September 22, 1995

P. 219————"…in order to remold steel…" – *Los Angeles Times*, September 23, 1995

P. 219————"It's very encouraging" – *Los Angeles Times*, Sept. 22, 1995

P. 219————"We've got a deal" – *Los Angeles Times*, March 5, 1996

P. 224————"It's hard to walk away…" – Los Angeles Times, Nov. 17, 1998

Chapter 16

P. 229————Months later I recounted… – *Los Angeles Times*, Jan. 7, 2007

P. 232————Although Waxman's fear… – *Los Angeles Times*, Feb. 1, 1986

P. 234————"The Sinkhole that ate…" – Frank del Olmo, *Los Angeles Times*, Sept. 13, 1985

Chapter 17

Chapter 18

Chapter 19

Chapter 20

Chapter 21

P. 310———What in the world, he asked… – Steve Lopez column in *Los Angeles Times*, May 30, 2007

P. 313———"Los Angeles cannot survive half-rich and half poor" – Zev Yaroslavsky, *Los Angeles Times*, April 7, 2000

Chapter 23

P. 330———"Evolved from an upstart…" – *Los Angeles Times*, November 28, 2014

P. 331———"I decided that I would grab" – Vin Scully taped remarks at Zev Yaroslavsky retirement event, Nov. 17, 2014

Index

"*Zev's Los Angeles* is a compelling history of our city's last half century, as conveyed through the life of one of our most impactful leaders.

Zev Yaroslavsky's career in public service spanned Los Angeles' emergence as a global city and some of its most trying times. His personal story is essential to understanding where our city is today, and where L.A. and the nation's cities are headed in the future. A must read for anyone curious about leadership and governing in changing and challenging times."

— *Los Angeles Mayor Karen Bass*

"In his upcoming memoir, Zev Yaroslavsky takes readers on an uplifting and inspiring journey of personal faith, public service, and the shaping of Los Angeles. The son of Jewish immigrants from Ukraine, his story is a quintessentially American one. From modest beginnings, Yaroslavsky left a lasting mark through his work on expanding health care, implementing innovative housing programs, and growing our city's public transportation network. Zev gives readers an inside look into the life of one of the most empathic and effective leaders I've known, as well as insight into the challenges he overcame along the way. This memoir is for any reader looking for inspiration about their own ability to effect change in their community."

— *U.S. Senator Alex Padilla (D-Calif.)*

"*Zev's Los Angeles* is a peerless guide to the history, politics, and culture of the City of Angels. No one knows L.A. better. And no one conveys it in precisely this way—spellbinding, unvarnished, and yet elegant. It reads as if Zev were doing what he does best–holding court with that mix of photographic recall, a penchant for the piquant, the unmistakable no-nonsense style, and the staggering command of policy. This book is, at once, the story of one man's undying commitment to his city, a brilliant and revealing biography of L.A., and a first-class primer on how to forge good governance at the local level. It should be of interest to all who are interested in how a city works—and how it should work."

— *David Myers, Distinguished Professor and Sady and Ludwig Kahn Chair in Jewish History, University of California, Los Angeles*

"Politicians often avoid risk until they are forced to do the right thing. Not Zev. With little political upside, he aggressively stood up for all civil rights, stared down LAPD bullies, and championed women's rights. Throughout his 40-year career, he wielded political power not for himself, but to right wrongs. He passionately lived up to his oath of office—to faithfully protect and defend the Constitution. He has earned my respect and my friendship."

— *Connie Rice, Civil Rights Lawyer, Author of* Power Concedes Nothing

"Zev Yaroslavsky played a central role in nearly every major Los Angeles public policy issue from his 1975 upset city council election to his retirement as a county supervisor in 2014. This remarkable political autobiography chronicles one person's journey through L.A.'s modern history, with acute perceptions, deep feeling, and detailed insider recollections of key players and dramas. It's an invaluable resource for students of public service in troubled times, and for those who hope to understand this complicated, ever-hopeful, and diverse region."

— *Raphael J. Sonenshein, Executive Director, Pat Brown Institute for Public Affairs, California State University, Los Angeles*

"In this compelling memoir, Zev Yaroslavsky chronicles Los Angeles' evolution into one of the world's great cultural capitals and his role in that transformation. From Disney Hall and the Hollywood Bowl, to the L.A. Opera, to the region's museums and more—his influence in expanding L.A.'s cultural footprint is a remarkable legacy. I have been privileged to share many of the challenges and exciting moments in that history."

— *James Conlon, Music Director, Los Angeles Opera, International Conductor*

"At a time of highly polarized, partisan politics, Zev Yaroslavsky's memoir offers an insightful and very personal view of an era when Los Angeles leaders came together to tackle the most difficult issues facing the region, from police accountability and preserving green space, to protecting the region's fragile safety net and expanding accessibility to the arts. *Zev's Los Angeles: From Boyle Heights to the Halls of Power* is required reading for students of leadership and government, and aspiring policymakers on what it takes to be an effective, issue-oriented leader."

— *Miguel Santana, President and CEO of the Weingart Foundation*

CPSIA information can be obtained
at www.ICGtesting.com
Printed in the USA
JSHW040213120523
41630JS00002B/2

9 798887 191676